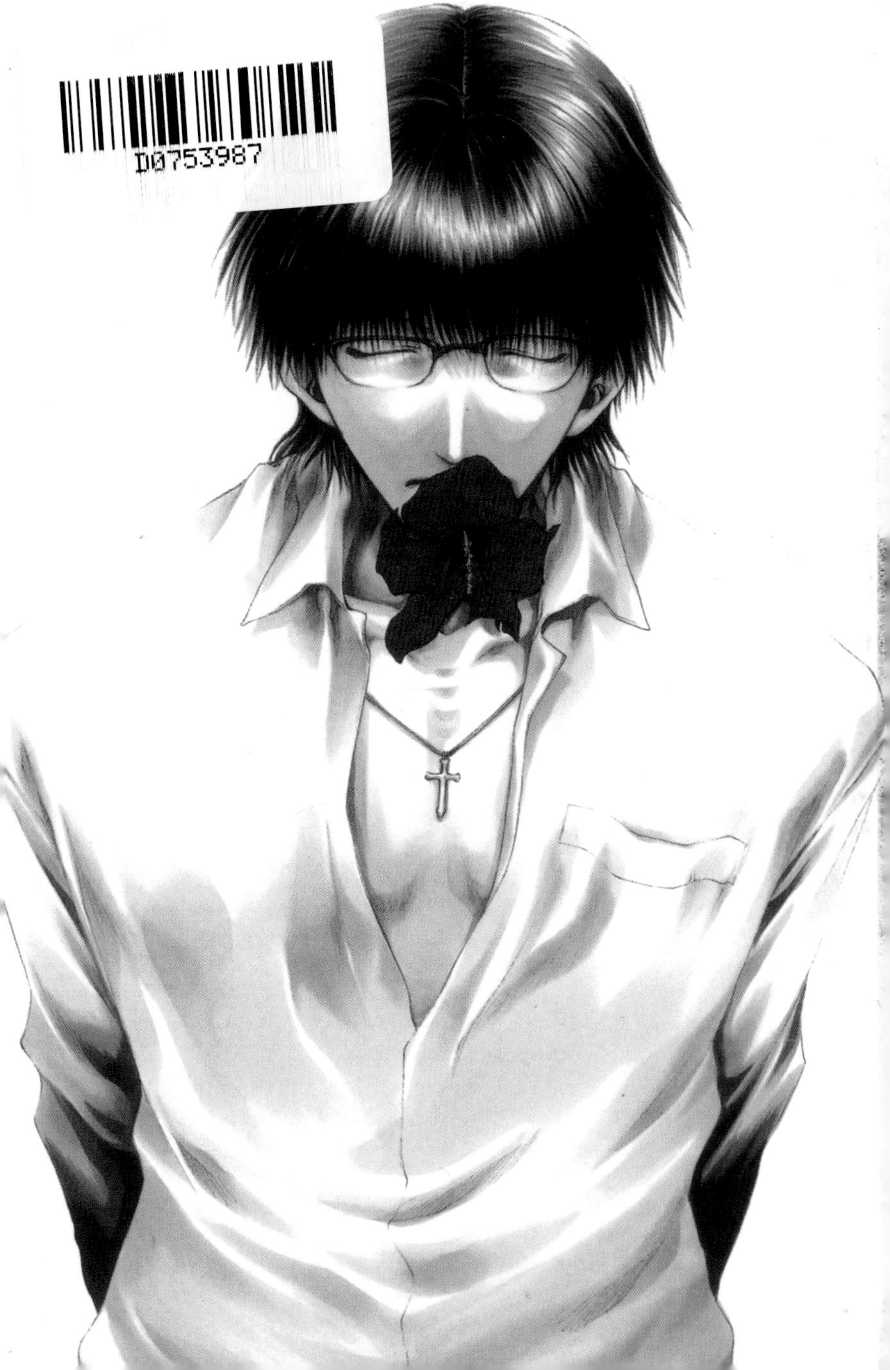

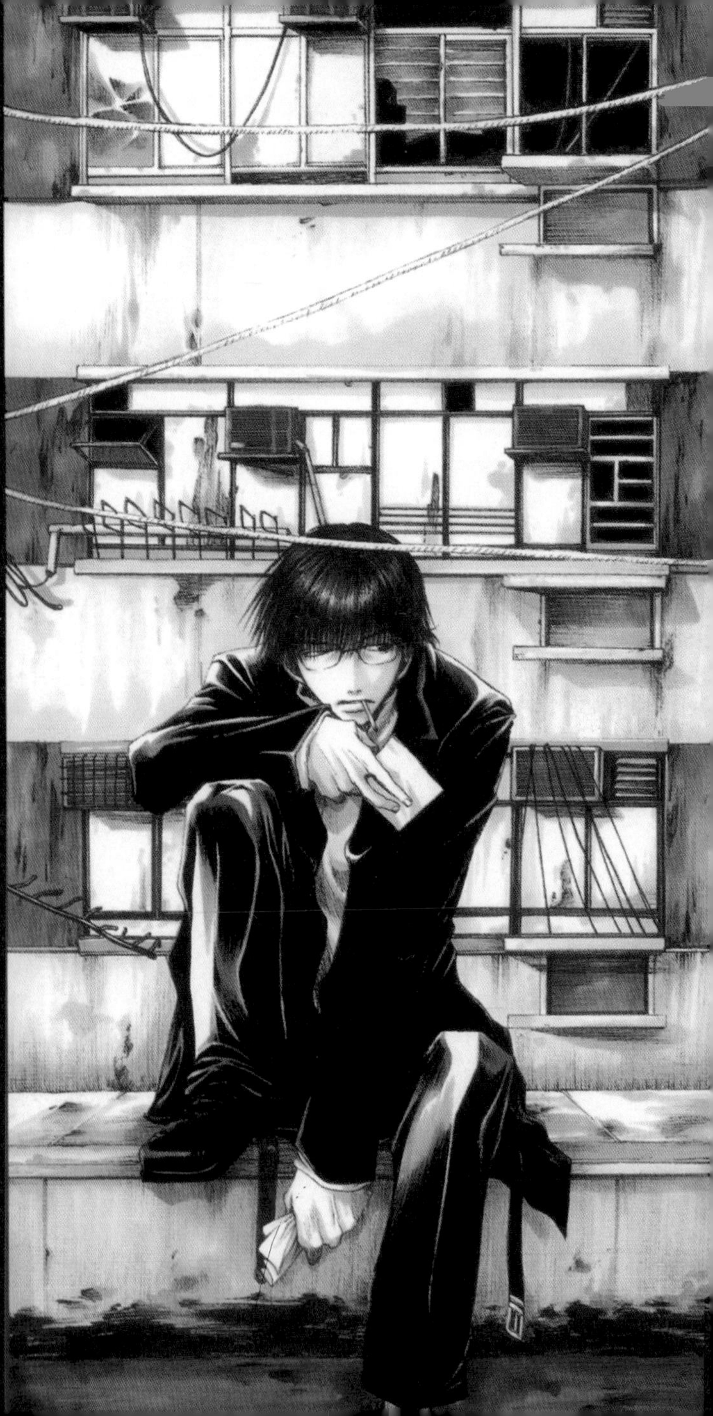

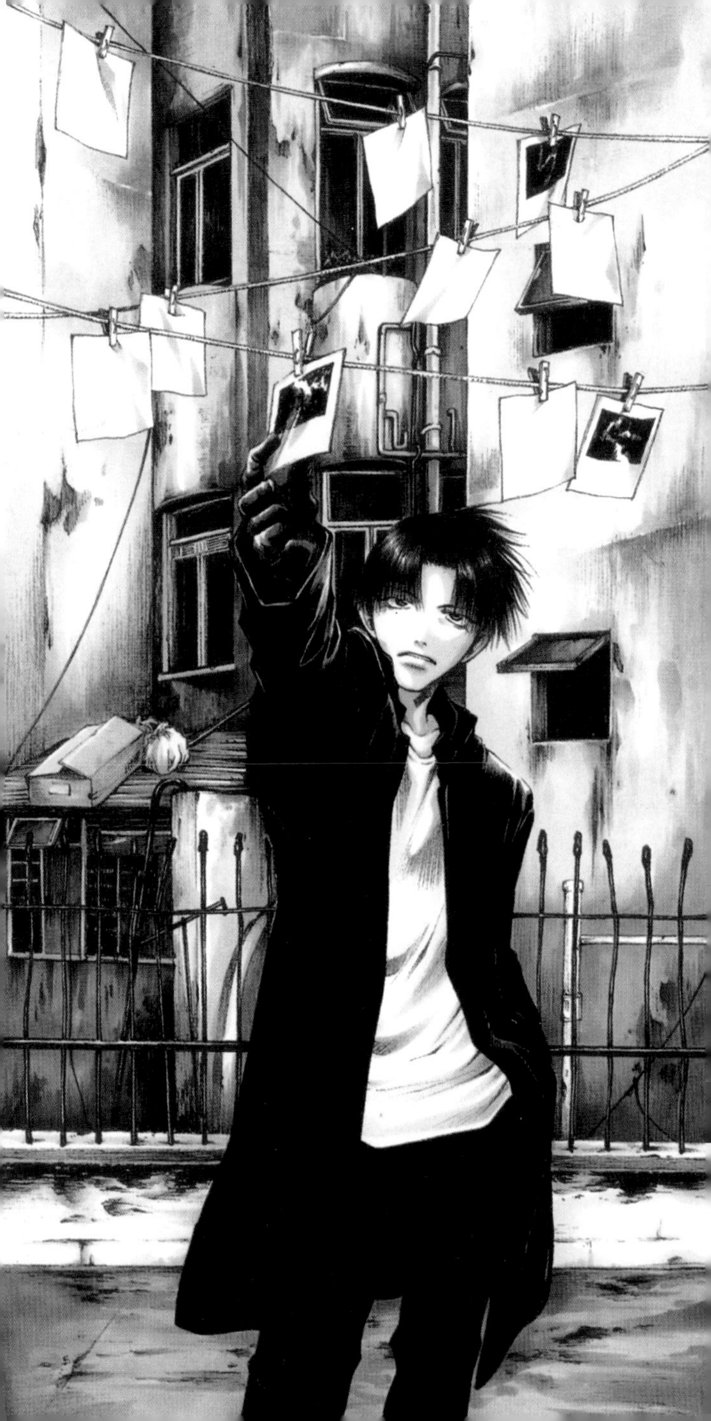

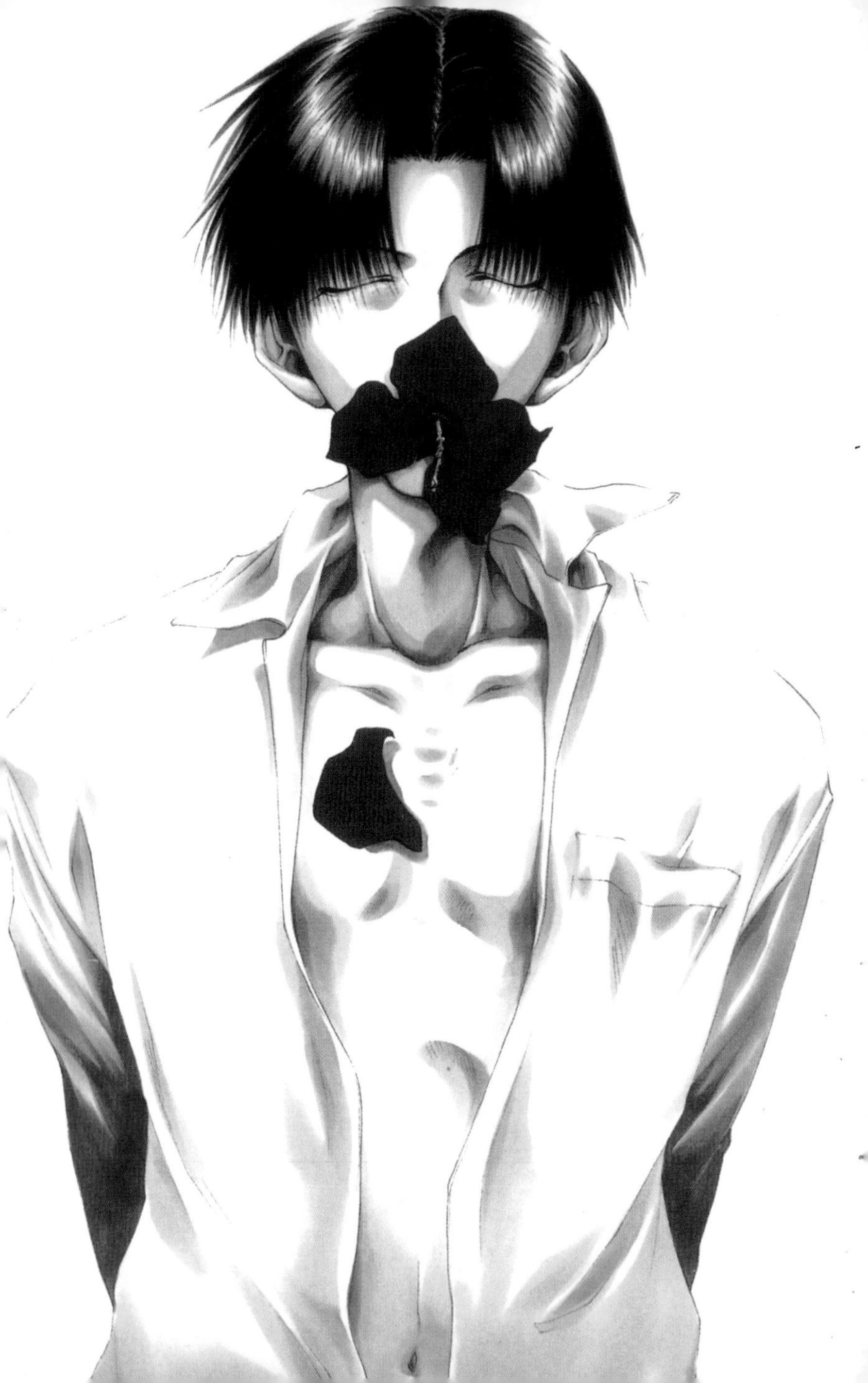

WILD ADAPTER

vol.1

by Kazuya Minekura

HAMBURG // LONDON // LOS ANGELES // TOKYO

Wild Adapter Volume 1
Created by Kazuya Minekura

Translation - Alexis Kirsch
English Adaptaion - Christine Boylan
Retouch and Lettering - Gavin Hignight and Jennifer Carbajal
Production Artist - Michael Paolilli
Graphic Designer - Louis Csontos

Editor - Lillian Diaz-Przybyl
Digital Imaging Manager - Chris Buford
Pre-Production Supervisor - Erika Terriquez
Art Director - Anne Marie Horne
Production Manager - Elisabeth Brizzi
VP of Production - Ron Klamert
Editor-in-Chief - Rob Tokar
Publisher - Mike Kiley
President and C.O.O. - John Parker
C.E.O. and Chief Creative Officer - Stuart Levy

A **TOKYOPOP** Manga

TOKYOPOP Inc.
5900 Wilshire Blvd. Suite 2000
Los Angeles, CA 90036

E-mail: info@TOKYOPOP.com
Come visit us online at www.TOKYOPOP.com

ISBN: 978-1-59816-978-2

First TOKYOPOP printing: February 2007
10 9 8 7 6 5 4 3 2 1
Printed in the USA

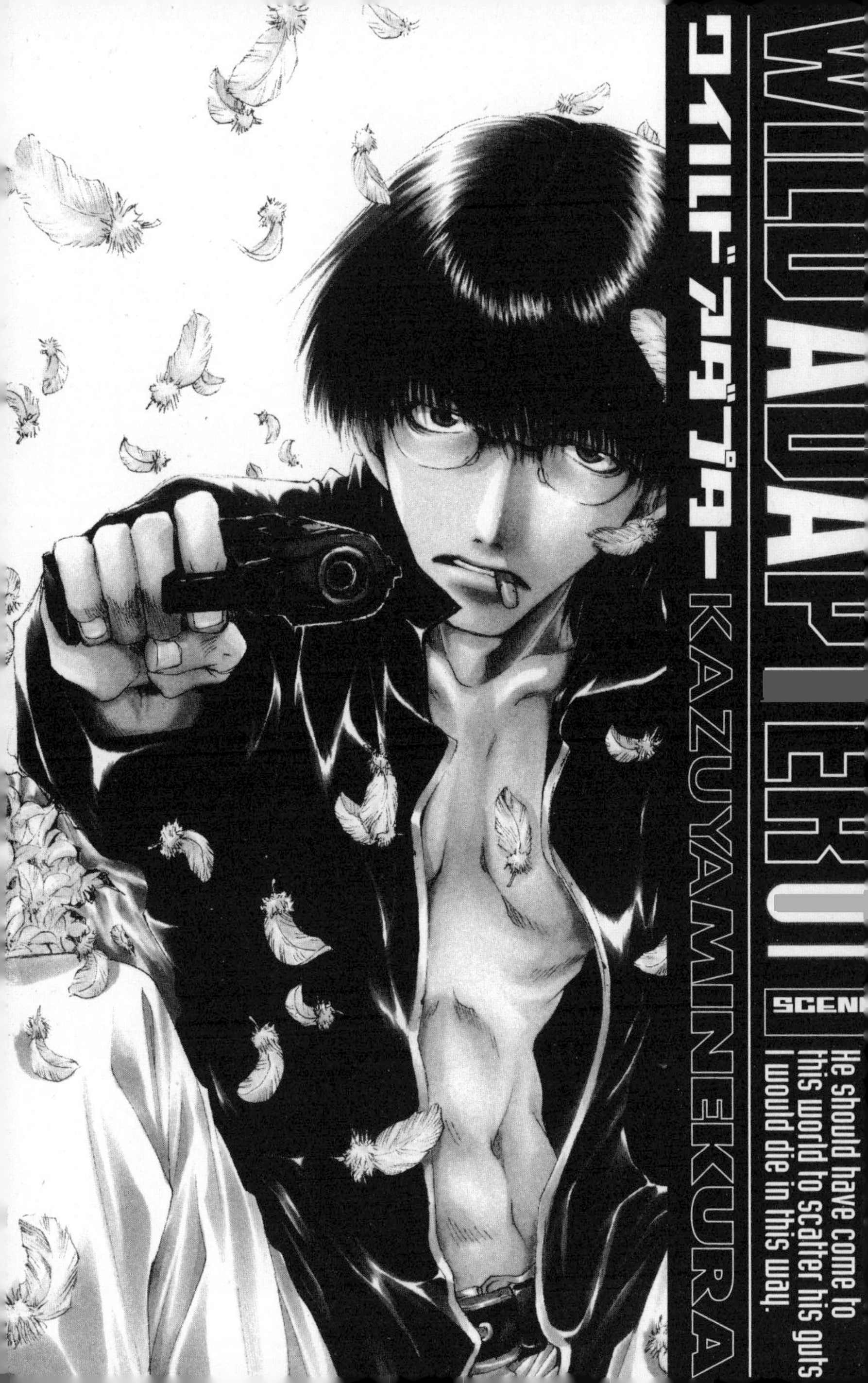
WILD ADAPTER 01
ワイルドアダプター
KAZUYA MINEKURA
SCEN
He should have come to
this world to scatter his guts
I would die in this way.

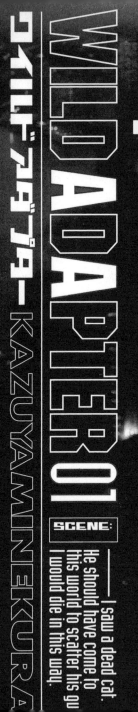

WILD ADAPTER 01

SCENE:

——I saw a dead cat.
He should have come to
this world to scatter his gu
I would die in this way.

ワイルドアダプター—KAZUYA MINEKURA

CONTENTS

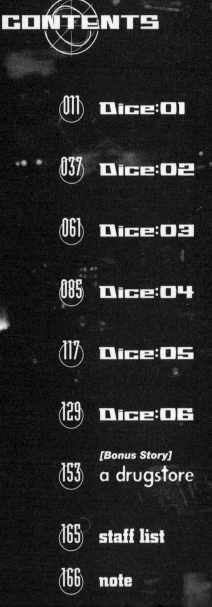

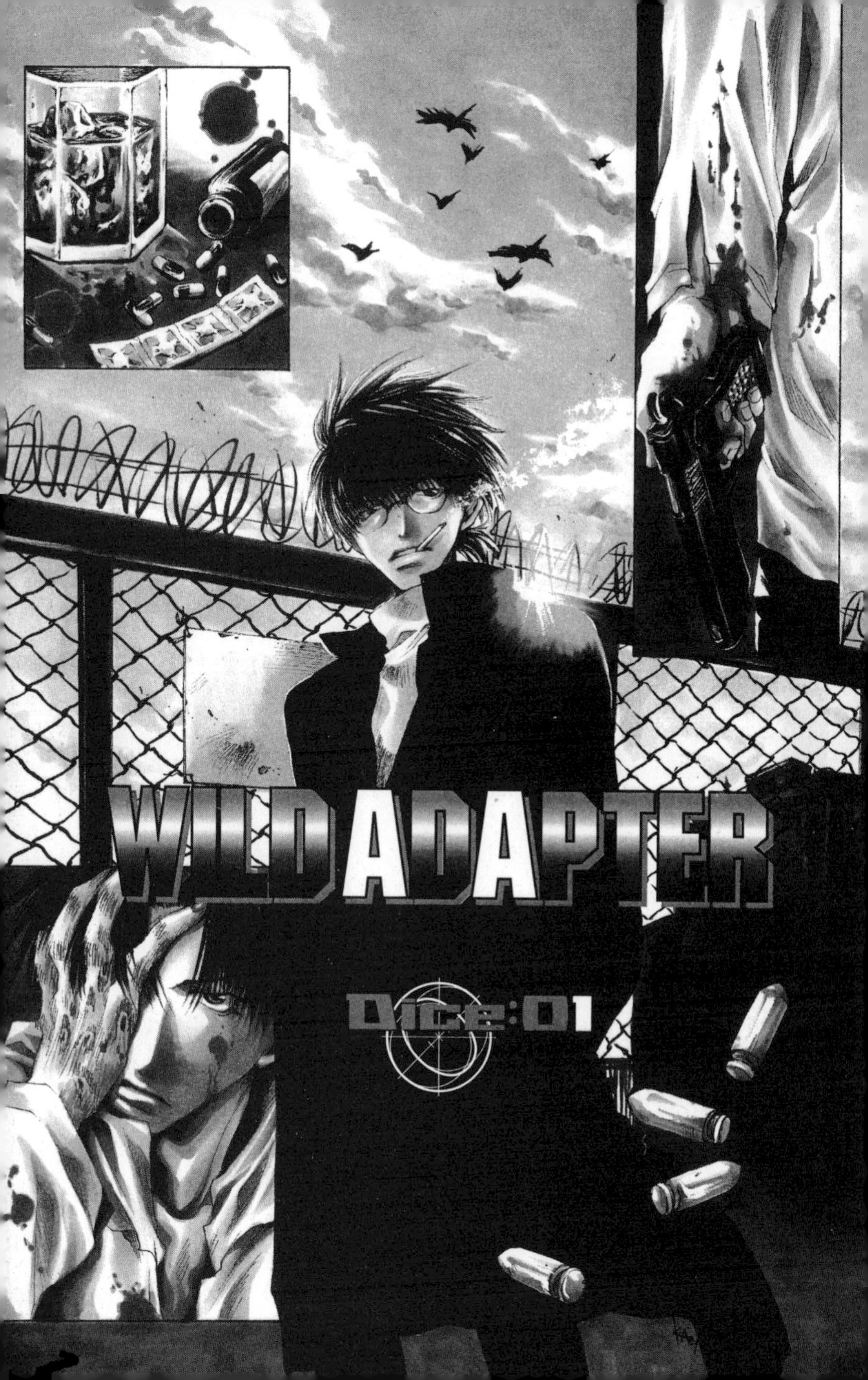
WILD ADAPTER
DICE:01

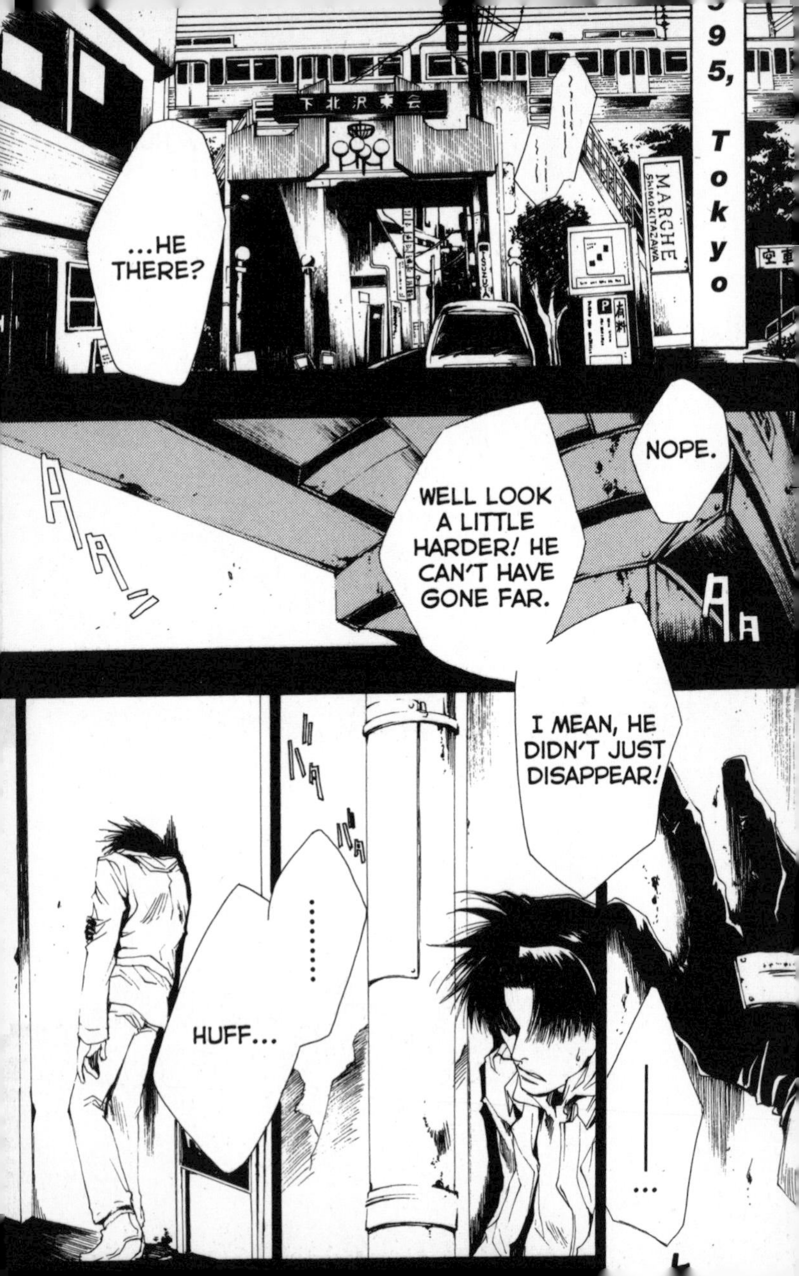

95, Tokyo
下北沢東会
MARCHE
SHIMOKITAZAWA
空車
...HE THERE?
NOPE.
WELL LOOK A LITTLE HARDER! HE CAN'T HAVE GONE FAR.
I MEAN, HE DIDN'T JUST DISAPPEAR!
—...
....
HUFF...

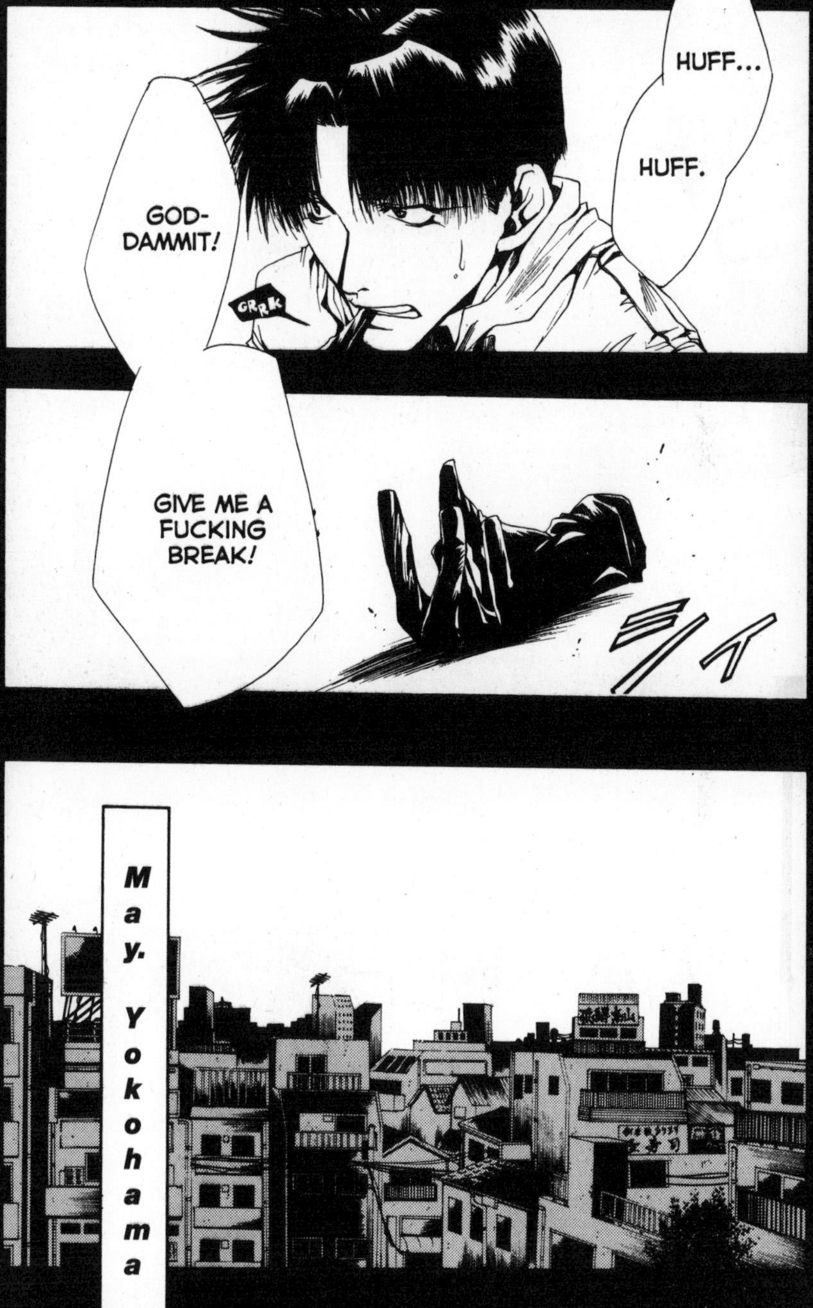
HUFF...
HUFF.
GOD-DAMMIT!
GRRK
GIVE ME A FUCKING BREAK!
May. Yokohama

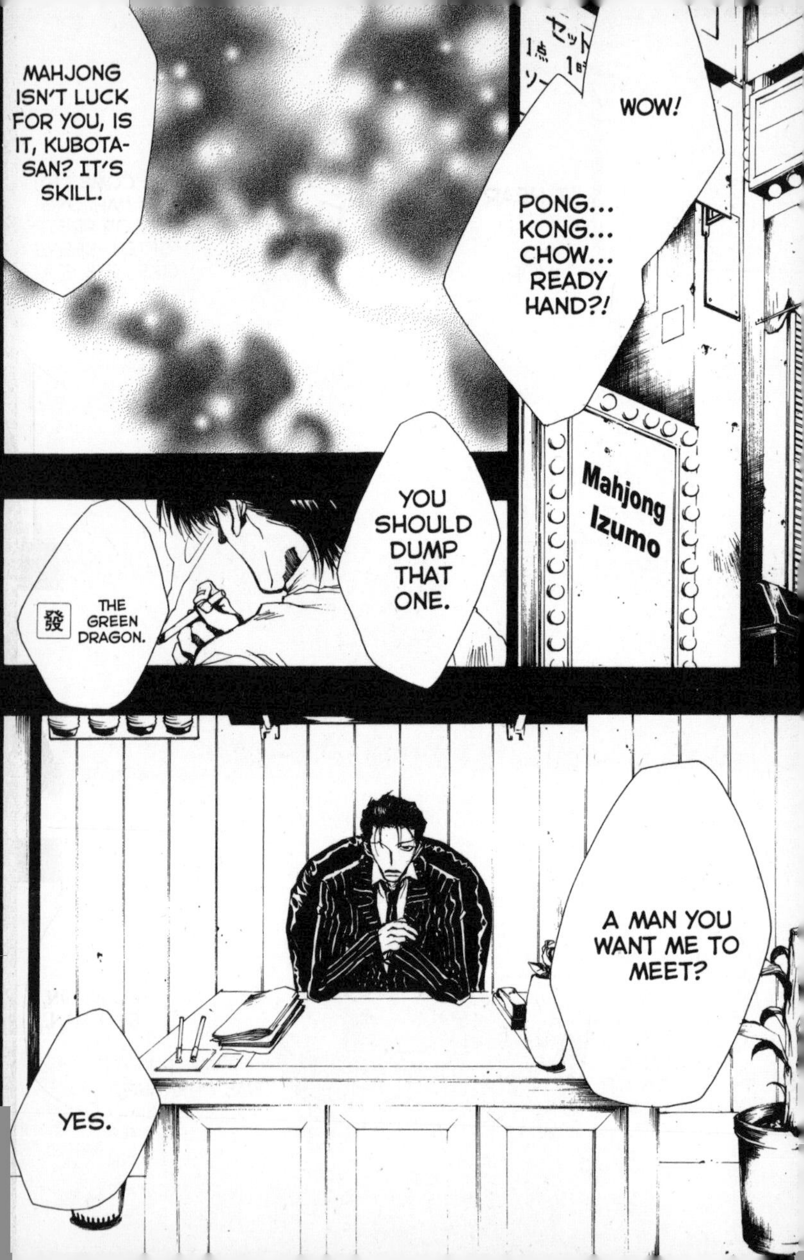
WOW!
PONG... KONG... CHOW... READY HAND?!
Mahjong Izumo
MAHJONG ISN'T LUCK FOR YOU, IS IT, KUBOTA-SAN? IT'S SKILL.
YOU SHOULD DUMP THAT ONE.
發 THE GREEN DRAGON.
A MAN YOU WANT ME TO MEET?
YES.

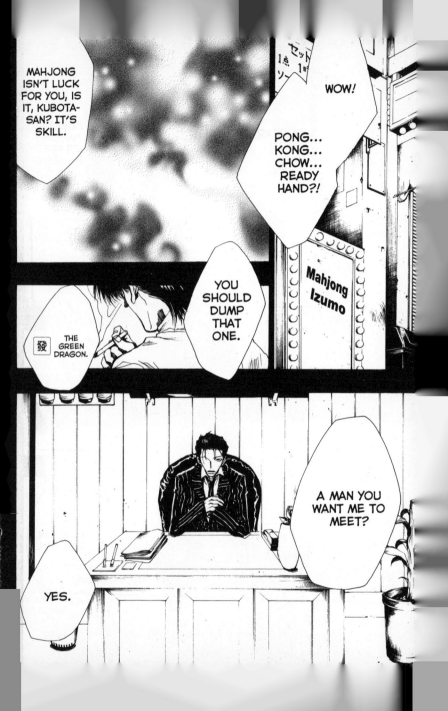

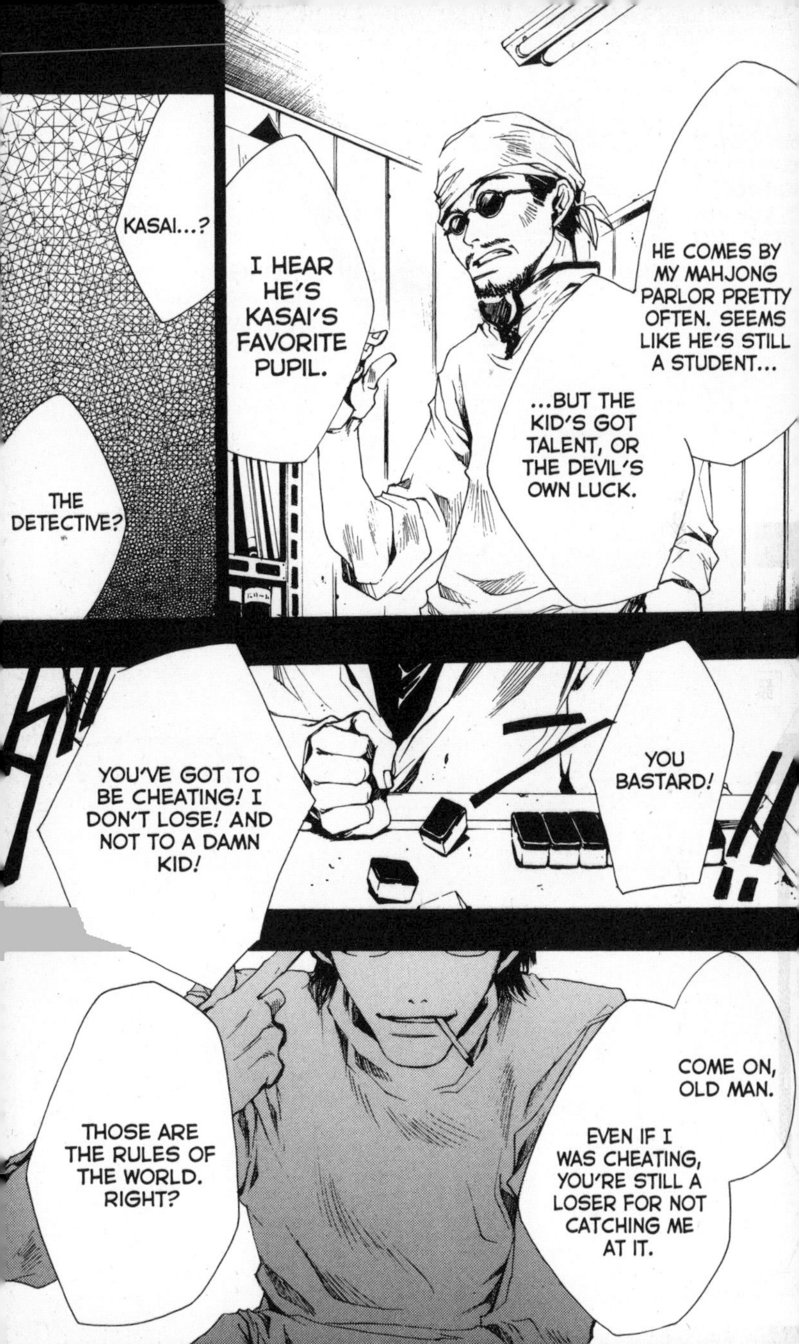
HE COMES BY MY MAHJONG PARLOR PRETTY OFTEN. SEEMS LIKE HE'S STILL A STUDENT...
...BUT THE KID'S GOT TALENT, OR THE DEVIL'S OWN LUCK.
I HEAR HE'S KASAI'S FAVORITE PUPIL.
KASAI...?
THE DETECTIVE?
YOU BASTARD!
YOU'VE GOT TO BE CHEATING! I DON'T LOSE! AND NOT TO A DAMN KID!
COME ON, OLD MAN.
EVEN IF I WAS CHEATING, YOU'RE STILL A LOSER FOR NOT CATCHING ME AT IT.
THOSE ARE THE RULES OF THE WORLD. RIGHT?

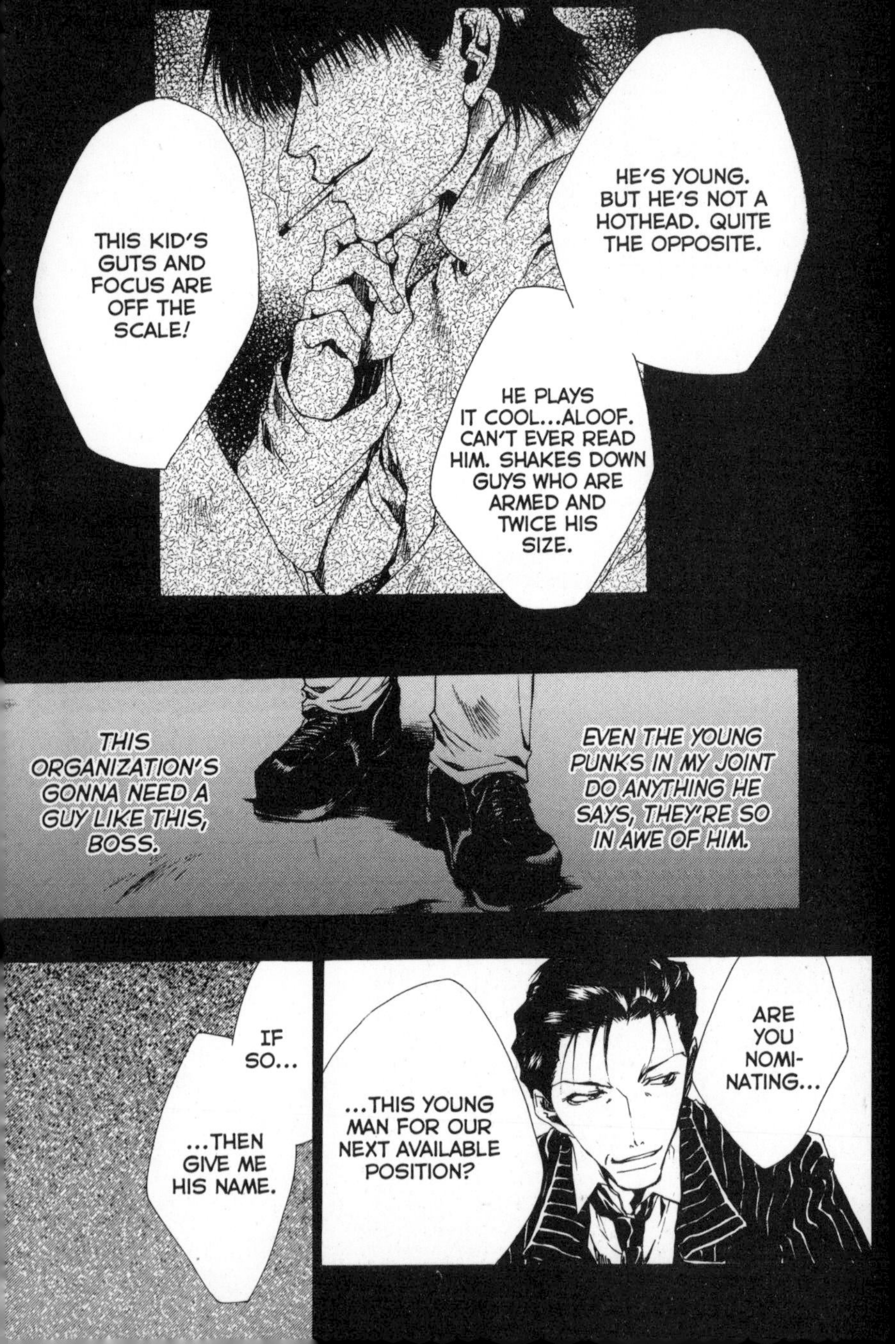
HE'S YOUNG. BUT HE'S NOT A HOTHEAD. QUITE THE OPPOSITE.
HE PLAYS IT COOL...ALOOF. CAN'T EVER READ HIM. SHAKES DOWN GUYS WHO ARE ARMED AND TWICE HIS SIZE.
THIS KID'S GUTS AND FOCUS ARE OFF THE SCALE!
EVEN THE YOUNG PUNKS IN MY JOINT DO ANYTHING HE SAYS, THEY'RE SO IN AWE OF HIM.
THIS ORGANIZATION'S GONNA NEED A GUY LIKE THIS, BOSS.
ARE YOU NOMI-NATING...
...THIS YOUNG MAN FOR OUR NEXT AVAILABLE POSITION?
IF SO...
...THEN GIVE ME HIS NAME.

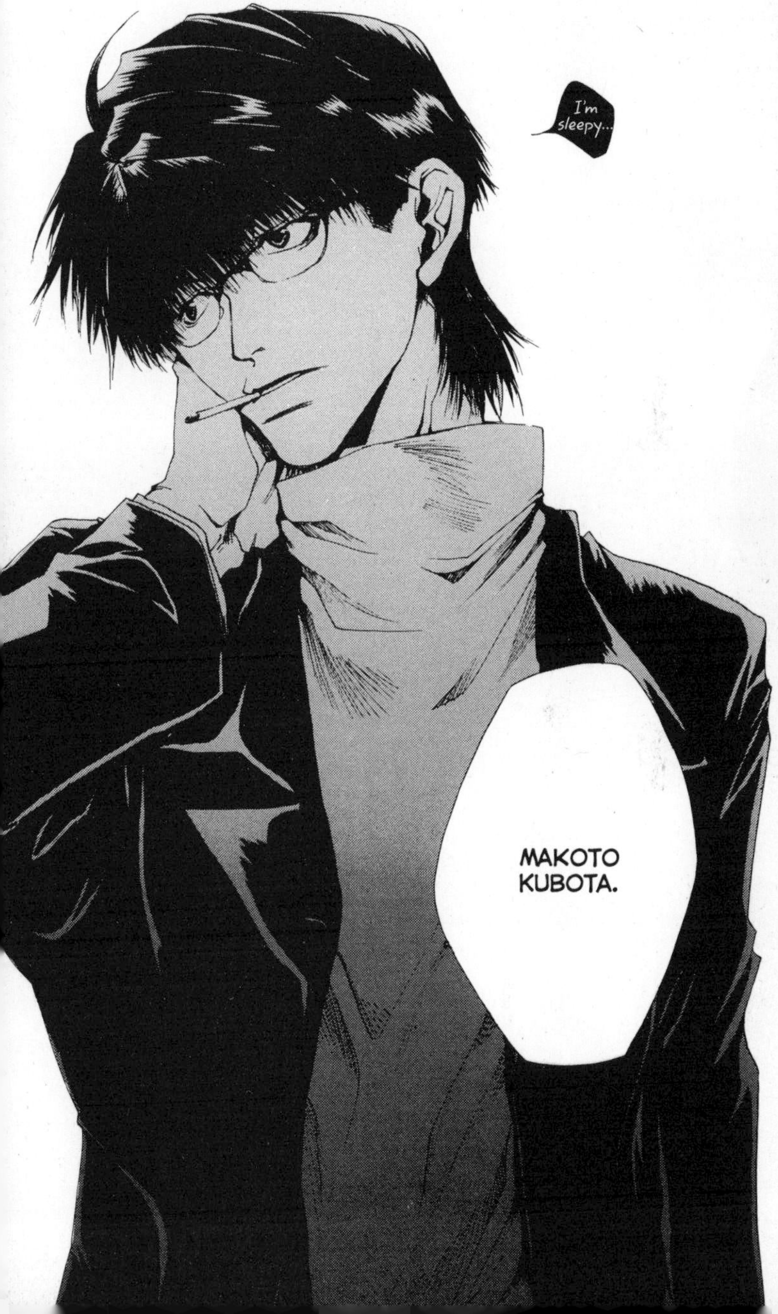
I'm sleepy...
MAKOTO KUBOTA.

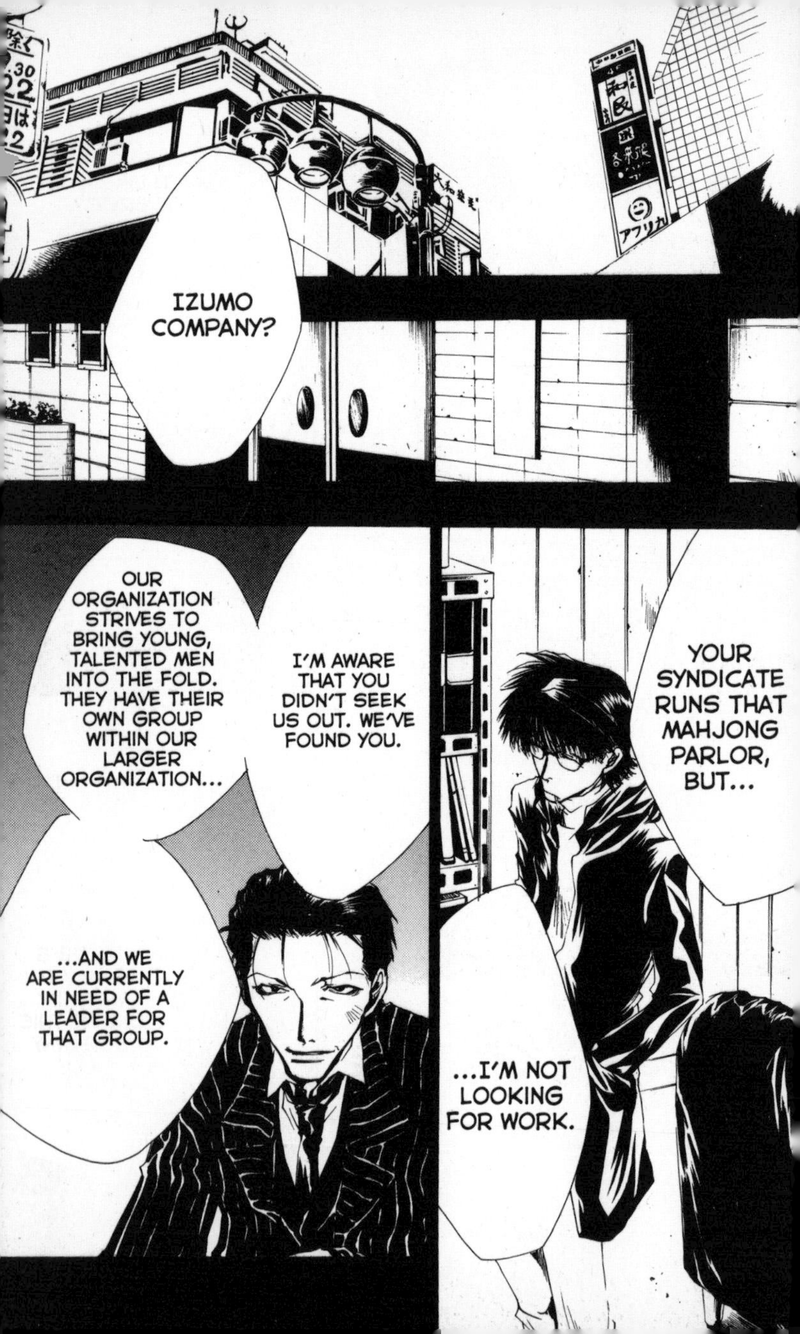
IZUMO COMPANY?
YOUR SYNDICATE RUNS THAT MAHJONG PARLOR, BUT...
...I'M NOT LOOKING FOR WORK.
I'M AWARE THAT YOU DIDN'T SEEK US OUT. WE'VE FOUND YOU.
OUR ORGANIZATION STRIVES TO BRING YOUNG, TALENTED MEN INTO THE FOLD. THEY HAVE THEIR OWN GROUP WITHIN OUR LARGER ORGANIZATION...
...AND WE ARE CURRENTLY IN NEED OF A LEADER FOR THAT GROUP.

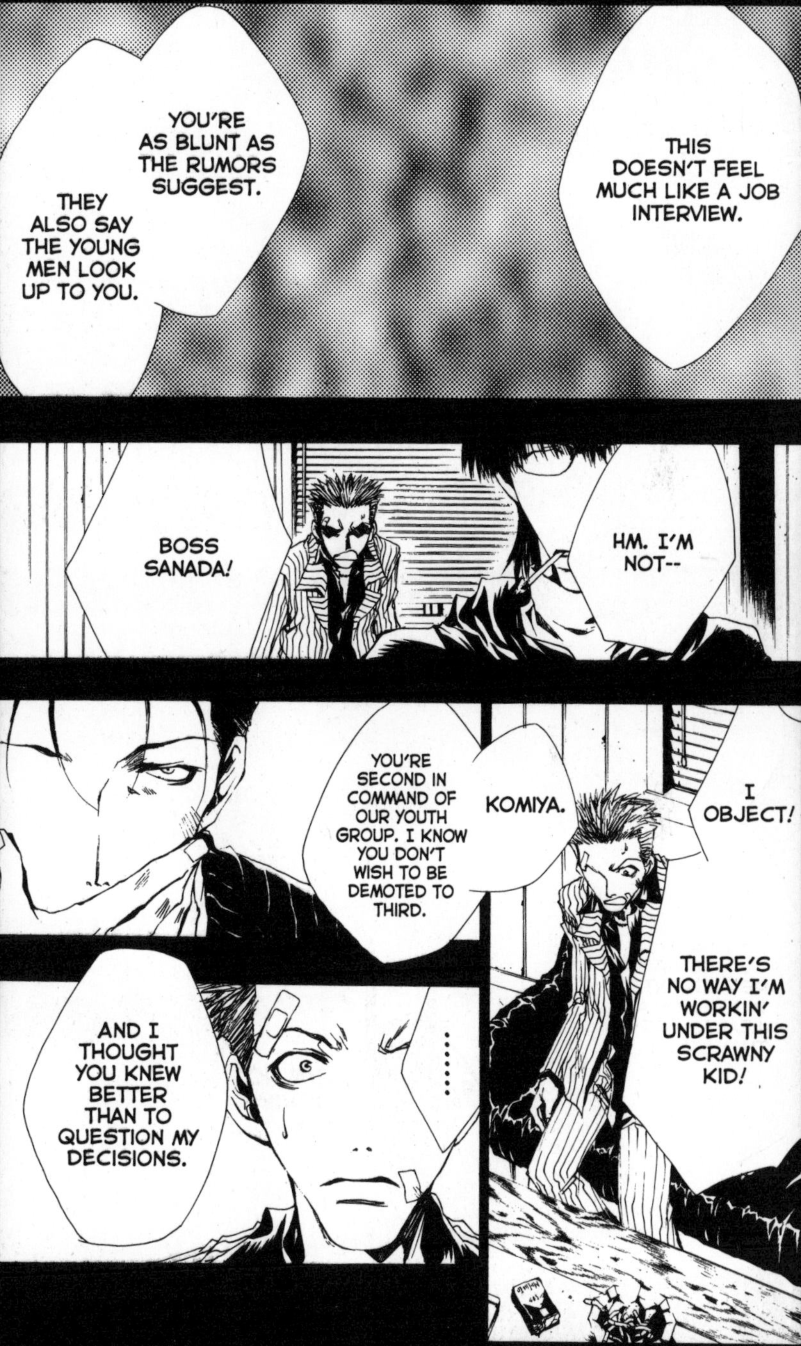
THIS DOESN'T FEEL MUCH LIKE A JOB INTERVIEW.
YOU'RE AS BLUNT AS THE RUMORS SUGGEST.
THEY ALSO SAY THE YOUNG MEN LOOK UP TO YOU.
HM. I'M NOT--
BOSS SANADA!
I OBJECT!
THERE'S NO WAY I'M WORKIN' UNDER THIS SCRAWNY KID!
KOMIYA.
YOU'RE SECOND IN COMMAND OF OUR YOUTH GROUP. I KNOW YOU DON'T WISH TO BE DEMOTED TO THIRD.
......
AND I THOUGHT YOU KNEW BETTER THAN TO QUESTION MY DECISIONS.

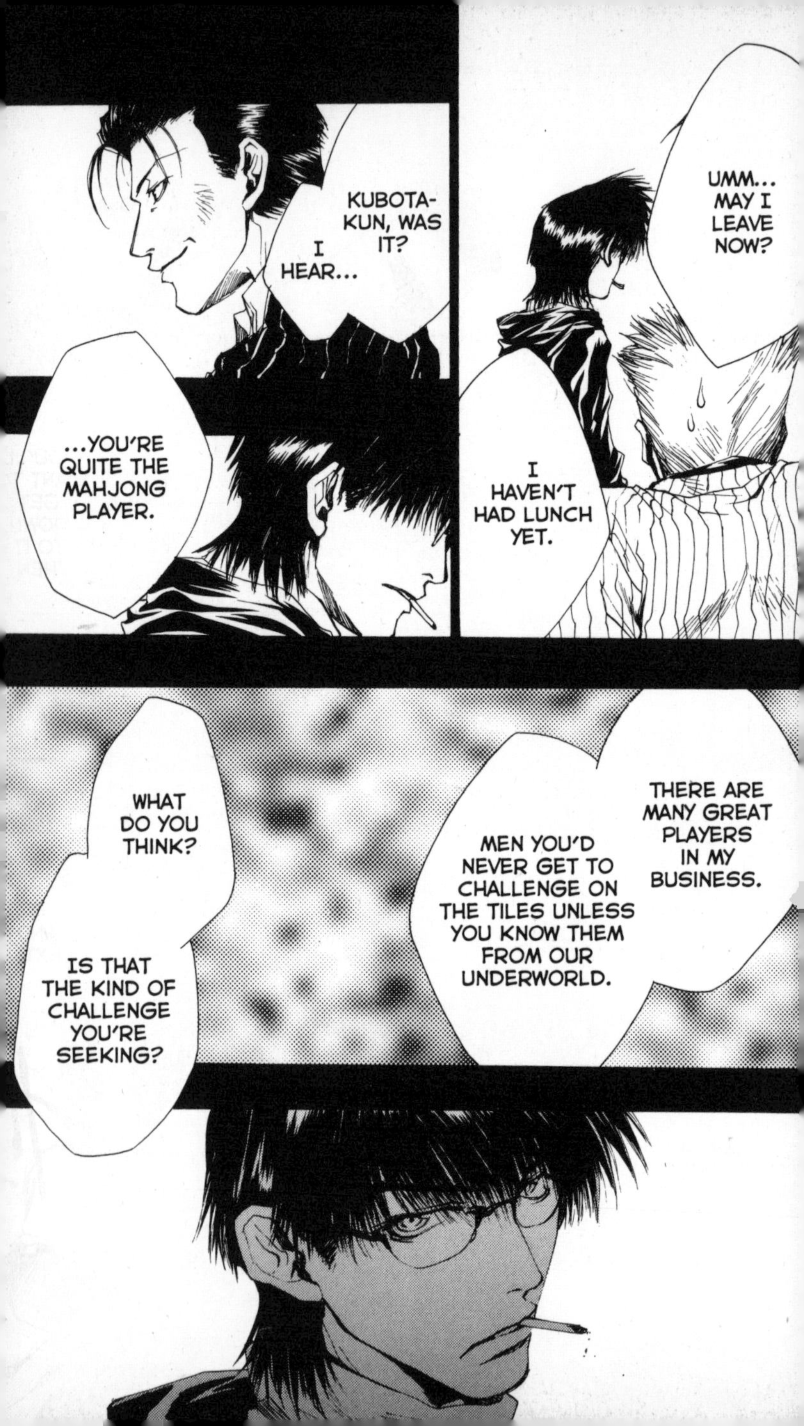
UMM... MAY I LEAVE NOW?
I HAVEN'T HAD LUNCH YET.
KUBOTA-KUN, WAS IT?
I HEAR...
...YOU'RE QUITE THE MAHJONG PLAYER.
THERE ARE MANY GREAT PLAYERS IN MY BUSINESS.
MEN YOU'D NEVER GET TO CHALLENGE ON THE TILES UNLESS YOU KNOW THEM FROM OUR UNDERWORLD.
WHAT DO YOU THINK?
IS THAT THE KIND OF CHALLENGE YOU'RE SEEKING?

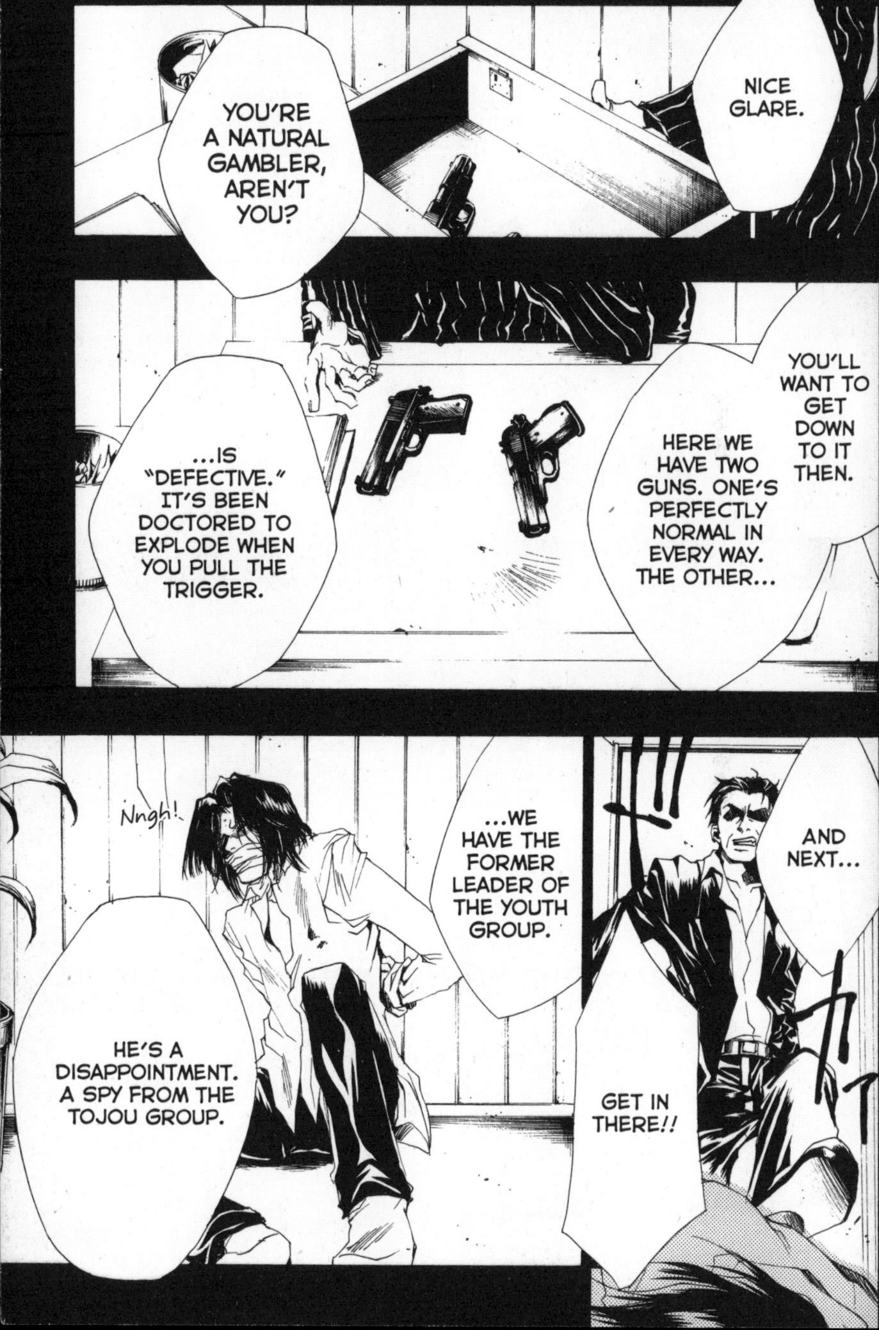
NICE GLARE.
YOU'RE A NATURAL GAMBLER, AREN'T YOU?
YOU'LL WANT TO GET DOWN TO IT THEN.
HERE WE HAVE TWO GUNS. ONE'S PERFECTLY NORMAL IN EVERY WAY. THE OTHER...
...IS "DEFECTIVE." IT'S BEEN DOCTORED TO EXPLODE WHEN YOU PULL THE TRIGGER.
AND NEXT...
GET IN THERE!!
...WE HAVE THE FORMER LEADER OF THE YOUTH GROUP.
Nngh!
HE'S A DISAPPOINTMENT. A SPY FROM THE TOJOU GROUP.

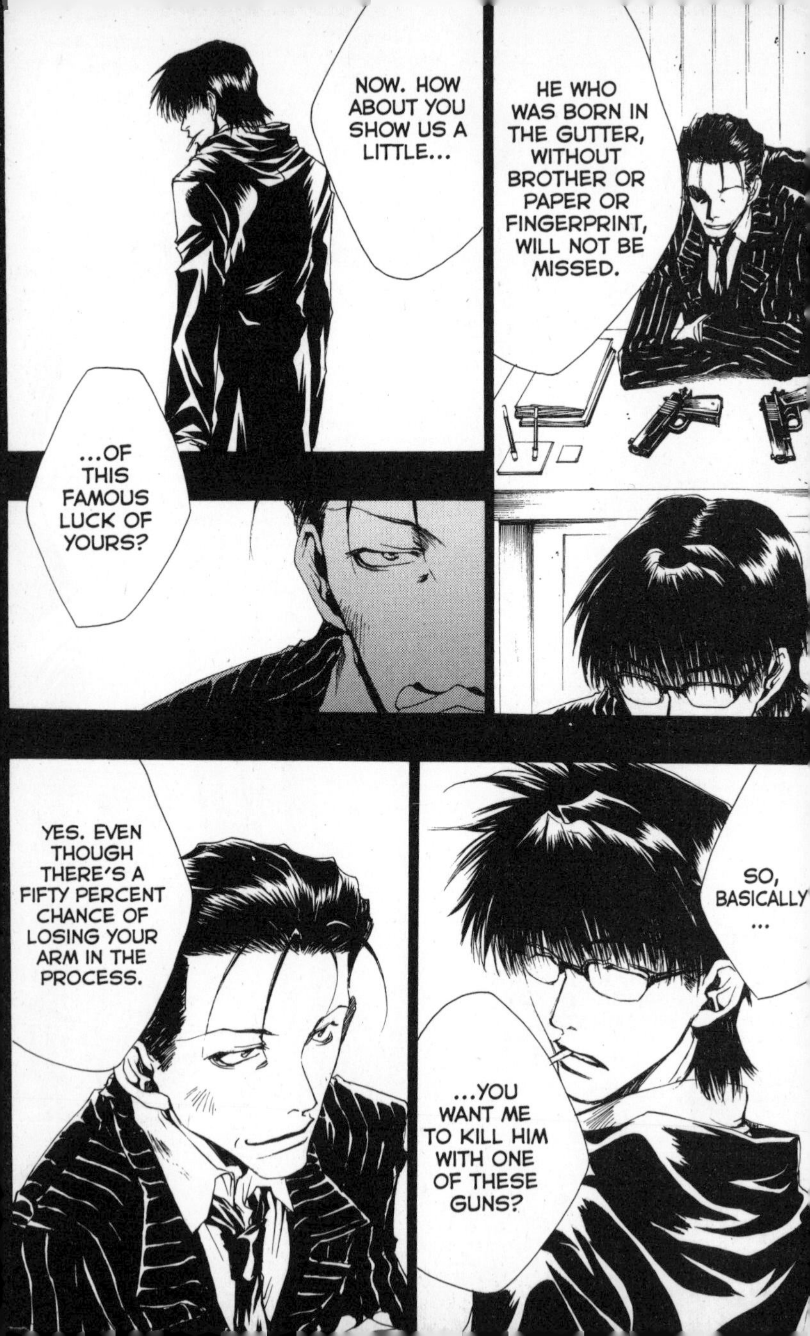
HE WHO WAS BORN IN THE GUTTER, WITHOUT BROTHER OR PAPER OR FINGERPRINT, WILL NOT BE MISSED.
NOW. HOW ABOUT YOU SHOW US A LITTLE...
...OF THIS FAMOUS LUCK OF YOURS?
SO, BASICALLY...
...YOU WANT ME TO KILL HIM WITH ONE OF THESE GUNS?
YES. EVEN THOUGH THERE'S A FIFTY PERCENT CHANCE OF LOSING YOUR ARM IN THE PROCESS.

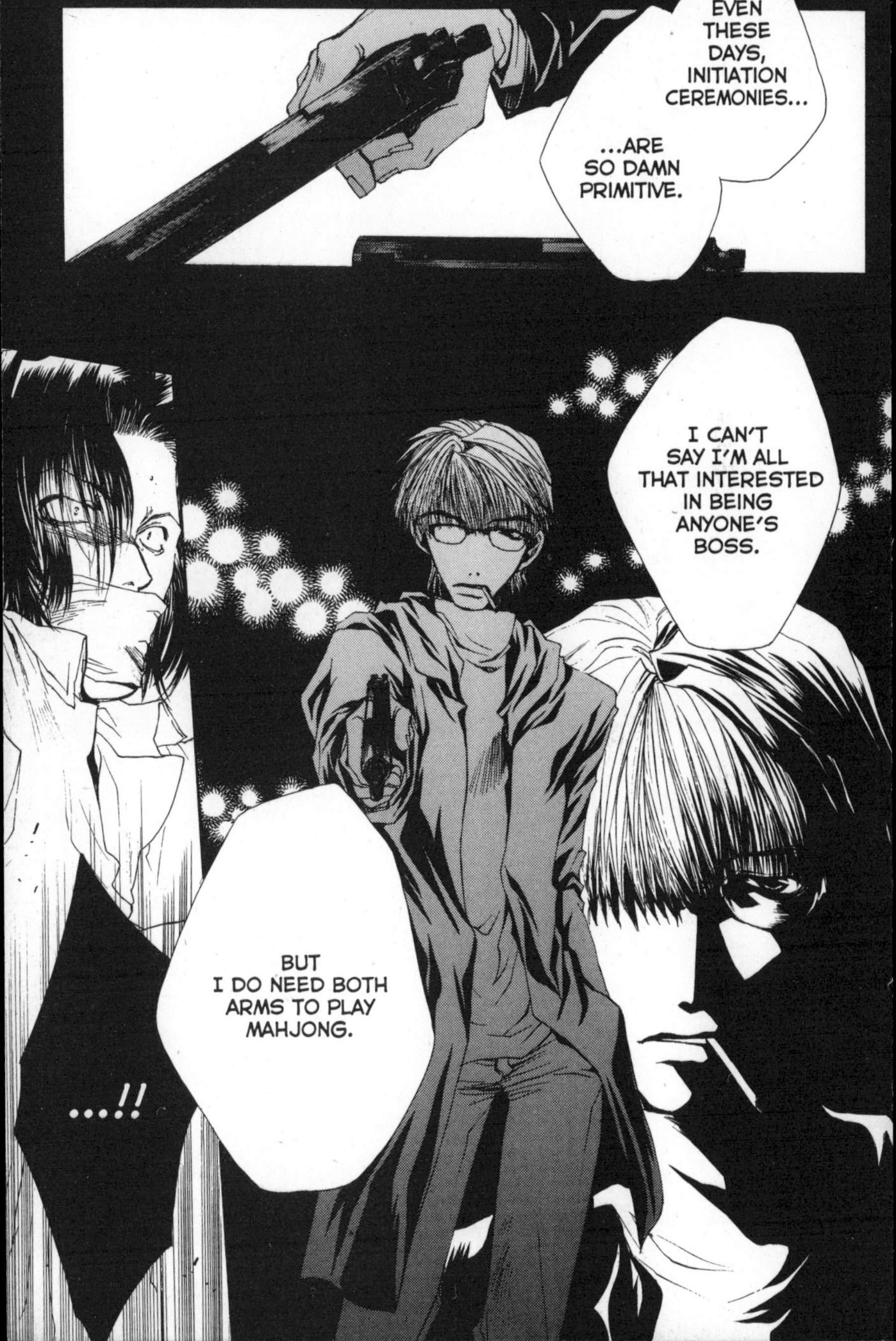
EVEN THESE DAYS, INITIATION CEREMONIES...
...ARE SO DAMN PRIMITIVE.
I CAN'T SAY I'M ALL THAT INTERESTED IN BEING ANYONE'S BOSS.
BUT I DO NEED BOTH ARMS TO PLAY MAHJONG.
...!!

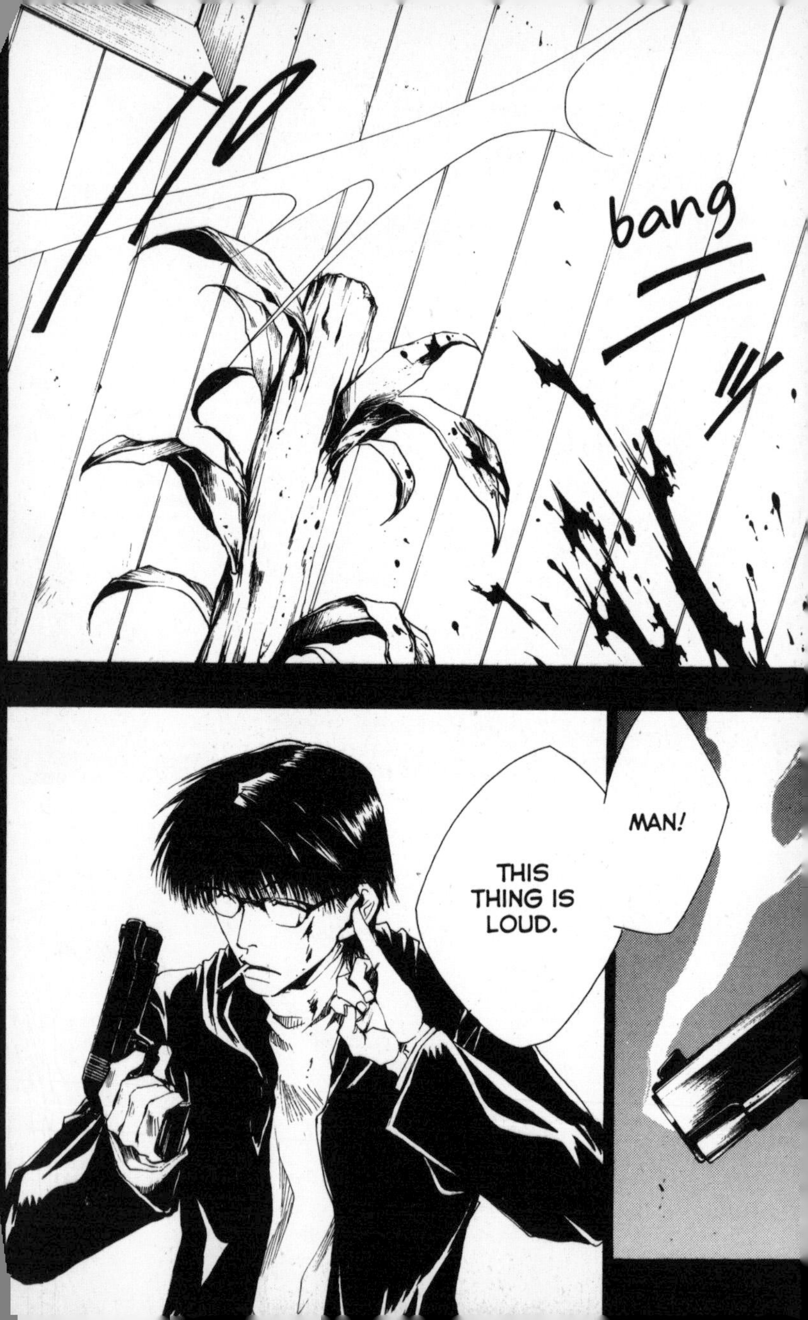
bang
MAN!
THIS THING IS LOUD.

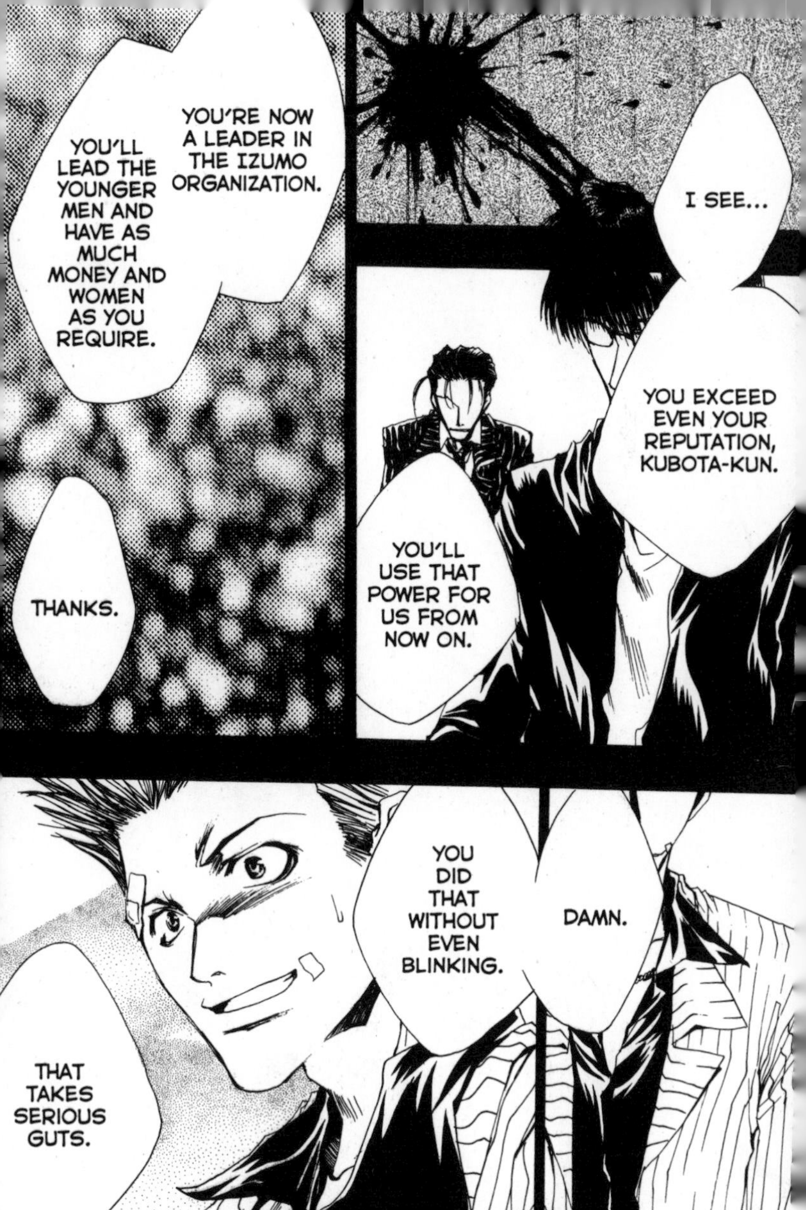
I SEE...
YOU EXCEED EVEN YOUR REPUTATION, KUBOTA-KUN.
YOU'LL USE THAT POWER FOR US FROM NOW ON.
YOU'RE NOW A LEADER IN THE IZUMO ORGANIZATION.
YOU'LL LEAD THE YOUNGER MEN AND HAVE AS MUCH MONEY AND WOMEN AS YOU REQUIRE.
THANKS.
DAMN.
YOU DID THAT WITHOUT EVEN BLINKING.
THAT TAKES SERIOUS GUTS.

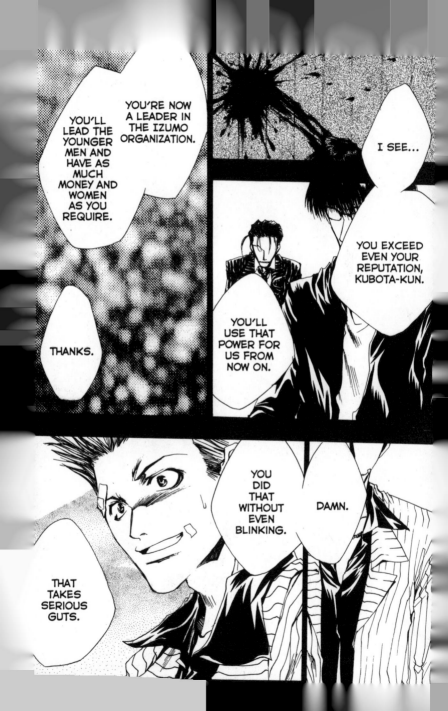

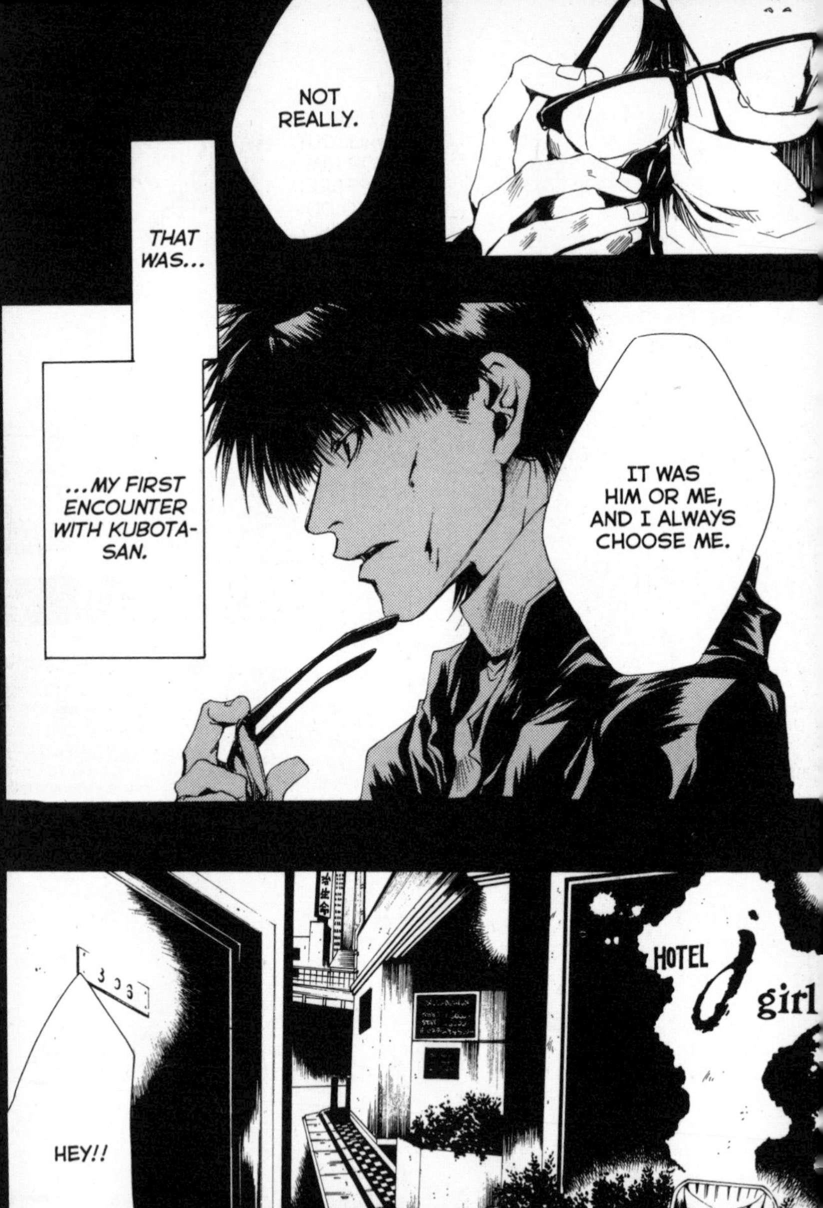
NOT REALLY.
THAT WAS...
IT WAS HIM OR ME, AND I ALWAYS CHOOSE ME.
...MY FIRST ENCOUNTER WITH KUBOTA-SAN.
HOTEL
girl
HEY!!

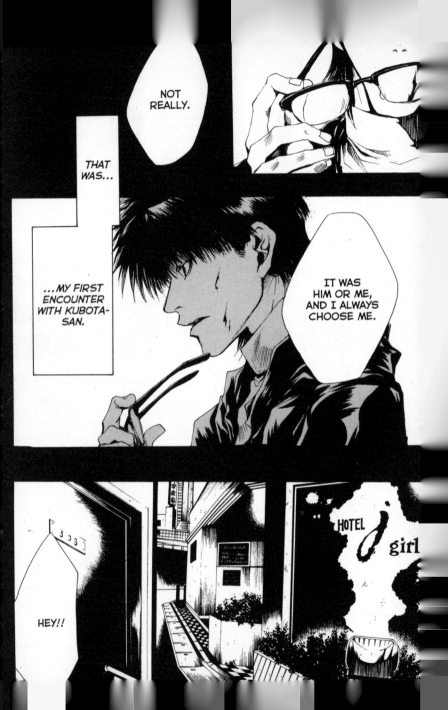

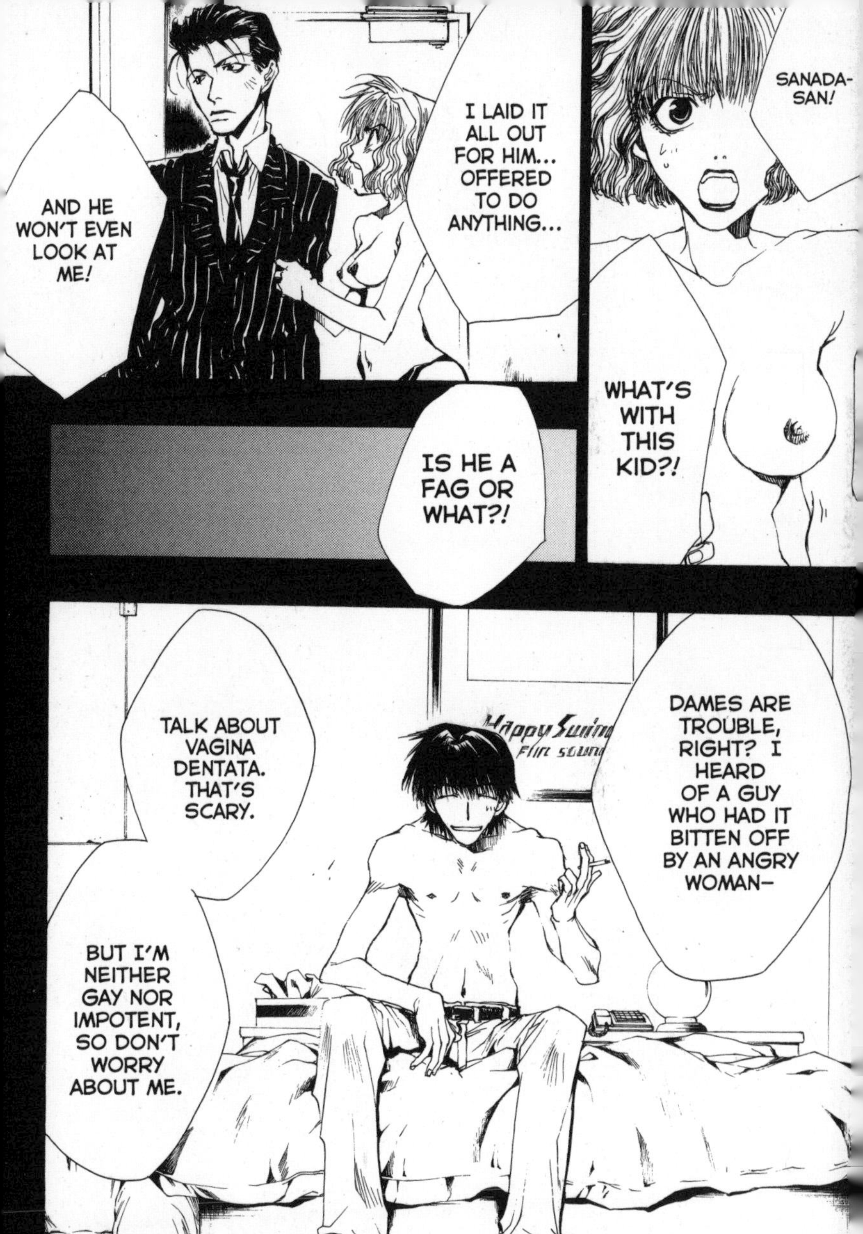
SANADA-SAN!
WHAT'S WITH THIS KID?!
I LAID IT ALL OUT FOR HIM... OFFERED TO DO ANYTHING...
AND HE WON'T EVEN LOOK AT ME!
IS HE A FAG OR WHAT?!
DAMES ARE TROUBLE, RIGHT? I HEARD OF A GUY WHO HAD IT BITTEN OFF BY AN ANGRY WOMAN–
TALK ABOUT VAGINA DENTATA. THAT'S SCARY.
BUT I'M NEITHER GAY NOR IMPOTENT, SO DON'T WORRY ABOUT ME.

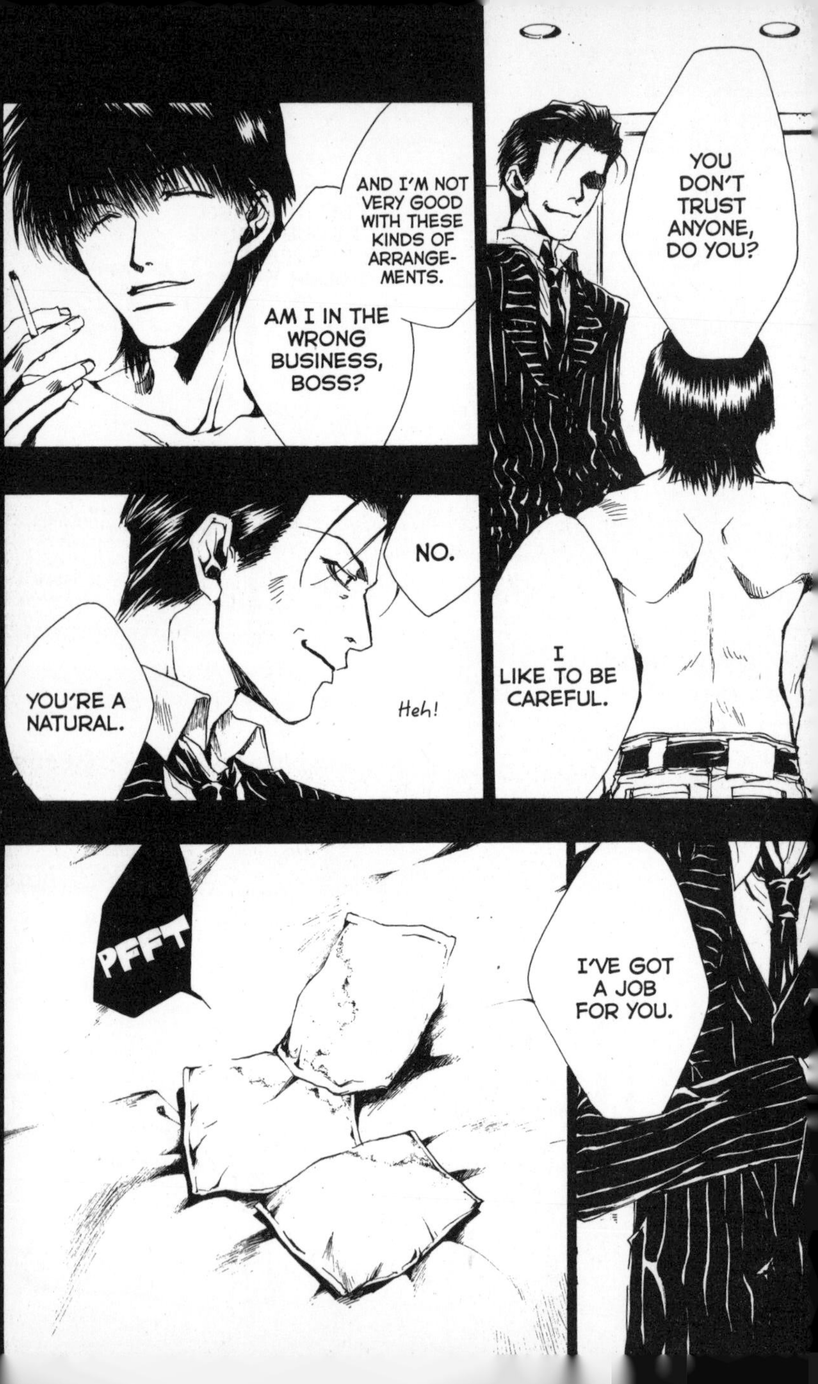
YOU DON'T TRUST ANYONE, DO YOU?
I LIKE TO BE CAREFUL.
AND I'M NOT VERY GOOD WITH THESE KINDS OF ARRANGE-MENTS.
AM I IN THE WRONG BUSINESS, BOSS?
NO.
Heh!
YOU'RE A NATURAL.
I'VE GOT A JOB FOR YOU.
PFFT

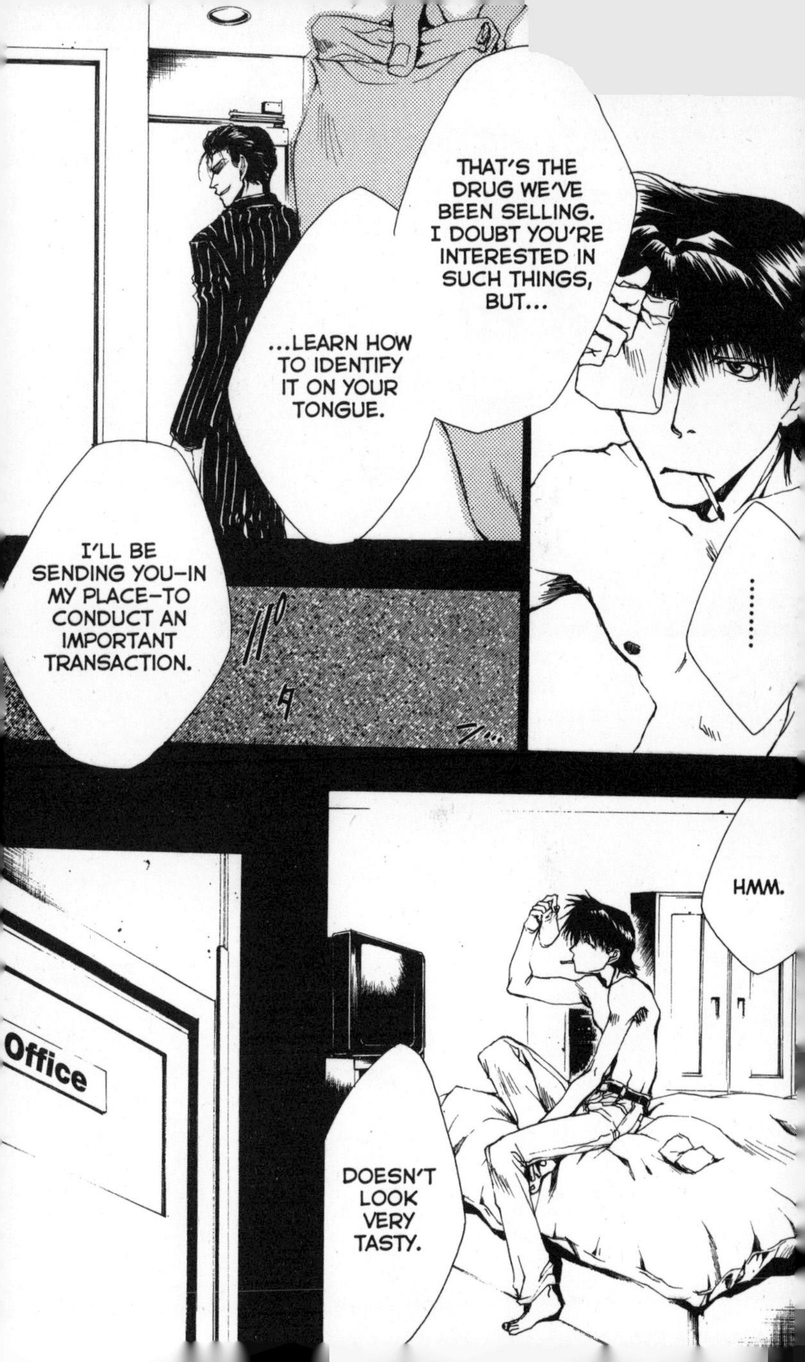
THAT'S THE DRUG WE'VE BEEN SELLING. I DOUBT YOU'RE INTERESTED IN SUCH THINGS, BUT...
...LEARN HOW TO IDENTIFY IT ON YOUR TONGUE.
I'LL BE SENDING YOU—IN MY PLACE—TO CONDUCT AN IMPORTANT TRANSACTION.
......
HMM.
DOESN'T LOOK VERY TASTY.
Office

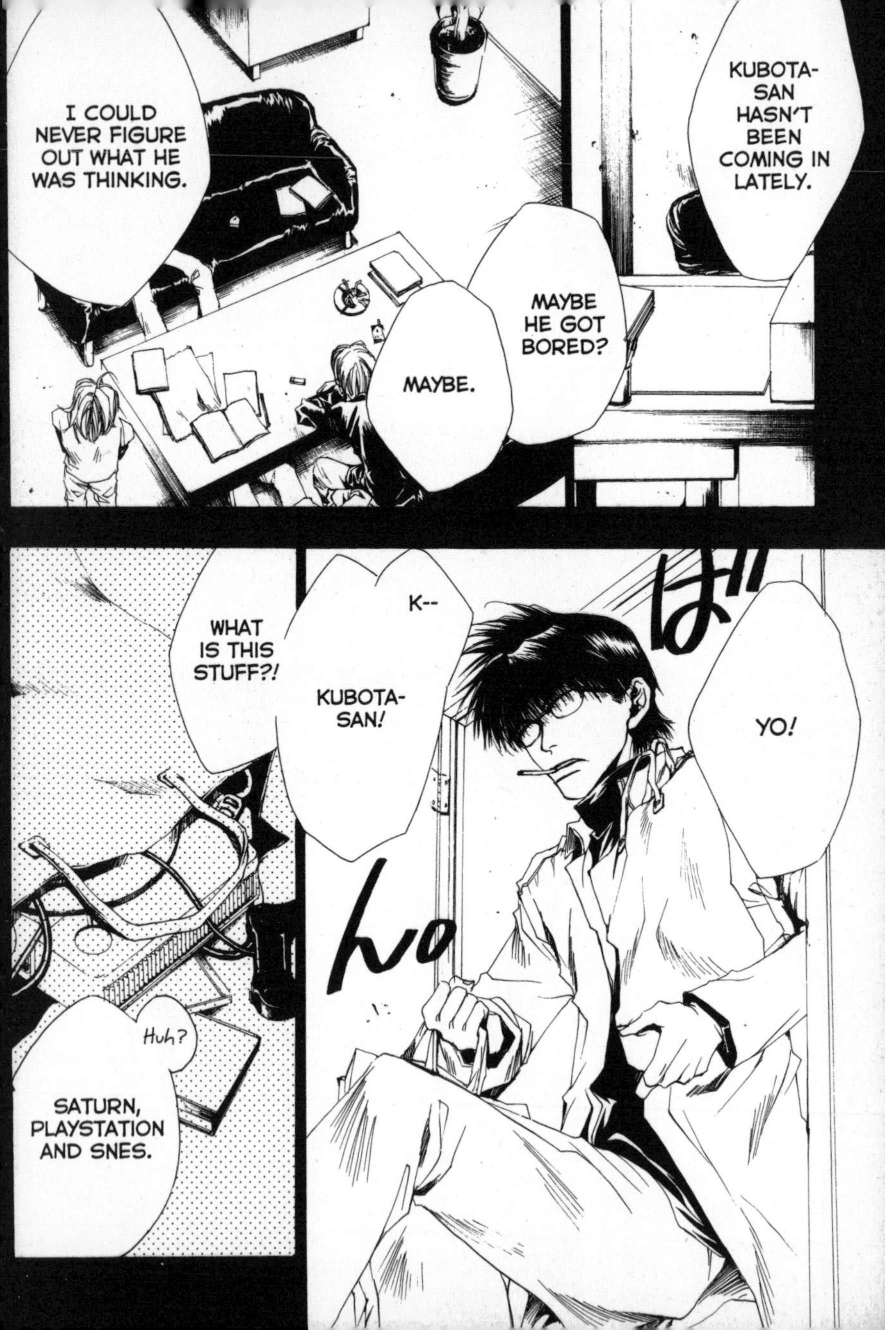
KUBOTA-SAN HASN'T BEEN COMING IN LATELY.
MAYBE HE GOT BORED?
MAYBE.
I COULD NEVER FIGURE OUT WHAT HE WAS THINKING.
ば
YO!
K--
KUBOTA-SAN!
ho
WHAT IS THIS STUFF?!
Huh?
SATURN, PLAYSTATION AND SNES.

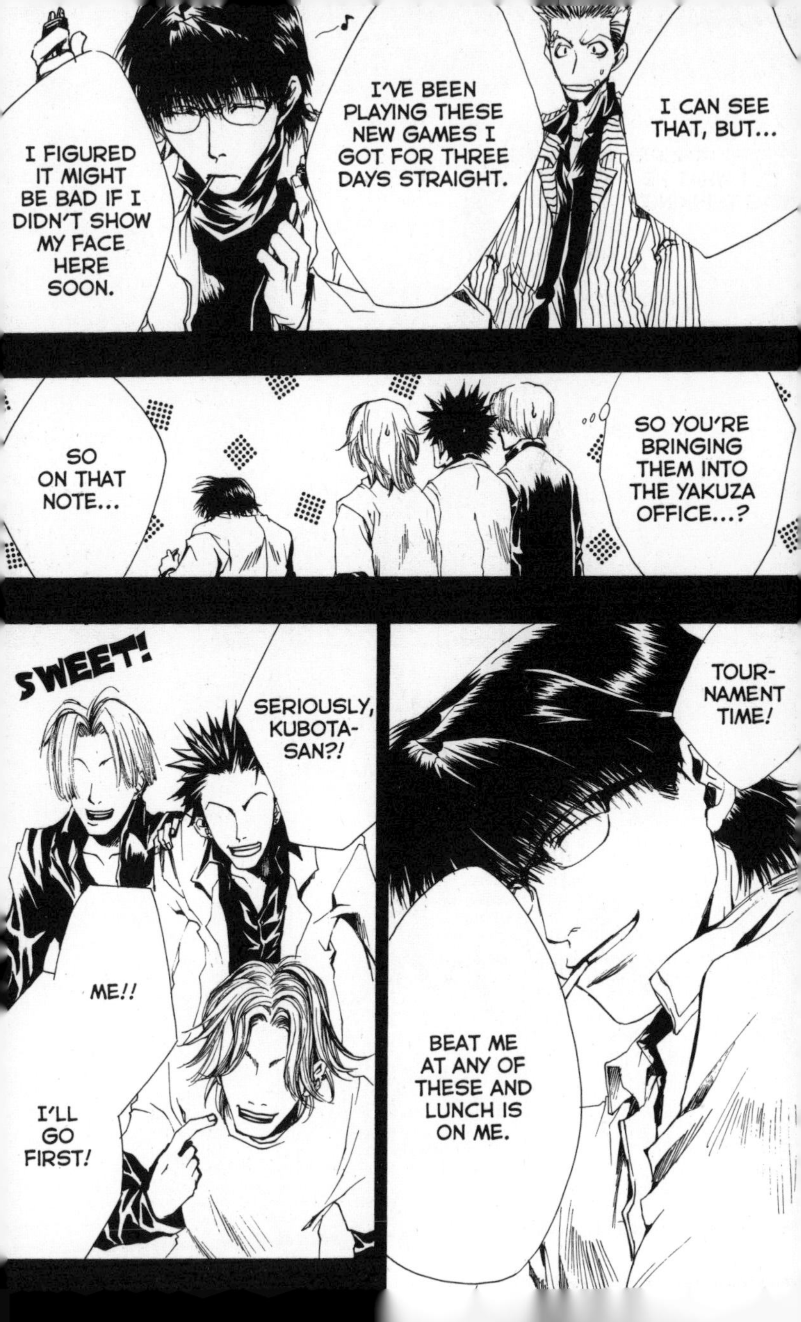
I CAN SEE THAT, BUT...
I'VE BEEN PLAYING THESE NEW GAMES I GOT FOR THREE DAYS STRAIGHT.
I FIGURED IT MIGHT BE BAD IF I DIDN'T SHOW MY FACE HERE SOON.
SO YOU'RE BRINGING THEM INTO THE YAKUZA OFFICE...?
SO ON THAT NOTE...
TOUR-NAMENT TIME!
BEAT ME AT ANY OF THESE AND LUNCH IS ON ME.
SERIOUSLY, KUBOTA-SAN?!
SWEET!
ME!!
I'LL GO FIRST!

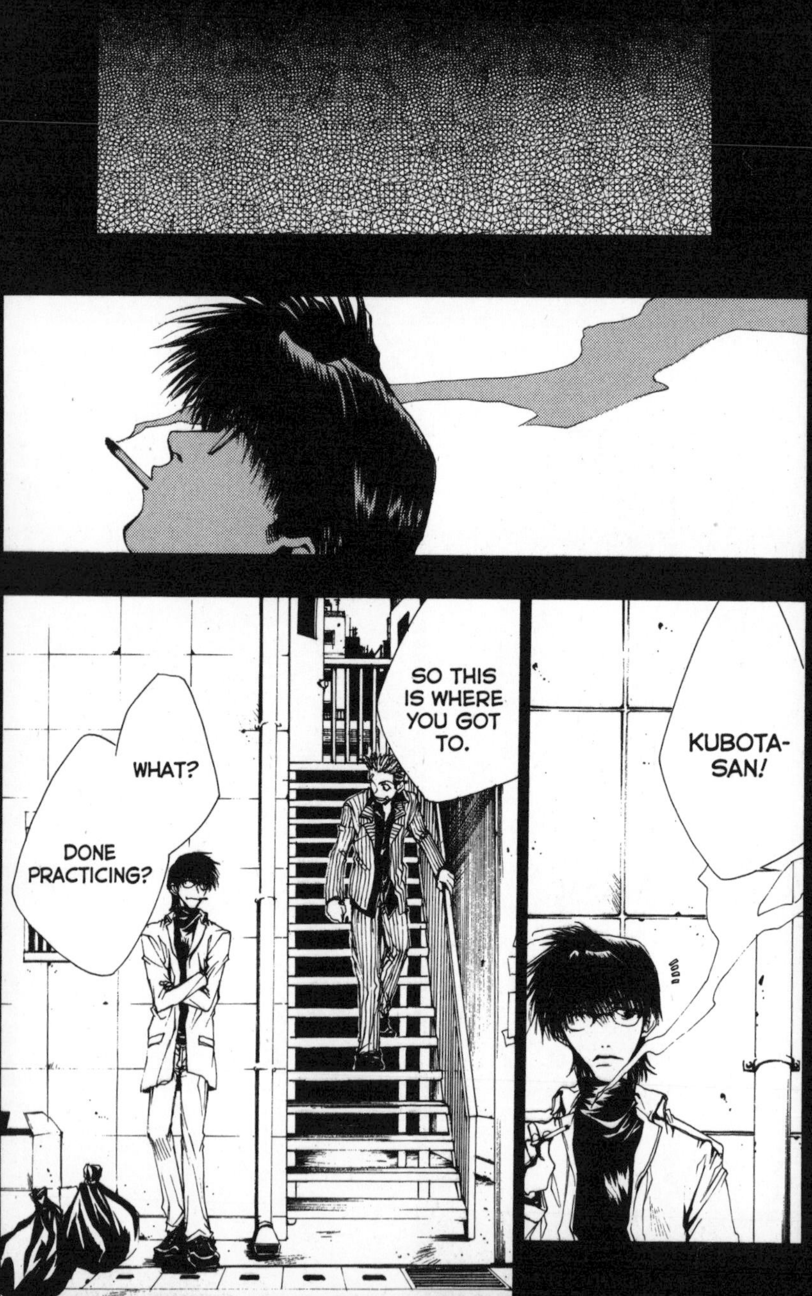
KUBOTA-SAN!
SO THIS IS WHERE YOU GOT TO.
WHAT?
DONE PRACTICING?

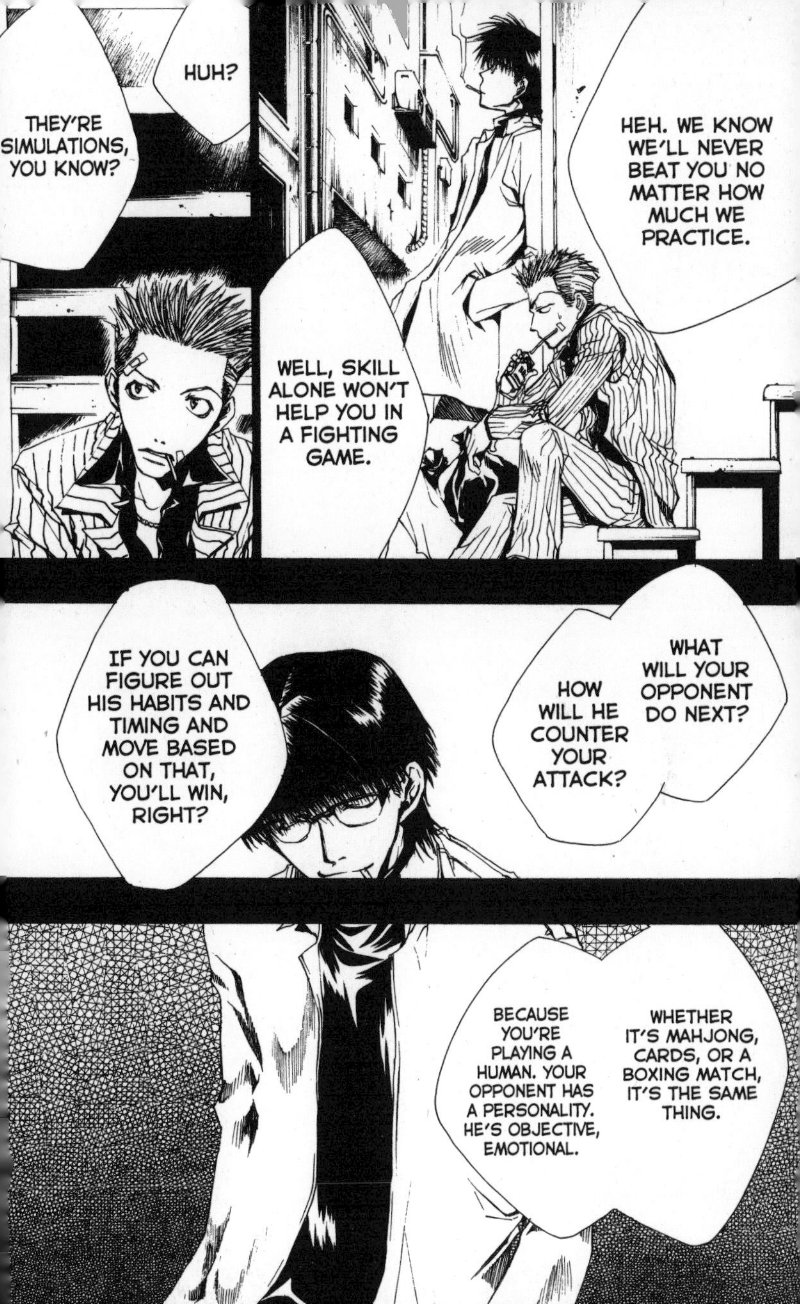
HEH. WE KNOW WE'LL NEVER BEAT YOU NO MATTER HOW MUCH WE PRACTICE.
WELL, SKILL ALONE WON'T HELP YOU IN A FIGHTING GAME.
HUH?
THEY'RE SIMULATIONS, YOU KNOW?
WHAT WILL YOUR OPPONENT DO NEXT?
HOW WILL HE COUNTER YOUR ATTACK?
IF YOU CAN FIGURE OUT HIS HABITS AND TIMING AND MOVE BASED ON THAT, YOU'LL WIN, RIGHT?
WHETHER IT'S MAHJONG, CARDS, OR A BOXING MATCH, IT'S THE SAME THING.
BECAUSE YOU'RE PLAYING A HUMAN. YOUR OPPONENT HAS A PERSONALITY. HE'S OBJECTIVE, EMOTIONAL.

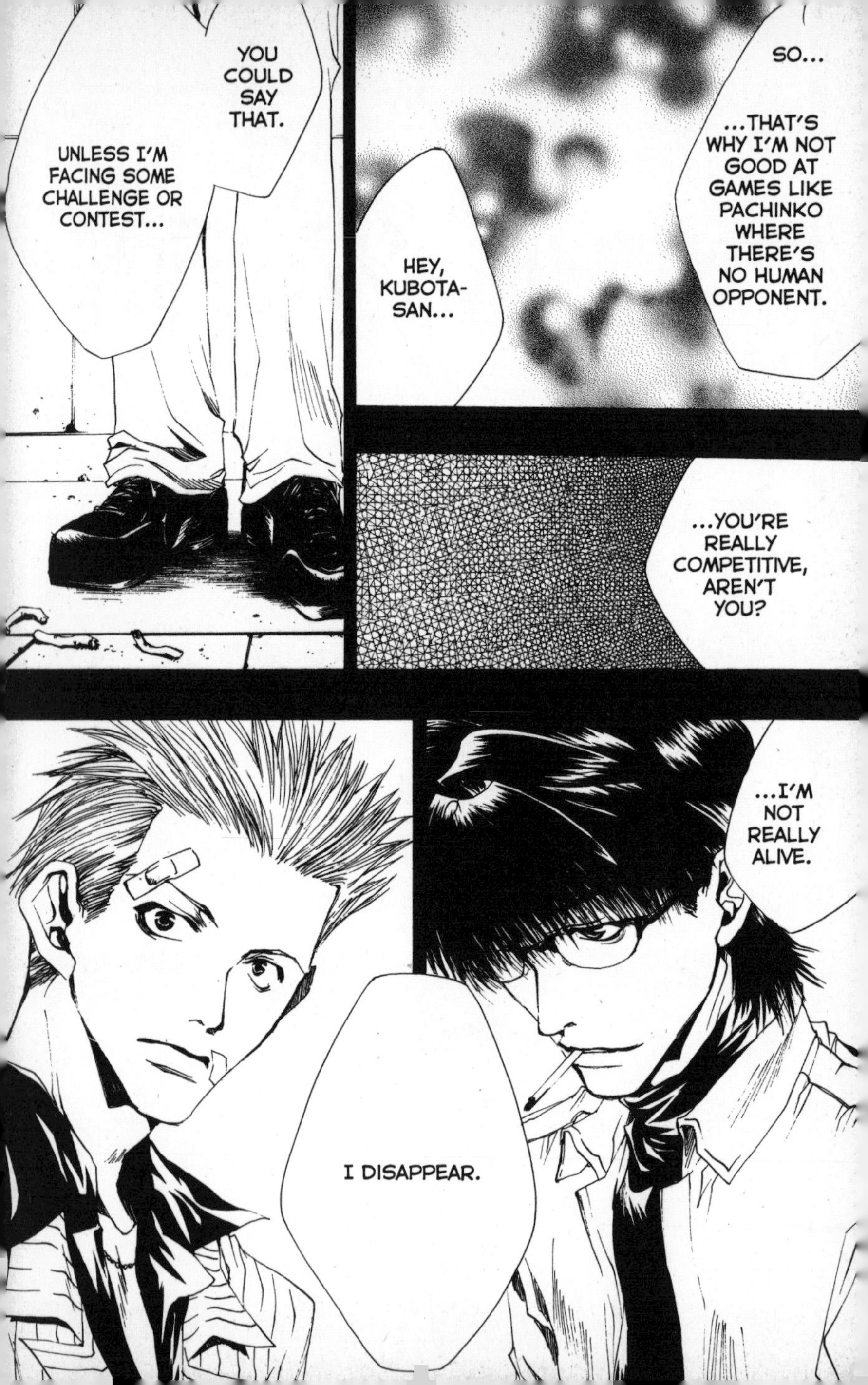
SO...
...THAT'S WHY I'M NOT GOOD AT GAMES LIKE PACHINKO WHERE THERE'S NO HUMAN OPPONENT.
HEY, KUBOTA-SAN...
...YOU'RE REALLY COMPETITIVE, AREN'T YOU?
YOU COULD SAY THAT.
UNLESS I'M FACING SOME CHALLENGE OR CONTEST...
...I'M NOT REALLY ALIVE.
I DISAPPEAR.

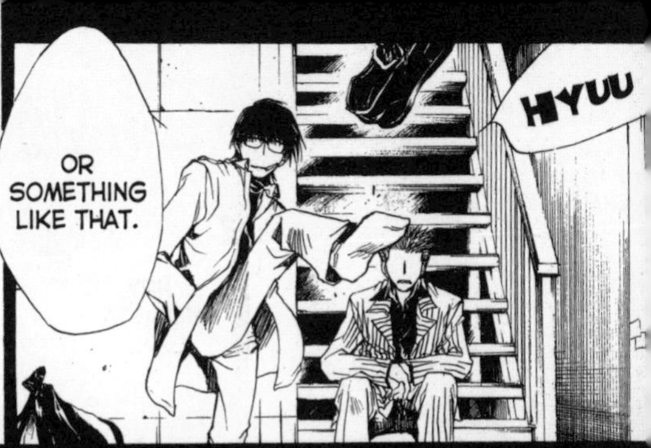
HYUU
OR SOMETHING LIKE THAT.

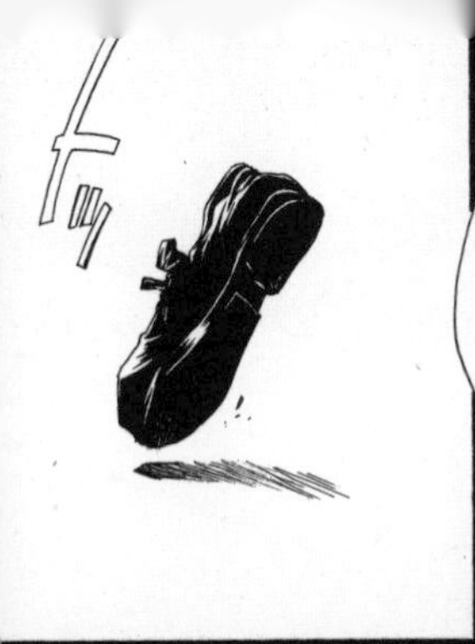
トッ

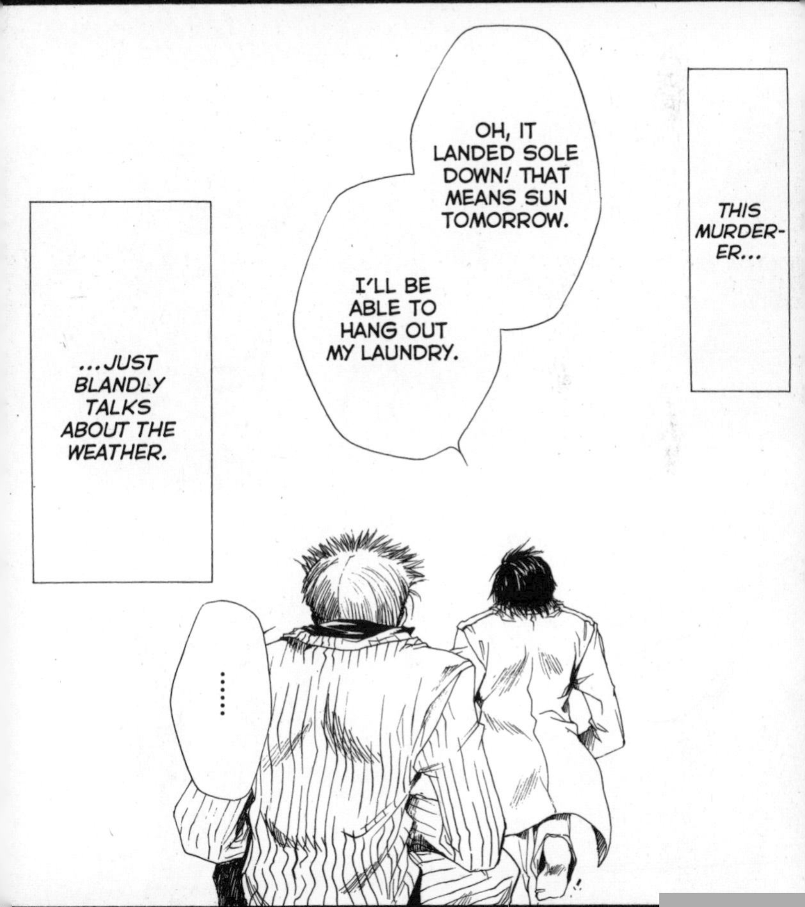
THIS MURDER-ER...
OH, IT LANDED SOLE DOWN! THAT MEANS SUN TOMORROW.
I'LL BE ABLE TO HANG OUT MY LAUNDRY.
...JUST BLANDLY TALKS ABOUT THE WEATHER.
......

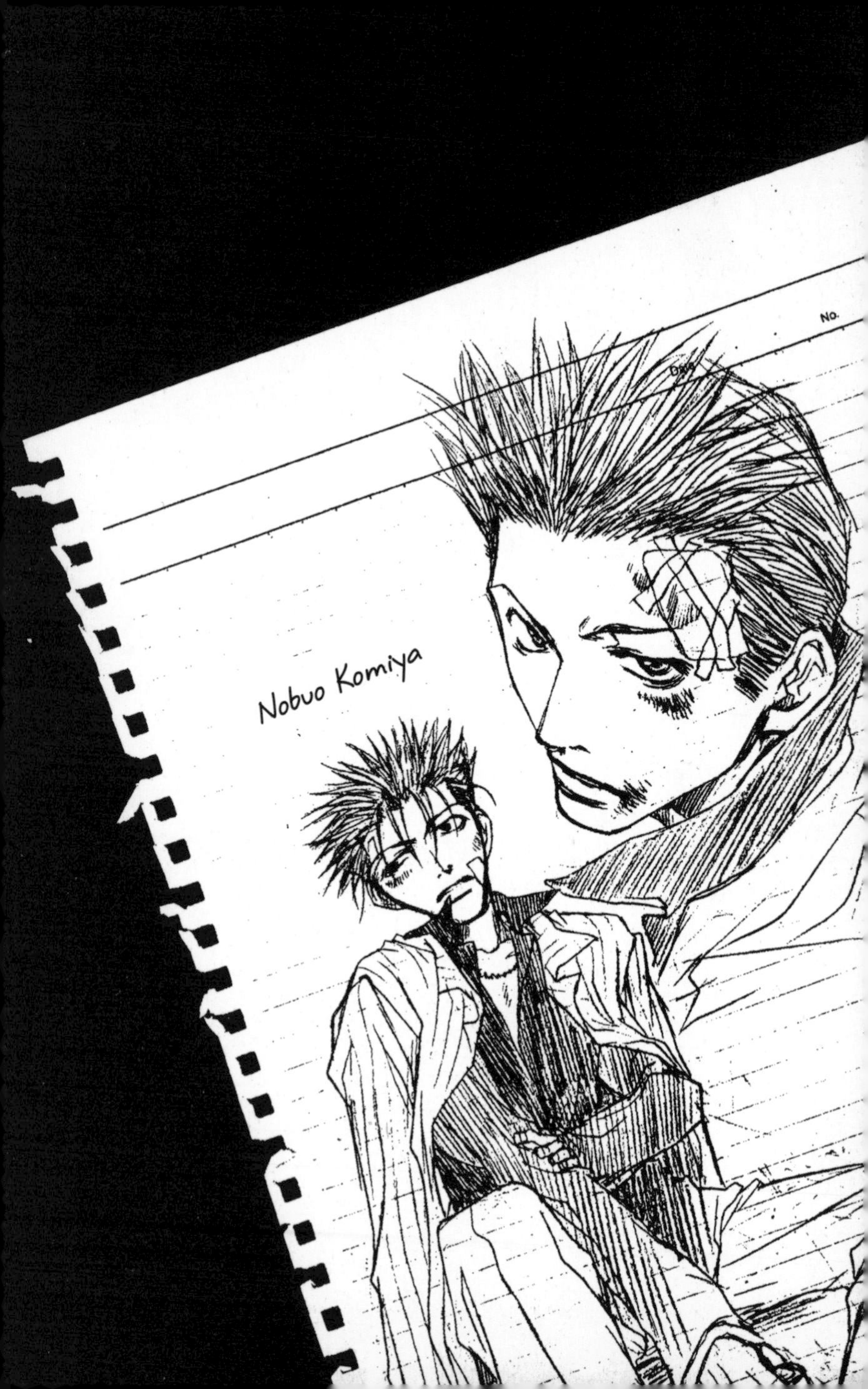
No.
Nobuo Komiya

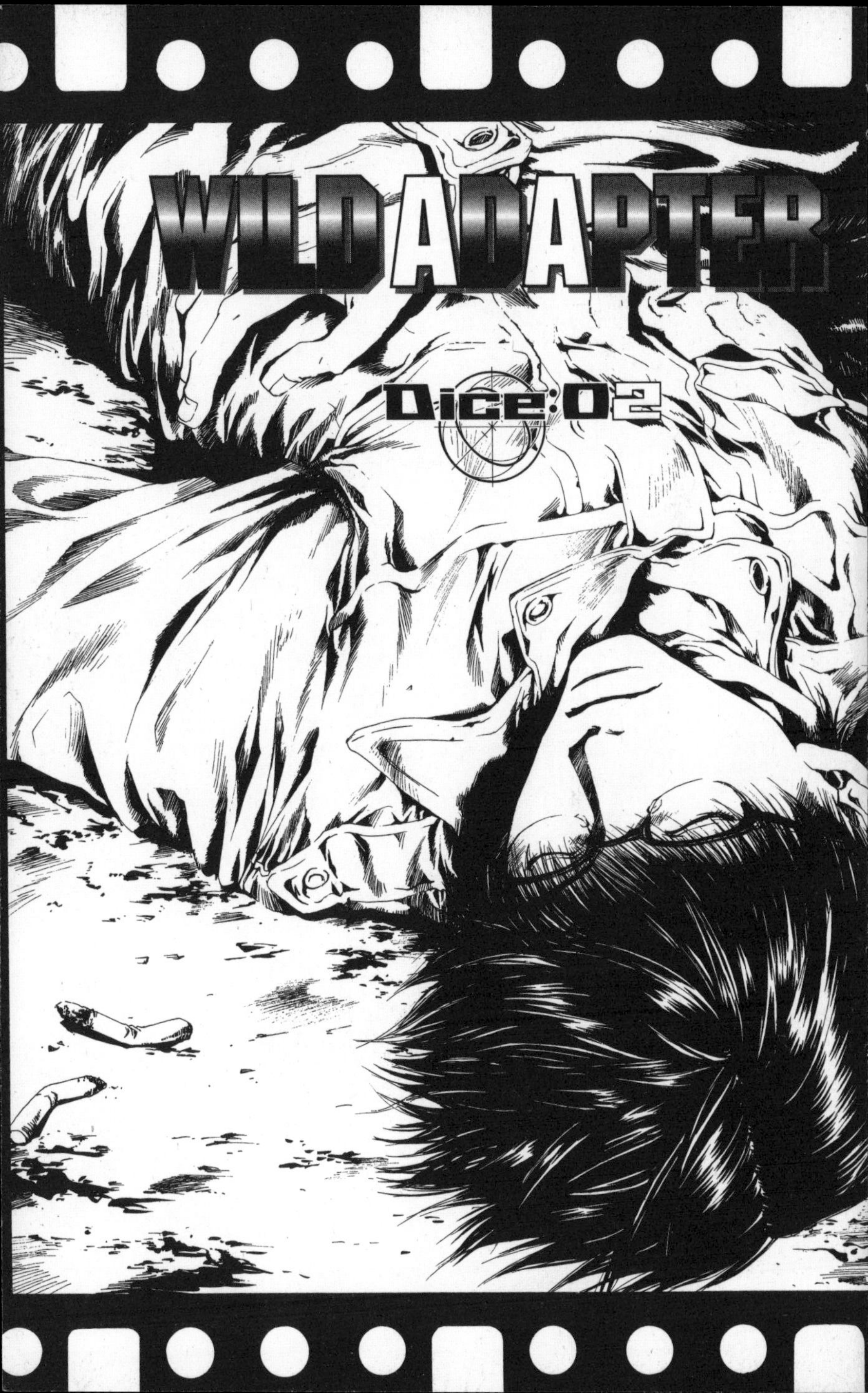
WILD ADAPTER
Dice:02

The more human we become...

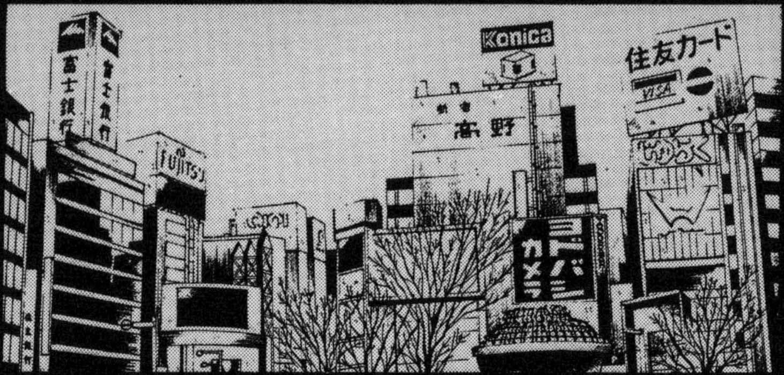

Konica
住友カード

...the more animalistic we are.

~Ryunosuke Akutagawa, *Words of a Dwarf.*

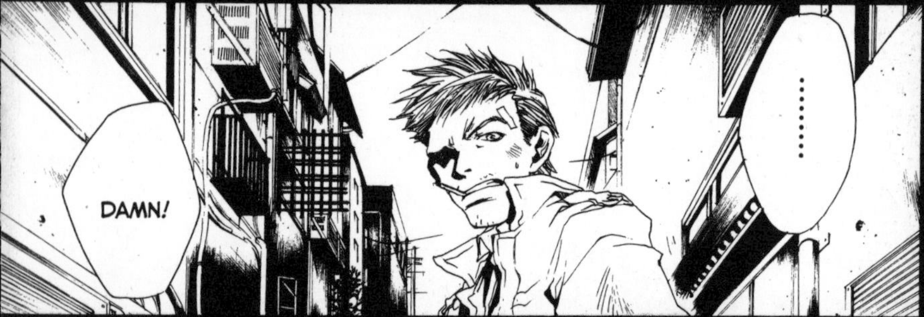

....
DAMN!

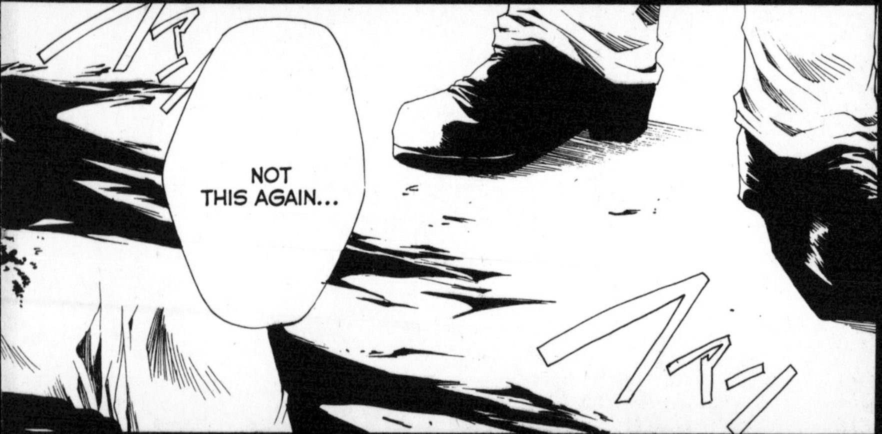

NOT THIS AGAIN...

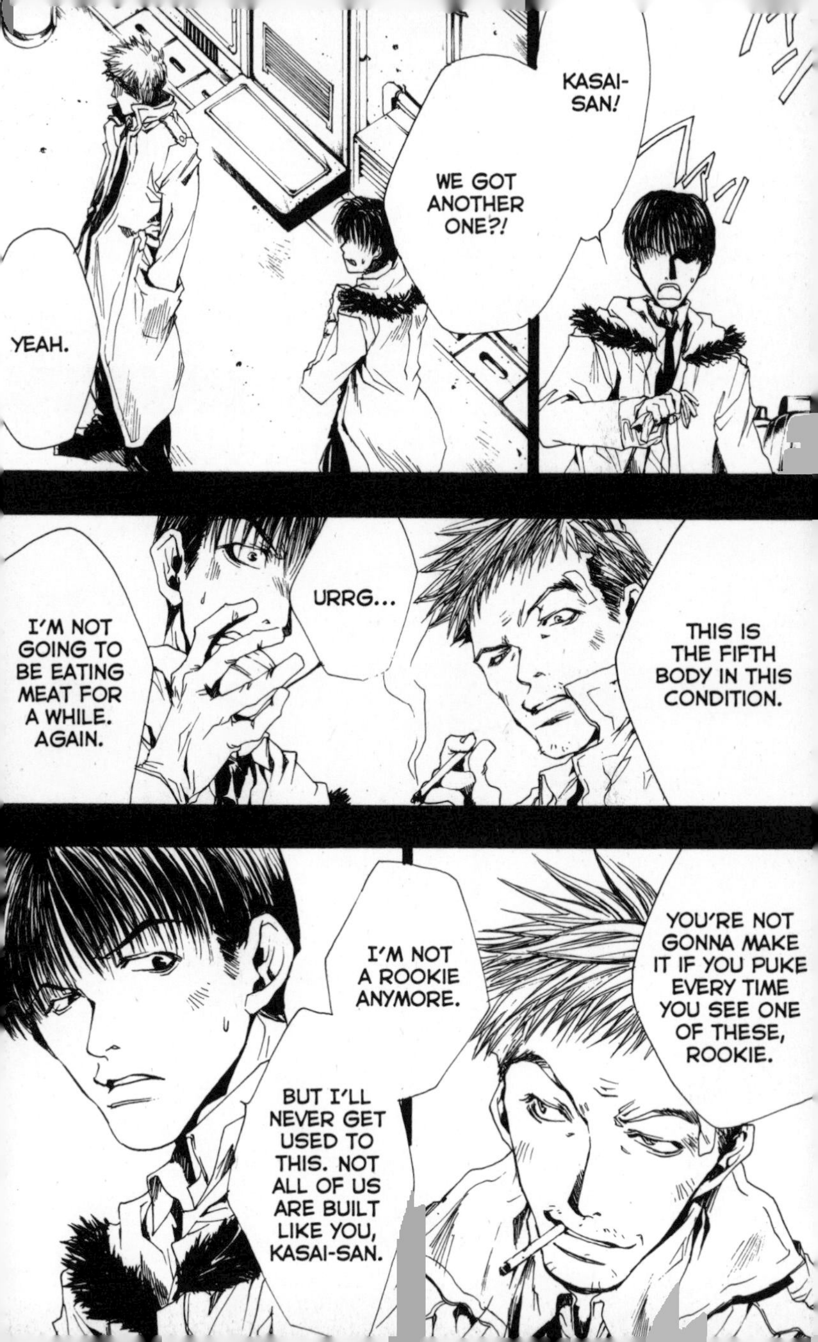
KASAI-SAN!
WE GOT ANOTHER ONE?!
YEAH.
THIS IS THE FIFTH BODY IN THIS CONDITION.
URRG...
I'M NOT GOING TO BE EATING MEAT FOR A WHILE. AGAIN.
YOU'RE NOT GONNA MAKE IT IF YOU PUKE EVERY TIME YOU SEE ONE OF THESE, ROOKIE.
I'M NOT A ROOKIE ANYMORE.
BUT I'LL NEVER GET USED TO THIS. NOT ALL OF US ARE BUILT LIKE YOU, KASAI-SAN.

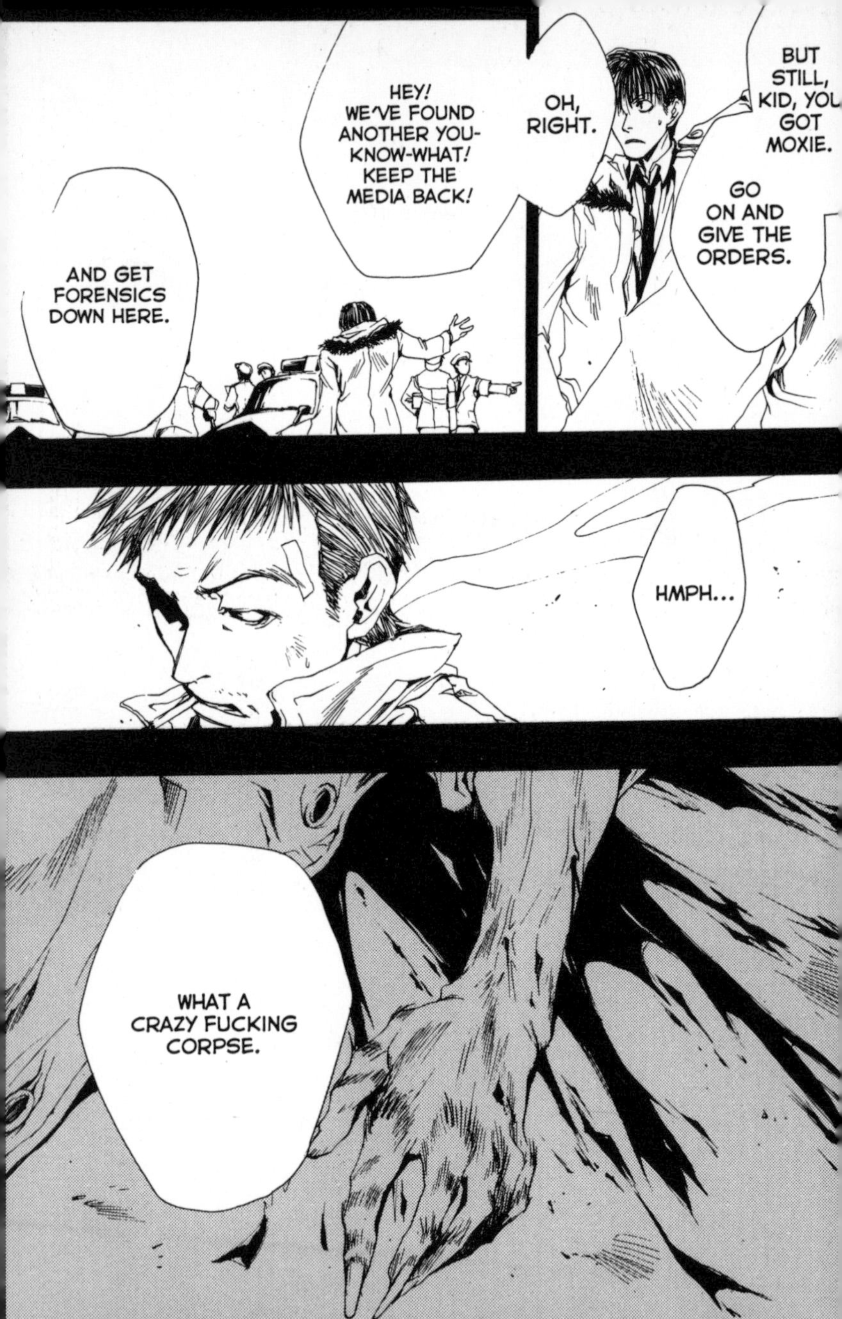
BUT STILL, KID, YOU GOT MOXIE.
GO ON AND GIVE THE ORDERS.
OH, RIGHT.
HEY! WE'VE FOUND ANOTHER YOU-KNOW-WHAT! KEEP THE MEDIA BACK!
AND GET FORENSICS DOWN HERE.
HMPH...
WHAT A CRAZY FUCKING CORPSE.

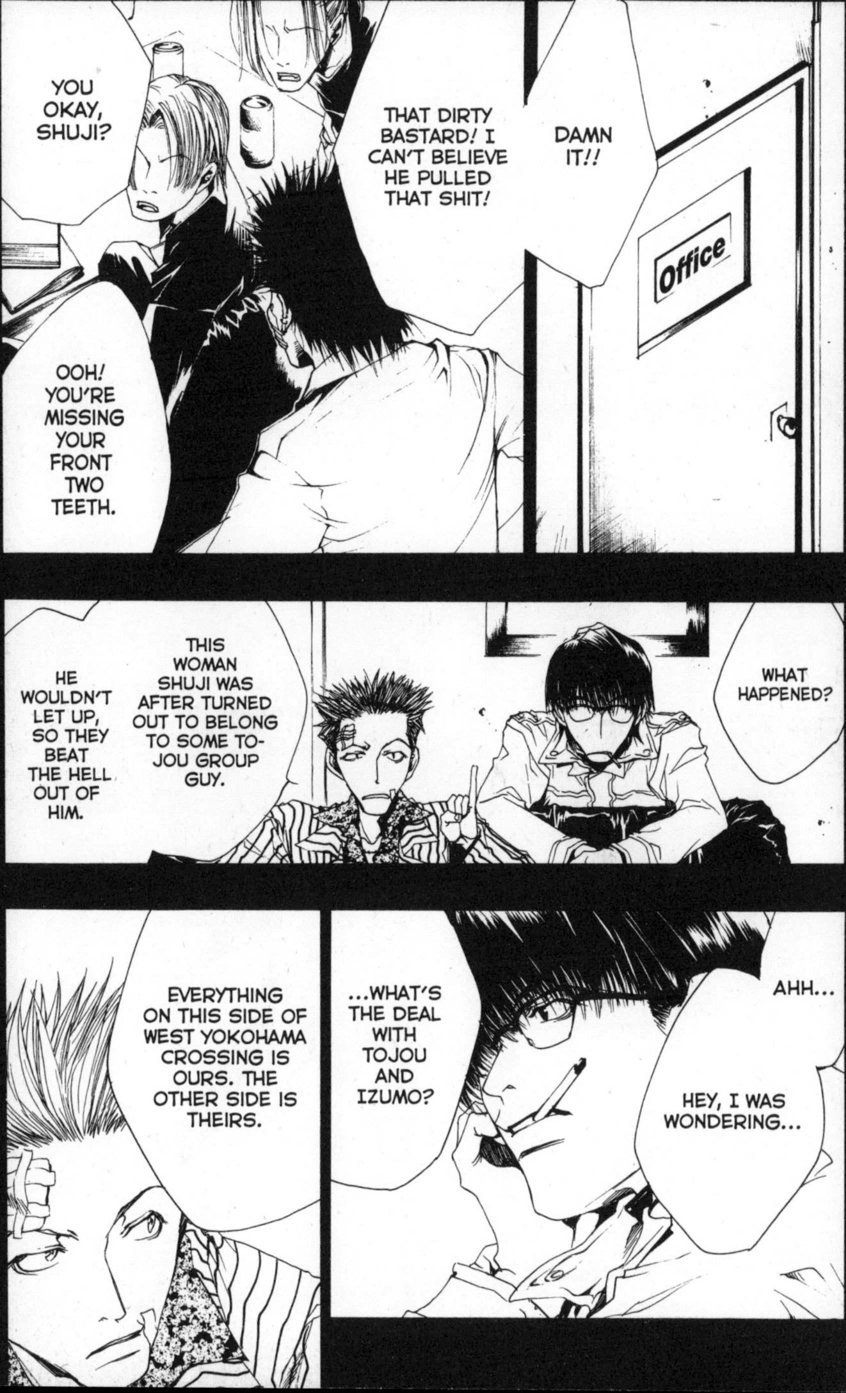
DAMN IT!!
THAT DIRTY BASTARD! I CAN'T BELIEVE HE PULLED THAT SHIT!
YOU OKAY, SHUJI?
OOH! YOU'RE MISSING YOUR FRONT TWO TEETH.
Office
WHAT HAPPENED?
THIS WOMAN SHUJI WAS AFTER TURNED OUT TO BELONG TO SOME TO-JOU GROUP GUY.
HE WOULDN'T LET UP, SO THEY BEAT THE HELL OUT OF HIM.
AHH...
HEY, I WAS WONDERING...
...WHAT'S THE DEAL WITH TOJOU AND IZUMO?
EVERYTHING ON THIS SIDE OF WEST YOKOHAMA CROSSING IS OURS. THE OTHER SIDE IS THEIRS.

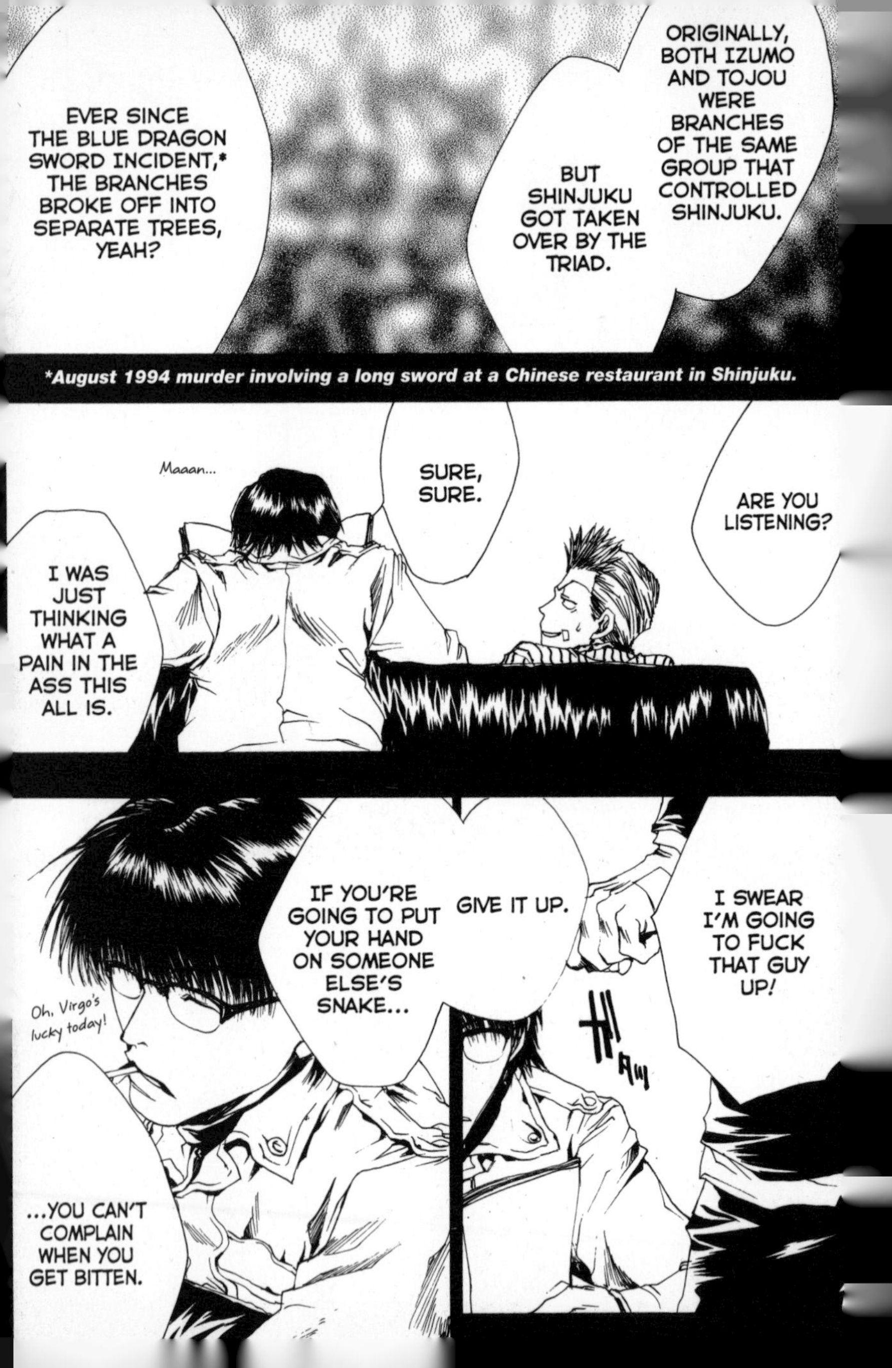
ORIGINALLY, BOTH IZUMO AND TOJOU WERE BRANCHES OF THE SAME GROUP THAT CONTROLLED SHINJUKU.
BUT SHINJUKU GOT TAKEN OVER BY THE TRIAD.
EVER SINCE THE BLUE DRAGON SWORD INCIDENT,* THE BRANCHES BROKE OFF INTO SEPARATE TREES, YEAH?
ARE YOU LISTENING?
SURE, SURE.
Maaan...
I WAS JUST THINKING WHAT A PAIN IN THE ASS THIS ALL IS.
I SWEAR I'M GOING TO FUCK THAT GUY UP!
GIVE IT UP.
IF YOU'RE GOING TO PUT YOUR HAND ON SOMEONE ELSE'S SNAKE...
Oh, Virgo's lucky today!
...YOU CAN'T COMPLAIN WHEN YOU GET BITTEN.

***August 1994 murder involving a long sword at a Chinese restaurant in Shinjuku.**

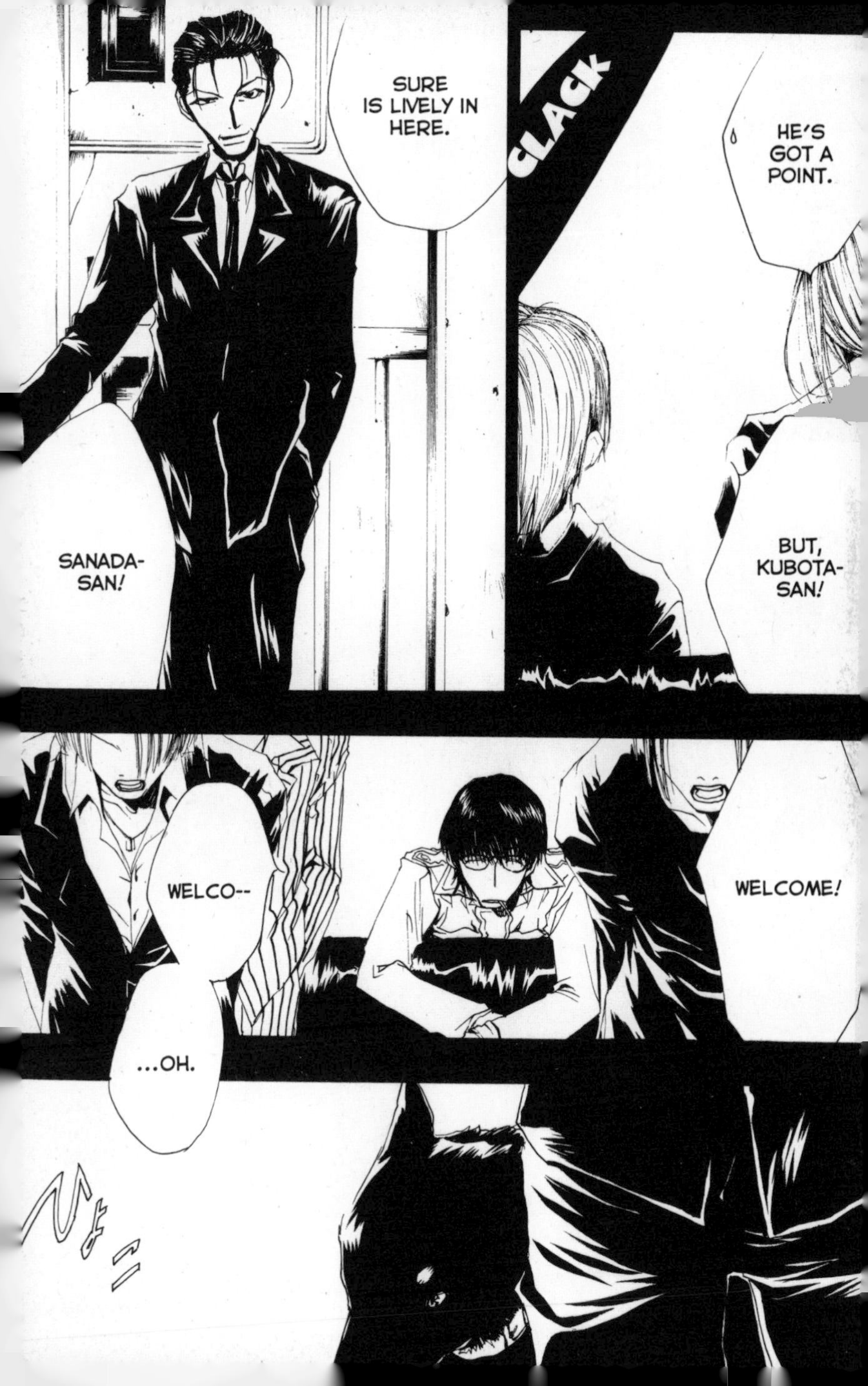

CLACK
HE'S GOT A POINT.
BUT, KUBOTA-SAN!
SURE IS LIVELY IN HERE.
SANADA-SAN!
WELCOME!
WELCO--
...OH.
ひょこ

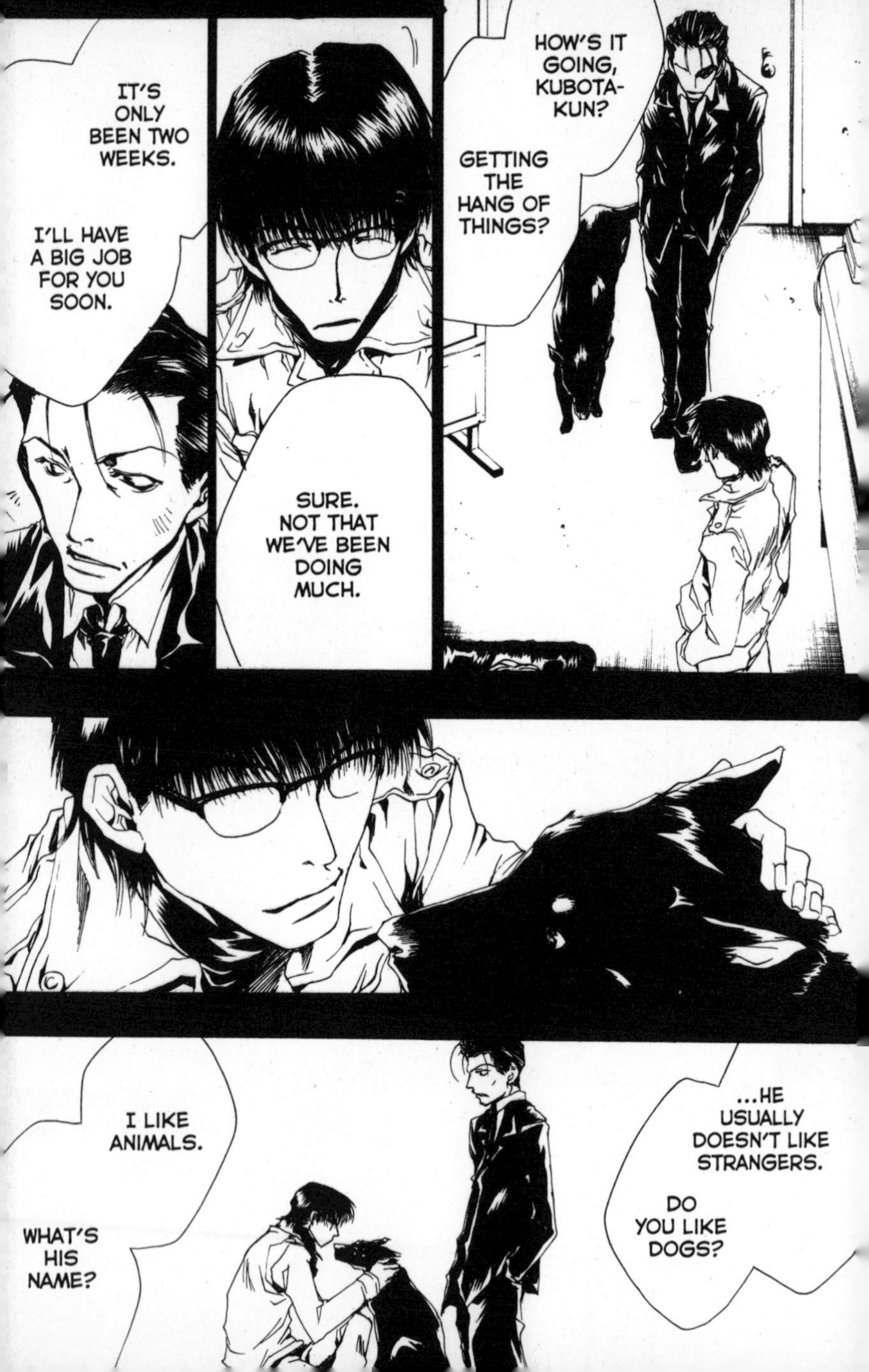
HOW'S IT GOING, KUBOTA-KUN?
GETTING THE HANG OF THINGS?
SURE. NOT THAT WE'VE BEEN DOING MUCH.
IT'S ONLY BEEN TWO WEEKS.
I'LL HAVE A BIG JOB FOR YOU SOON.
...HE USUALLY DOESN'T LIKE STRANGERS.
DO YOU LIKE DOGS?
I LIKE ANIMALS.
WHAT'S HIS NAME?

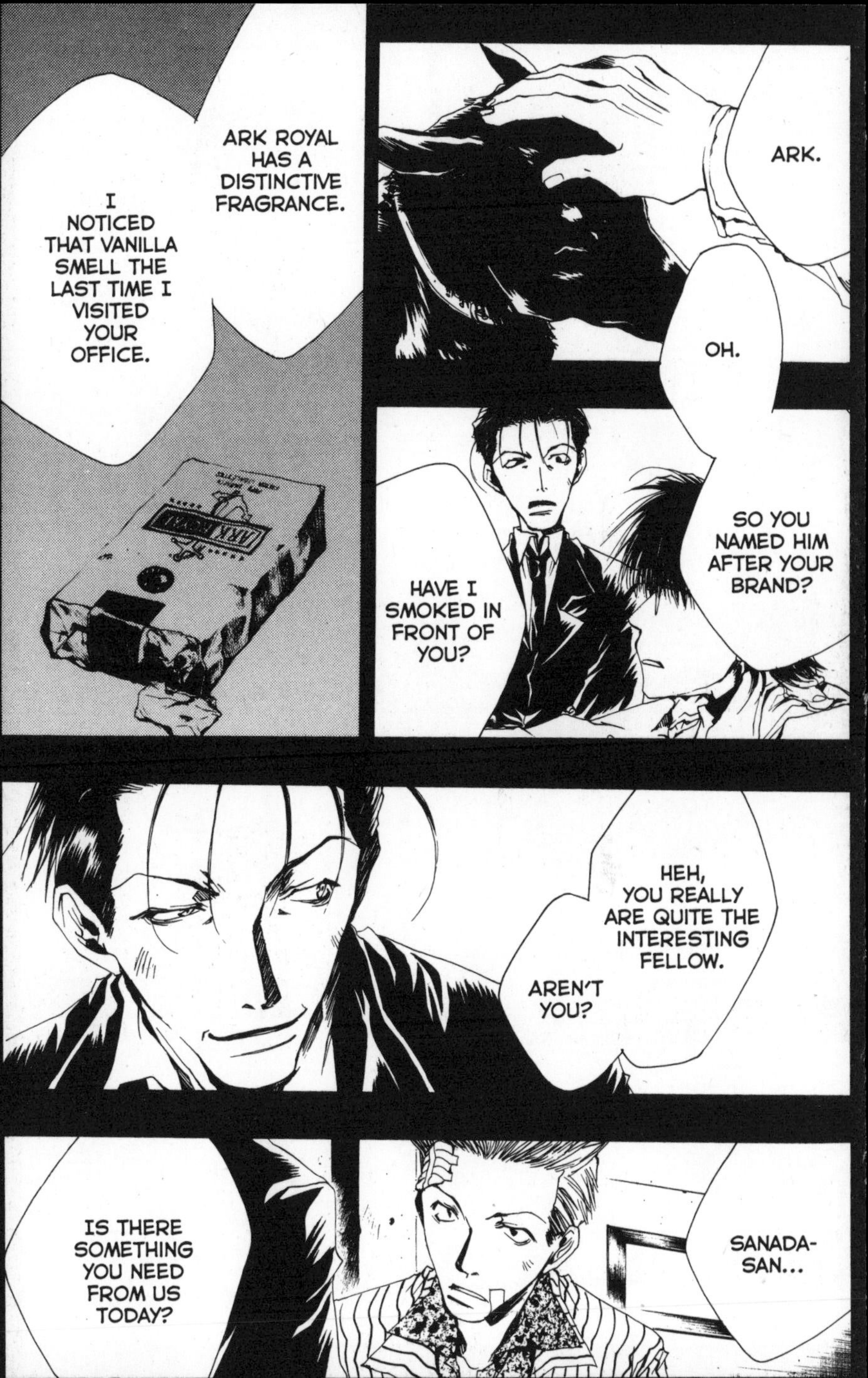
ARK.
OH.
SO YOU NAMED HIM AFTER YOUR BRAND?
HAVE I SMOKED IN FRONT OF YOU?
ARK ROYAL HAS A DISTINCTIVE FRAGRANCE.
I NOTICED THAT VANILLA SMELL THE LAST TIME I VISITED YOUR OFFICE.
HEH, YOU REALLY ARE QUITE THE INTERESTING FELLOW.
AREN'T YOU?
SANADA-SAN...
IS THERE SOMETHING YOU NEED FROM US TODAY?

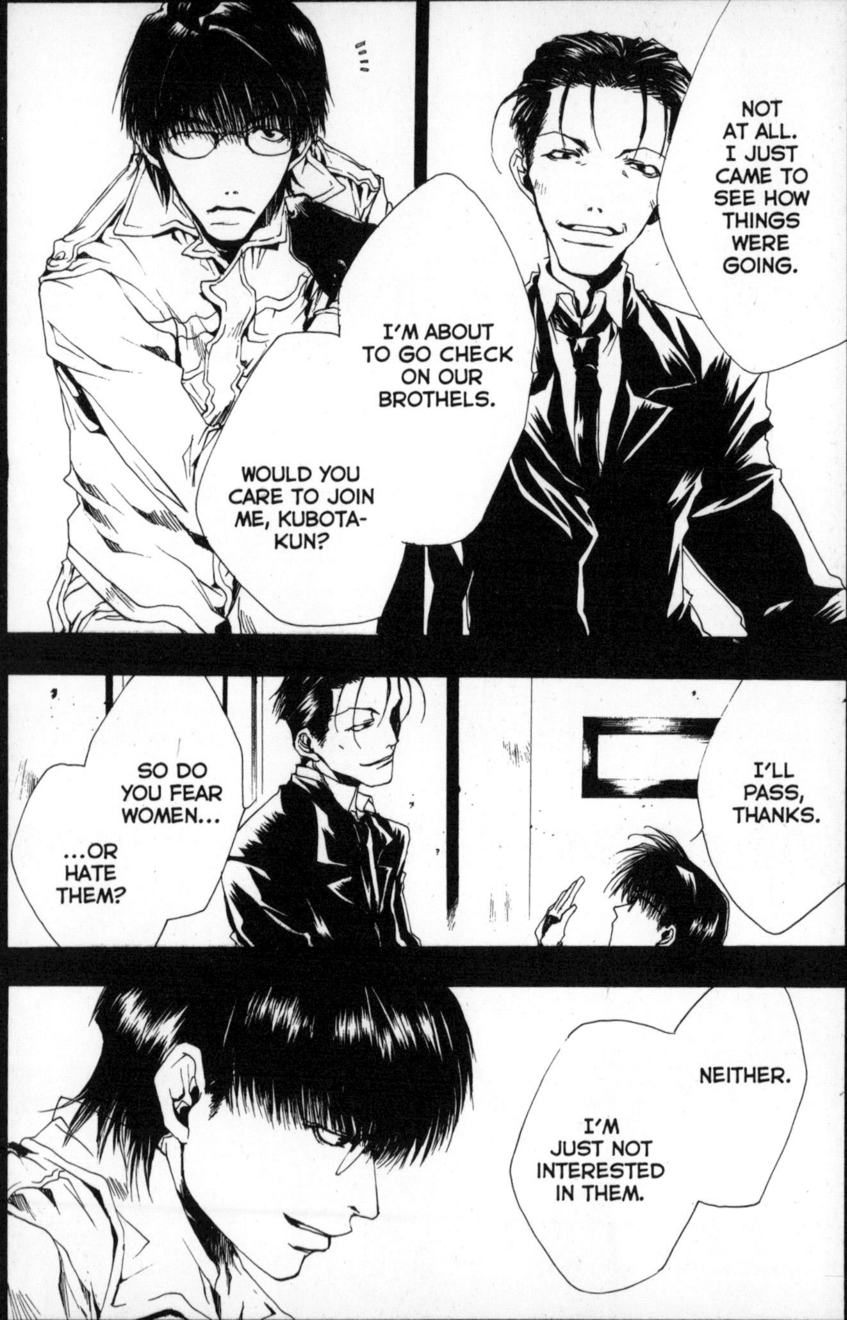
NOT AT ALL. I JUST CAME TO SEE HOW THINGS WERE GOING.
I'M ABOUT TO GO CHECK ON OUR BROTHELS.
WOULD YOU CARE TO JOIN ME, KUBOTA-KUN?
I'LL PASS, THANKS.
SO DO YOU FEAR WOMEN...
...OR HATE THEM?
NEITHER.
I'M JUST NOT INTERESTED IN THEM.

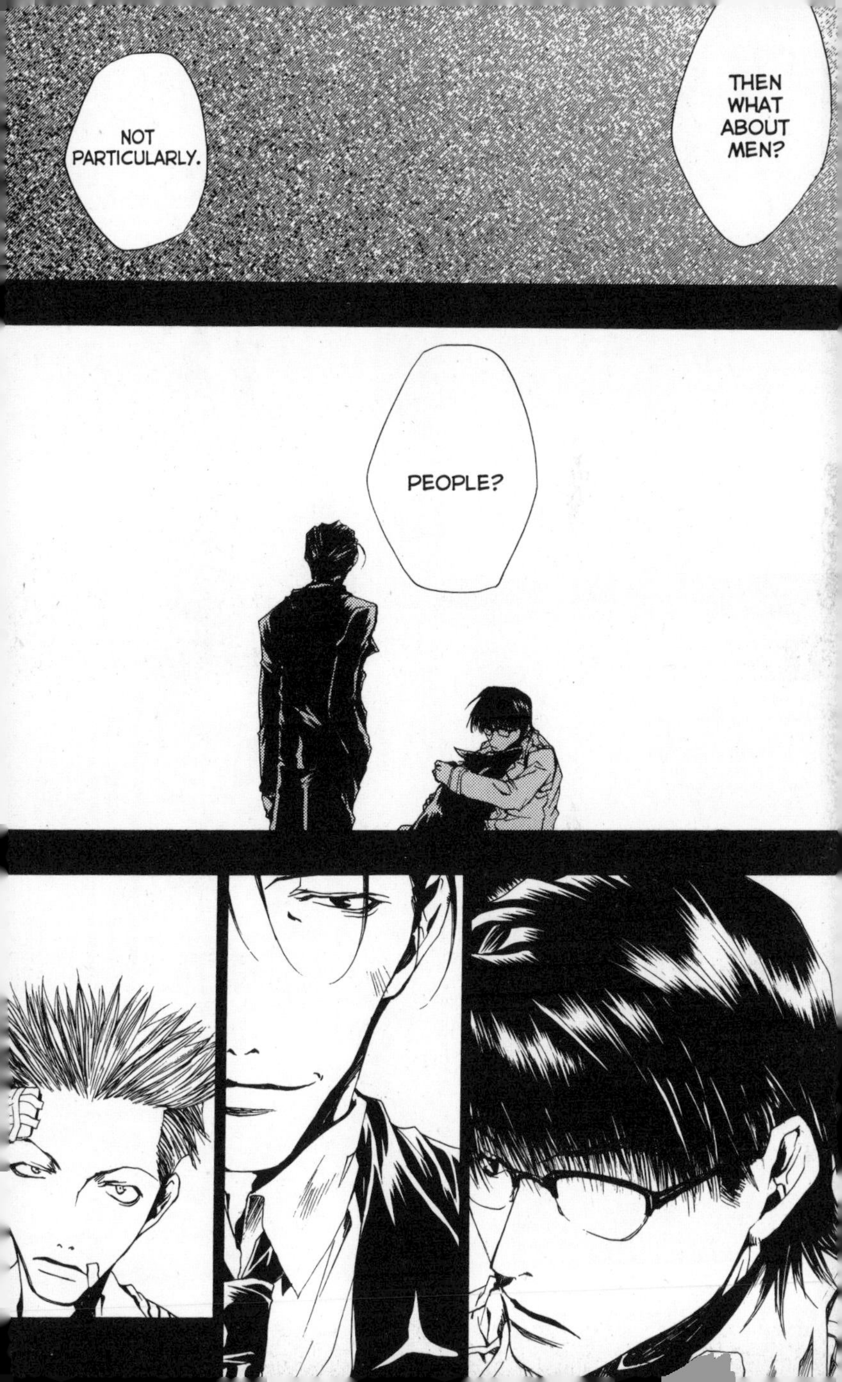
THEN WHAT ABOUT MEN?
NOT PARTICULARLY.
PEOPLE?

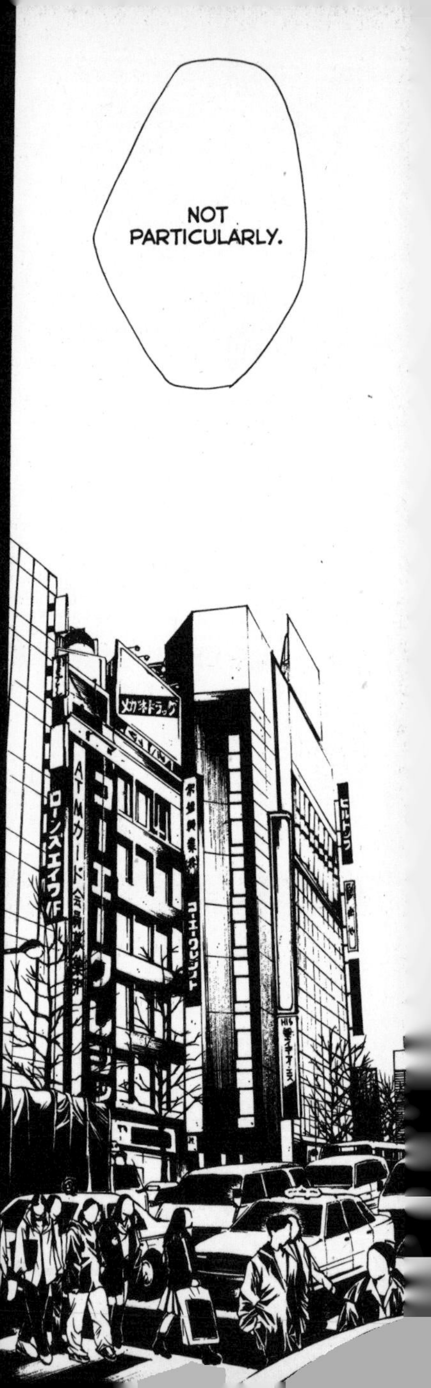
NOT PARTICULARLY.
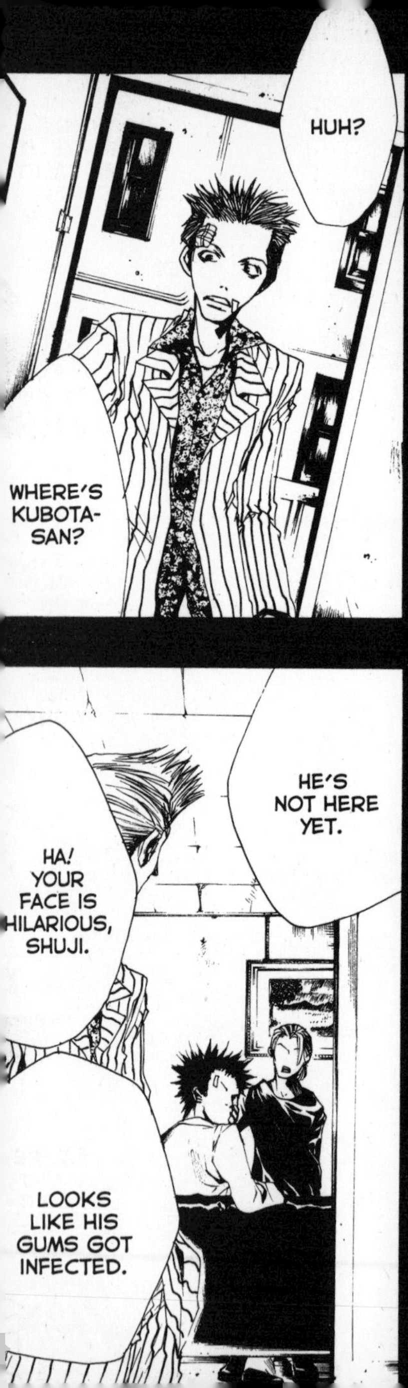
HUH?
WHERE'S KUBOTA-SAN?
HE'S NOT HERE YET.
HA! YOUR FACE IS HILARIOUS, SHUJI.
LOOKS LIKE HIS GUMS GOT INFECTED.

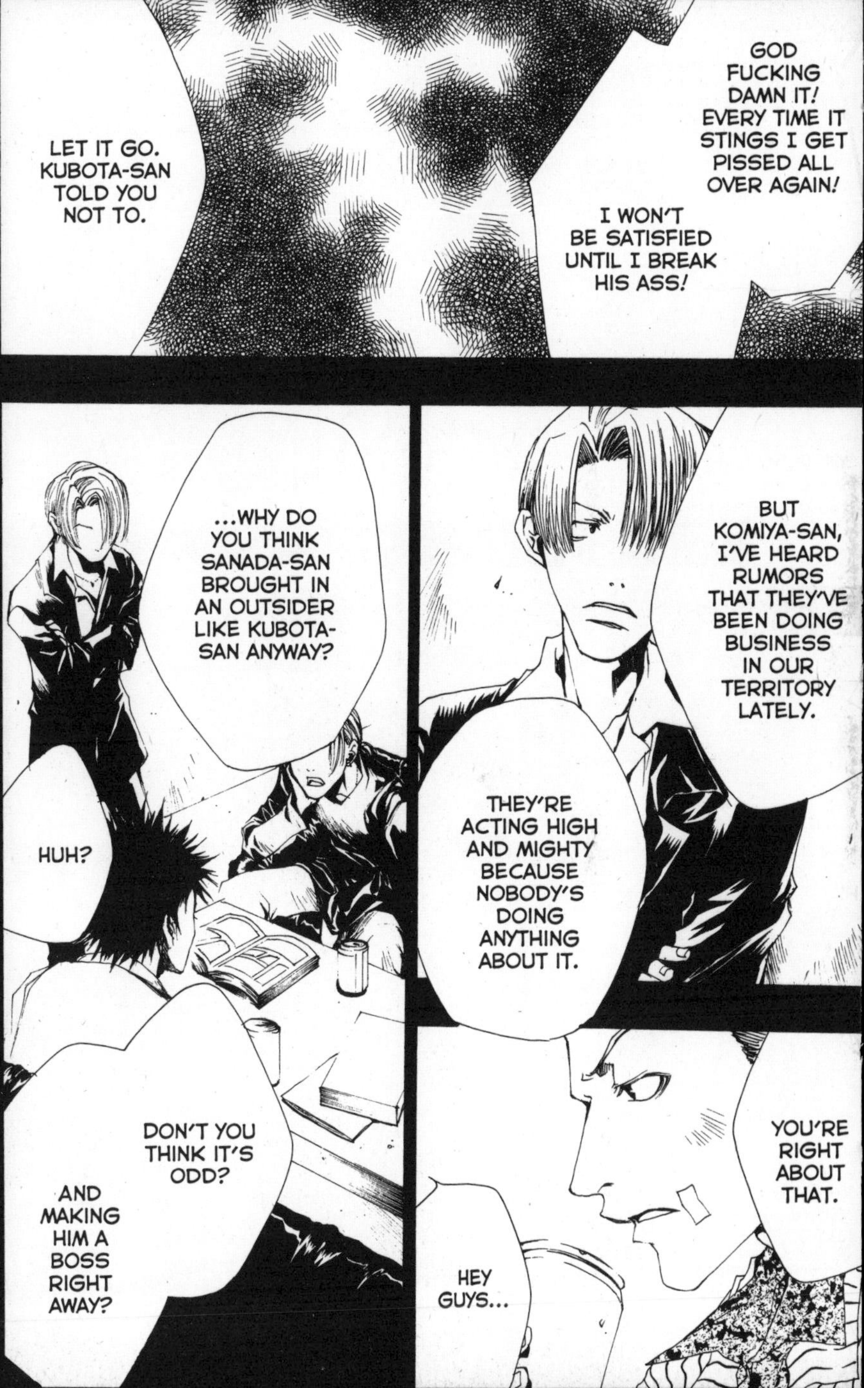
GOD FUCKING DAMN IT! EVERY TIME IT STINGS I GET PISSED ALL OVER AGAIN!
I WON'T BE SATISFIED UNTIL I BREAK HIS ASS!
LET IT GO. KUBOTA-SAN TOLD YOU NOT TO.
BUT KOMIYA-SAN, I'VE HEARD RUMORS THAT THEY'VE BEEN DOING BUSINESS IN OUR TERRITORY LATELY.
THEY'RE ACTING HIGH AND MIGHTY BECAUSE NOBODY'S DOING ANYTHING ABOUT IT.
YOU'RE RIGHT ABOUT THAT.
HEY GUYS...
...WHY DO YOU THINK SANADA-SAN BROUGHT IN AN OUTSIDER LIKE KUBOTA-SAN ANYWAY?
HUH?
DON'T YOU THINK IT'S ODD?
AND MAKING HIM A BOSS RIGHT AWAY?

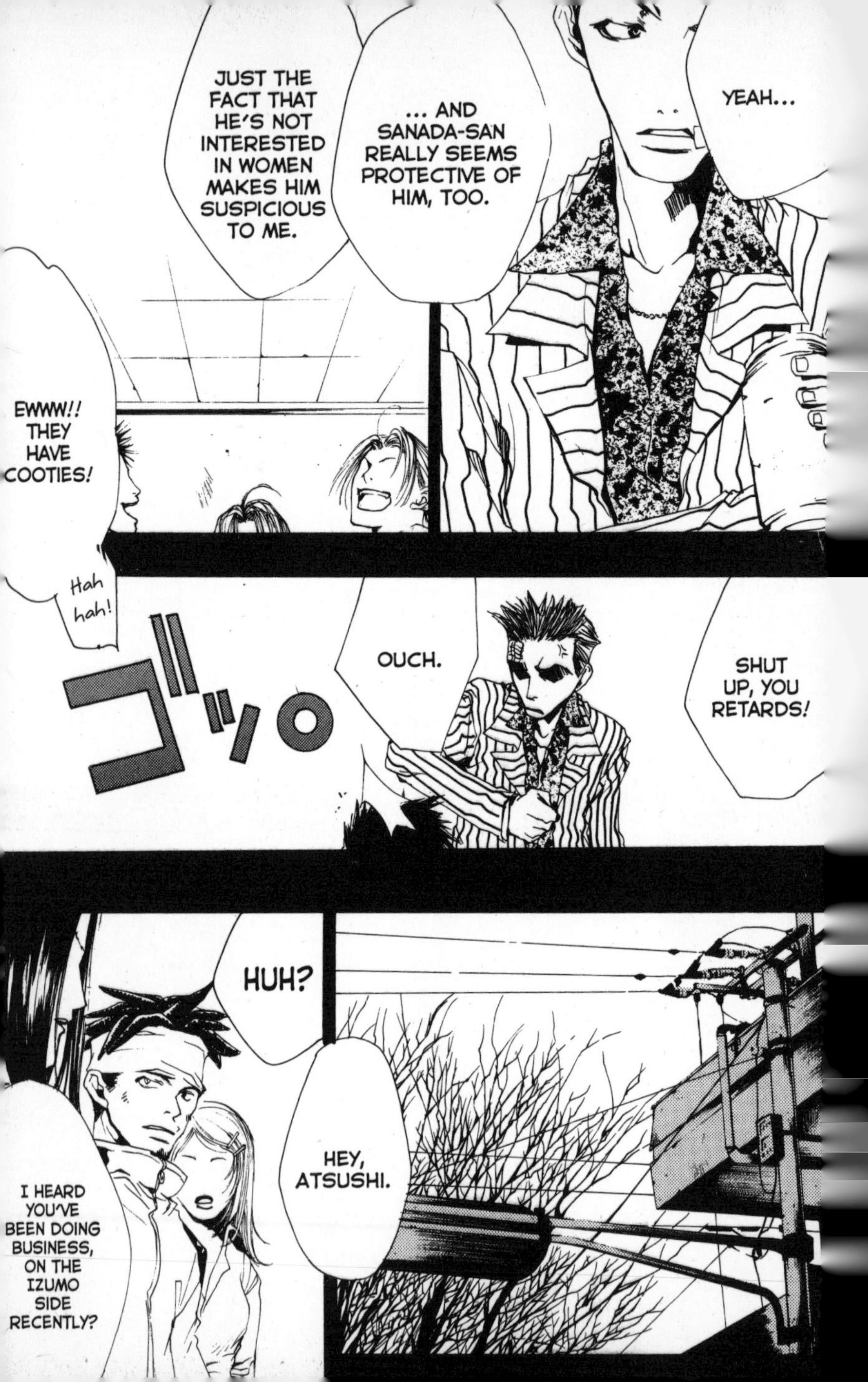
JUST THE FACT THAT HE'S NOT INTERESTED IN WOMEN MAKES HIM SUSPICIOUS TO ME.
... AND SANADA-SAN REALLY SEEMS PROTECTIVE OF HIM, TOO.
YEAH...
EWWW!! THEY HAVE COOTIES!
SHUT UP, YOU RETARDS!
OUCH.
Hah hah!
ゴッ
HEY, ATSUSHI.
HUH?
I HEARD YOU'VE BEEN DOING BUSINESS, ON THE IZUMO SIDE RECENTLY?

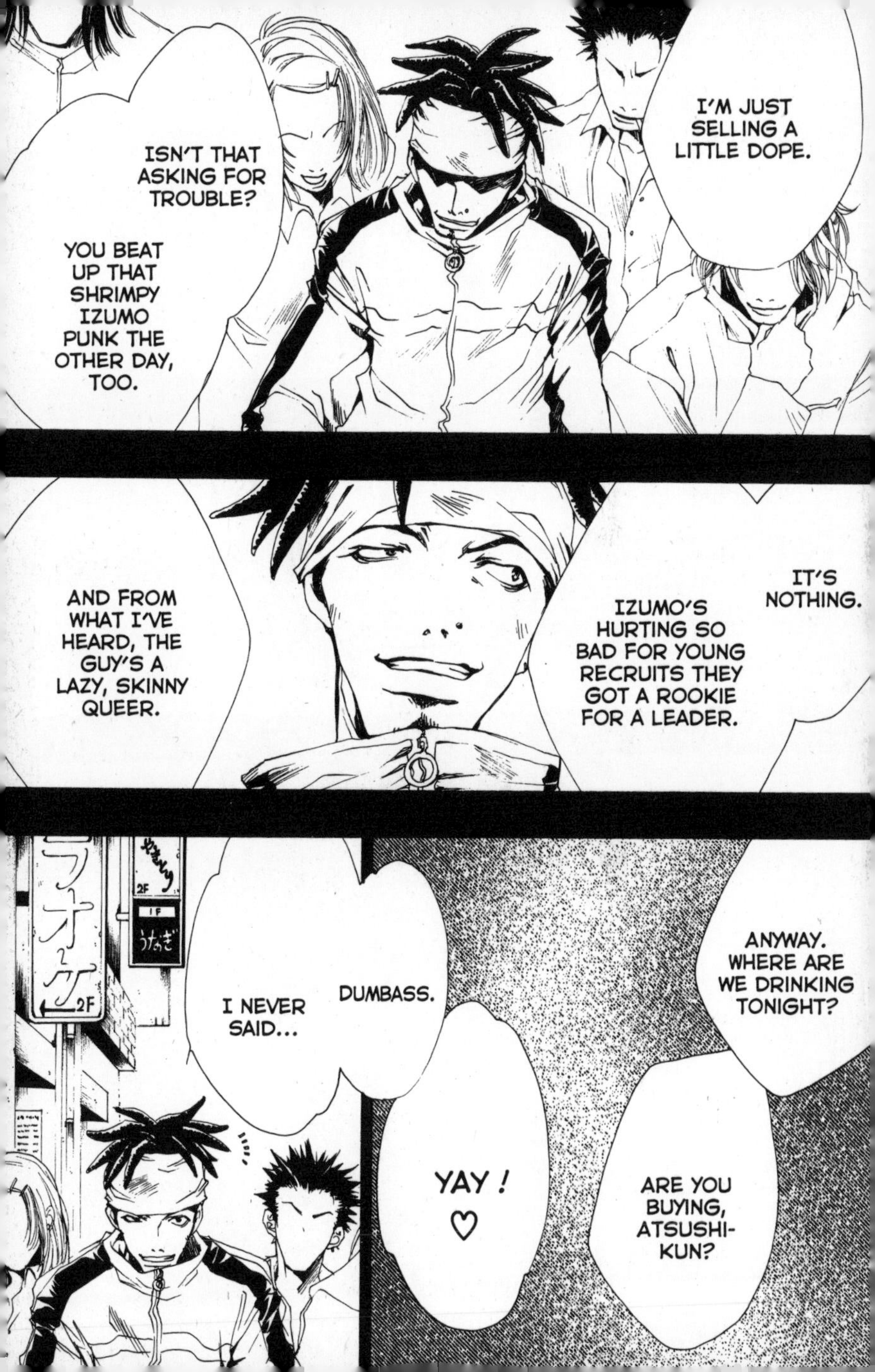
I'M JUST SELLING A LITTLE DOPE.
ISN'T THAT ASKING FOR TROUBLE?
YOU BEAT UP THAT SHRIMPY IZUMO PUNK THE OTHER DAY, TOO.
IT'S NOTHING.
IZUMO'S HURTING SO BAD FOR YOUNG RECRUITS THEY GOT A ROOKIE FOR A LEADER.
AND FROM WHAT I'VE HEARD, THE GUY'S A LAZY, SKINNY QUEER.
ANYWAY. WHERE ARE WE DRINKING TONIGHT?
ARE YOU BUYING, ATSUSHI-KUN?
YAY! ♡
DUMBASS.
I NEVER SAID...

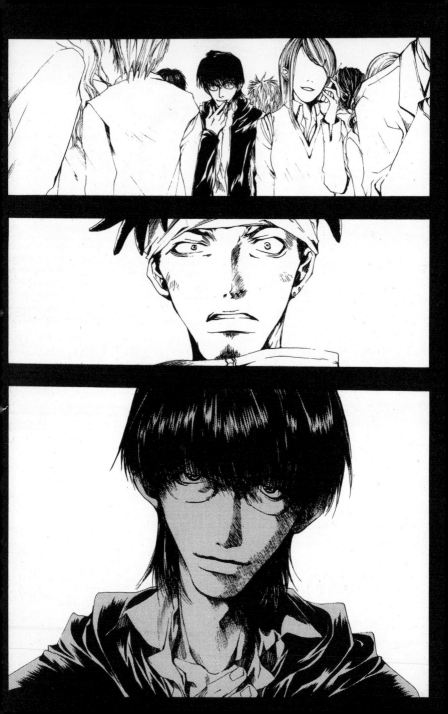

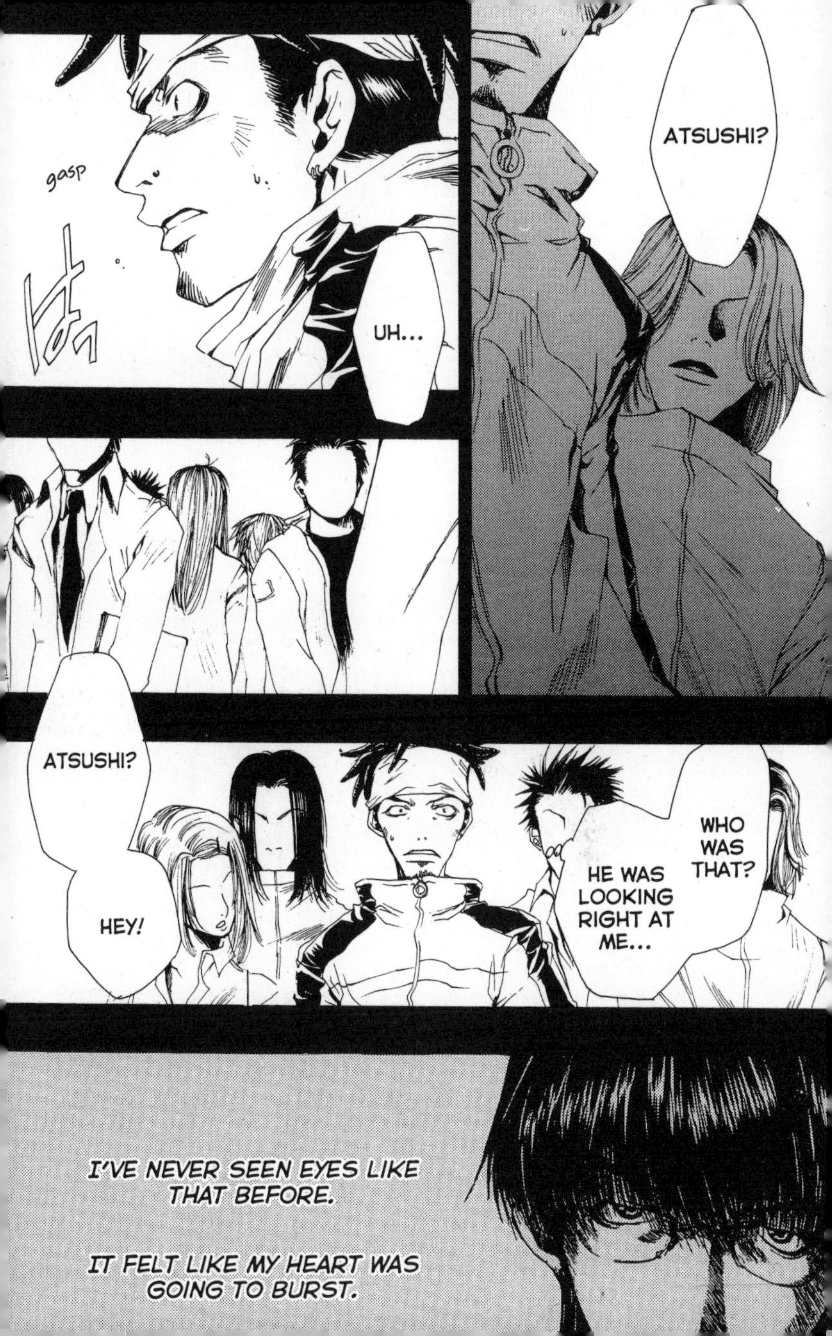
ATSUSHI?
gasp
はっ
UH...
WHO WAS THAT?
HE WAS LOOKING RIGHT AT ME...
ATSUSHI?
HEY!
I'VE NEVER SEEN EYES LIKE THAT BEFORE.
IT FELT LIKE MY HEART WAS GOING TO BURST.

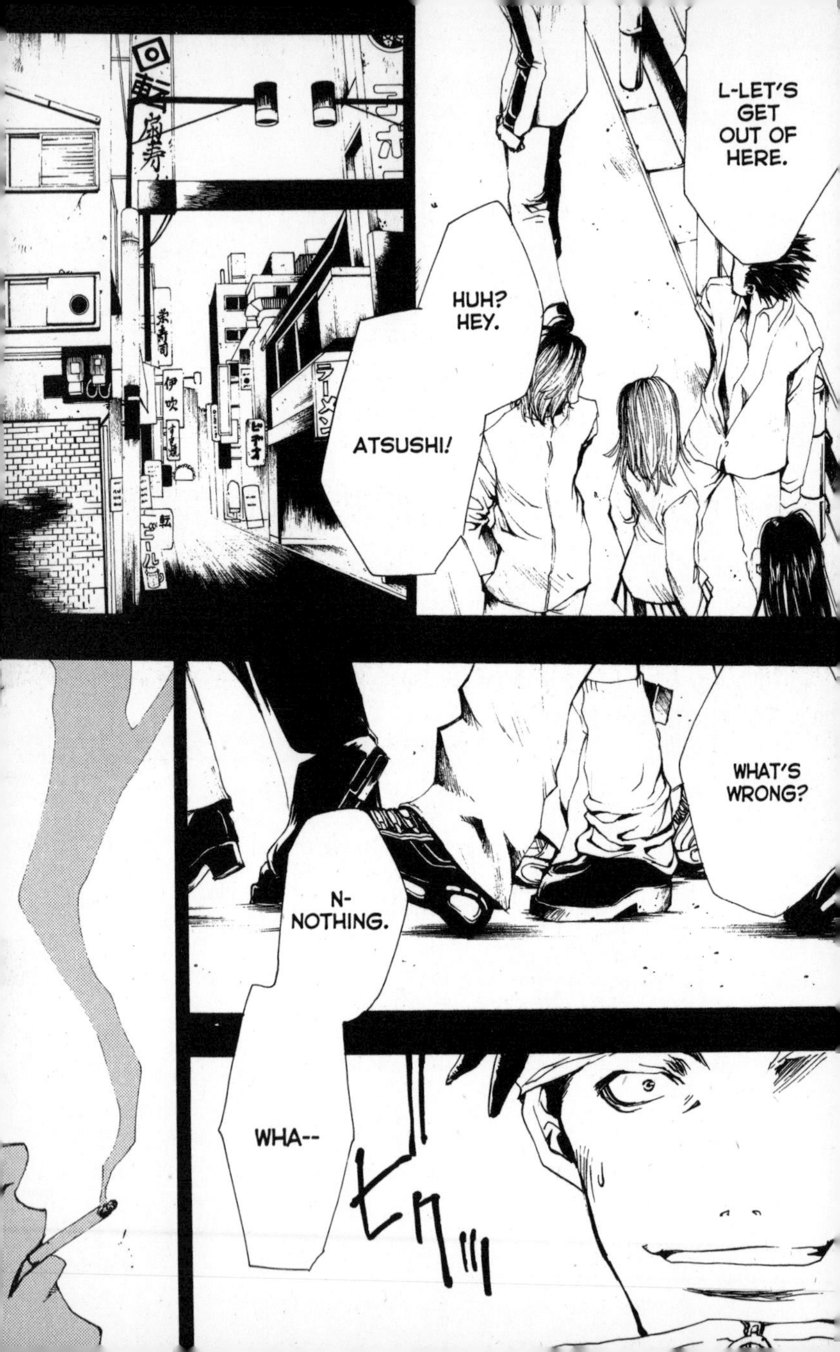
L-LET'S GET OUT OF HERE.
HUH? HEY.
ATSUSHI!
WHAT'S WRONG?
N-NOTHING.
WHA--

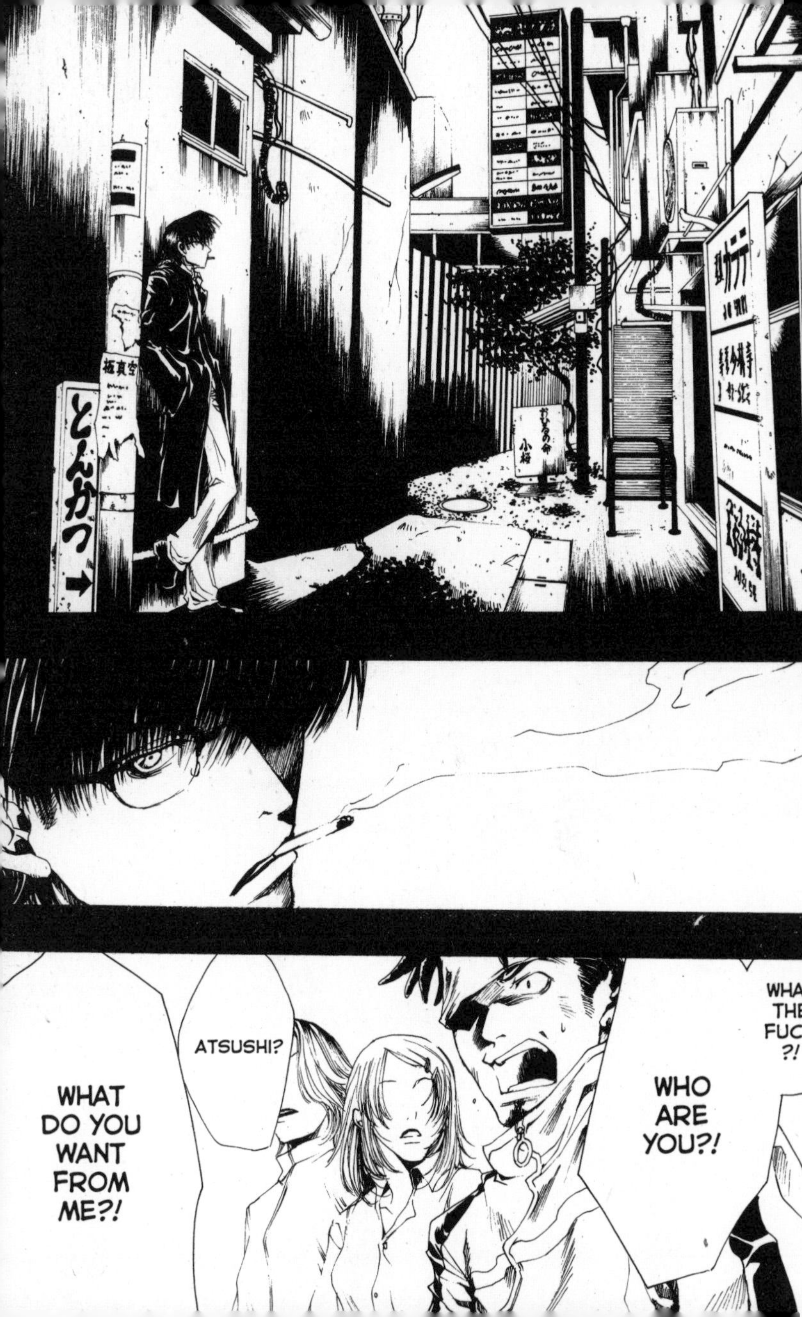
とんかつ
WHAT THE FUCK?!
WHO ARE YOU?!
ATSUSHI?
WHAT DO YOU WANT FROM ME?!

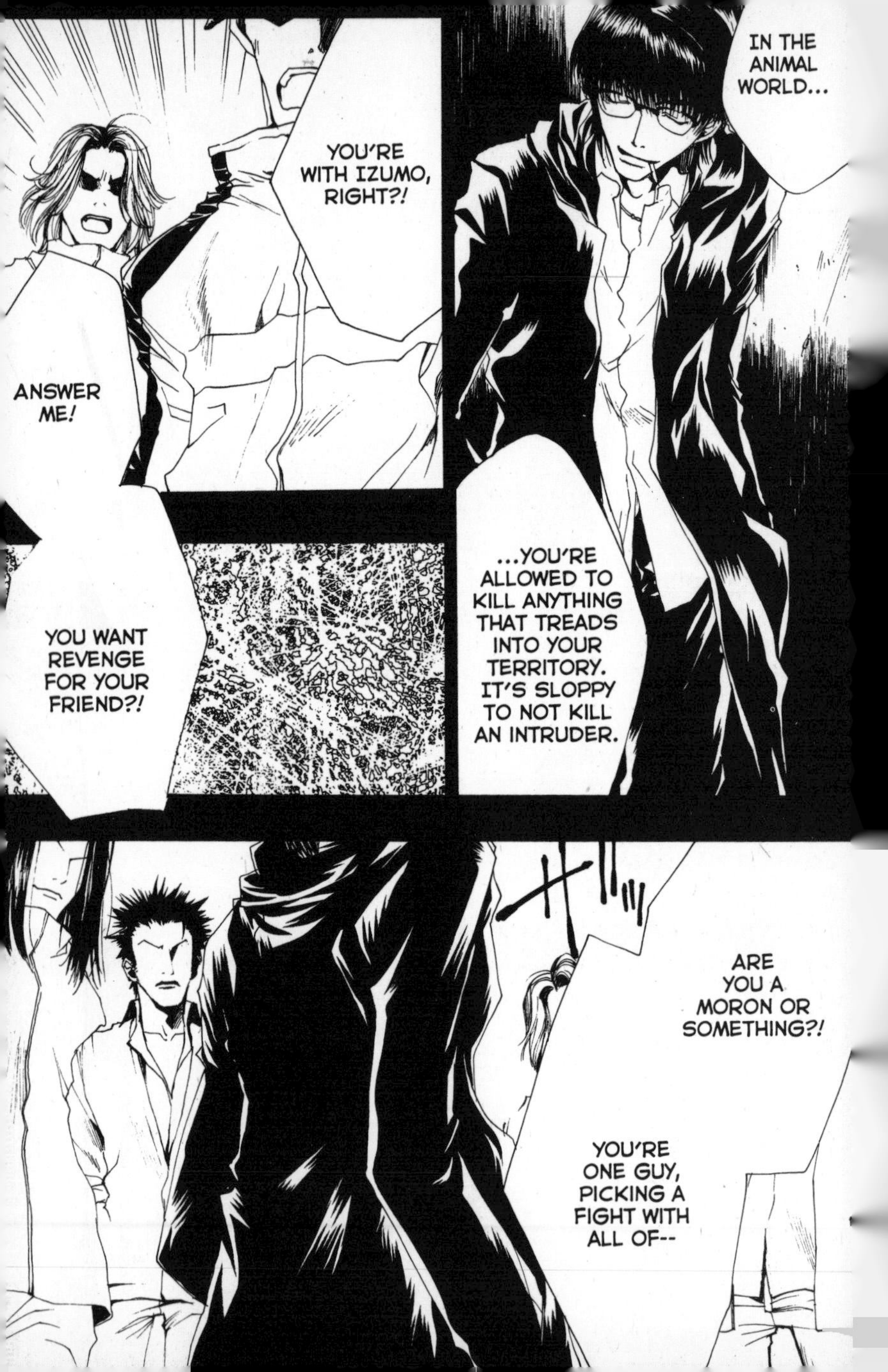
IN THE ANIMAL WORLD...
...YOU'RE ALLOWED TO KILL ANYTHING THAT TREADS INTO YOUR TERRITORY. IT'S SLOPPY TO NOT KILL AN INTRUDER.
YOU'RE WITH IZUMO, RIGHT?!
ANSWER ME!
YOU WANT REVENGE FOR YOUR FRIEND?!
ARE YOU A MORON OR SOMETHING?!
YOU'RE ONE GUY, PICKING A FIGHT WITH ALL OF--

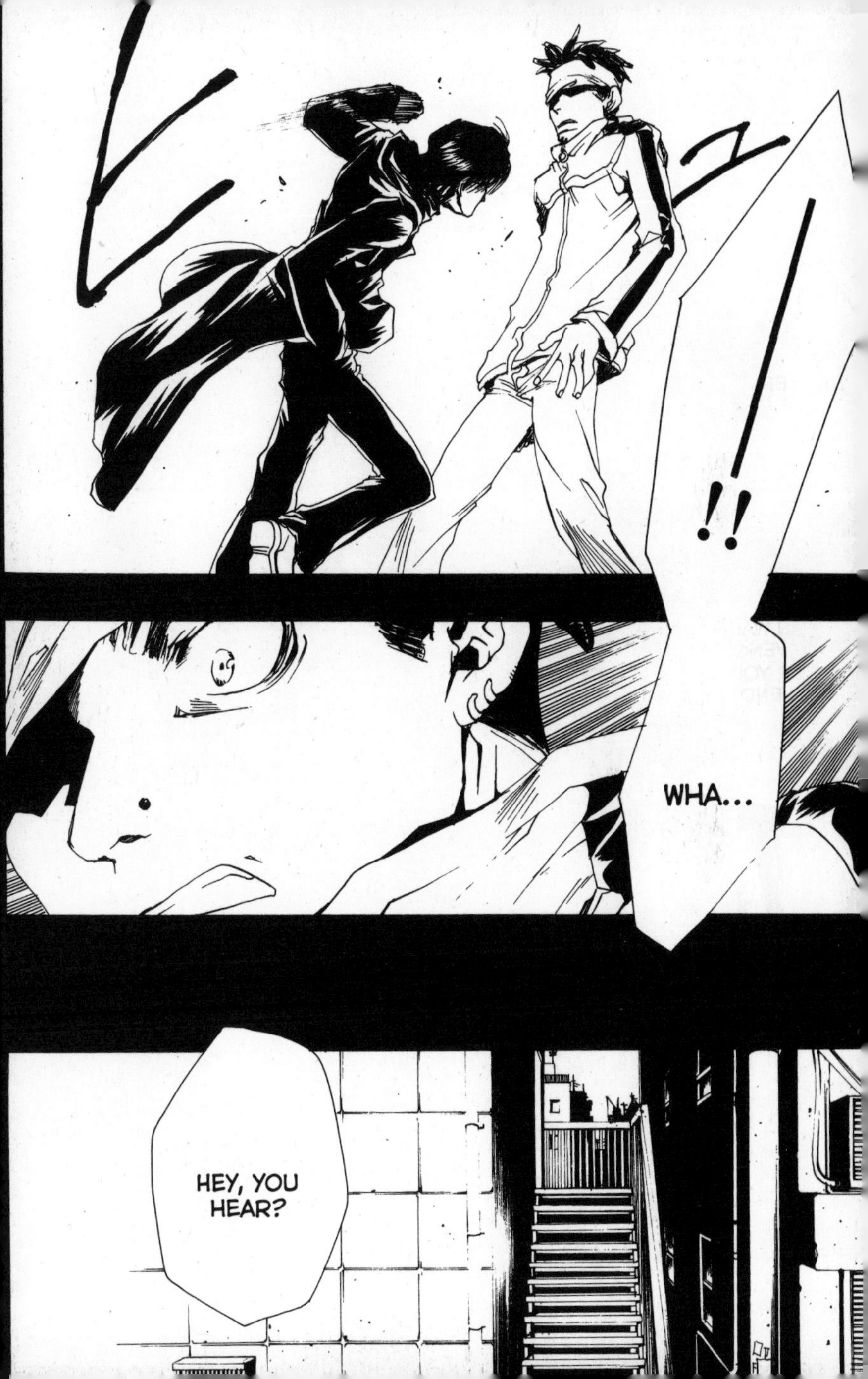
!!
WHA...
HEY, YOU
HEAR?

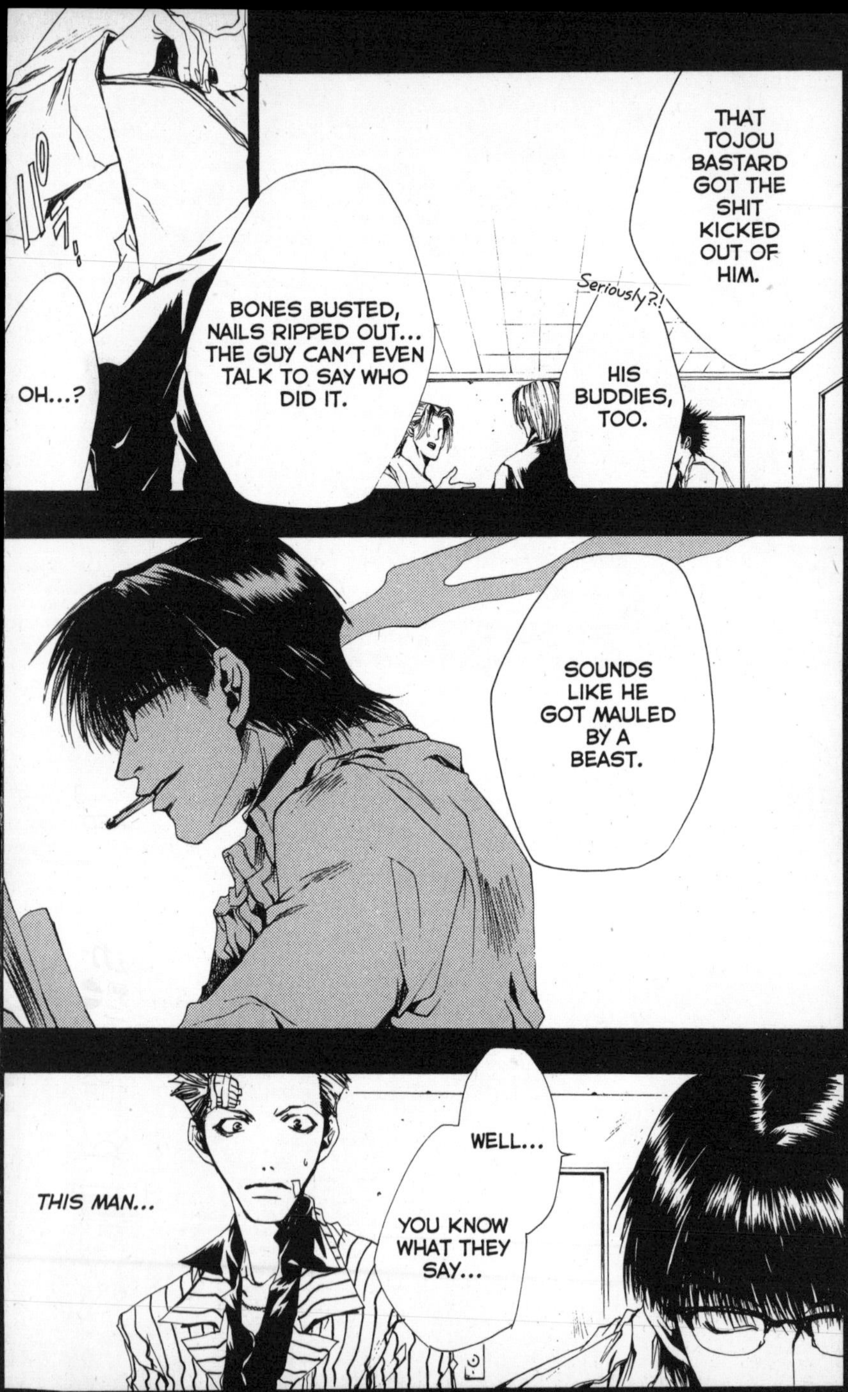
THAT TOJOU BASTARD GOT THE SHIT KICKED OUT OF HIM.
Seriously?!
HIS BUDDIES, TOO.
BONES BUSTED, NAILS RIPPED OUT... THE GUY CAN'T EVEN TALK TO SAY WHO DID IT.
OH...?
SOUNDS LIKE HE GOT MAULED BY A BEAST.
WELL...
YOU KNOW WHAT THEY SAY...
THIS MAN...

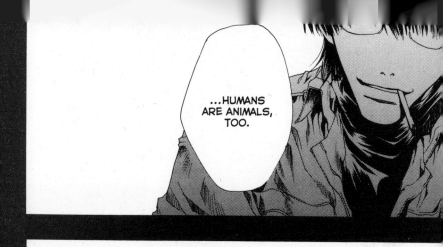

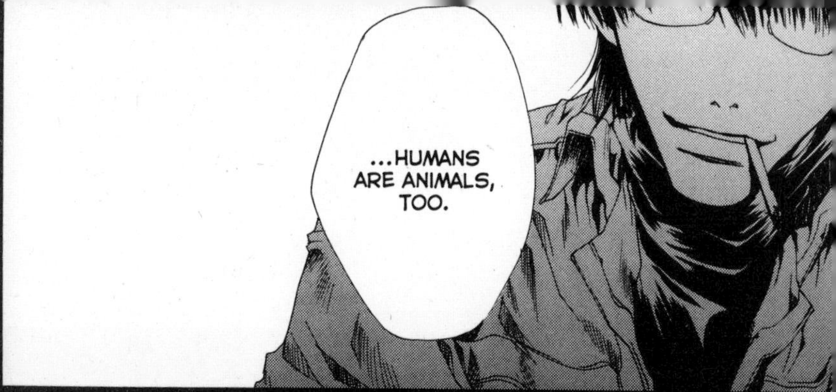
...HUMANS ARE ANIMALS, TOO.

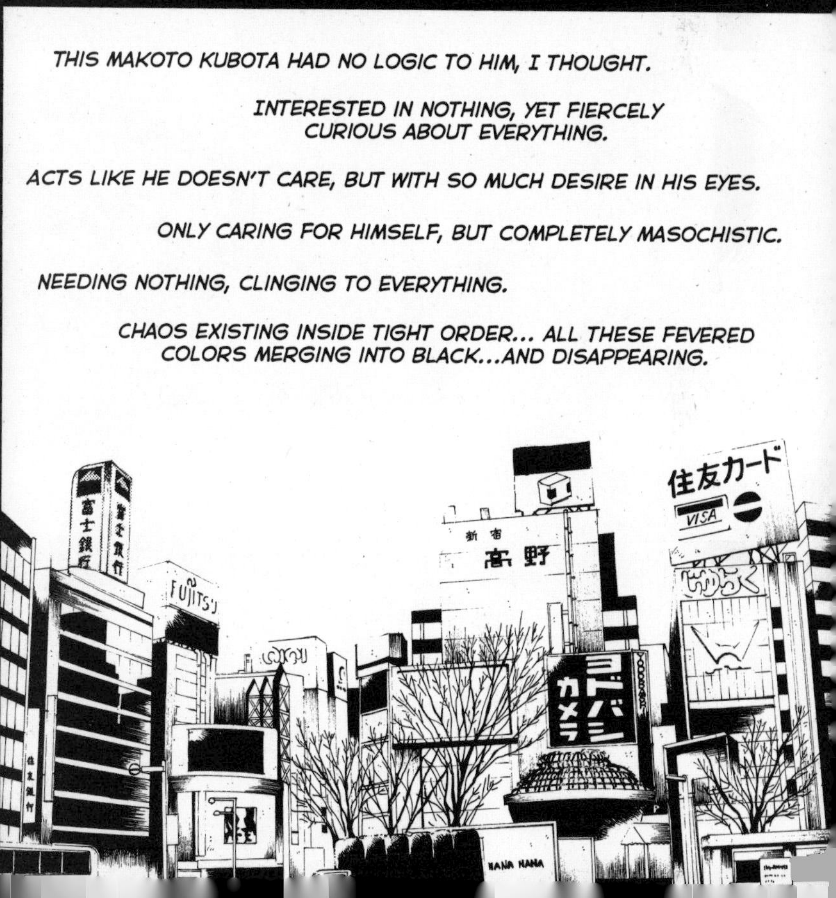
THIS MAKOTO KUBOTA HAD NO LOGIC TO HIM, I THOUGHT.
INTERESTED IN NOTHING, YET FIERCELY CURIOUS ABOUT EVERYTHING.
ACTS LIKE HE DOESN'T CARE, BUT WITH SO MUCH DESIRE IN HIS EYES.
ONLY CARING FOR HIMSELF, BUT COMPLETELY MASOCHISTIC.
NEEDING NOTHING, CLINGING TO EVERYTHING.
CHAOS EXISTING INSIDE TIGHT ORDER... ALL THESE FEVERED COLORS MERGING INTO BLACK...AND DISAPPEARING.
住友カード
VISA
新宿
高野
ヨドバシカメラ
富士銀行
FUJITSU
HANA HANA

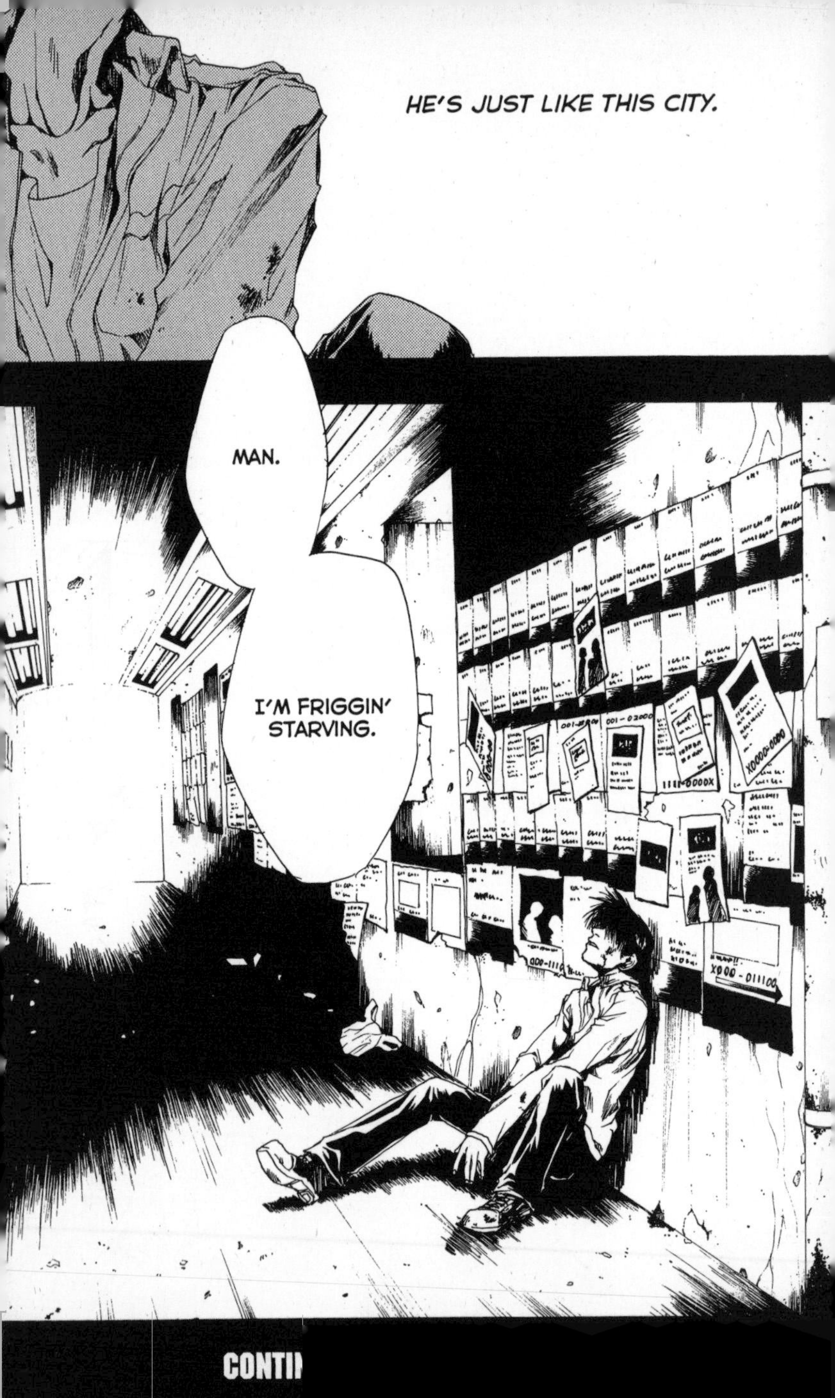
HE'S JUST LIKE THIS CITY.
MAN.
I'M FRIGGIN' STARVING.
CONTIN

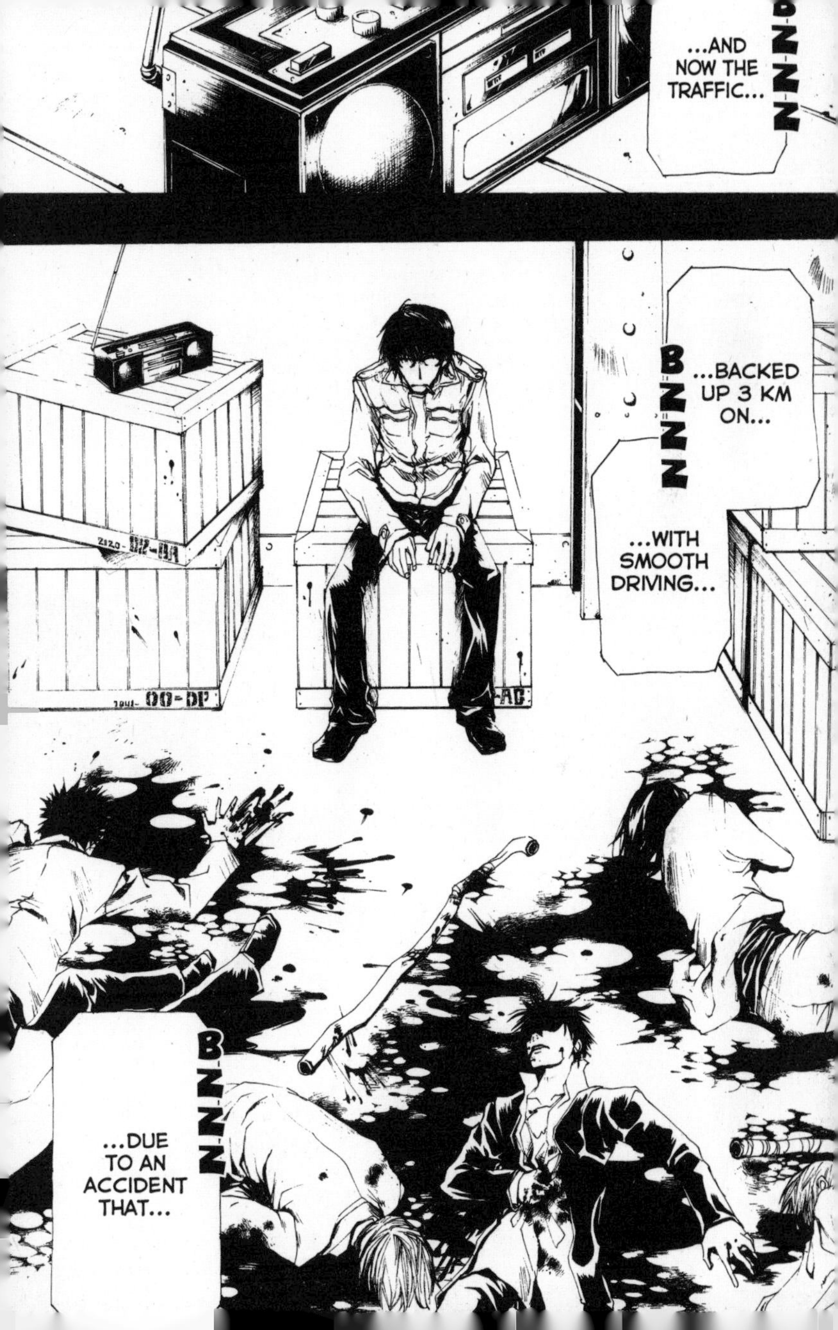
...AND NOW THE TRAFFIC...
ZZZ
...BACKED UP 3 KM ON...
BZZZ
...WITH SMOOTH DRIVING...
...DUE TO AN ACCIDENT THAT...
BZZZ

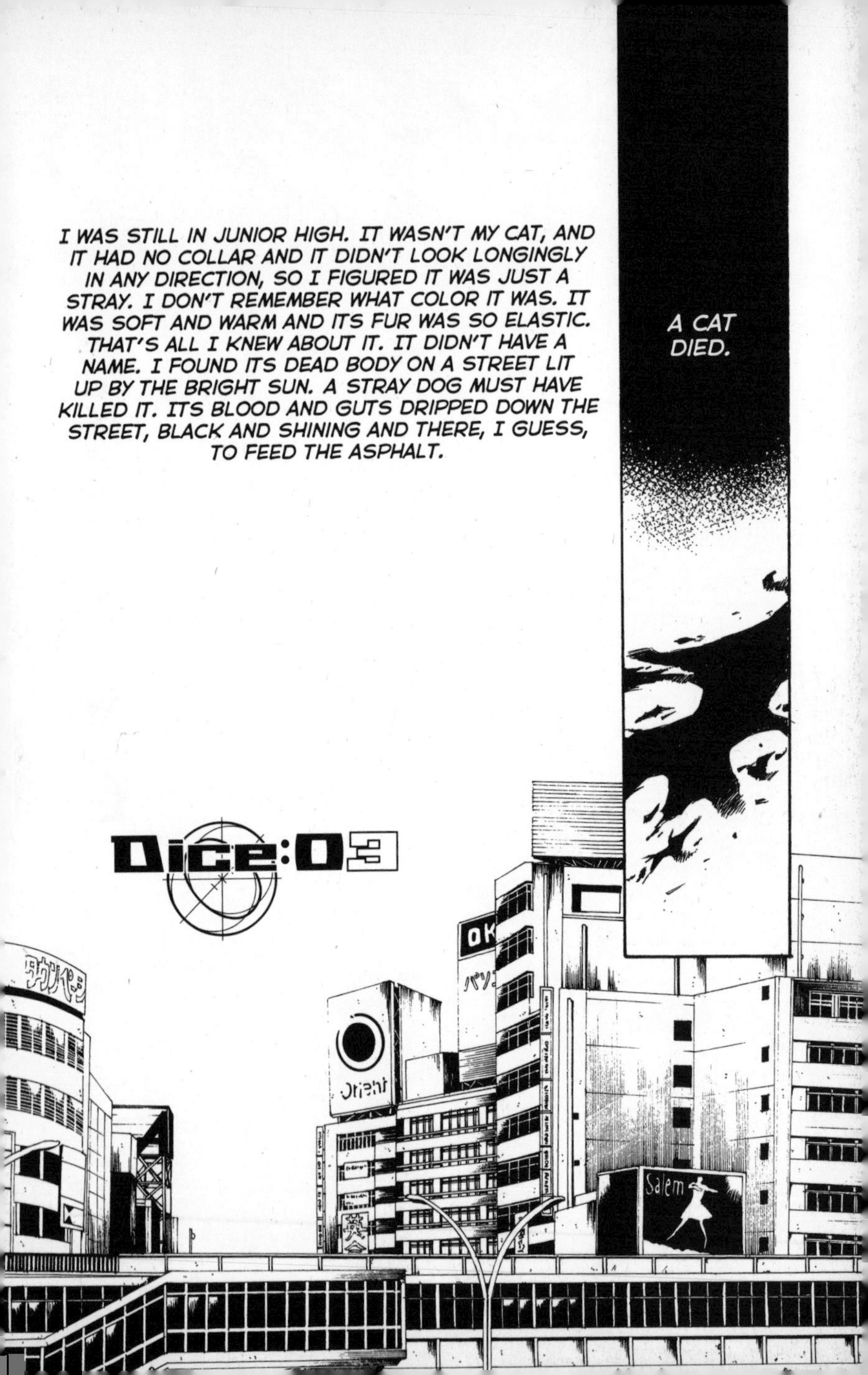
A CAT DIED.
I WAS STILL IN JUNIOR HIGH. IT WASN'T MY CAT, AND IT HAD NO COLLAR AND IT DIDN'T LOOK LONGINGLY IN ANY DIRECTION, SO I FIGURED IT WAS JUST A STRAY. I DON'T REMEMBER WHAT COLOR IT WAS. IT WAS SOFT AND WARM AND ITS FUR WAS SO ELASTIC. THAT'S ALL I KNEW ABOUT IT. IT DIDN'T HAVE A NAME. I FOUND ITS DEAD BODY ON A STREET LIT UP BY THE BRIGHT SUN. A STRAY DOG MUST HAVE KILLED IT. ITS BLOOD AND GUTS DRIPPED DOWN THE STREET, BLACK AND SHINING AND THERE, I GUESS, TO FEED THE ASPHALT.
DICE:03
OK
Orient
Salem

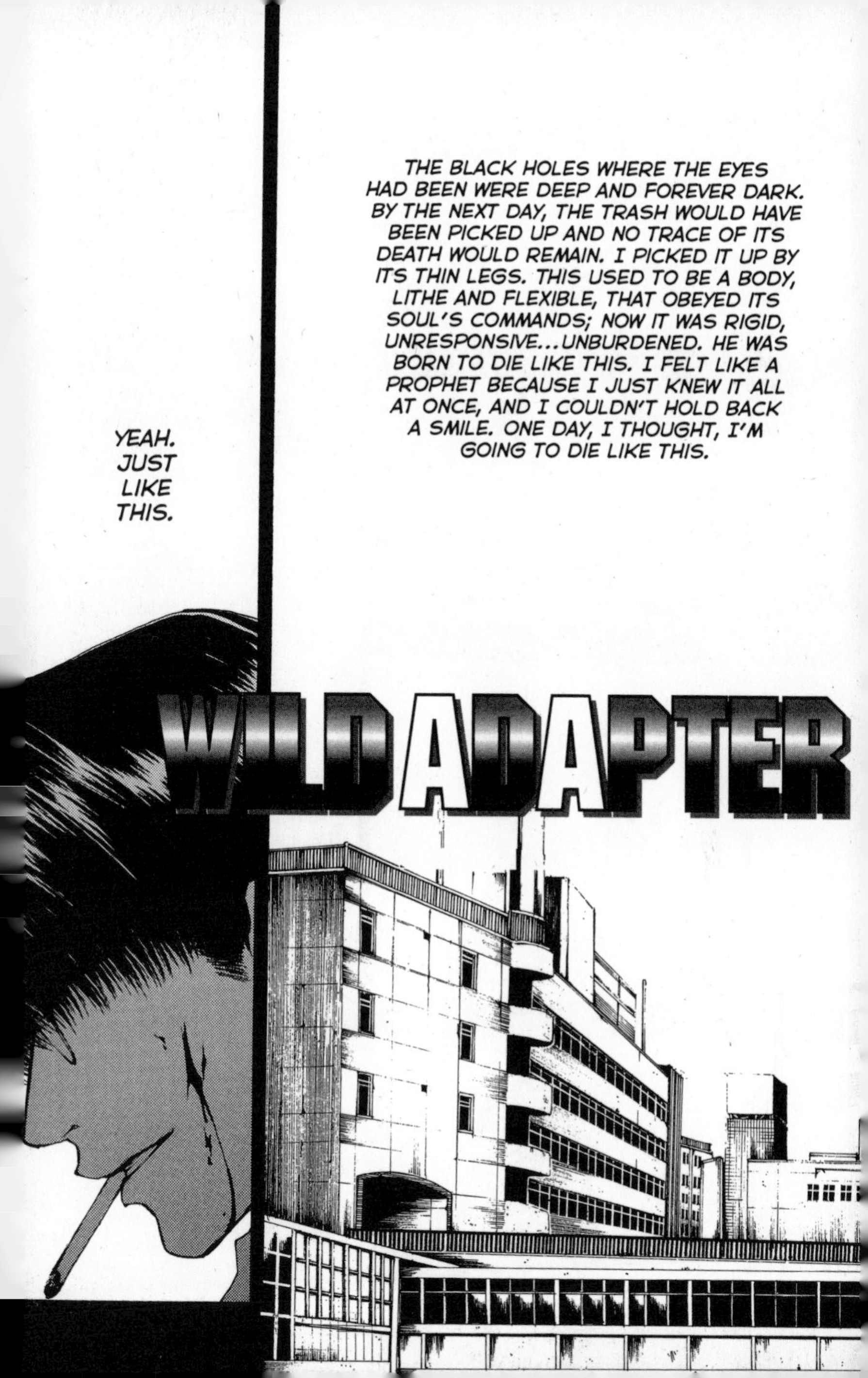
THE BLACK HOLES WHERE THE EYES HAD BEEN WERE DEEP AND FOREVER DARK. BY THE NEXT DAY, THE TRASH WOULD HAVE BEEN PICKED UP AND NO TRACE OF ITS DEATH WOULD REMAIN. I PICKED IT UP BY ITS THIN LEGS. THIS USED TO BE A BODY, LITHE AND FLEXIBLE, THAT OBEYED ITS SOUL'S COMMANDS; NOW IT WAS RIGID, UNRESPONSIVE...UNBURDENED. HE WAS BORN TO DIE LIKE THIS. I FELT LIKE A PROPHET BECAUSE I JUST KNEW IT ALL AT ONCE, AND I COULDN'T HOLD BACK A SMILE. ONE DAY, I THOUGHT, I'M GOING TO DIE LIKE THIS.
WILD ADAPTER
YEAH. JUST LIKE THIS.

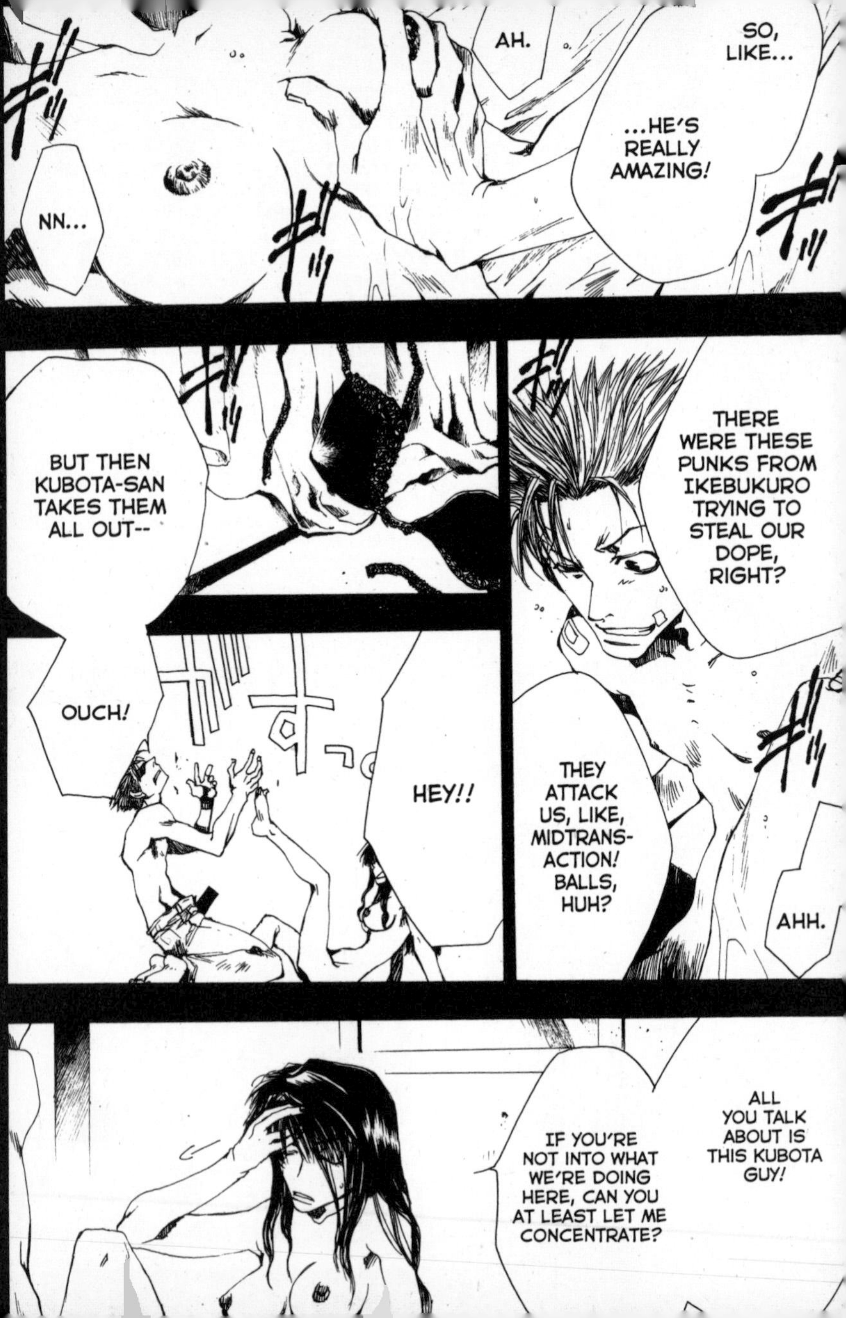
SO, LIKE...
...HE'S REALLY AMAZING!
AH.
NN...
THERE WERE THESE PUNKS FROM IKEBUKURO TRYING TO STEAL OUR DOPE, RIGHT?
THEY ATTACK US, LIKE, MIDTRANS-ACTION! BALLS, HUH?
AHH.
BUT THEN KUBOTA-SAN TAKES THEM ALL OUT--
すっ
HEY!!
OUCH!
ALL YOU TALK ABOUT IS THIS KUBOTA GUY!
IF YOU'RE NOT INTO WHAT WE'RE DOING HERE, CAN YOU AT LEAST LET ME CONCENTRATE?

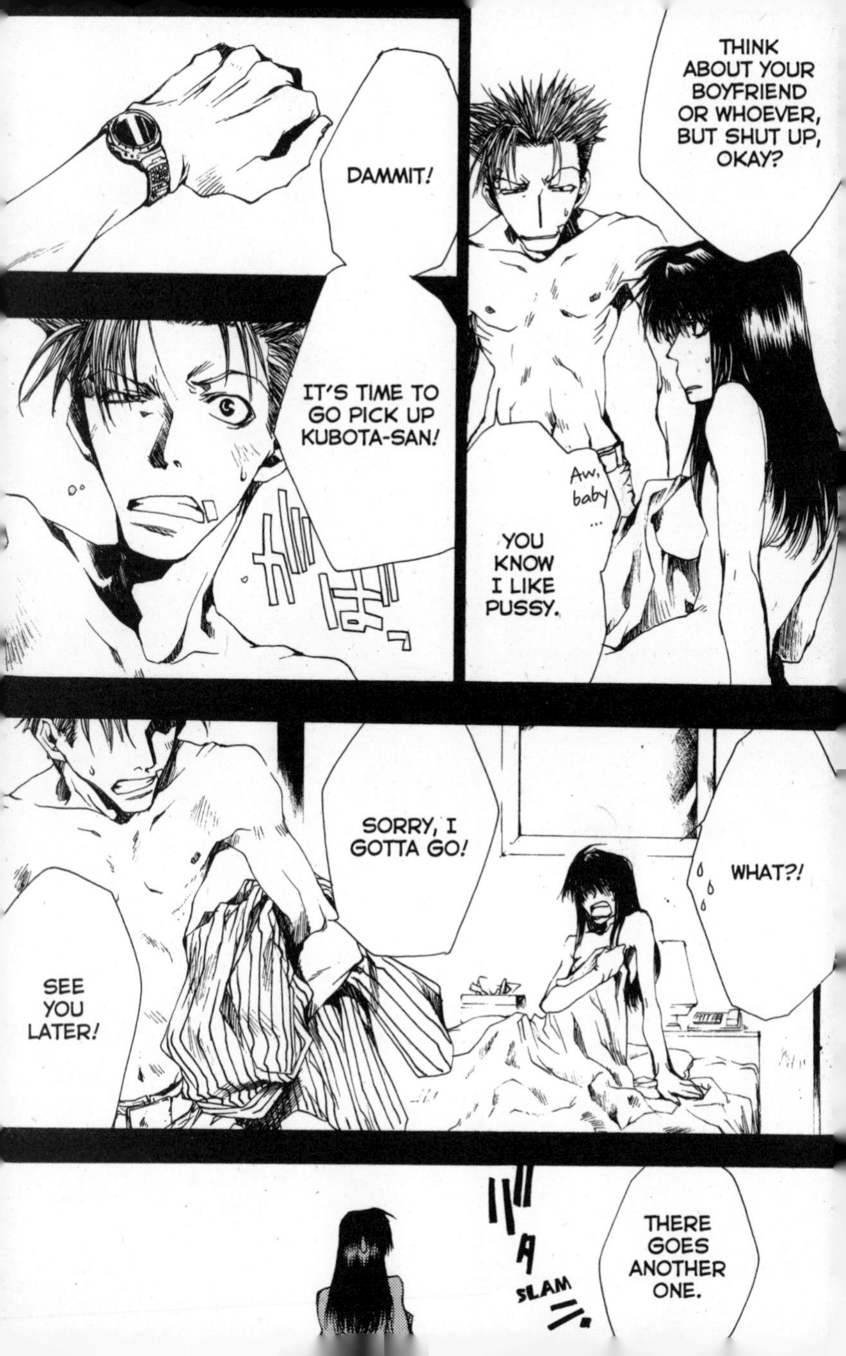
THINK ABOUT YOUR BOYFRIEND OR WHOEVER, BUT SHUT UP, OKAY?
Aw, baby...
YOU KNOW I LIKE PUSSY.
DAMMIT!
IT'S TIME TO GO PICK UP KUBOTA-SAN!
WHAT?!
SORRY, I GOTTA GO!
SEE YOU LATER!
THERE GOES ANOTHER ONE.
SLAM

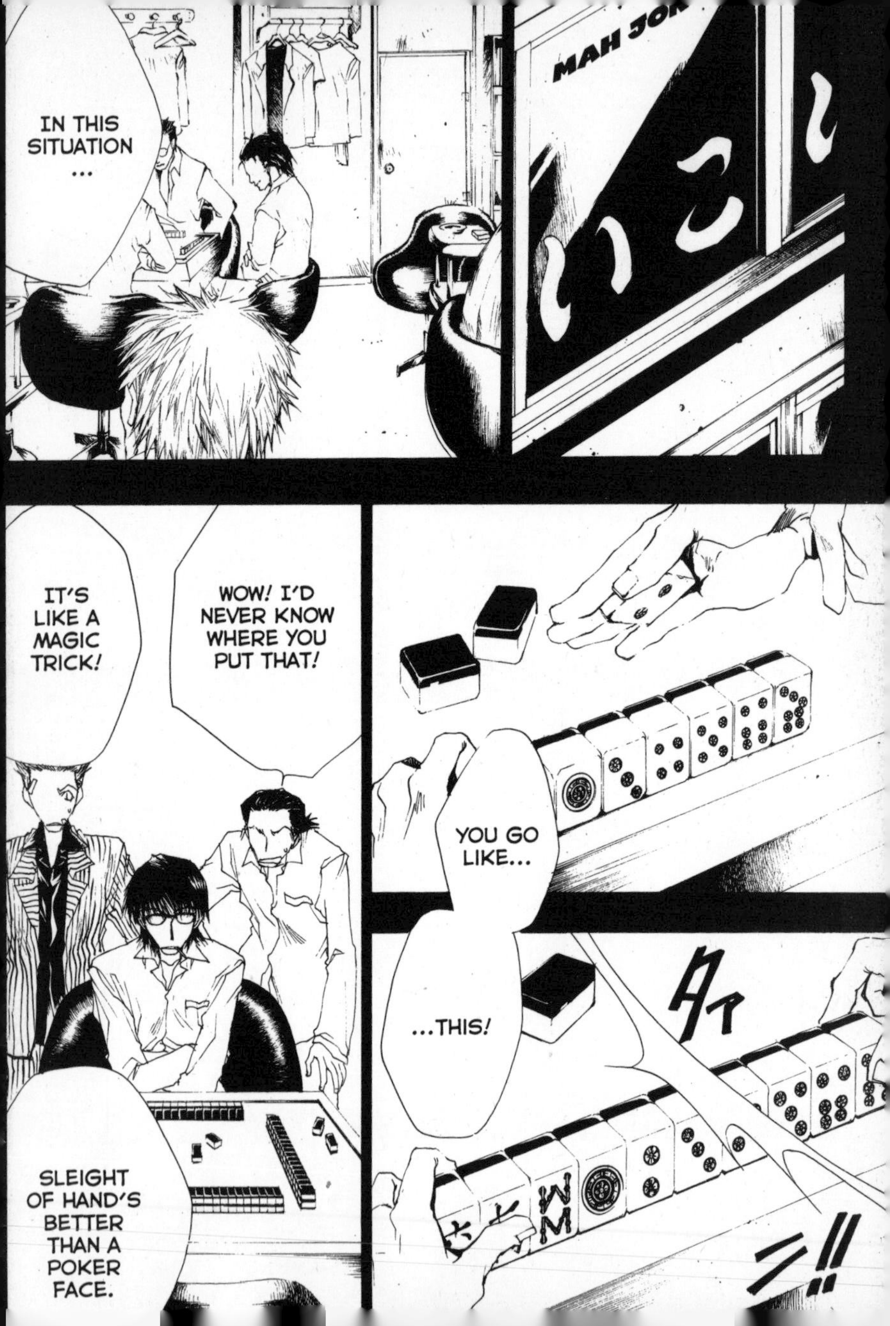
IN THIS SITUATION ...
YOU GO LIKE...
...THIS!
タァ
ン!!
WOW! I'D NEVER KNOW WHERE YOU PUT THAT!
IT'S LIKE A MAGIC TRICK!
SLEIGHT OF HAND'S BETTER THAN A POKER FACE.

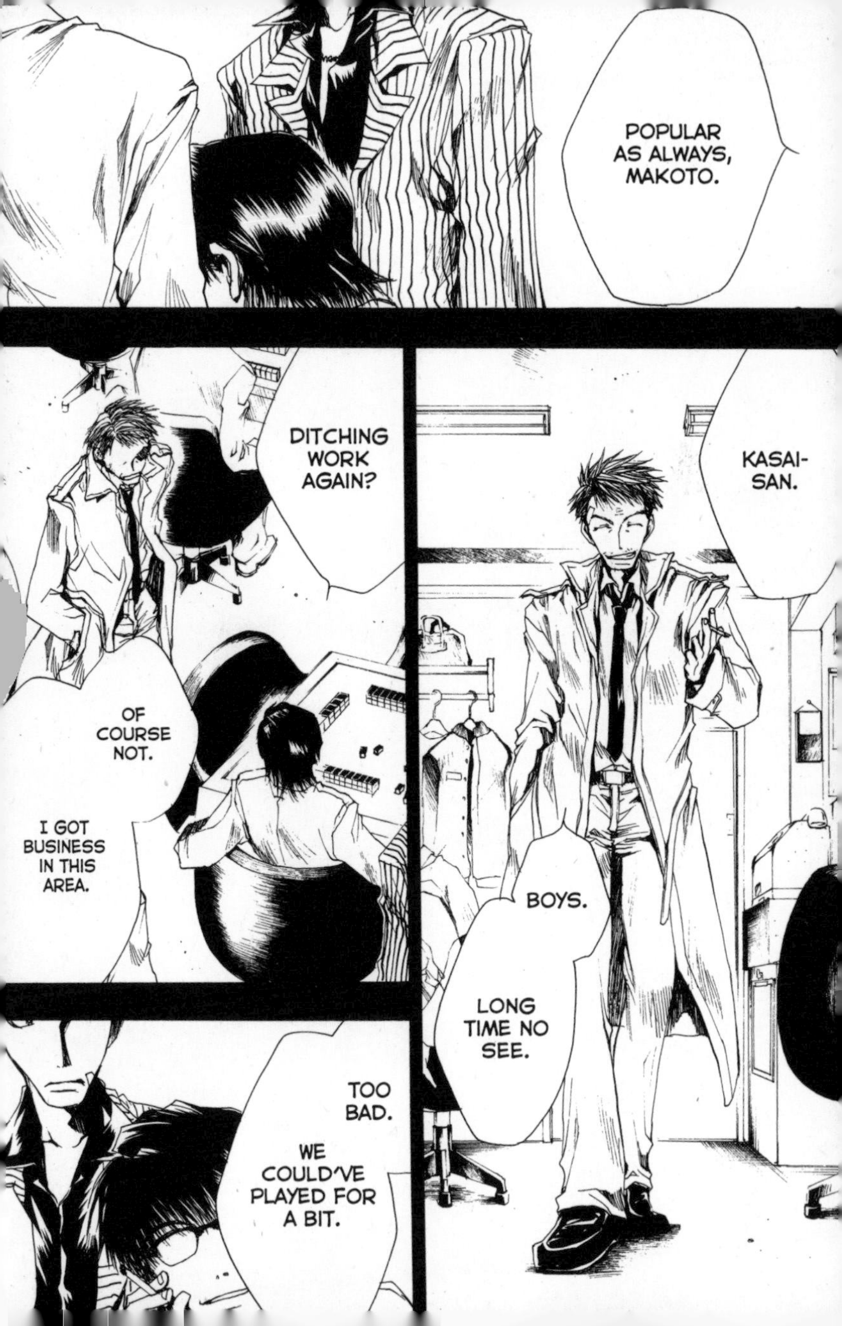
POPULAR AS ALWAYS, MAKOTO.
KASAI-SAN.
BOYS.
LONG TIME NO SEE.
DITCHING WORK AGAIN?
OF COURSE NOT.
I GOT BUSINESS IN THIS AREA.
TOO BAD.
WE COULD'VE PLAYED FOR A BIT.

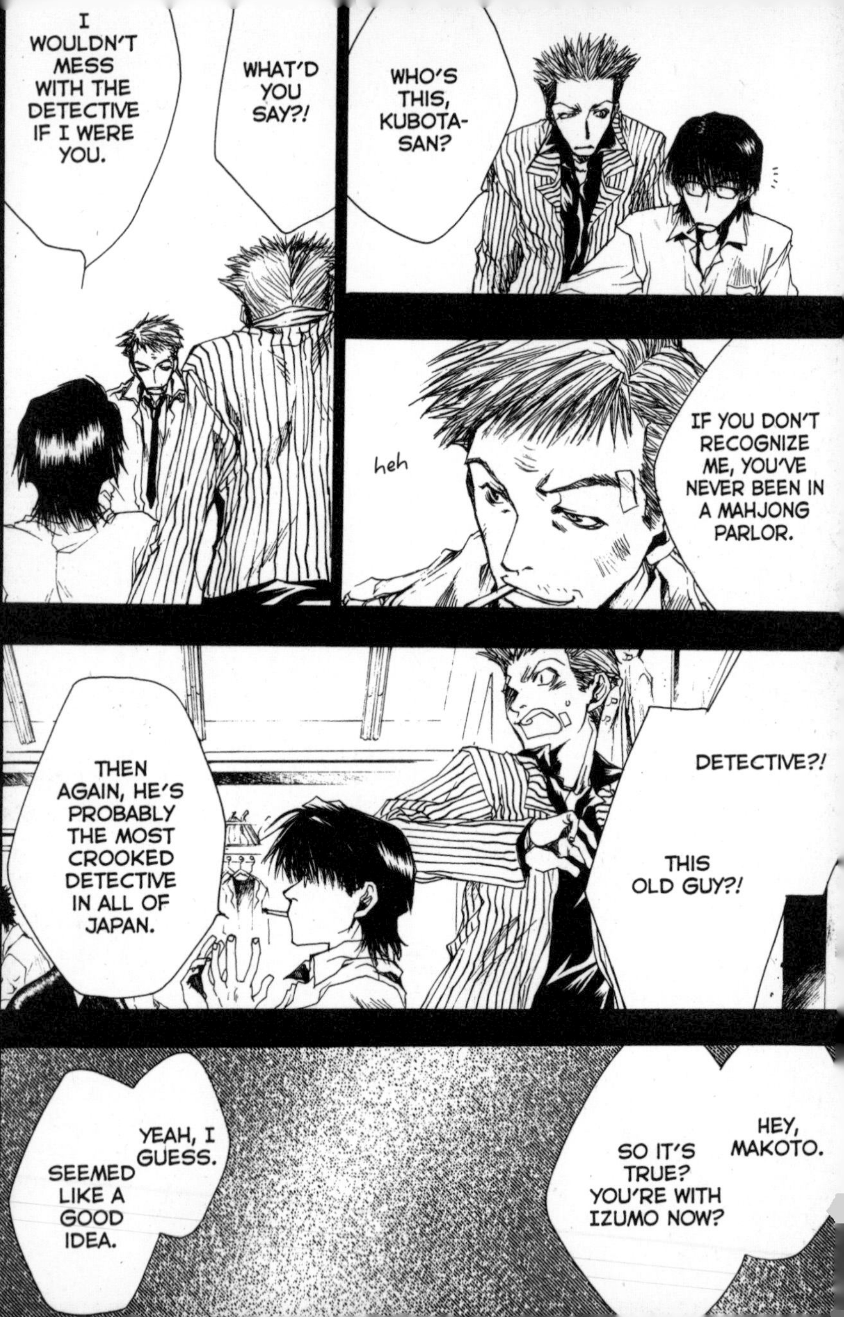
WHO'S THIS, KUBOTA-SAN?
IF YOU DON'T RECOGNIZE ME, YOU'VE NEVER BEEN IN A MAHJONG PARLOR.
heh
WHAT'D YOU SAY?!
I WOULDN'T MESS WITH THE DETECTIVE IF I WERE YOU.
DETECTIVE?!
THIS OLD GUY?!
THEN AGAIN, HE'S PROBABLY THE MOST CROOKED DETECTIVE IN ALL OF JAPAN.
HEY, MAKOTO.
SO IT'S TRUE? YOU'RE WITH IZUMO NOW?
YEAH, I GUESS.
SEEMED LIKE A GOOD IDEA.

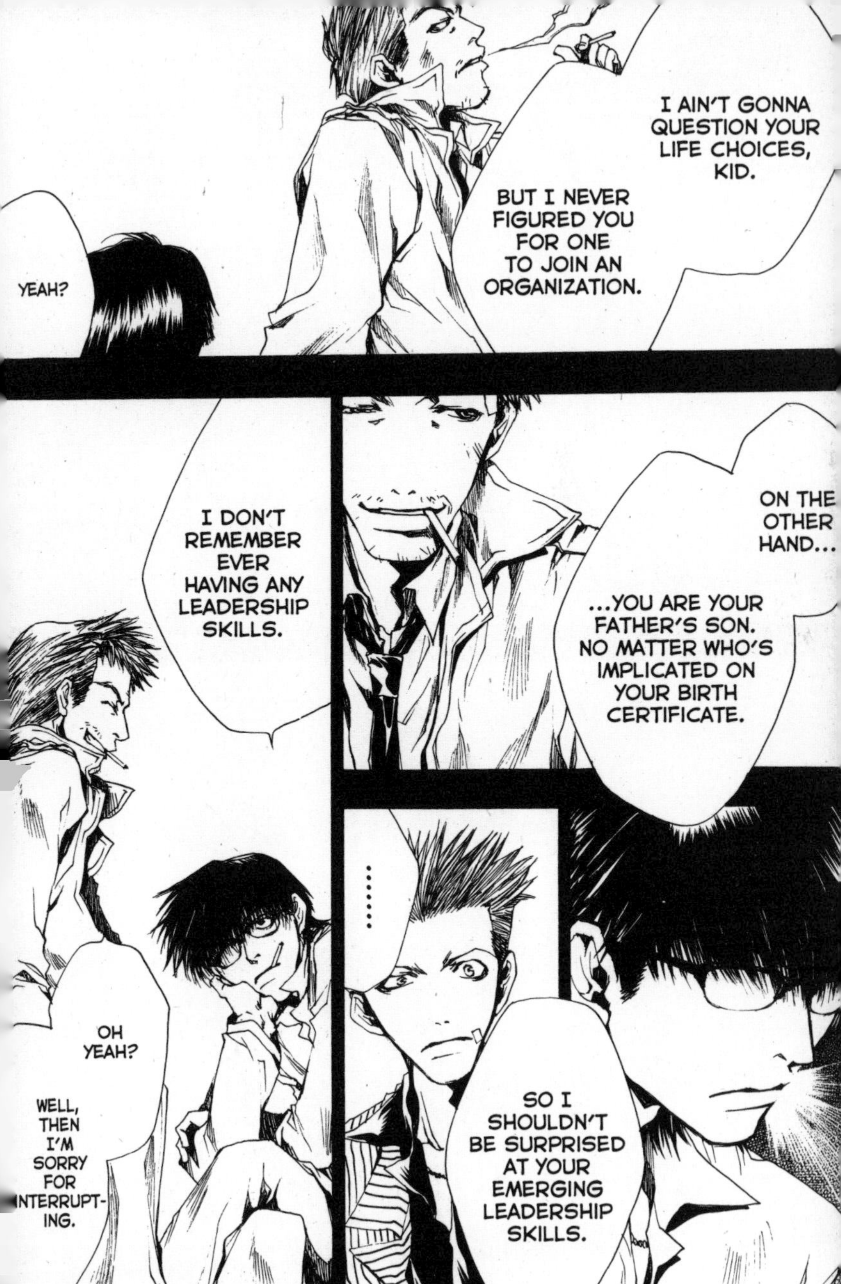
I AIN'T GONNA QUESTION YOUR LIFE CHOICES, KID.
BUT I NEVER FIGURED YOU FOR ONE TO JOIN AN ORGANIZATION.
YEAH?
ON THE OTHER HAND...
...YOU ARE YOUR FATHER'S SON. NO MATTER WHO'S IMPLICATED ON YOUR BIRTH CERTIFICATE.
I DON'T REMEMBER EVER HAVING ANY LEADERSHIP SKILLS.
SO I SHOULDN'T BE SURPRISED AT YOUR EMERGING LEADERSHIP SKILLS.
....
OH YEAH?
WELL, THEN I'M SORRY FOR INTERRUPT-ING.

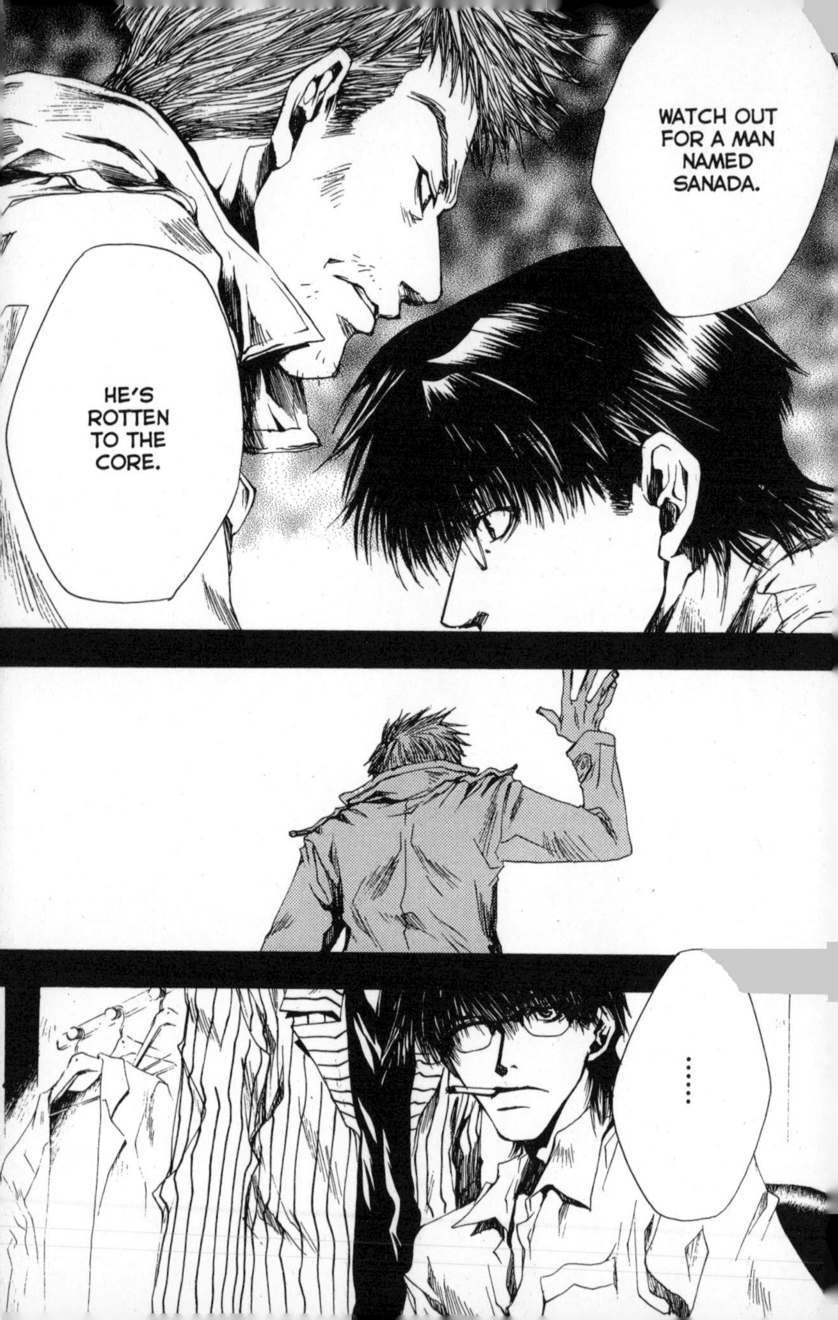
WATCH OUT FOR A MAN NAMED SANADA.
HE'S ROTTEN TO THE CORE.
......

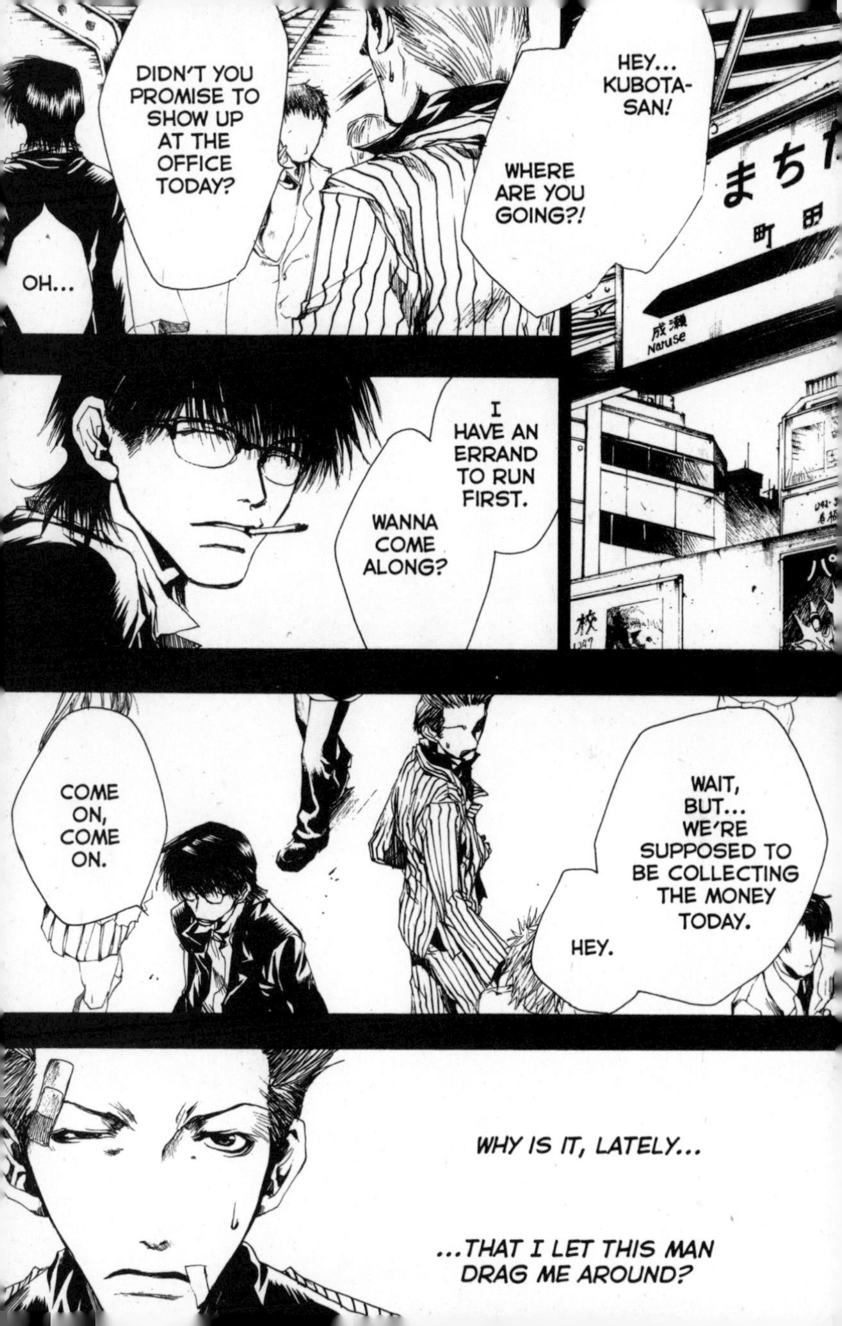

HEY... KUBOTA-SAN!
WHERE ARE YOU GOING?!
DIDN'T YOU PROMISE TO SHOW UP AT THE OFFICE TODAY?
OH...
I HAVE AN ERRAND TO RUN FIRST.
WANNA COME ALONG?
WAIT, BUT... WE'RE SUPPOSED TO BE COLLECTING THE MONEY TODAY.
HEY.
COME ON, COME ON.
WHY IS IT, LATELY...
...THAT I LET THIS MAN DRAG ME AROUND?

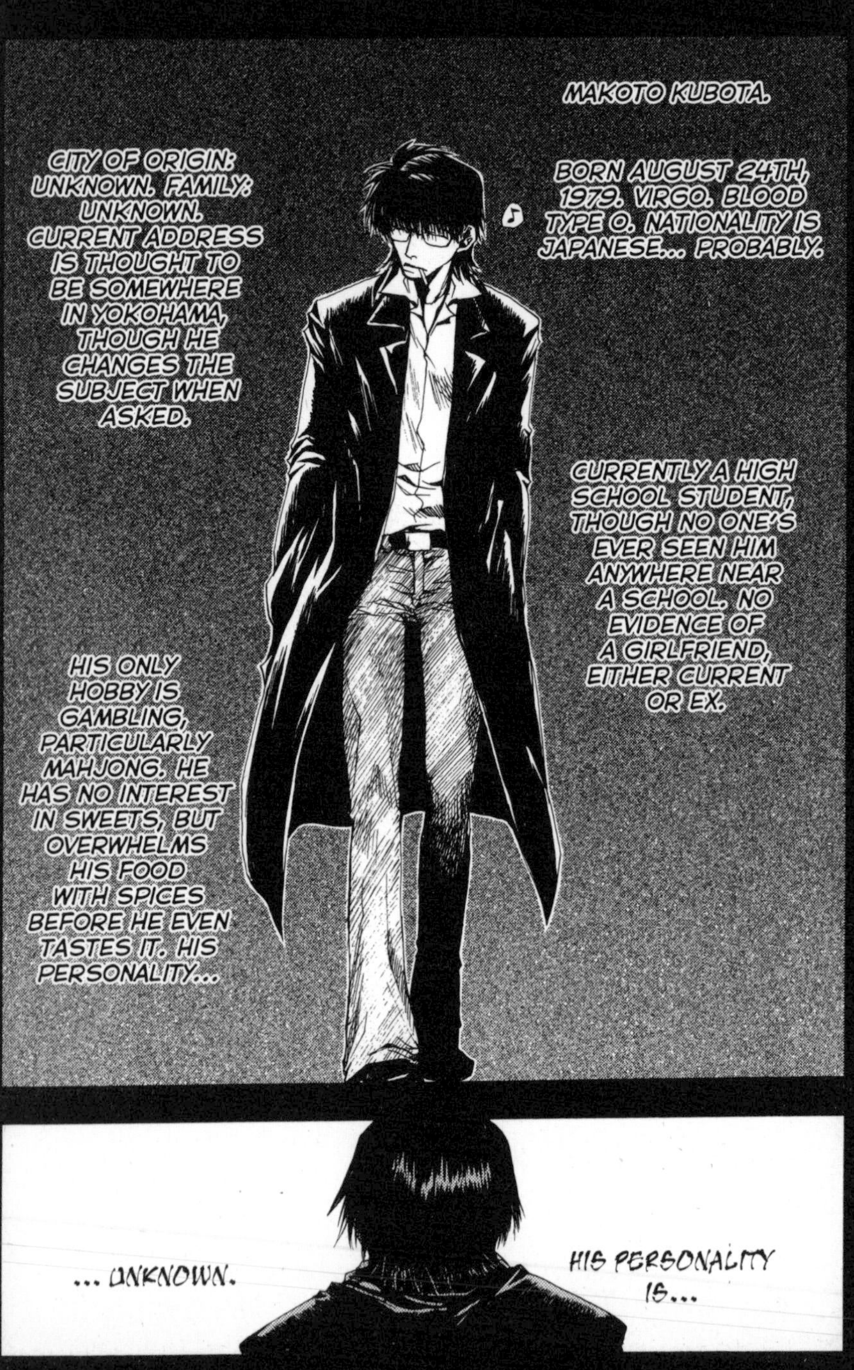
MAKOTO KUBOTA.
BORN AUGUST 24TH, 1979. VIRGO. BLOOD TYPE O. NATIONALITY IS JAPANESE... PROBABLY.
CITY OF ORIGIN: UNKNOWN. FAMILY: UNKNOWN. CURRENT ADDRESS IS THOUGHT TO BE SOMEWHERE IN YOKOHAMA, THOUGH HE CHANGES THE SUBJECT WHEN ASKED.
CURRENTLY A HIGH SCHOOL STUDENT, THOUGH NO ONE'S EVER SEEN HIM ANYWHERE NEAR A SCHOOL. NO EVIDENCE OF A GIRLFRIEND, EITHER CURRENT OR EX.
HIS ONLY HOBBY IS GAMBLING, PARTICULARLY MAHJONG. HE HAS NO INTEREST IN SWEETS, BUT OVERWHELMS HIS FOOD WITH SPICES BEFORE HE EVEN TASTES IT. HIS PERSONALITY...
HIS PERSONALITY IS...
... UNKNOWN.

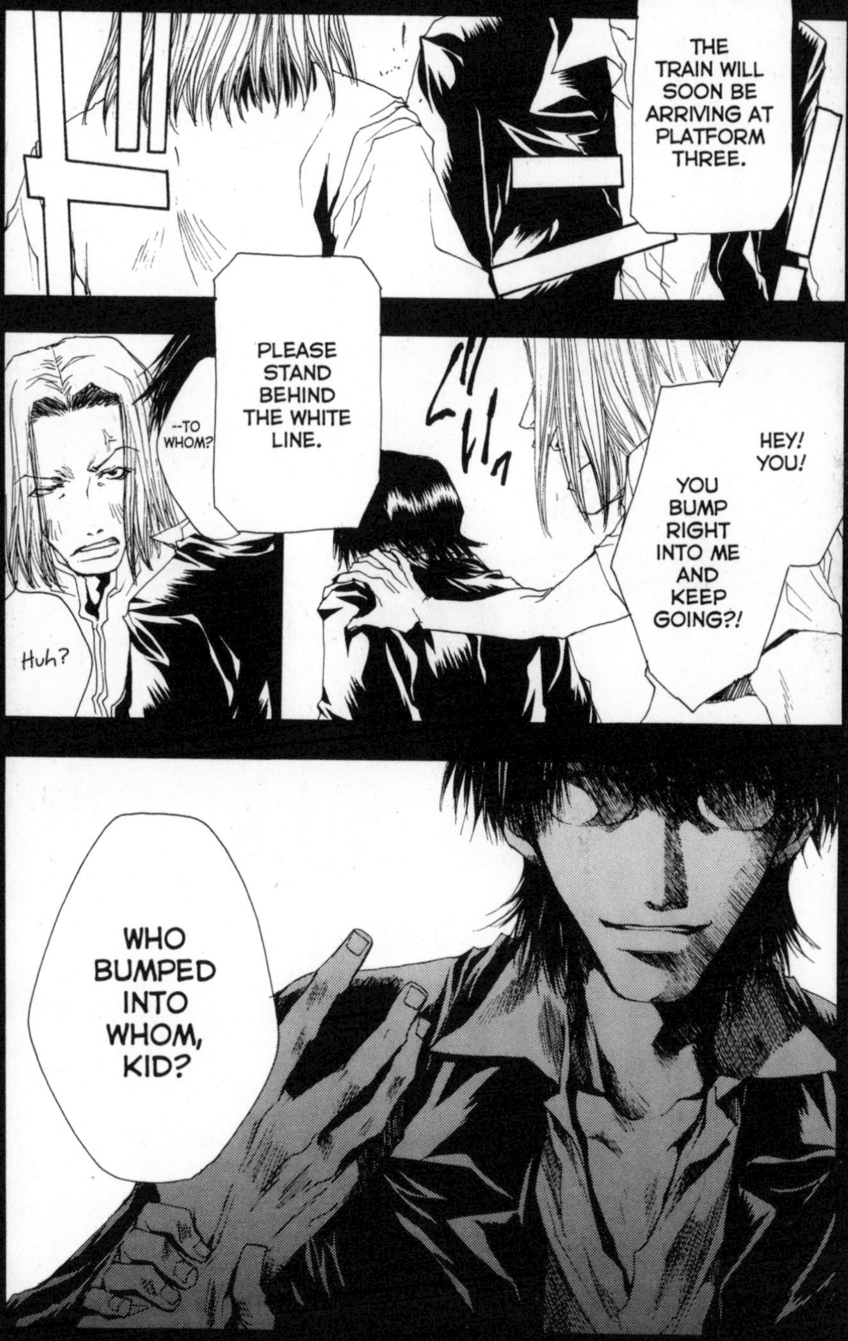
THE TRAIN WILL SOON BE ARRIVING AT PLATFORM THREE.
PLEASE STAND BEHIND THE WHITE LINE.
HEY! YOU!
YOU BUMP RIGHT INTO ME AND KEEP GOING?!
--TO WHOM?
Huh?
WHO BUMPED INTO WHOM, KID?

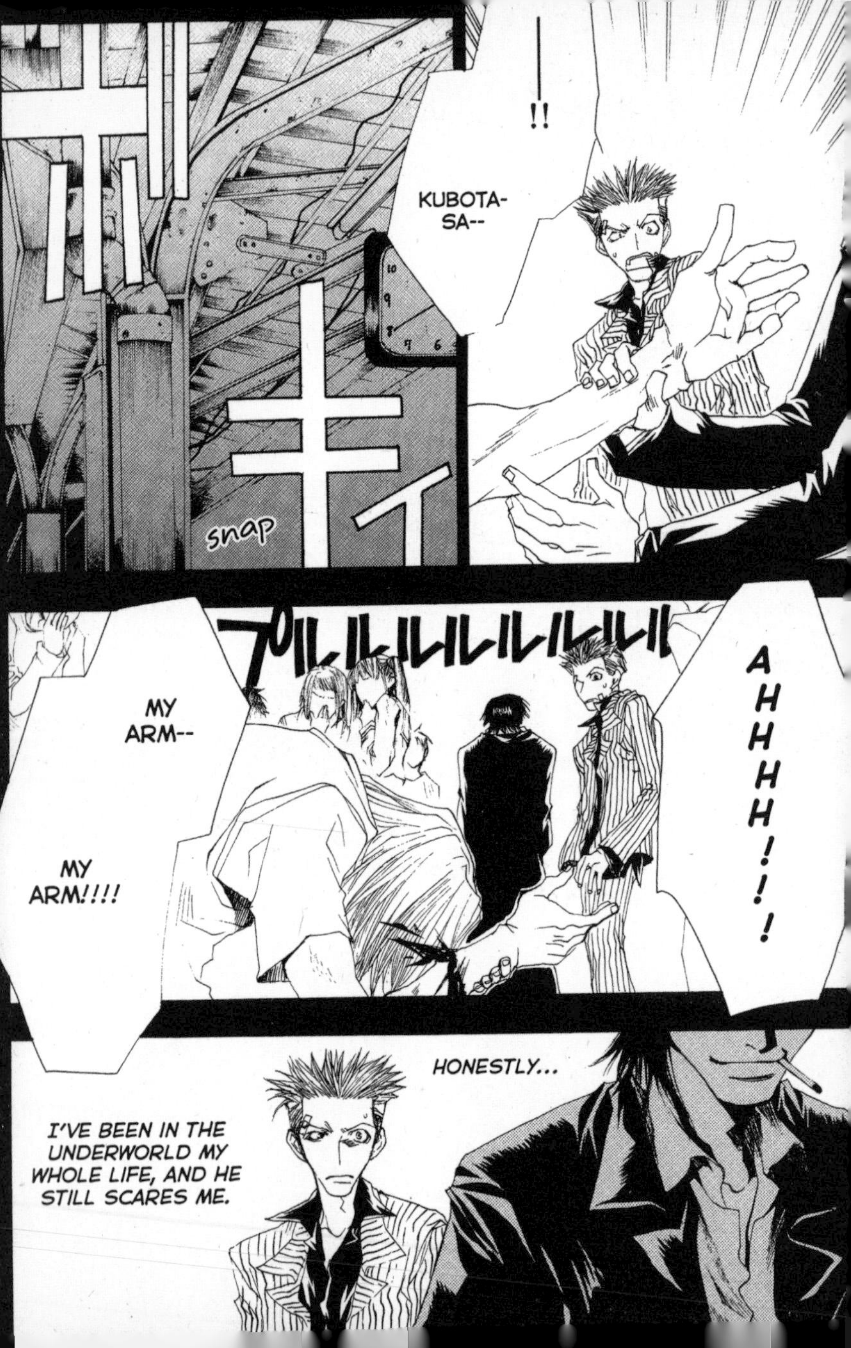
!!
KUBOTA-SA--
snap
AHHHH!!!!
MY ARM--
MY ARM!!!!
HONESTLY...
I'VE BEEN IN THE UNDERWORLD MY WHOLE LIFE, AND HE STILL SCARES ME.

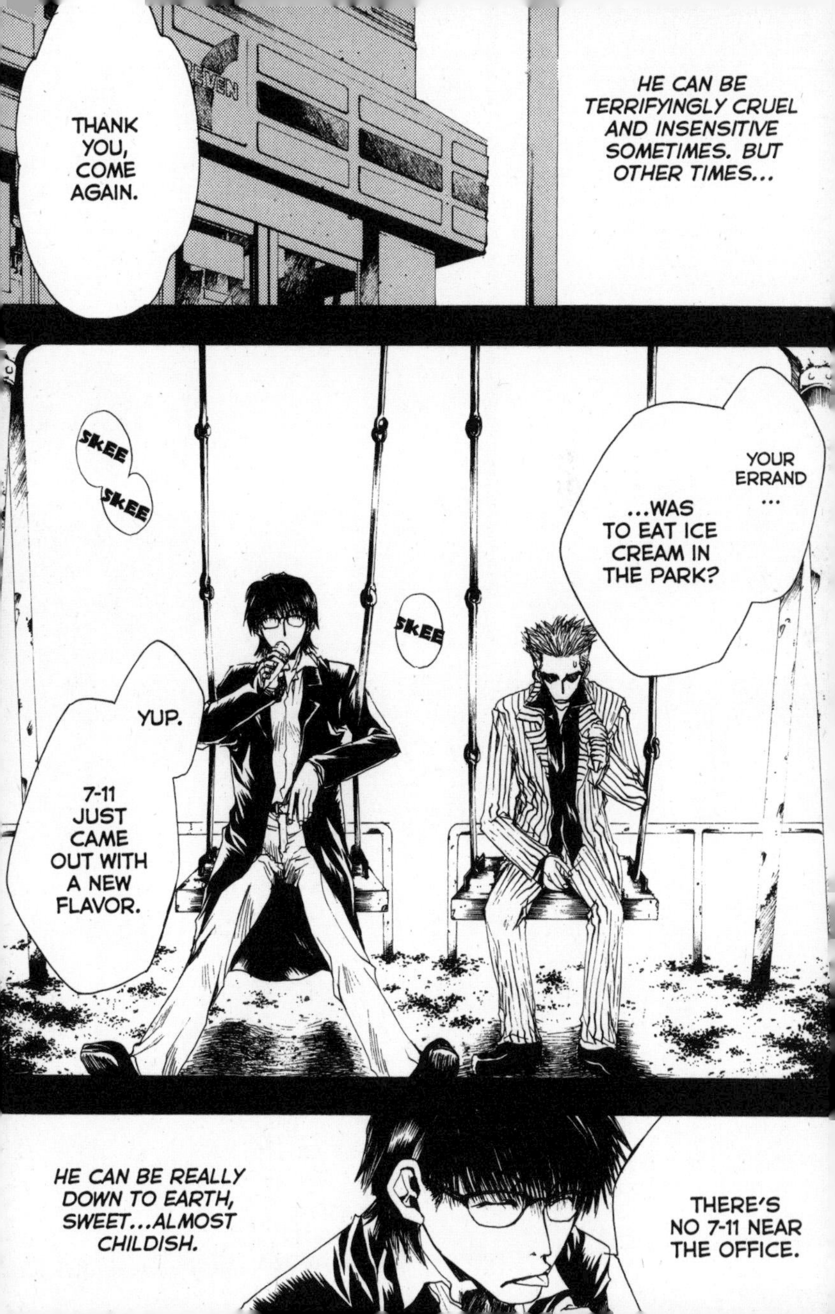
HE CAN BE TERRIFYINGLY CRUEL AND INSENSITIVE SOMETIMES. BUT OTHER TIMES...
THANK YOU, COME AGAIN.
YOUR ERRAND...
...WAS TO EAT ICE CREAM IN THE PARK?
SKEE
SKEE
SKEE
YUP.
7-11 JUST CAME OUT WITH A NEW FLAVOR.
THERE'S NO 7-11 NEAR THE OFFICE.
HE CAN BE REALLY DOWN TO EARTH, SWEET...ALMOST CHILDISH.

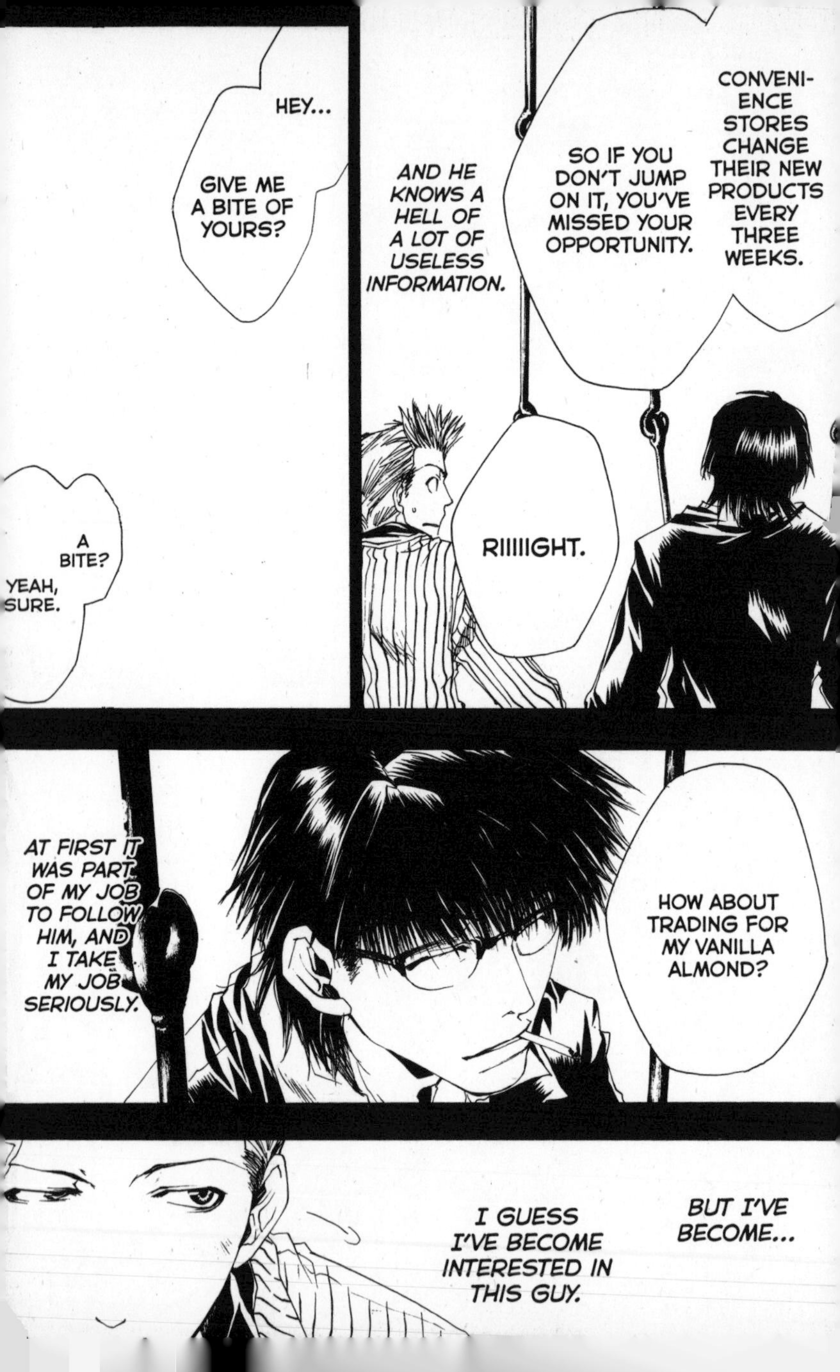
CONVENIENCE STORES CHANGE THEIR NEW PRODUCTS EVERY THREE WEEKS.
SO IF YOU DON'T JUMP ON IT, YOU'VE MISSED YOUR OPPORTUNITY.
AND HE KNOWS A HELL OF A LOT OF USELESS INFORMATION.
RIIIIIGHT.
HEY...
GIVE ME A BITE OF YOURS?
A BITE? YEAH, SURE.
HOW ABOUT TRADING FOR MY VANILLA ALMOND?
AT FIRST IT WAS PART OF MY JOB TO FOLLOW HIM, AND I TAKE MY JOB SERIOUSLY.
BUT I'VE BECOME...
I GUESS I'VE BECOME INTERESTED IN THIS GUY.

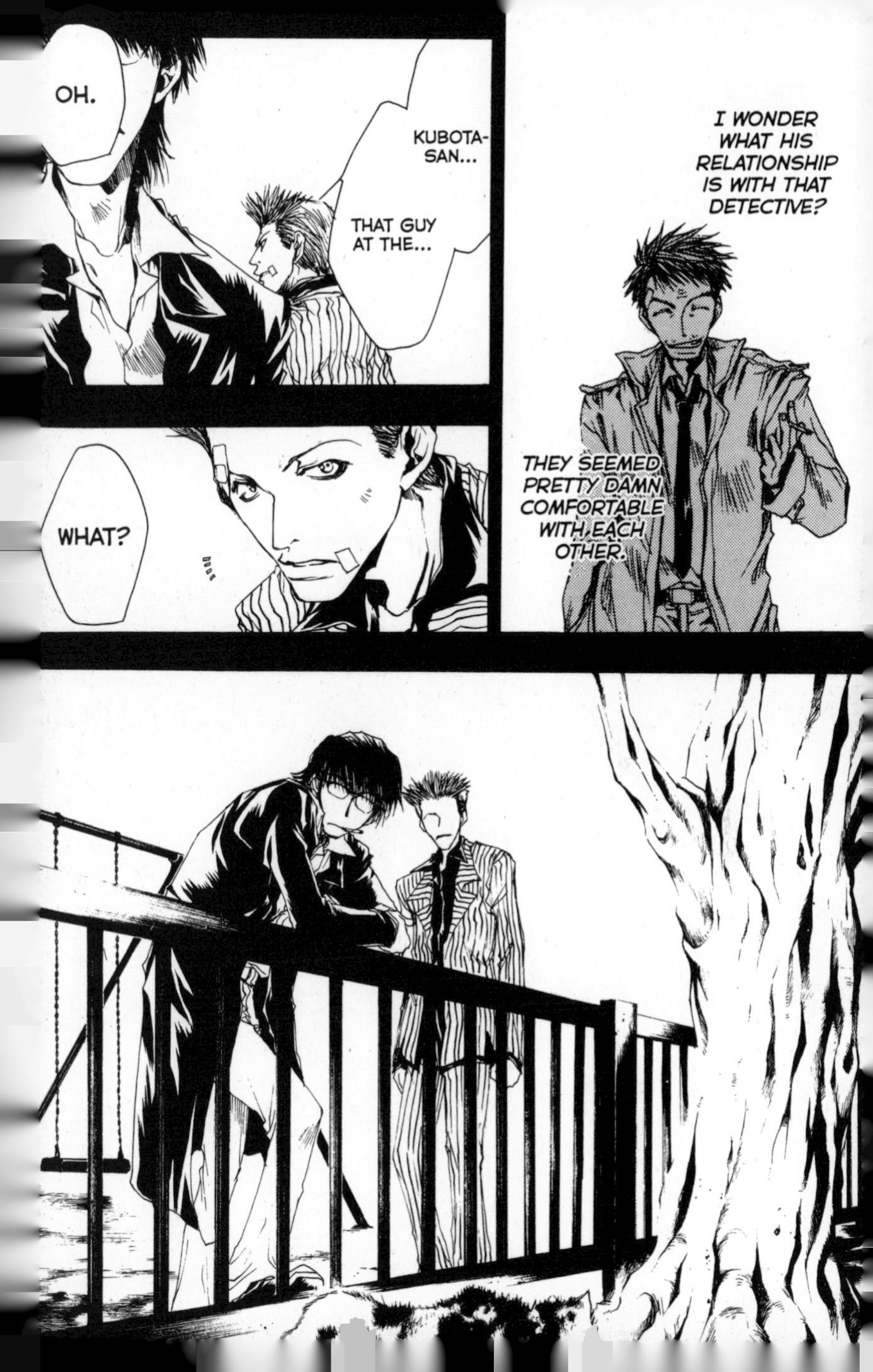
I WONDER WHAT HIS RELATIONSHIP IS WITH THAT DETECTIVE?
THEY SEEMED PRETTY DAMN COMFORTABLE WITH EACH OTHER.
KUBOTA-SAN...
THAT GUY AT THE...
OH.
WHAT?

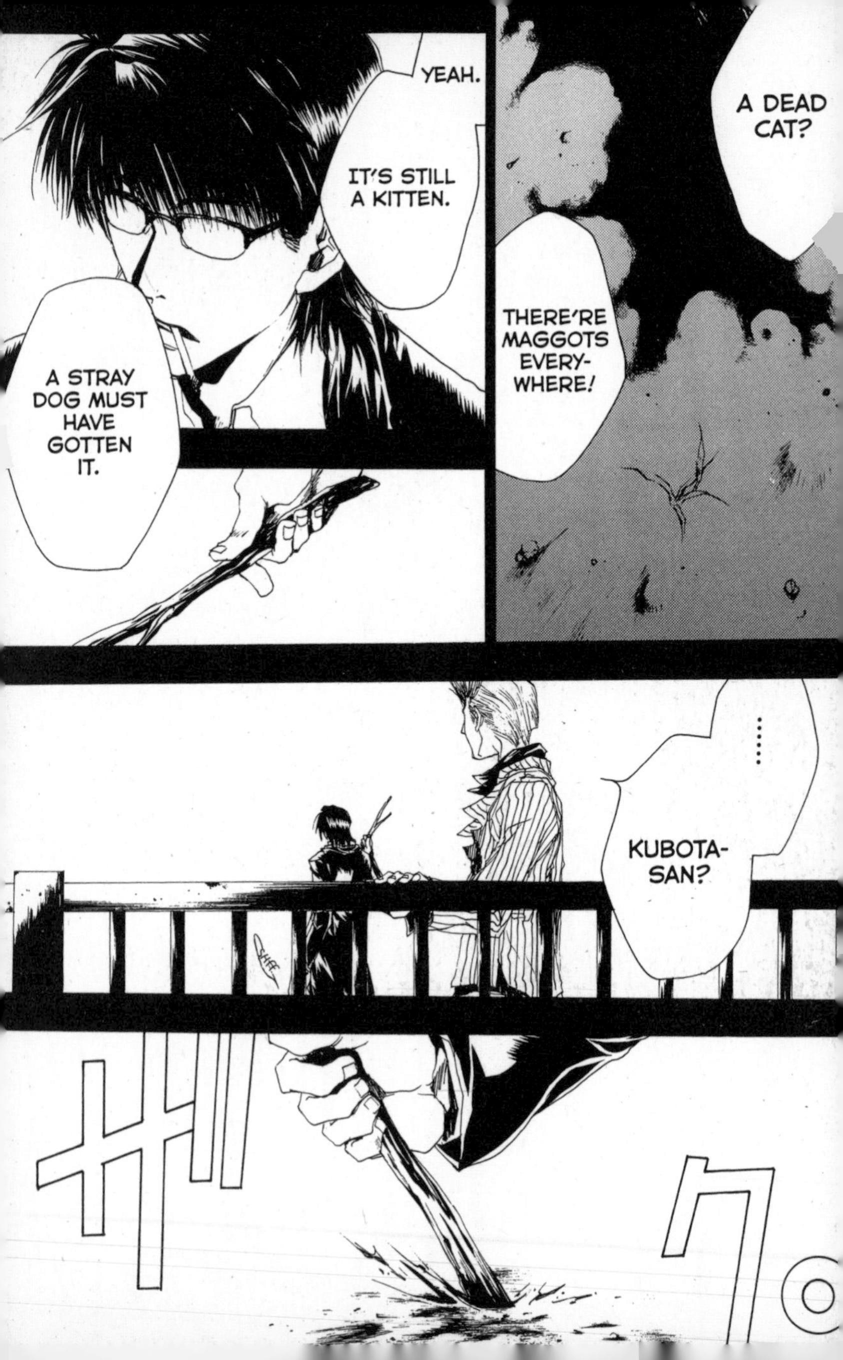
A DEAD CAT?
THERE'RE MAGGOTS EVERY-WHERE!
YEAH.
IT'S STILL A KITTEN.
A STRAY DOG MUST HAVE GOTTEN IT.
......
KUBOTA-SAN?
ザク。

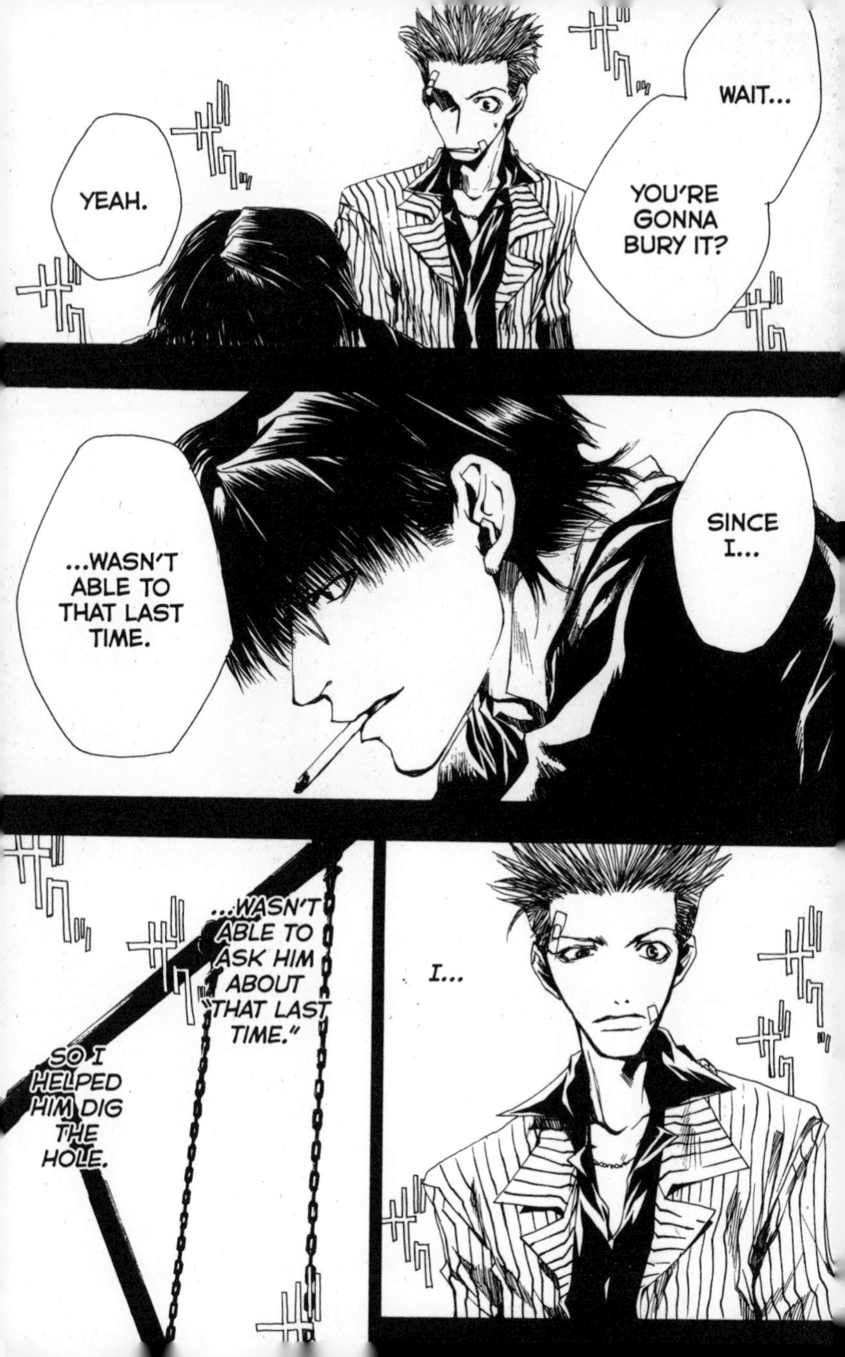
WAIT...
YOU'RE GONNA BURY IT?
YEAH.
SINCE I...
...WASN'T ABLE TO THAT LAST TIME.
I...
...WASN'T ABLE TO ASK HIM ABOUT "THAT LAST TIME."
SO I HELPED HIM DIG THE HOLE.

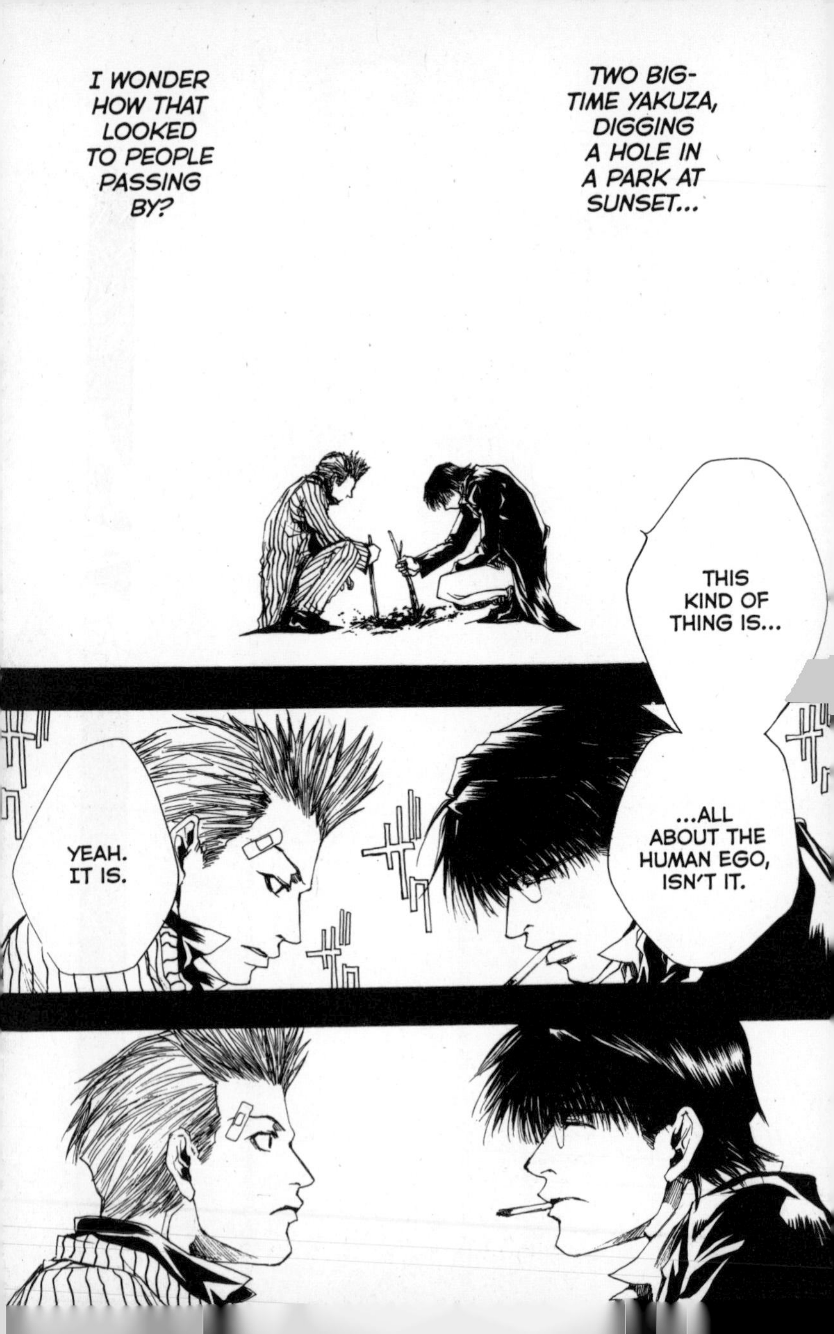
TWO BIG-TIME YAKUZA, DIGGING A HOLE IN A PARK AT SUNSET...
I WONDER HOW THAT LOOKED TO PEOPLE PASSING BY?
THIS KIND OF THING IS...
...ALL ABOUT THE HUMAN EGO, ISN'T IT.
YEAH. IT IS.

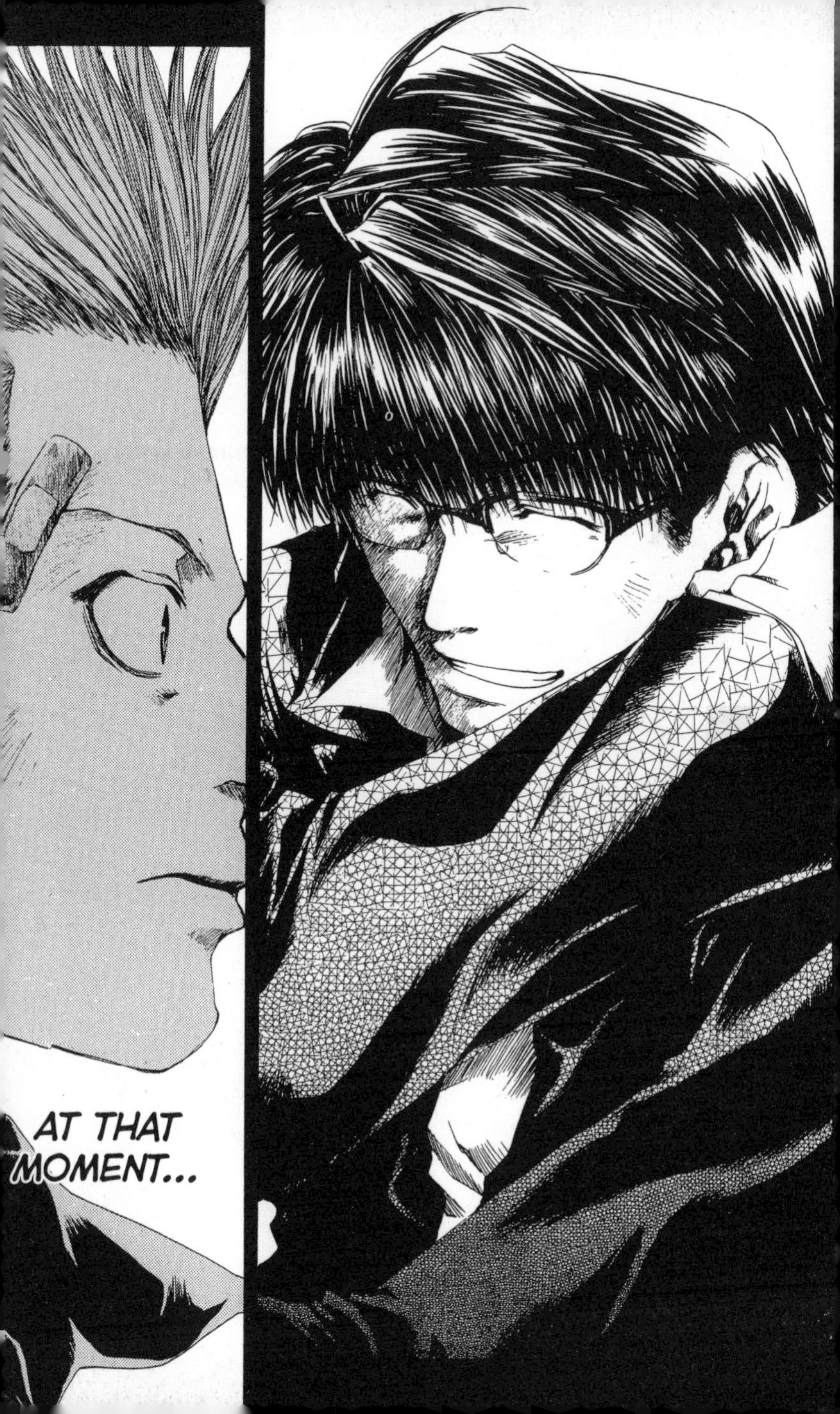
AT THAT MOMENT...

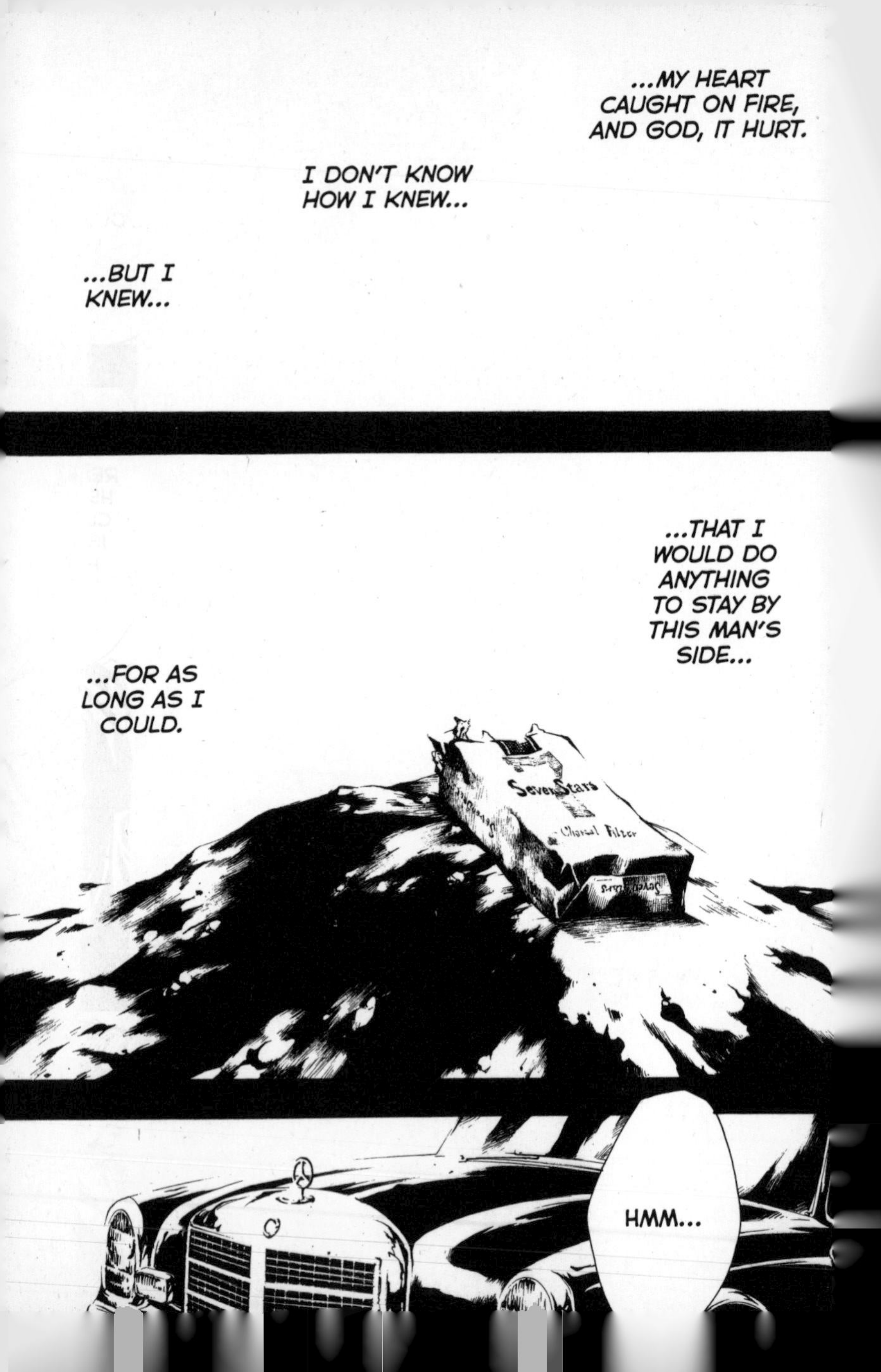
...MY HEART CAUGHT ON FIRE, AND GOD, IT HURT.
I DON'T KNOW HOW I KNEW...
...BUT I KNEW...
...THAT I WOULD DO ANYTHING TO STAY BY THIS MAN'S SIDE...
...FOR AS LONG AS I COULD.
Seven Stars
HMM...

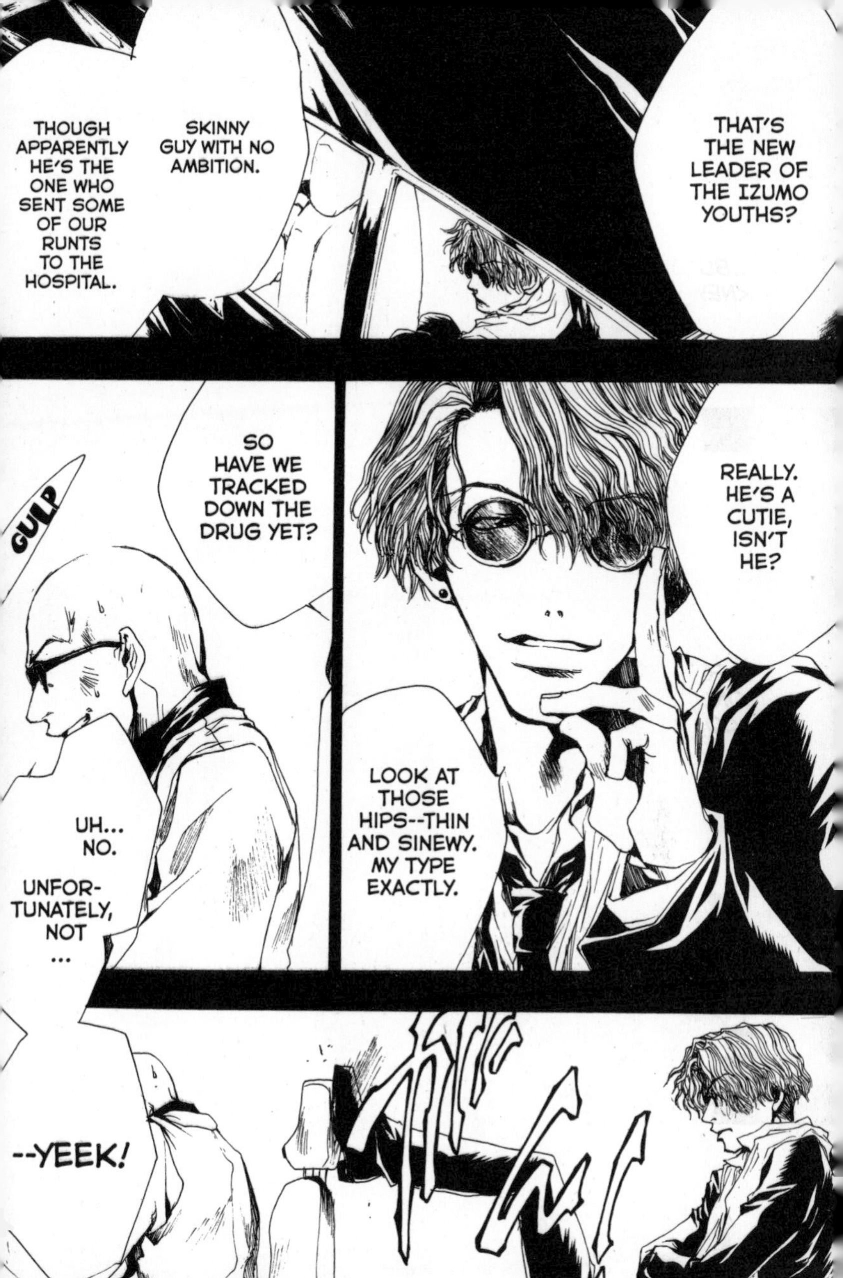
THAT'S THE NEW LEADER OF THE IZUMO YOUTHS?
SKINNY GUY WITH NO AMBITION.
THOUGH APPARENTLY HE'S THE ONE WHO SENT SOME OF OUR RUNTS TO THE HOSPITAL.
REALLY. HE'S A CUTIE, ISN'T HE?
LOOK AT THOSE HIPS--THIN AND SINEWY. MY TYPE EXACTLY.
SO HAVE WE TRACKED DOWN THE DRUG YET?
GULP
UH... NO.
UNFOR-TUNATELY, NOT ...
--YEEK!

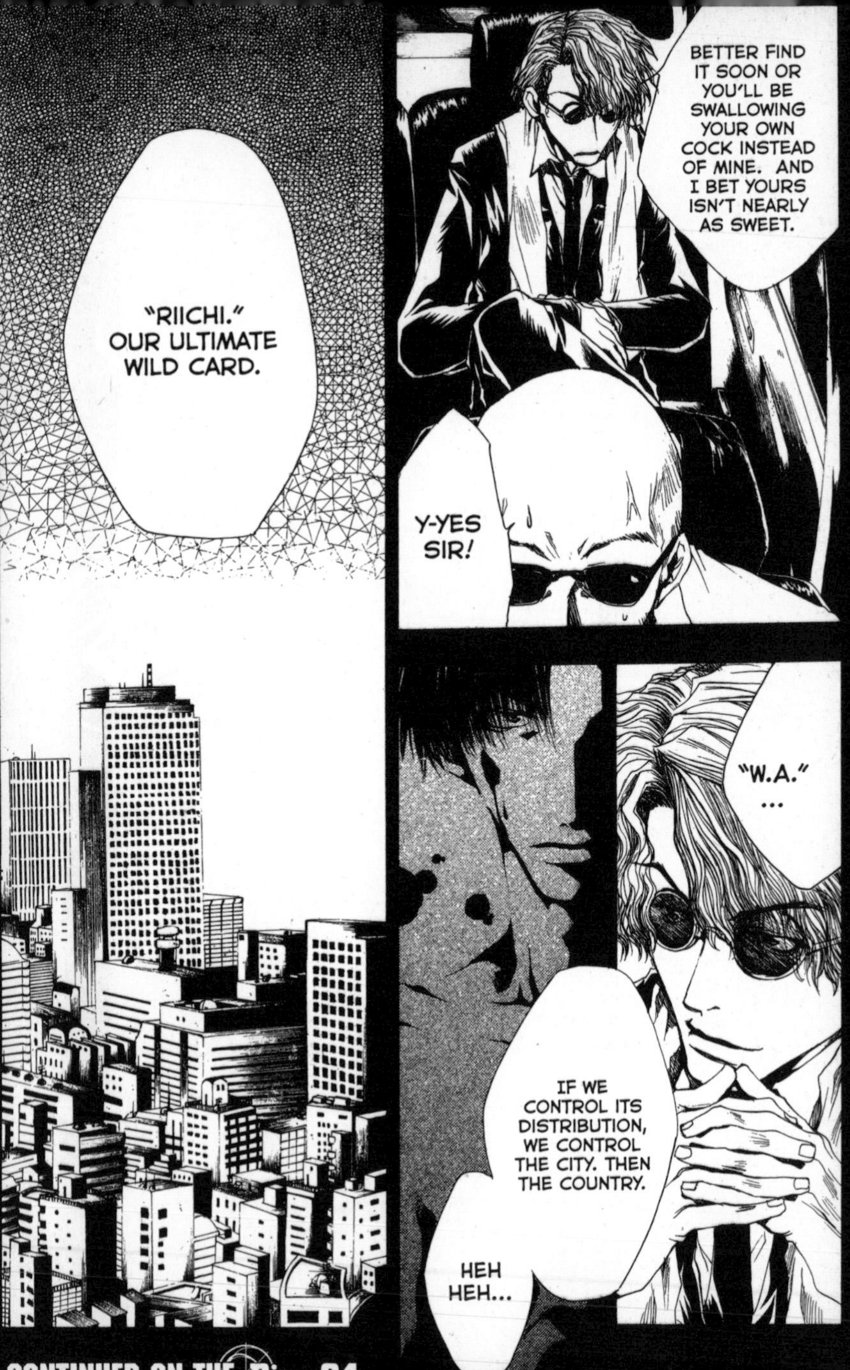
BETTER FIND IT SOON OR YOU'LL BE SWALLOWING YOUR OWN COCK INSTEAD OF MINE. AND I BET YOURS ISN'T NEARLY AS SWEET.
Y-YES SIR!
"W.A." ...
IF WE CONTROL ITS DISTRIBUTION, WE CONTROL THE CITY. THEN THE COUNTRY.
HEH HEH...
"RIICHI." OUR ULTIMATE WILD CARD.

CONTINUED ON THE Dice:04

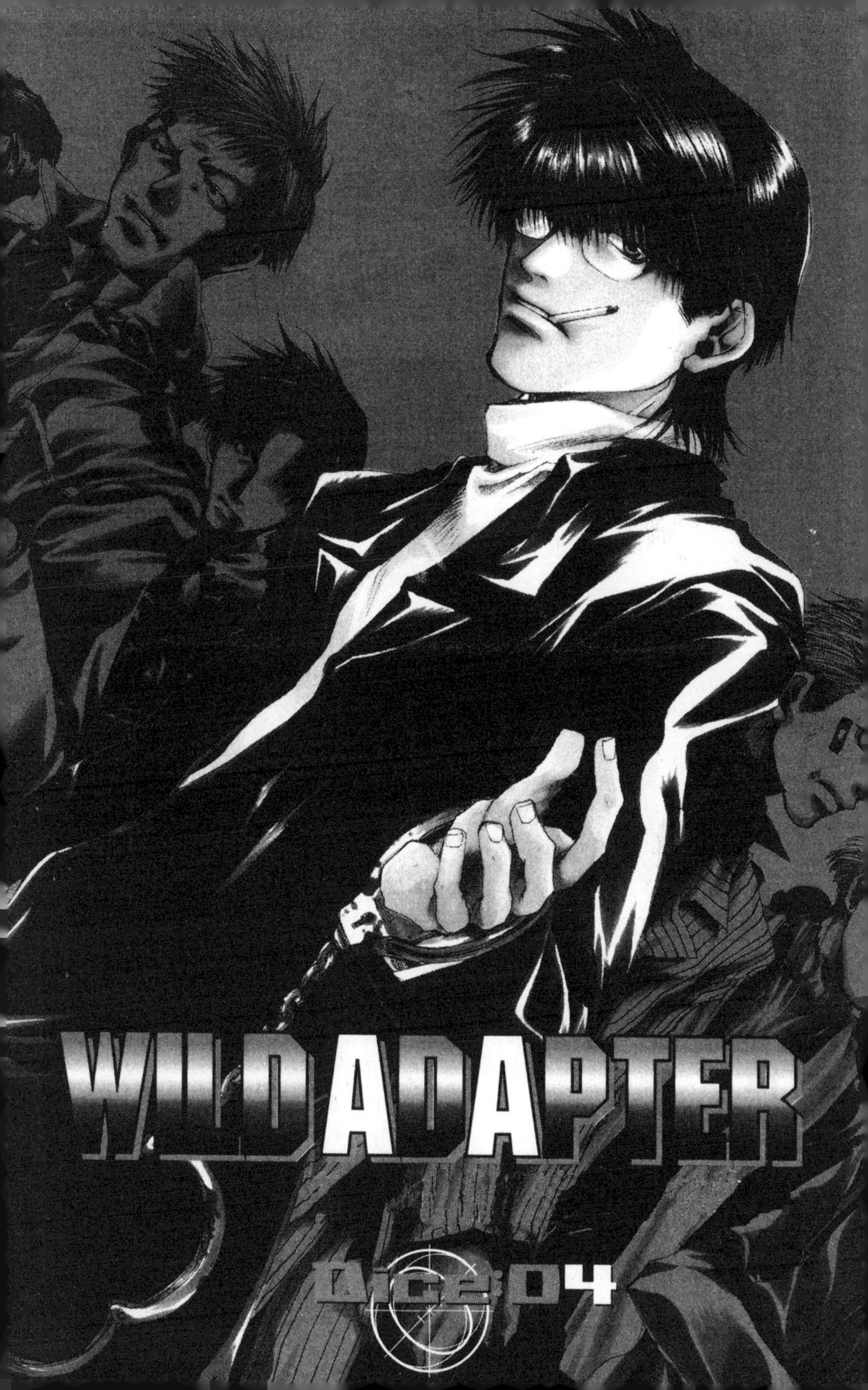
WILD ADAPTER
DICE:04

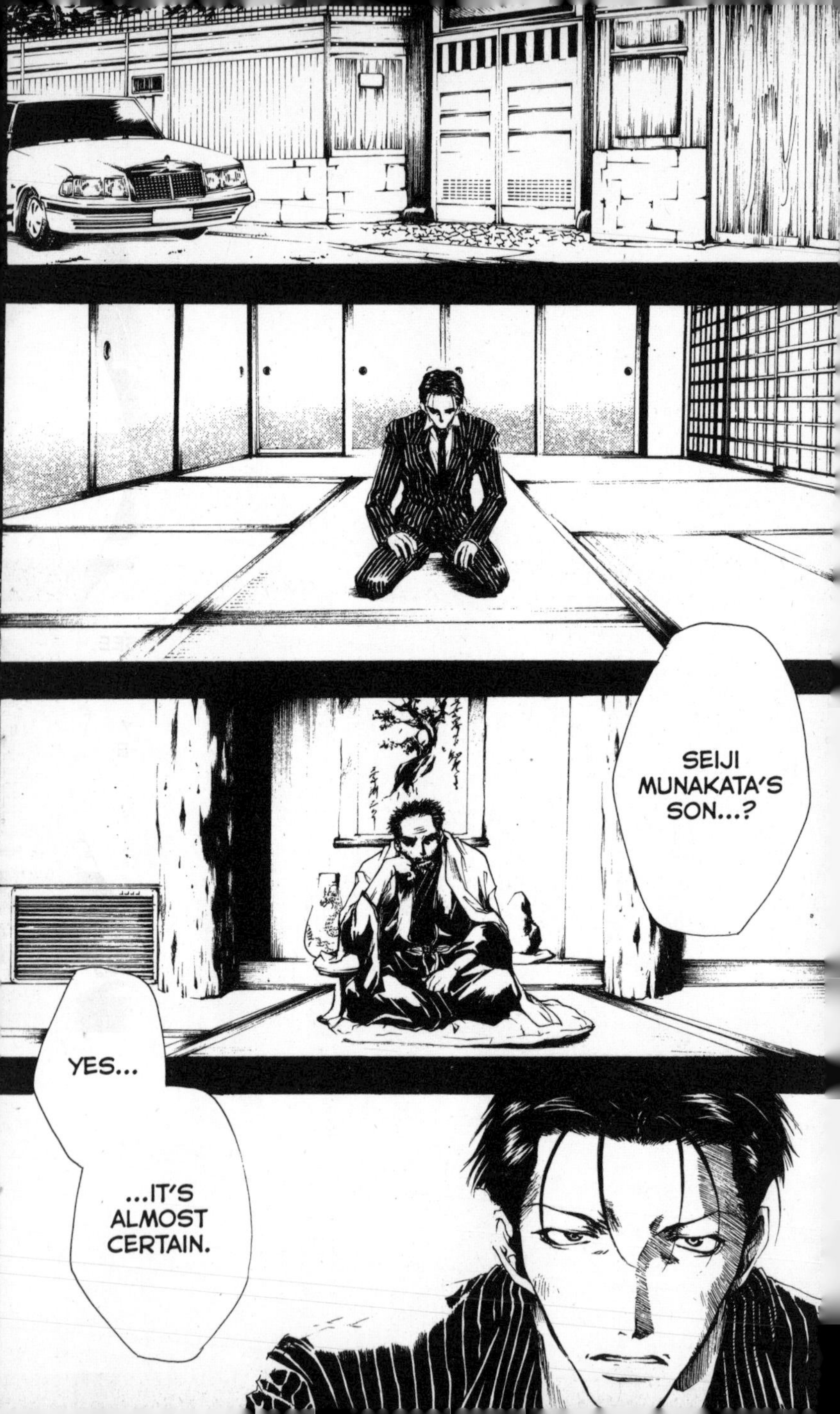
SEIJI MUNAKATA'S SON...?
YES...
...IT'S ALMOST CERTAIN.

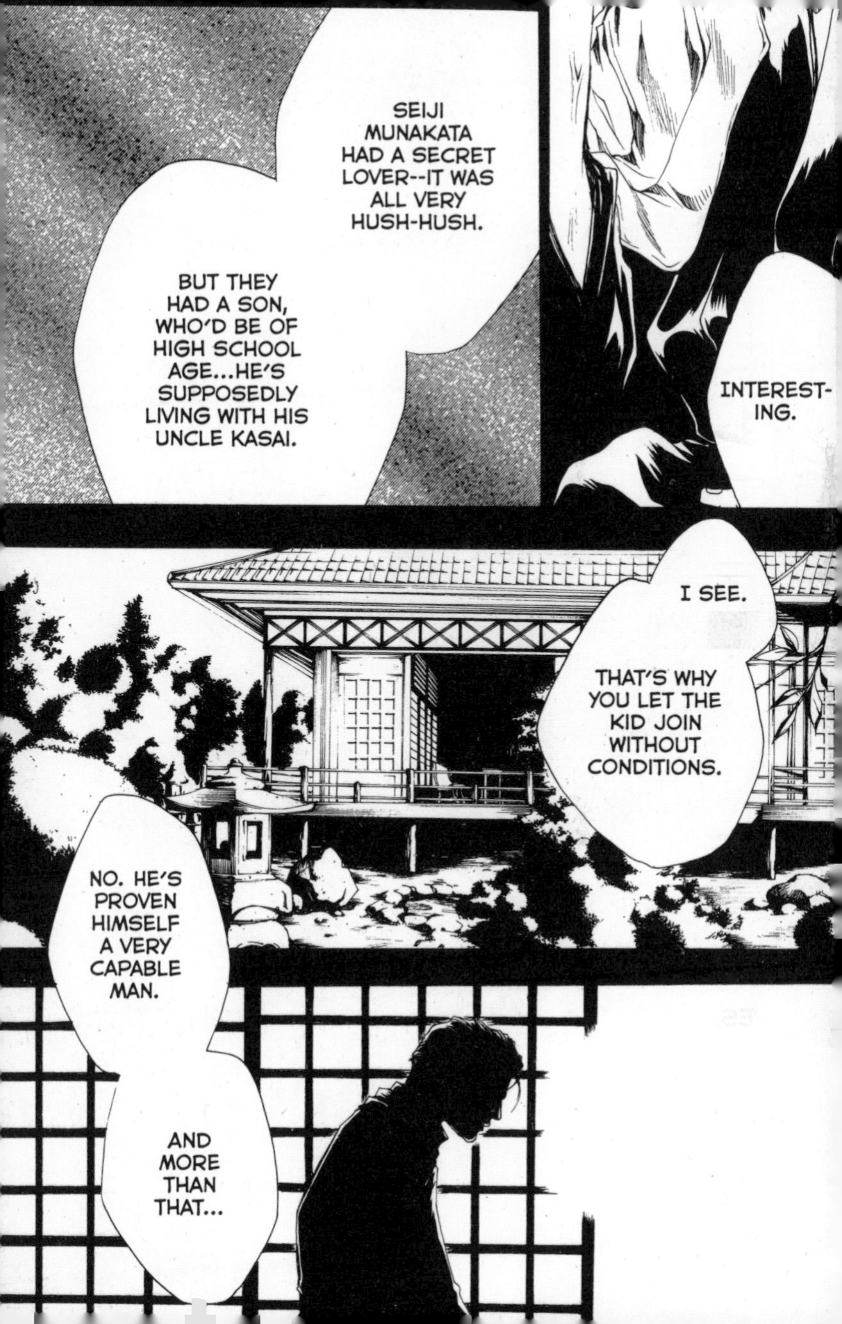
INTERESTING.
SEIJI MUNAKATA HAD A SECRET LOVER--IT WAS ALL VERY HUSH-HUSH.
BUT THEY HAD A SON, WHO'D BE OF HIGH SCHOOL AGE...HE'S SUPPOSEDLY LIVING WITH HIS UNCLE KASAI.
I SEE.
THAT'S WHY YOU LET THE KID JOIN WITHOUT CONDITIONS.
NO. HE'S PROVEN HIMSELF A VERY CAPABLE MAN.
AND MORE THAN THAT...

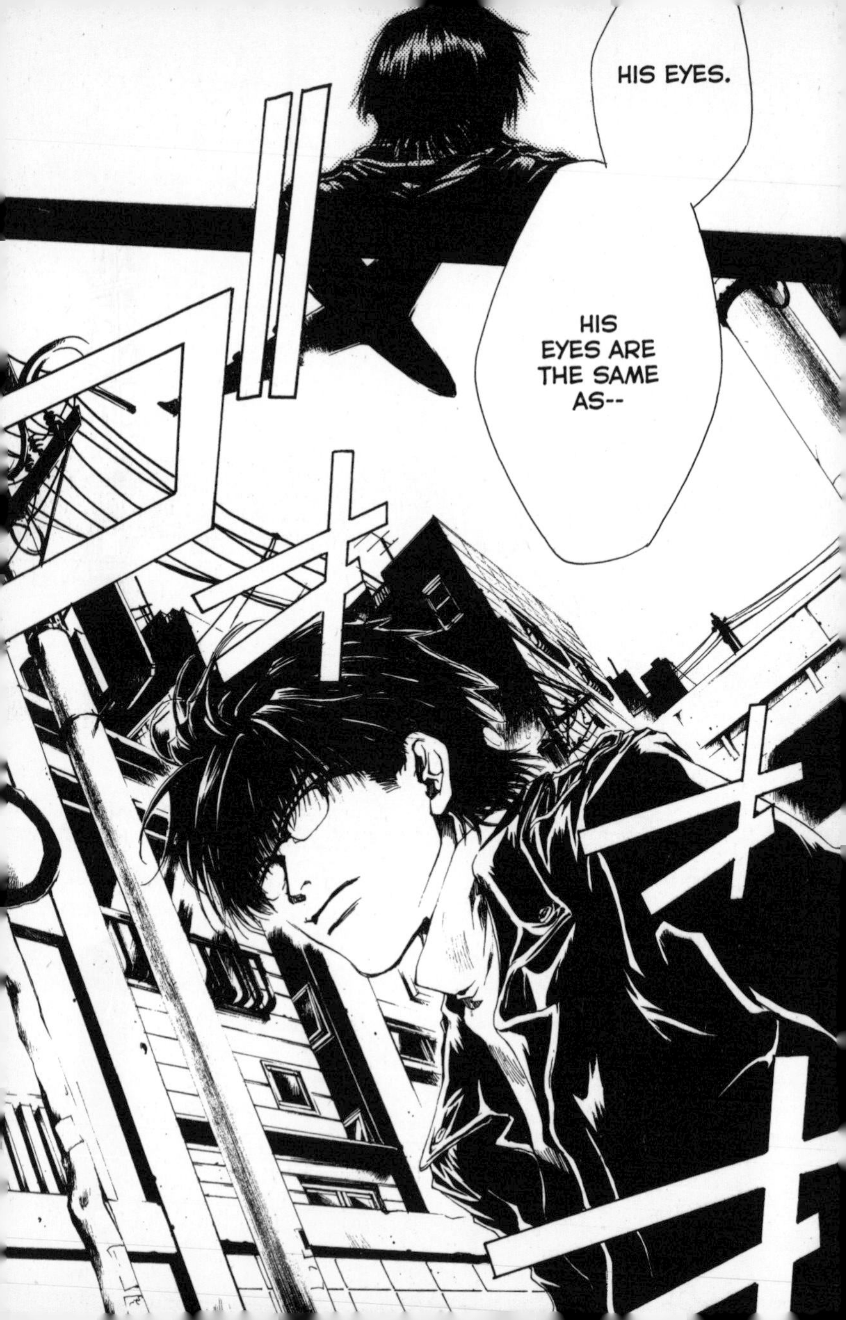
HIS EYES.
HIS EYES ARE THE SAME AS--

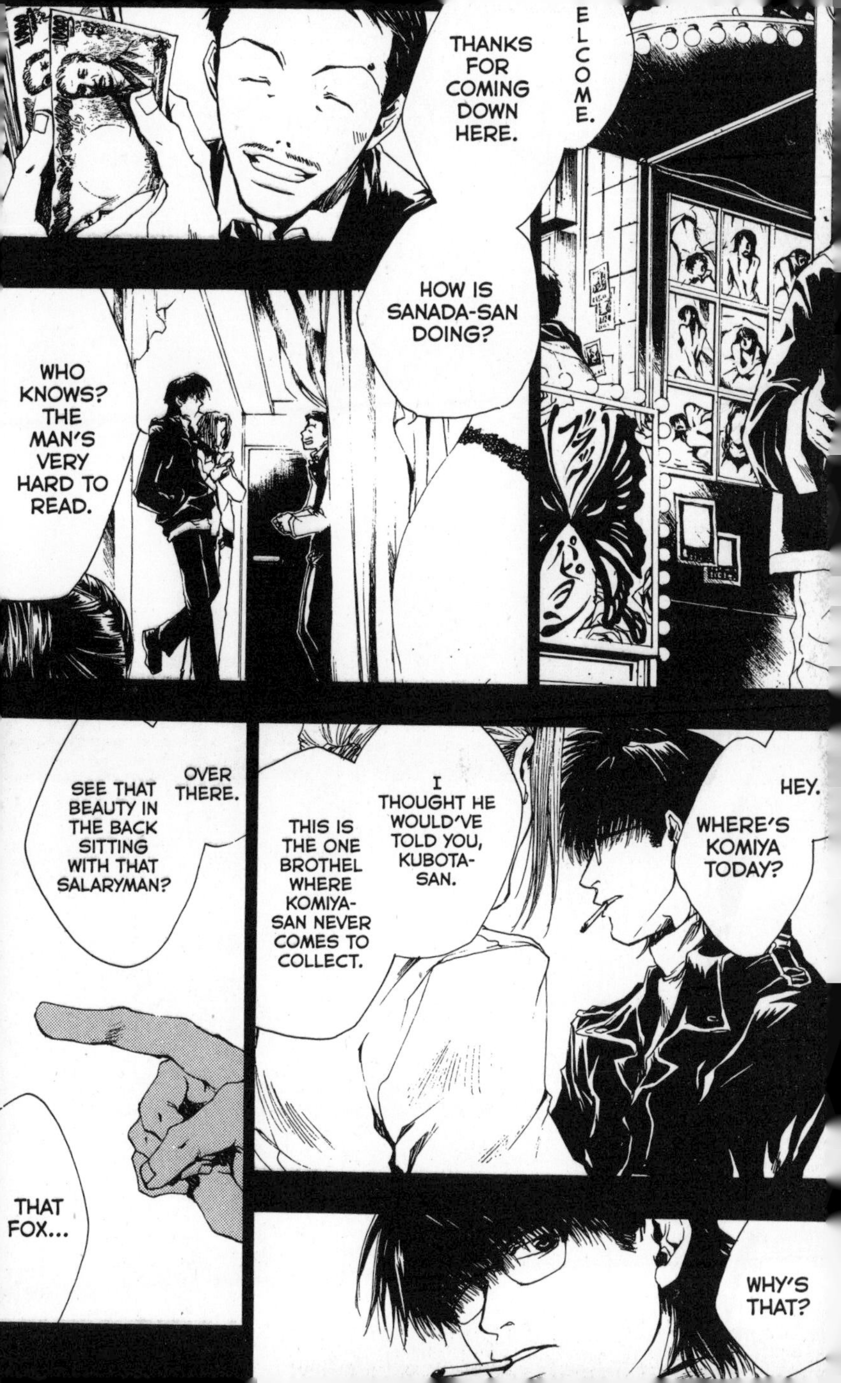
ELCOME.
THANKS FOR COMING DOWN HERE.
HOW IS SANADA-SAN DOING?
WHO KNOWS? THE MAN'S VERY HARD TO READ.
HEY.
WHERE'S KOMIYA TODAY?
I THOUGHT HE WOULD'VE TOLD YOU, KUBOTA-SAN.
THIS IS THE ONE BROTHEL WHERE KOMIYA-SAN NEVER COMES TO COLLECT.
WHY'S THAT?
OVER THERE.
SEE THAT BEAUTY IN THE BACK SITTING WITH THAT SALARYMAN?
THAT FOX...

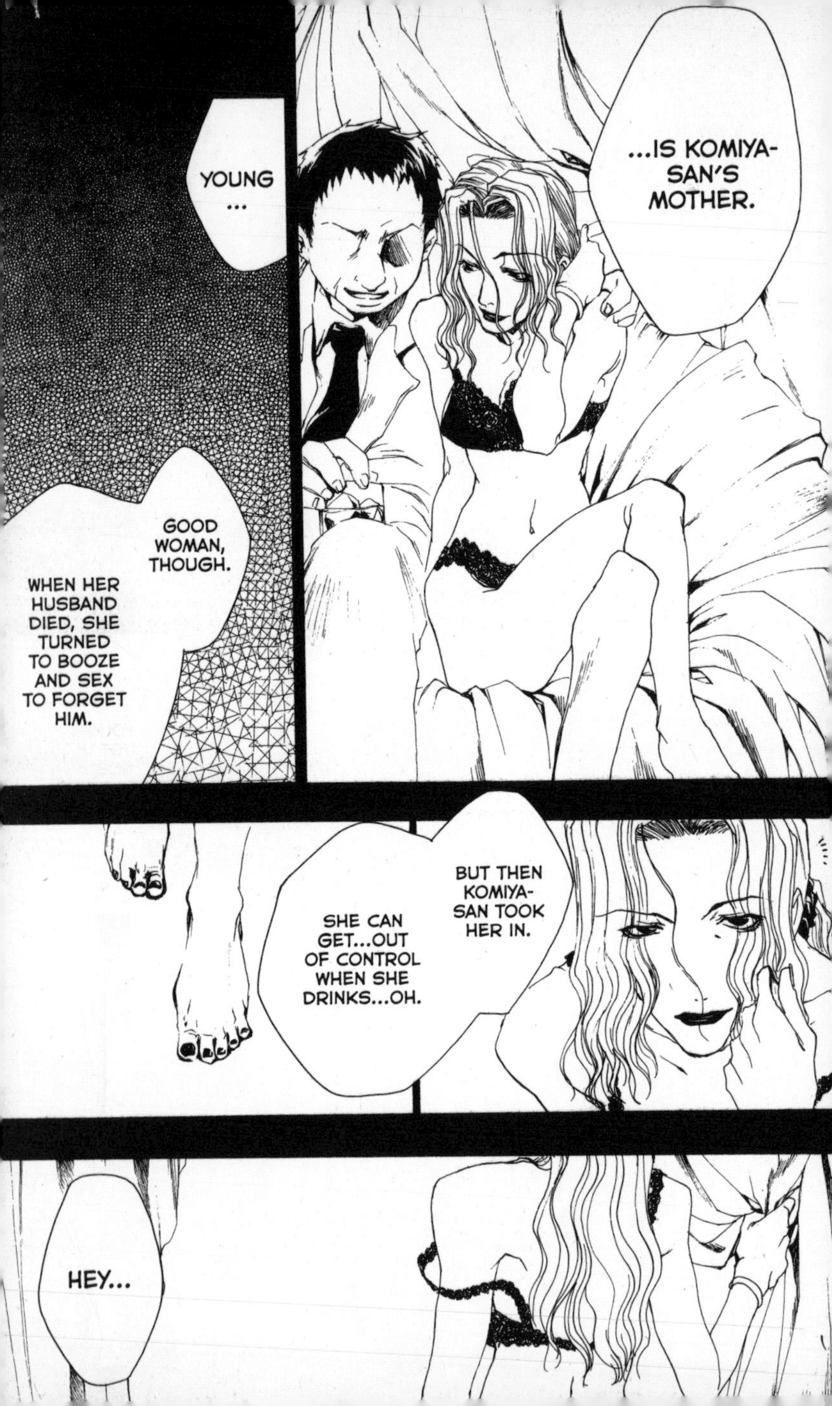
...IS KOMIYA-SAN'S MOTHER.
YOUNG ...
GOOD WOMAN, THOUGH.
WHEN HER HUSBAND DIED, SHE TURNED TO BOOZE AND SEX TO FORGET HIM.
BUT THEN KOMIYA-SAN TOOK HER IN.
SHE CAN GET...OUT OF CONTROL WHEN SHE DRINKS...OH.
HEY...

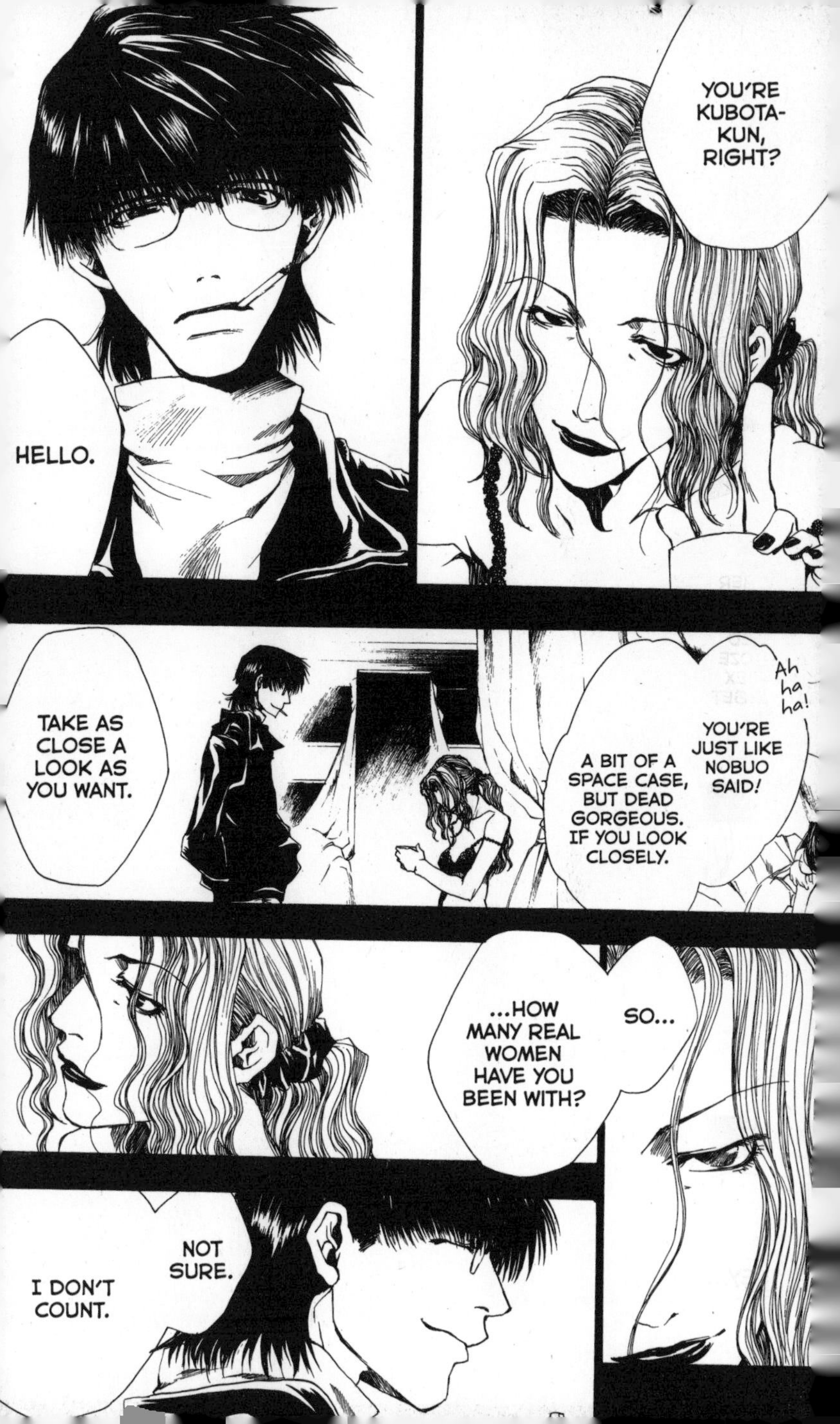
YOU'RE KUBOTA-KUN, RIGHT?
HELLO.
Ah ha ha!
YOU'RE JUST LIKE NOBUO SAID!
A BIT OF A SPACE CASE, BUT DEAD GORGEOUS. IF YOU LOOK CLOSELY.
TAKE AS CLOSE A LOOK AS YOU WANT.
SO...
...HOW MANY REAL WOMEN HAVE YOU BEEN WITH?
NOT SURE.
I DON'T COUNT.

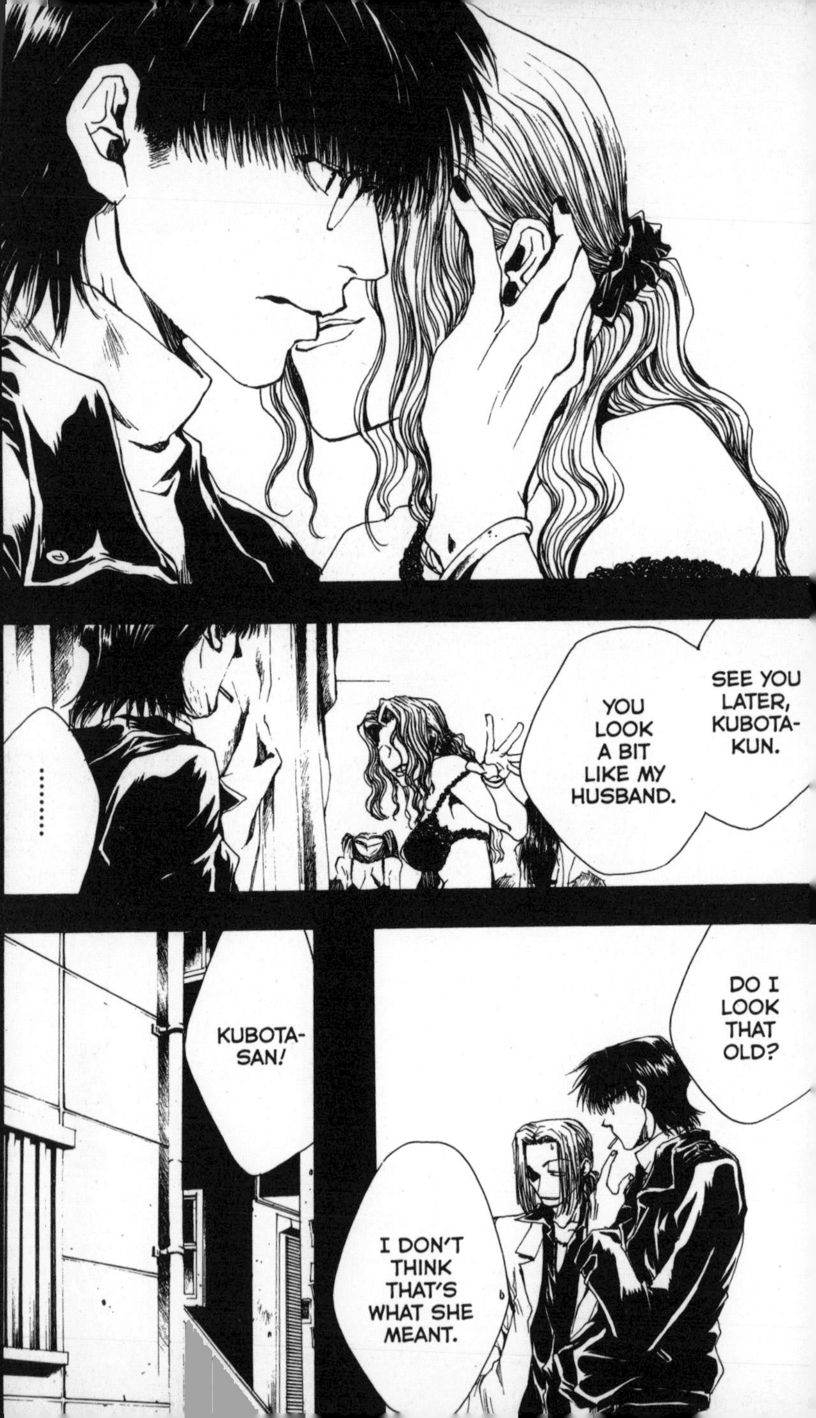
SEE YOU LATER, KUBOTA-KUN.
YOU LOOK A BIT LIKE MY HUSBAND.
......
DO I LOOK THAT OLD?
I DON'T THINK THAT'S WHAT SHE MEANT.
KUBOTA-SAN!

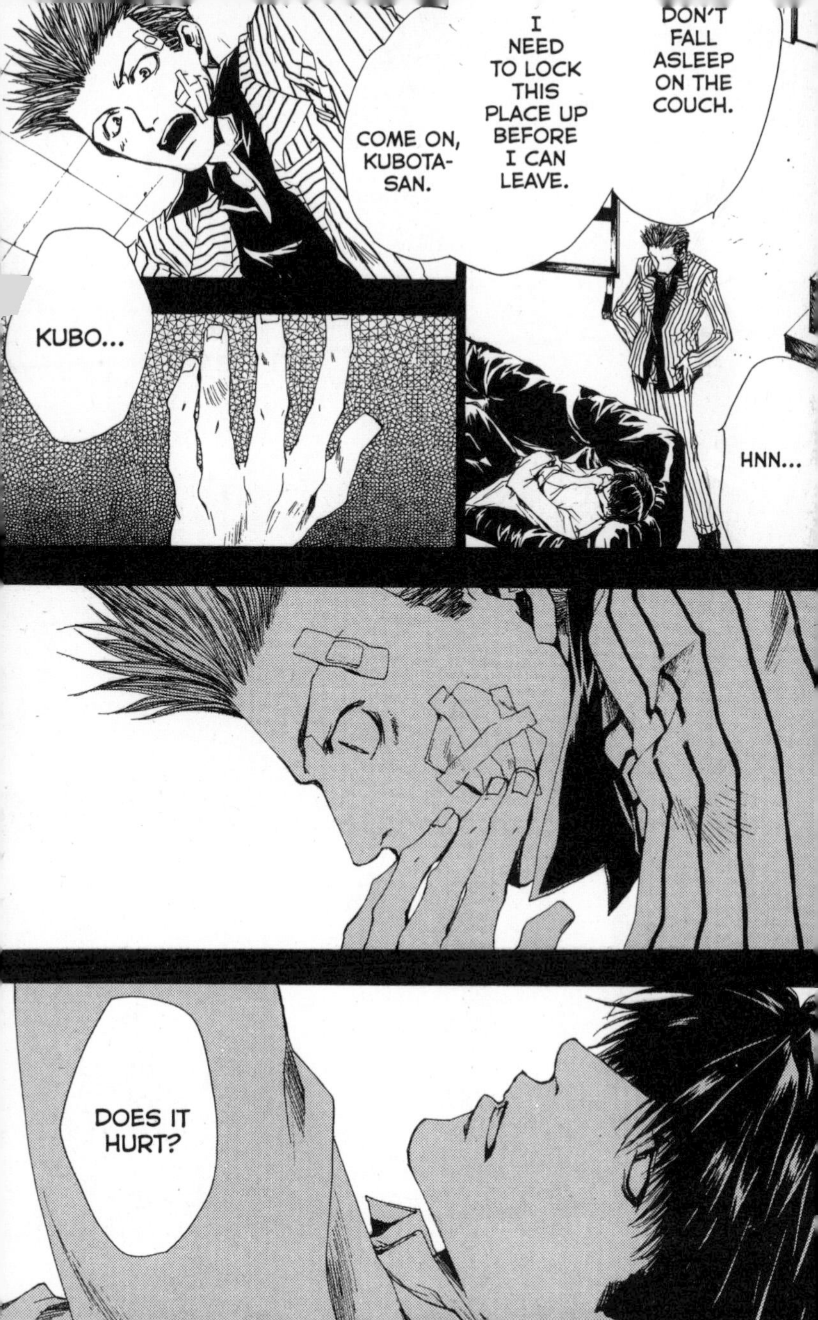
DON'T FALL ASLEEP ON THE COUCH.
I NEED TO LOCK THIS PLACE UP BEFORE I CAN LEAVE.
COME ON, KUBOTA-SAN.
HNN...
KUBO...
DOES IT HURT?

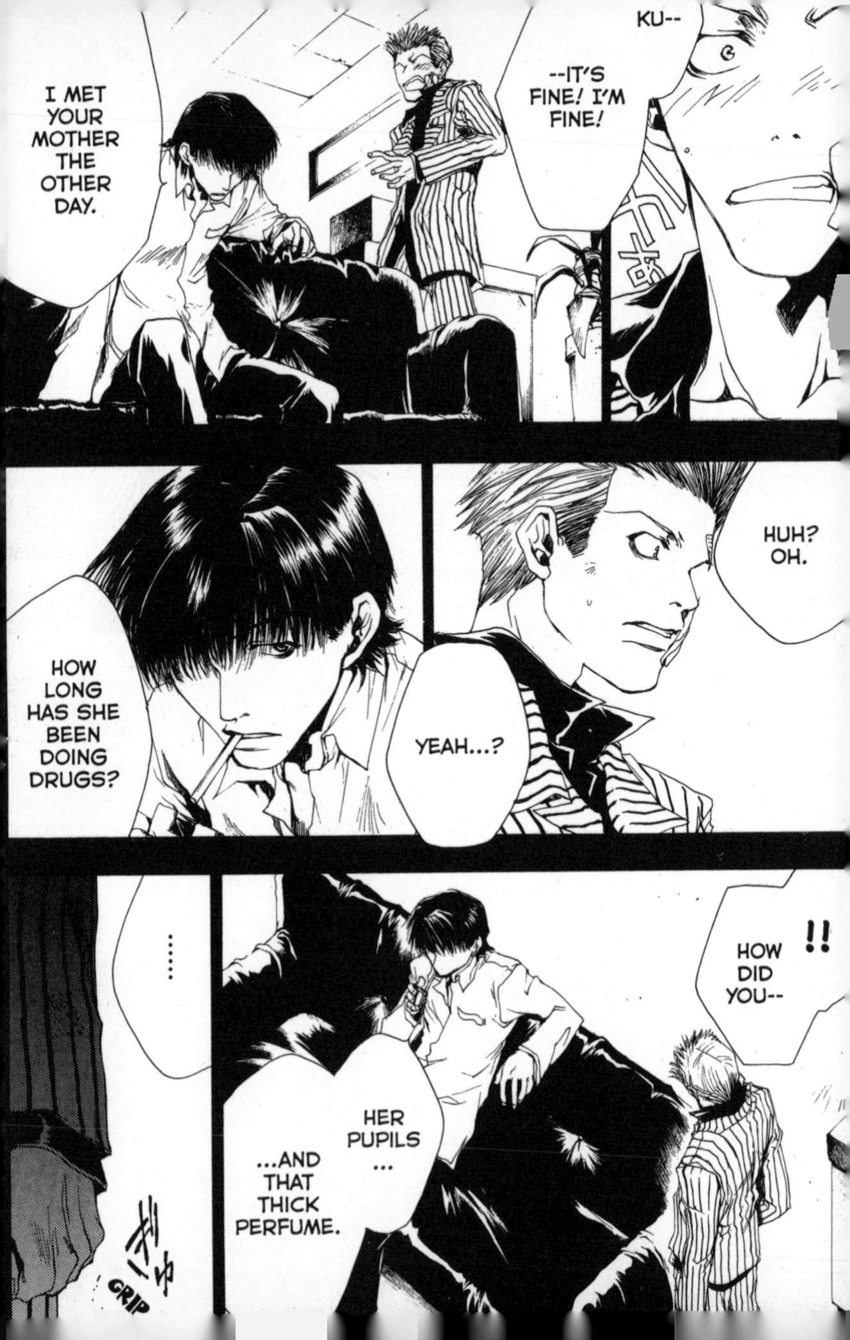
KU--
--IT'S FINE! I'M FINE!
I MET YOUR MOTHER THE OTHER DAY.
HUH? OH.
YEAH...?
HOW LONG HAS SHE BEEN DOING DRUGS?
!!
HOW DID YOU--
HER PUPILS ...
...AND THAT THICK PERFUME.
......
GRIP

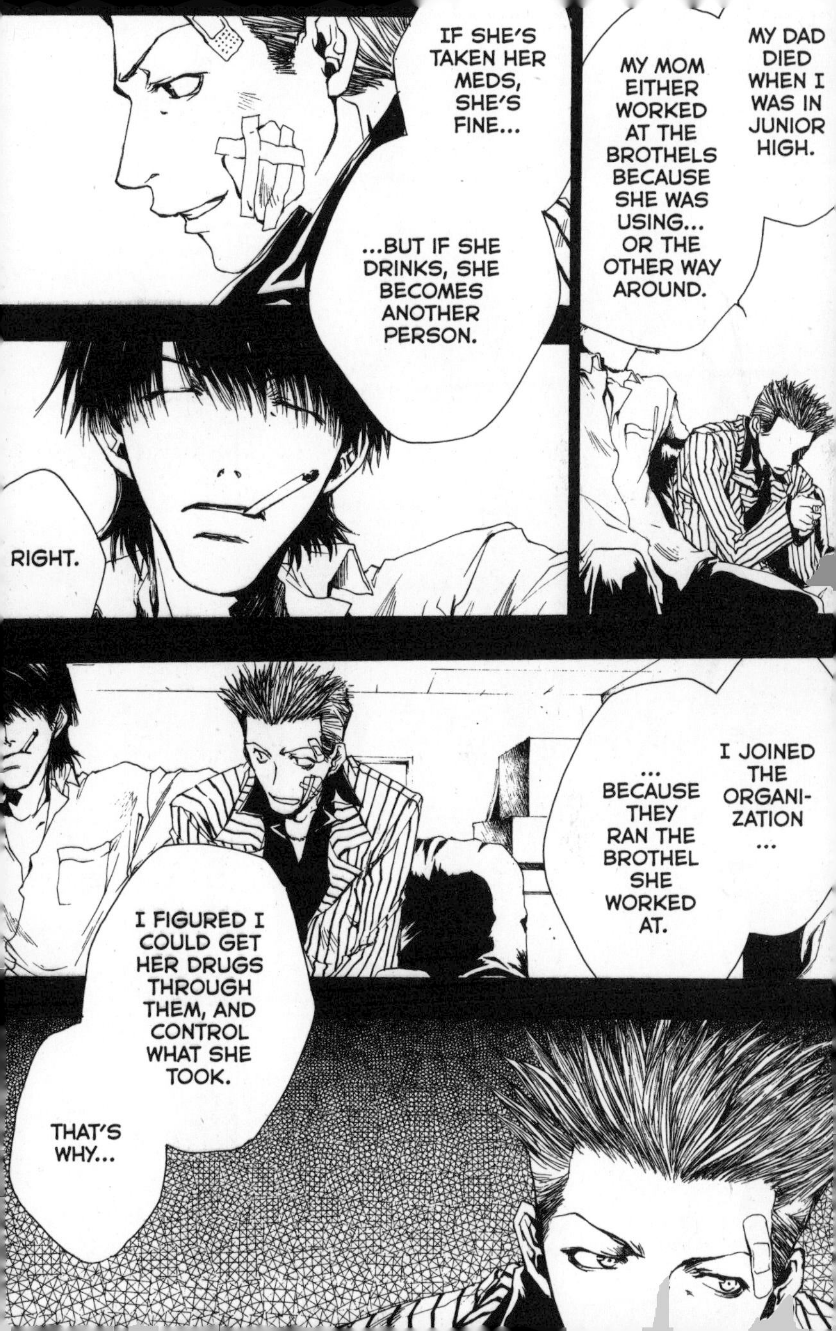
MY DAD DIED WHEN I WAS IN JUNIOR HIGH.
MY MOM EITHER WORKED AT THE BROTHELS BECAUSE SHE WAS USING... OR THE OTHER WAY AROUND.
IF SHE'S TAKEN HER MEDS, SHE'S FINE...
...BUT IF SHE DRINKS, SHE BECOMES ANOTHER PERSON.
RIGHT.
I JOINED THE ORGANIZATION...
...BECAUSE THEY RAN THE BROTHEL SHE WORKED AT.
I FIGURED I COULD GET HER DRUGS THROUGH THEM, AND CONTROL WHAT SHE TOOK.
THAT'S WHY...

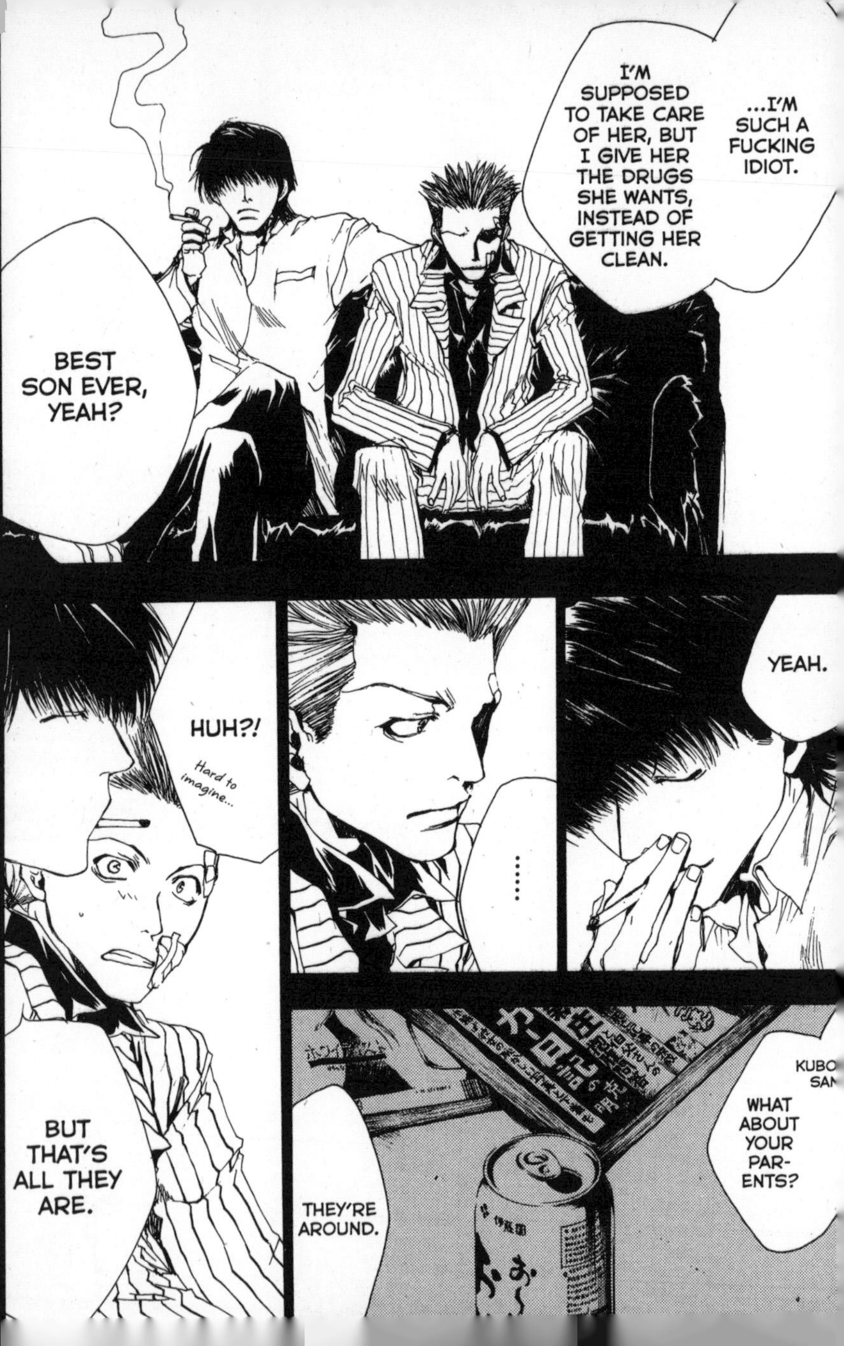
I'M SUPPOSED TO TAKE CARE OF HER, BUT I GIVE HER THE DRUGS SHE WANTS, INSTEAD OF GETTING HER CLEAN.
...I'M SUCH A FUCKING IDIOT.
BEST SON EVER, YEAH?
YEAH.
......
KUBO SAN
WHAT ABOUT YOUR PAR- ENTS?
THEY'RE AROUND.
HUH?!
Hard to imagine...
BUT THAT'S ALL THEY ARE.

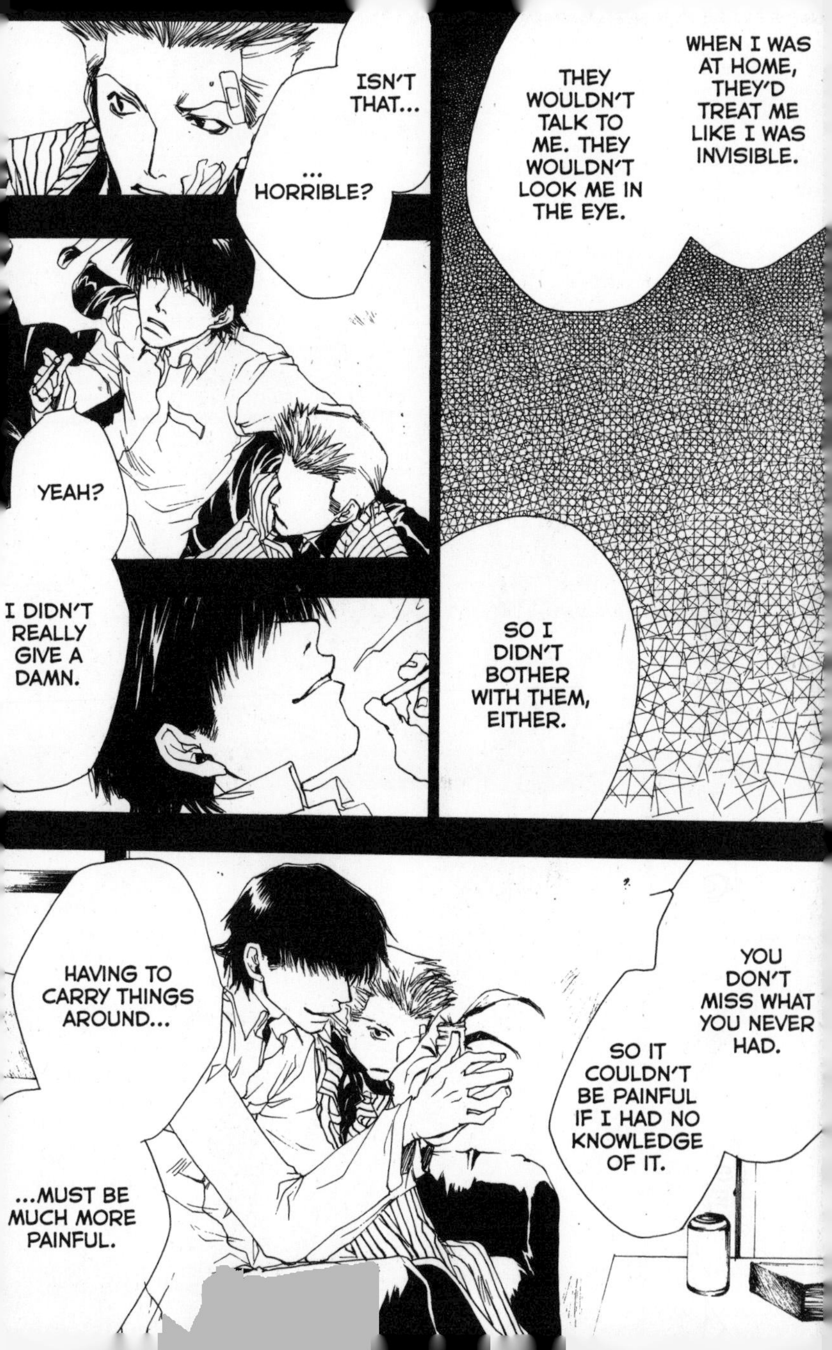
WHEN I WAS AT HOME, THEY'D TREAT ME LIKE I WAS INVISIBLE.
THEY WOULDN'T TALK TO ME. THEY WOULDN'T LOOK ME IN THE EYE.
SO I DIDN'T BOTHER WITH THEM, EITHER.
ISN'T THAT...
... HORRIBLE?
YEAH?
I DIDN'T REALLY GIVE A DAMN.
YOU DON'T MISS WHAT YOU NEVER HAD.
SO IT COULDN'T BE PAINFUL IF I HAD NO KNOWLEDGE OF IT.
HAVING TO CARRY THINGS AROUND...
...MUST BE MUCH MORE PAINFUL.

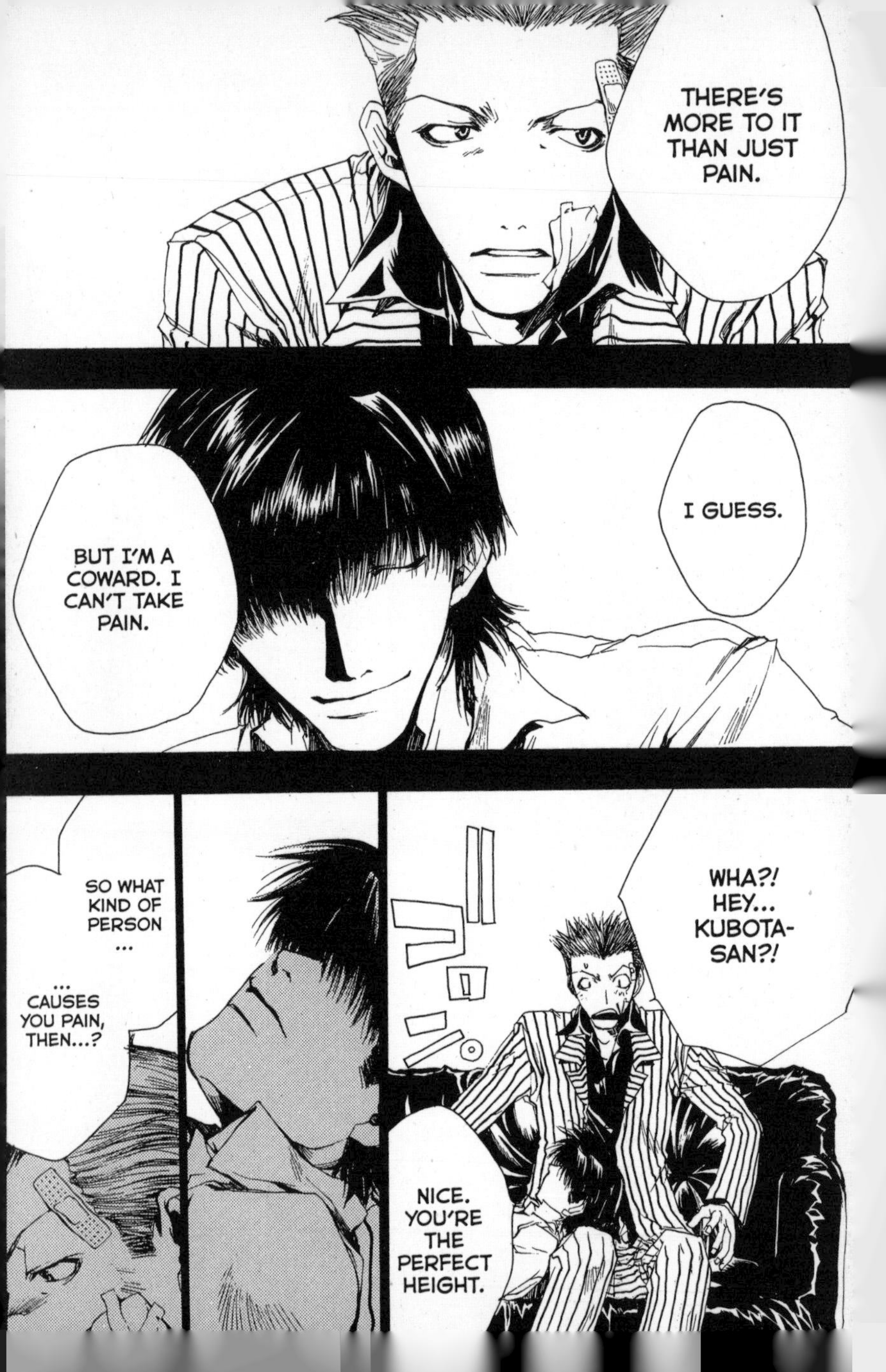
THERE'S MORE TO IT THAN JUST PAIN.
I GUESS.
BUT I'M A COWARD. I CAN'T TAKE PAIN.
WHA?! HEY... KUBOTA-SAN?!
NICE. YOU'RE THE PERFECT HEIGHT.
SO WHAT KIND OF PERSON ...
... CAUSES YOU PAIN, THEN...?

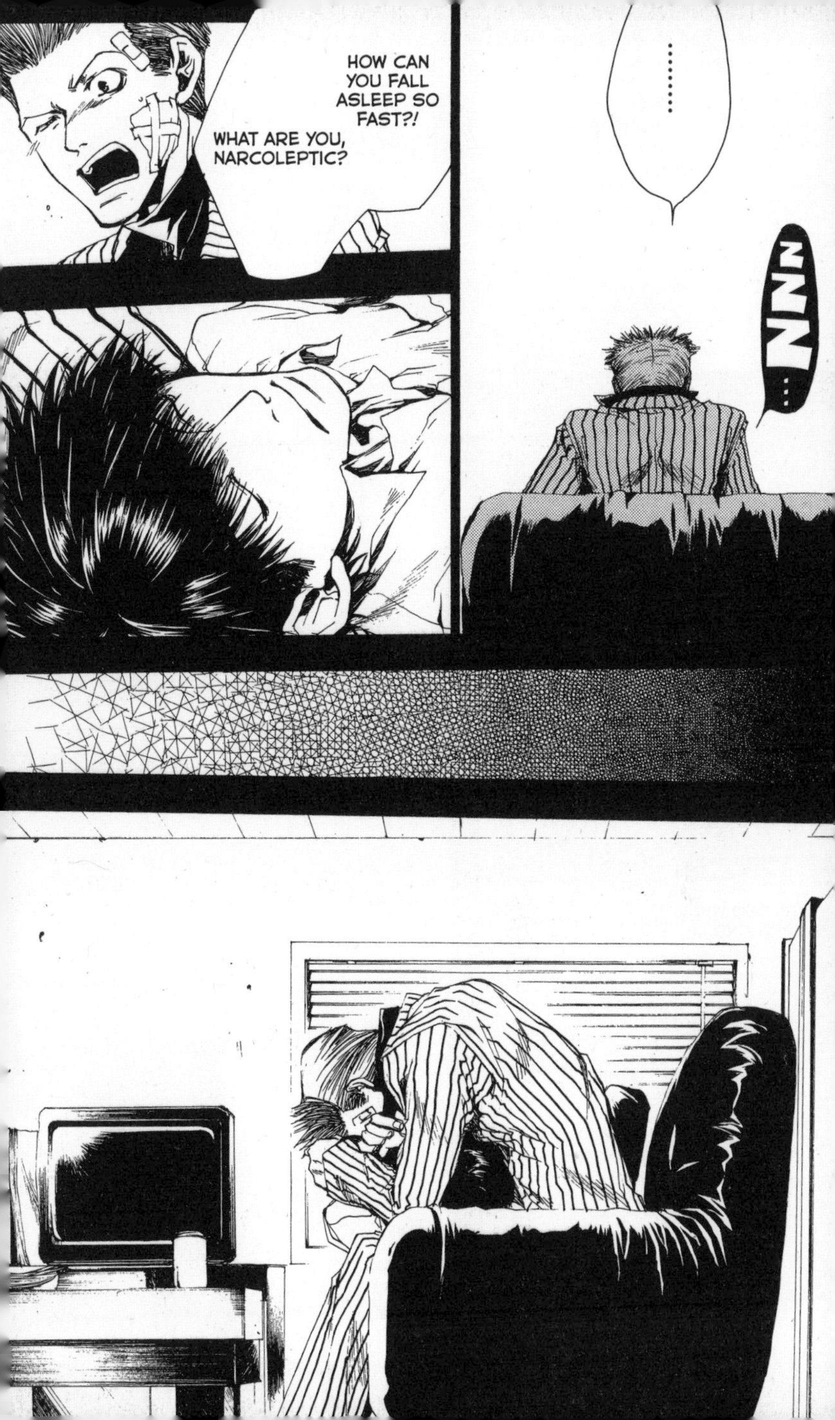

HOW CAN YOU FALL ASLEEP SO FAST?!
WHAT ARE YOU, NARCOLEPTIC?
......
...NNN

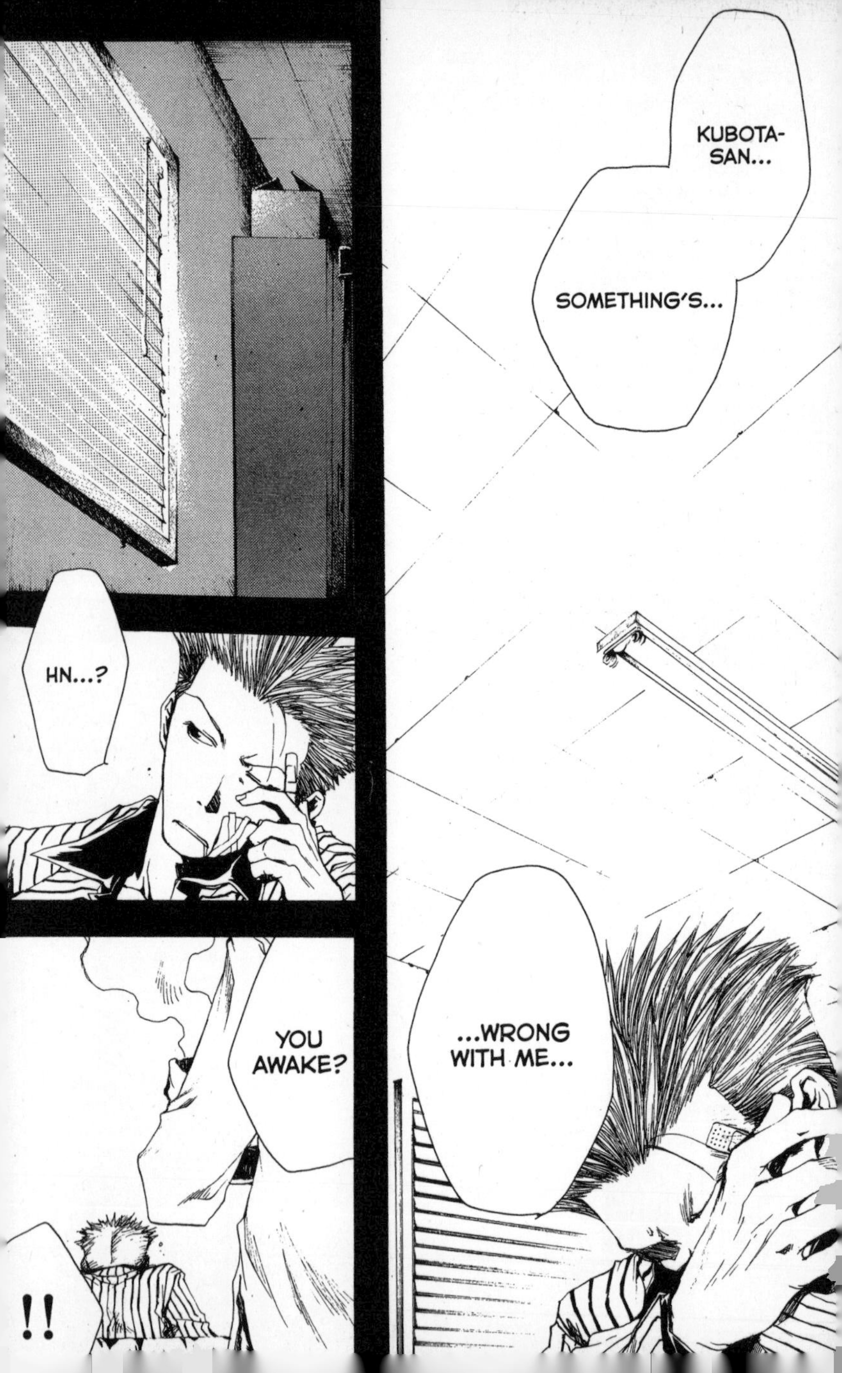
KUBOTA-SAN...
SOMETHING'S...
...WRONG WITH ME...
HN...?
YOU AWAKE?
!!

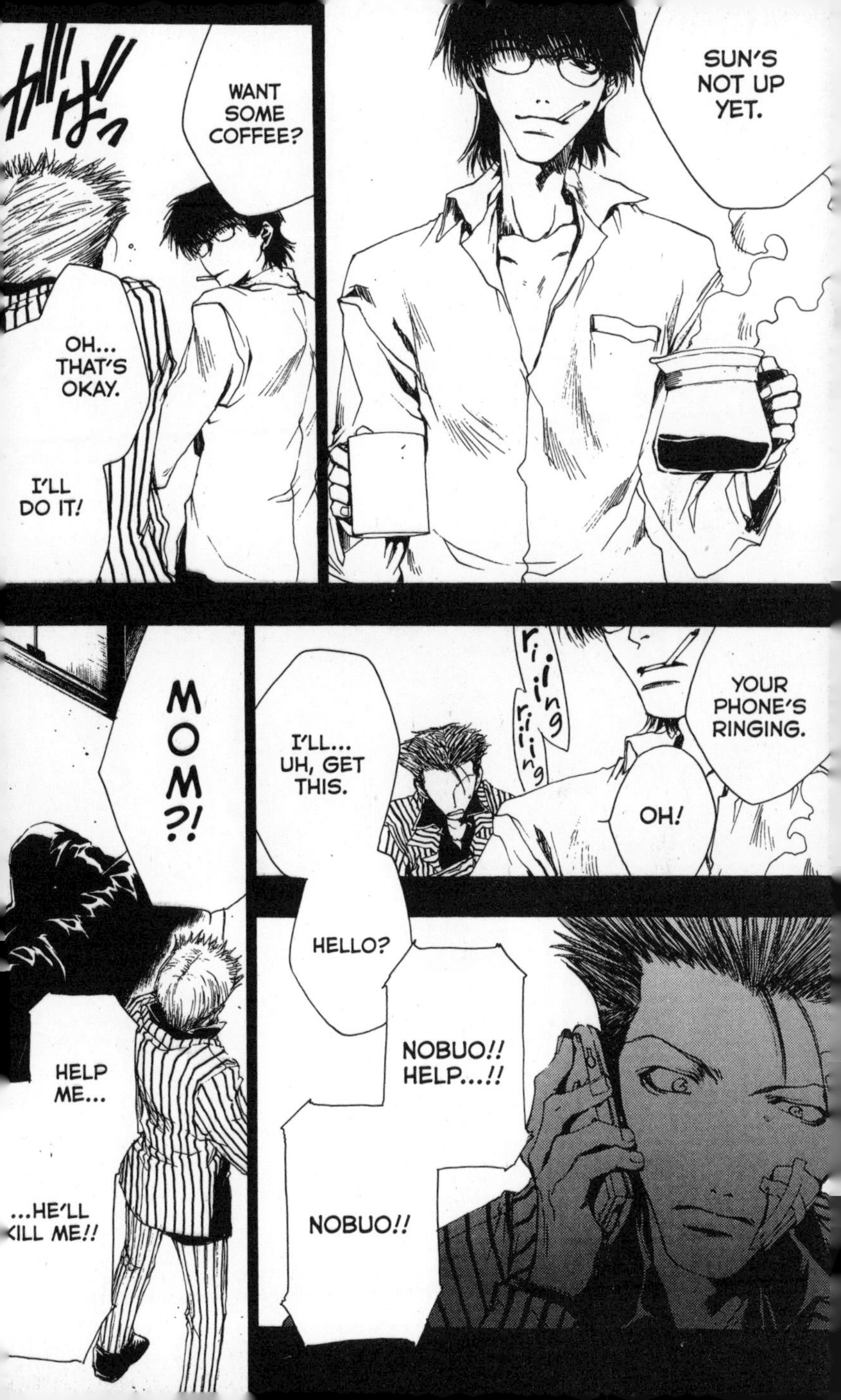
SUN'S NOT UP YET.
がばっ
WANT SOME COFFEE?
OH... THAT'S OKAY.
I'LL DO IT!
YOUR PHONE'S RINGING.
riiing riiing
OH!
I'LL... UH, GET THIS.
HELLO?
NOBUO!! HELP...!!
NOBUO!!
MOM?!
HELP ME...
...HE'LL KILL ME!!

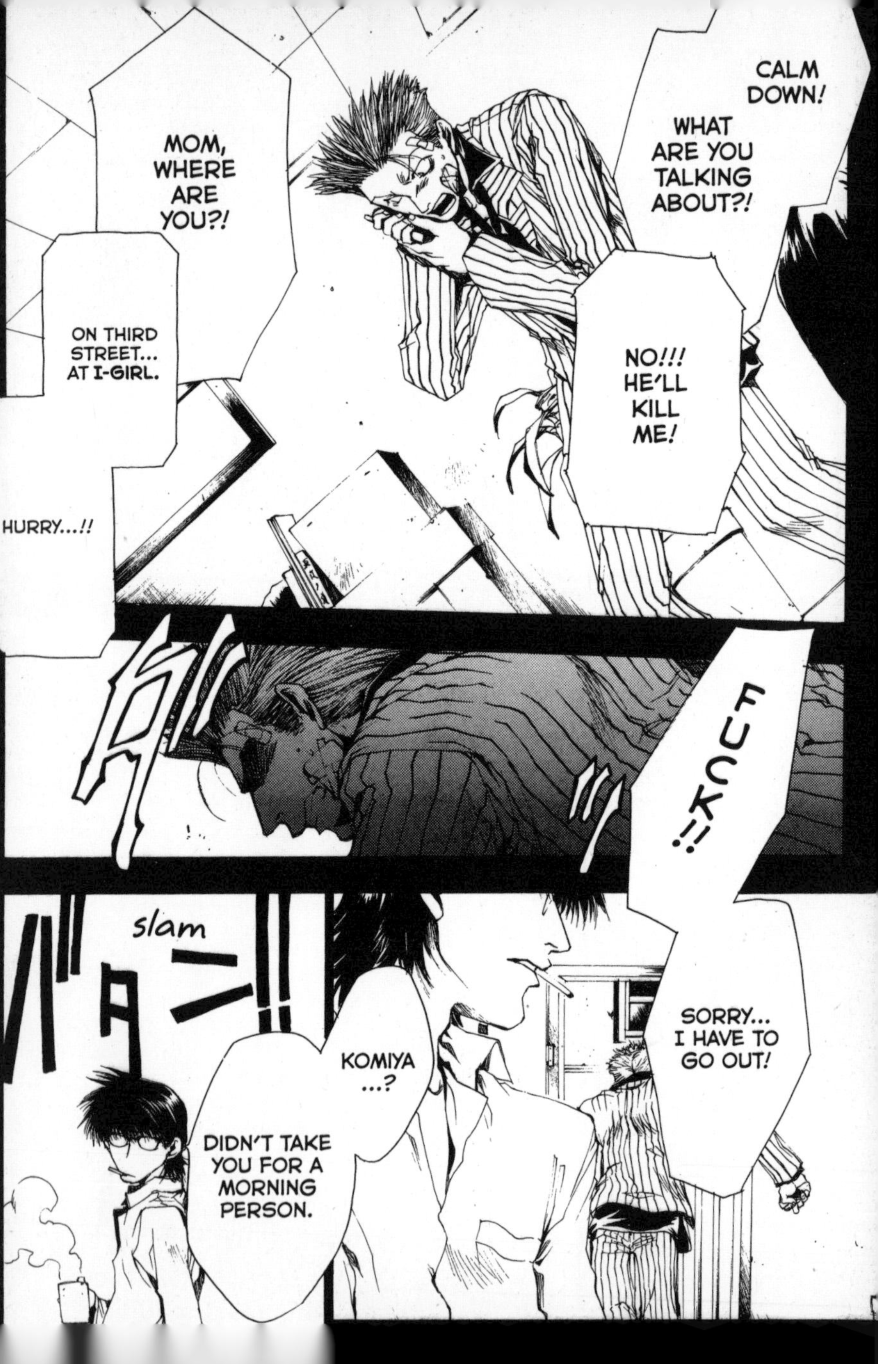
CALM DOWN!
WHAT ARE YOU TALKING ABOUT?!
NO!!! HE'LL KILL ME!
MOM, WHERE ARE YOU?!
ON THIRD STREET... AT I-GIRL.
HURRY...!!
FUCK!!
SORRY... I HAVE TO GO OUT!
slam
KOMIYA ...?
DIDN'T TAKE YOU FOR A MORNING PERSON.

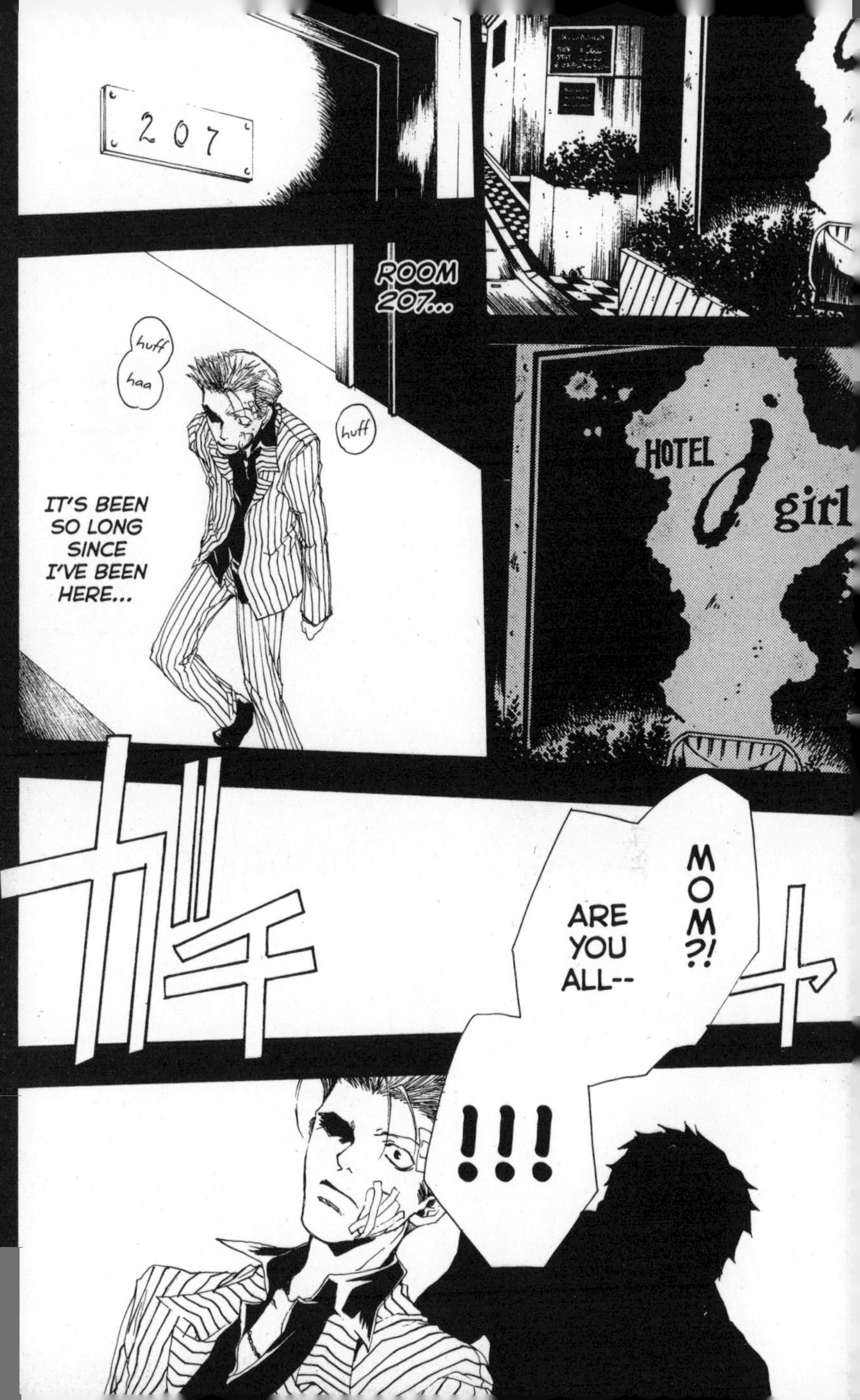
207
HOTEL girl
ROOM 207...
huff
haa
huff
IT'S BEEN SO LONG SINCE I'VE BEEN HERE...
MOM?! ARE YOU ALL--
ガチャ
!!!

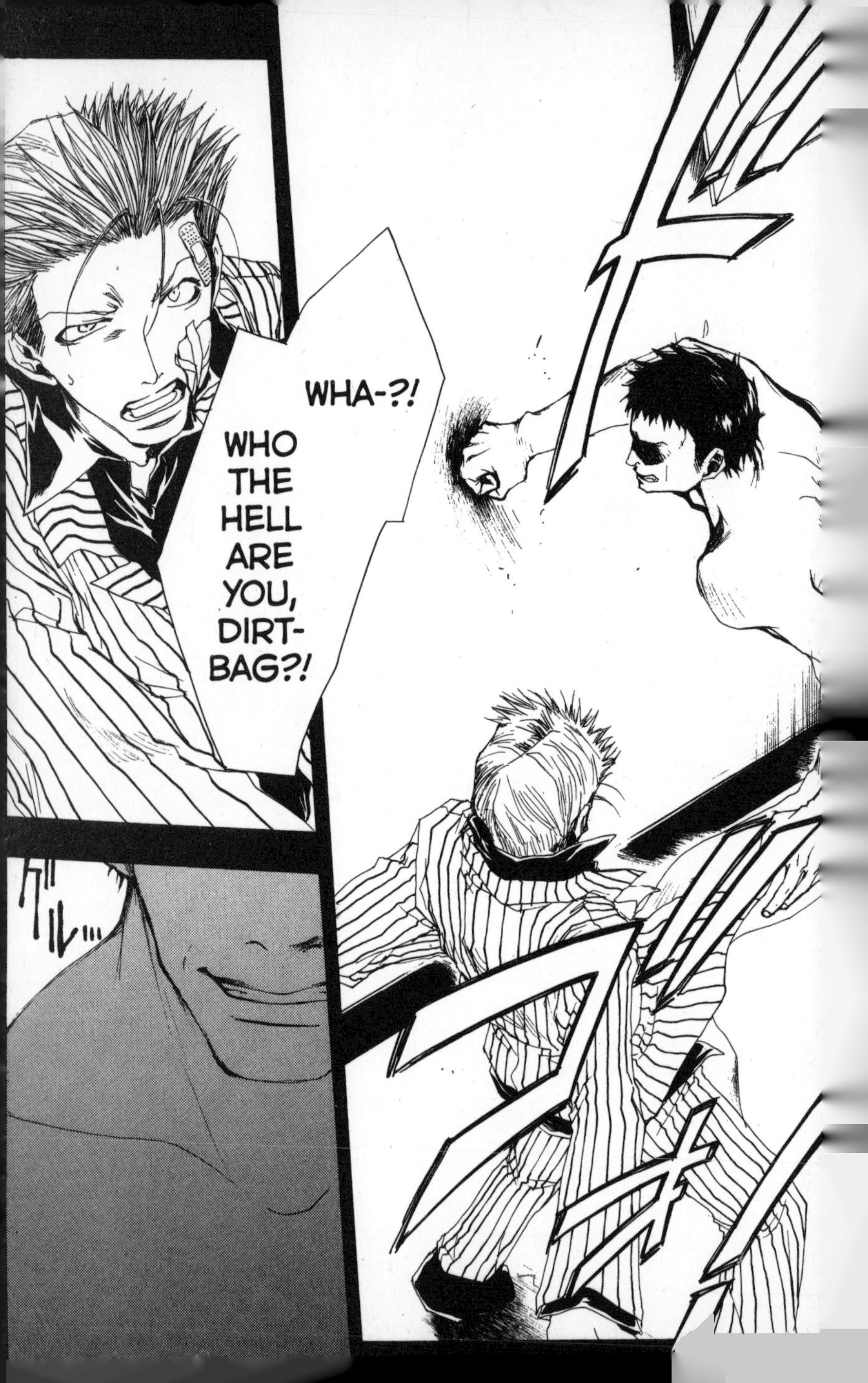
WHA-?!
WHO THE HELL ARE YOU, DIRT-BAG?!

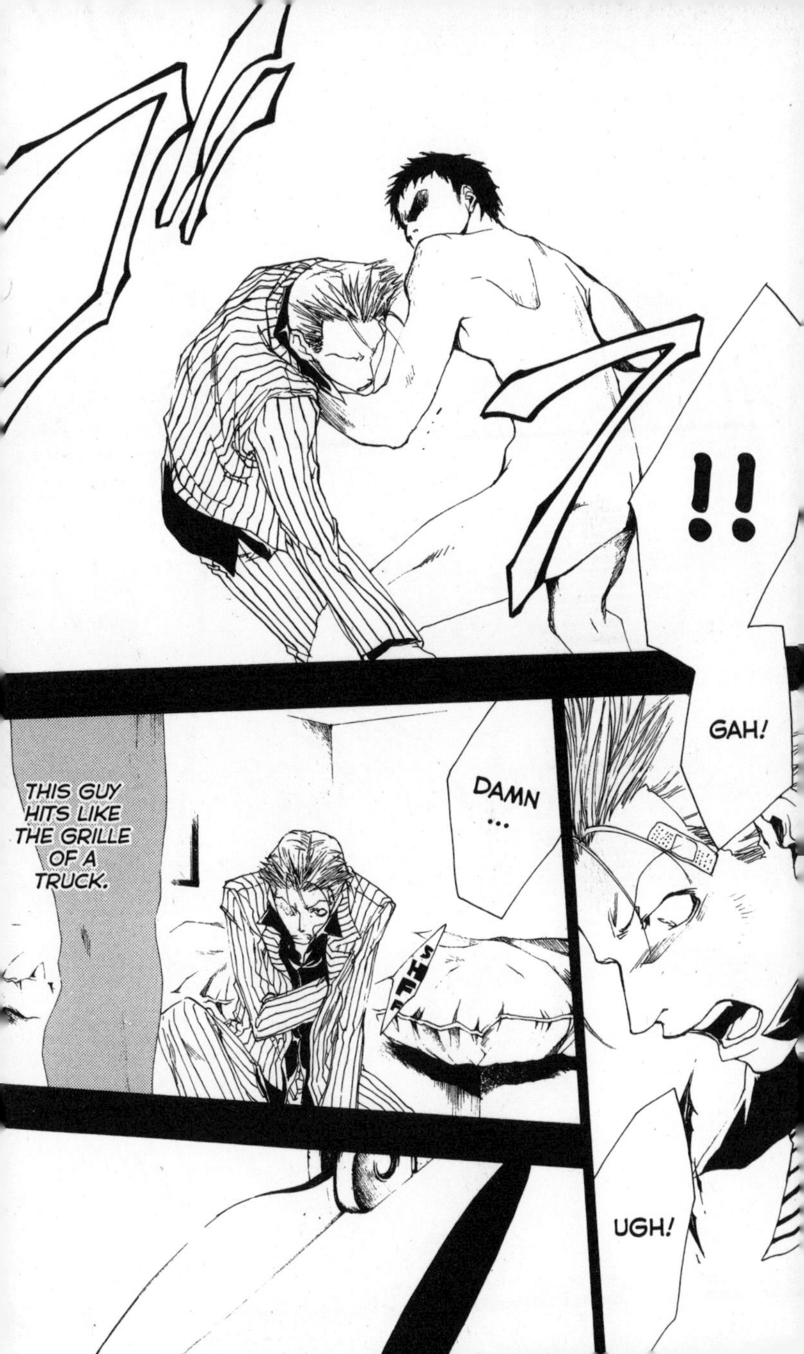
!!
GAH!
UGH!
DAMN ...
THIS GUY HITS LIKE THE GRILLE OF A TRUCK.

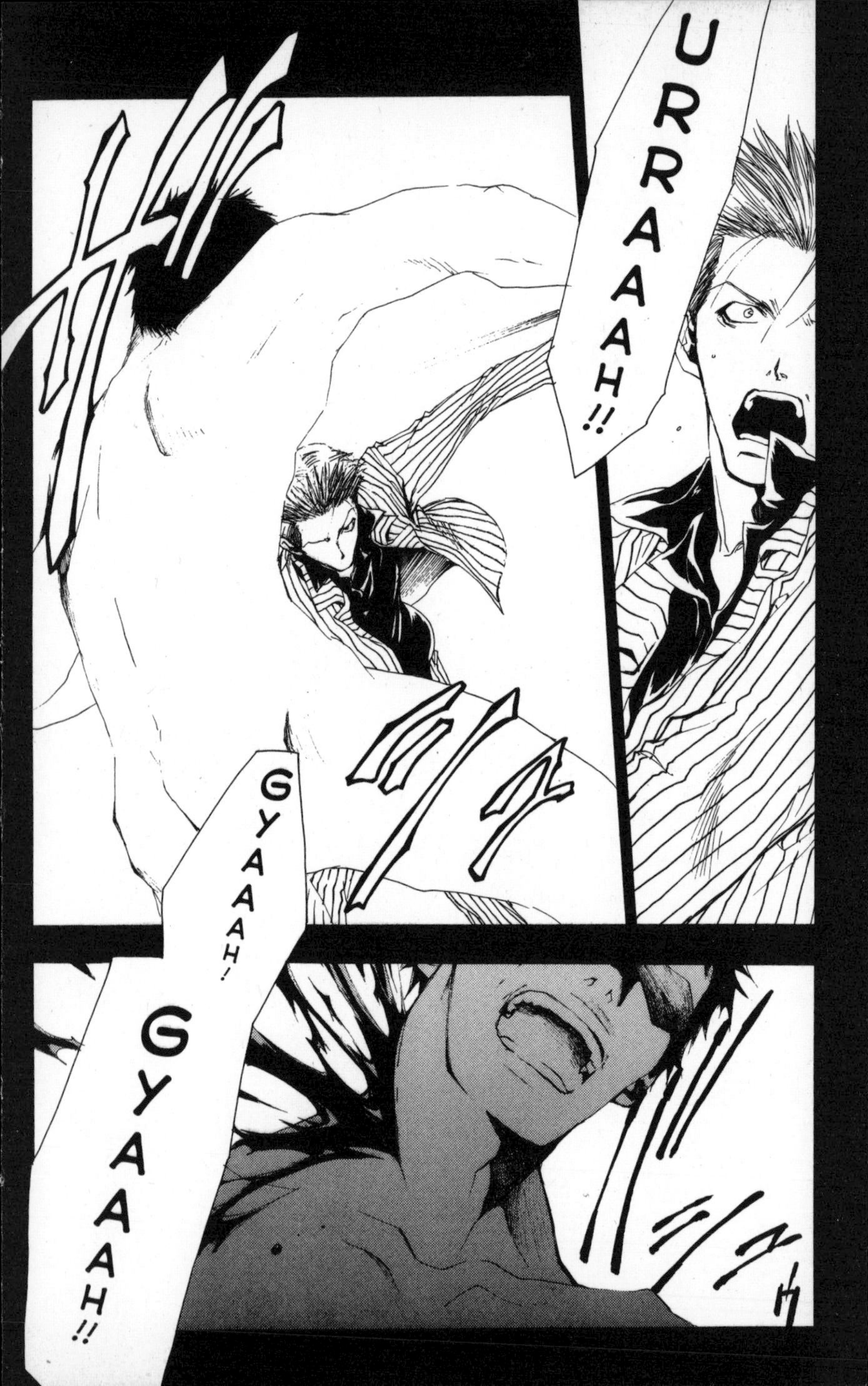
URRAAAAH!!
GYAAAH!
GYAAAH!!

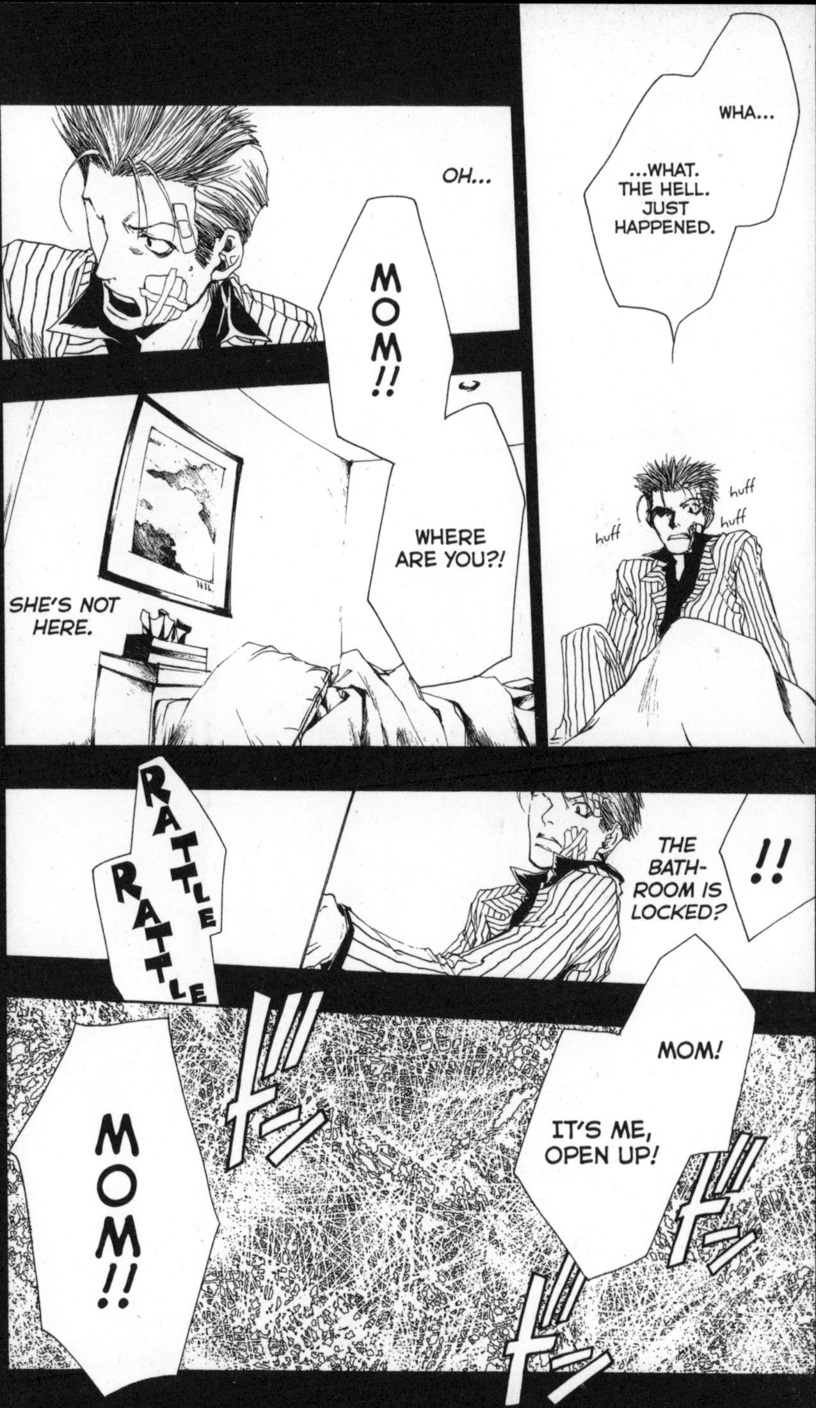
WHA...
...WHAT. THE HELL. JUST HAPPENED.
OH...
MOM!!
huff
huff
huff
WHERE ARE YOU?!
SHE'S NOT HERE.
!!
THE BATH-ROOM IS LOCKED?
RATTLE RATTLE
MOM!
IT'S ME, OPEN UP!
MOM!!

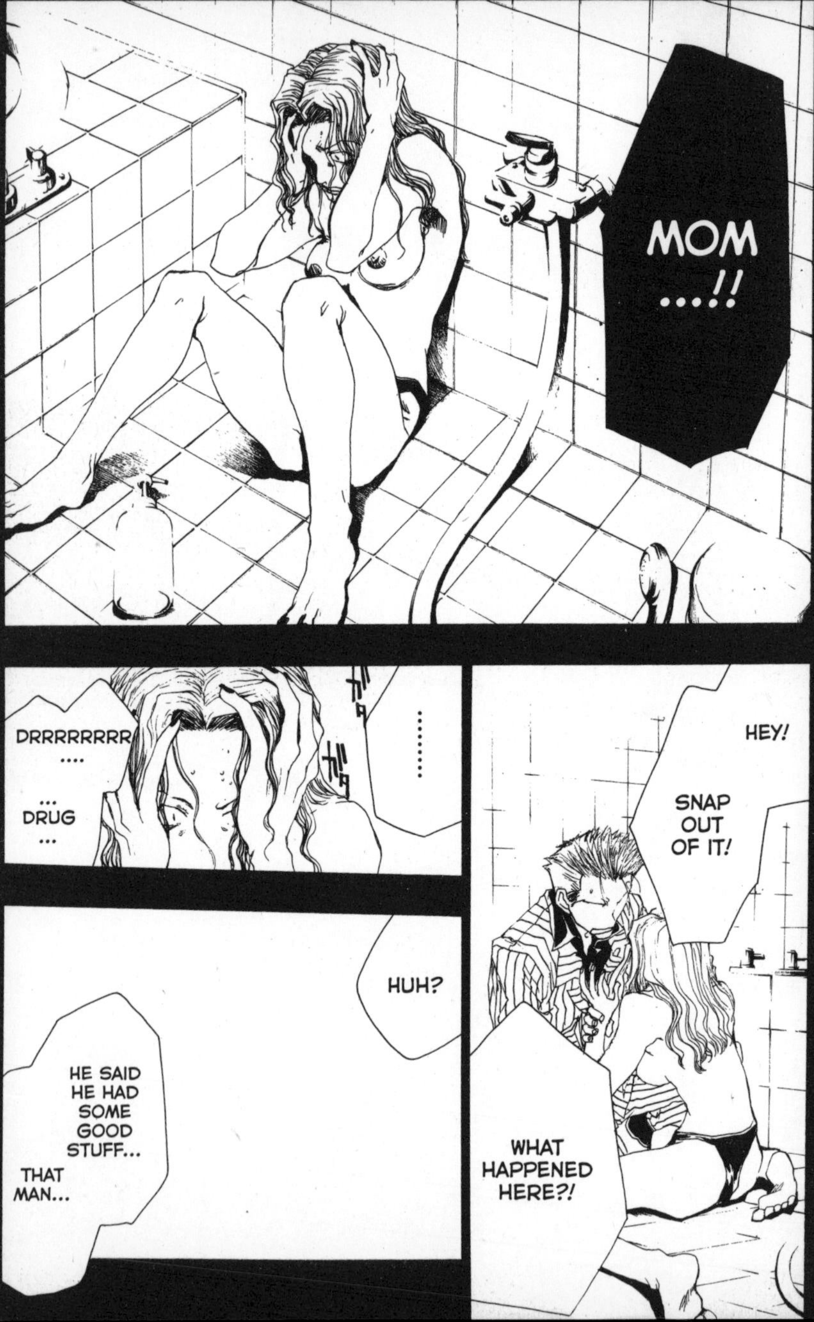
MOM ...!!
HEY!
SNAP OUT OF IT!
WHAT HAPPENED HERE?!
ガタ
ガタ
....
DRRRRRRRR ....
... DRUG ...
HUH?
HE SAID HE HAD SOME GOOD STUFF...
THAT MAN...

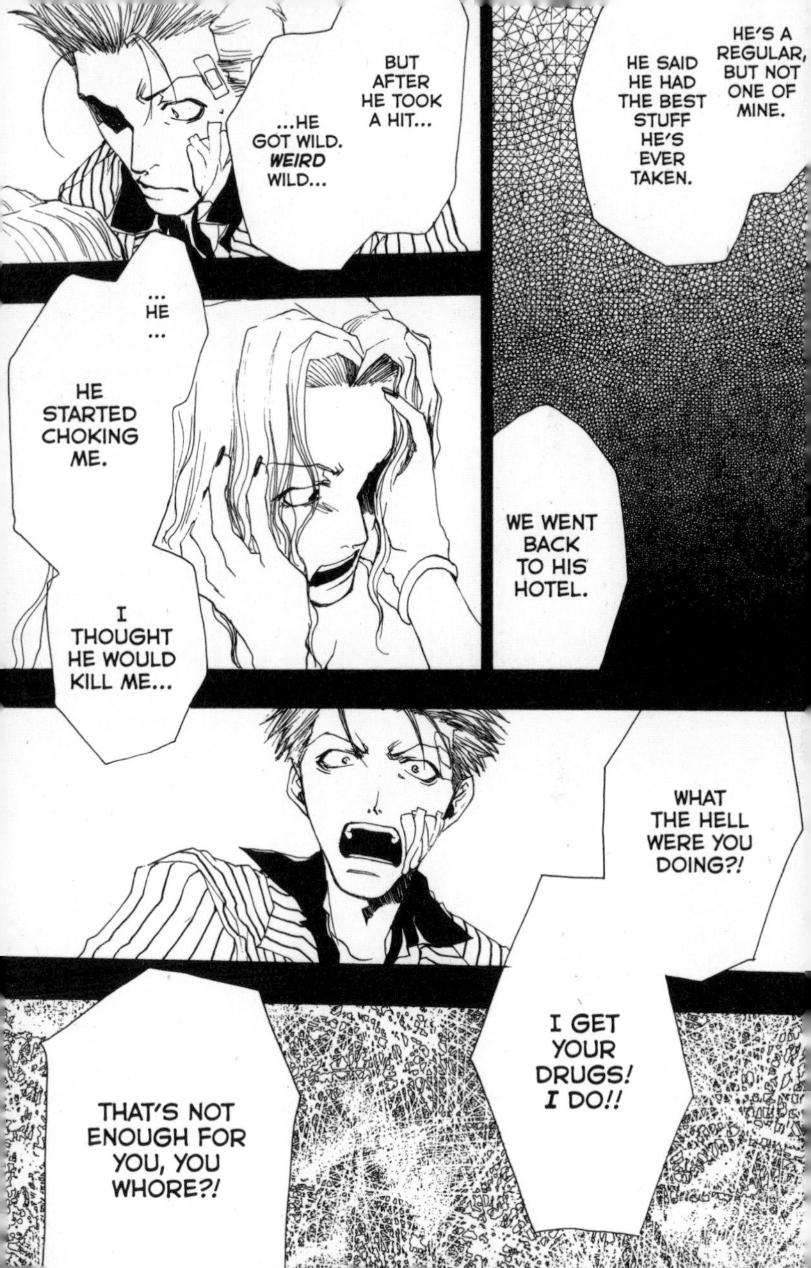
HE'S A REGULAR, BUT NOT ONE OF MINE.
HE SAID HE HAD THE BEST STUFF HE'S EVER TAKEN.
WE WENT BACK TO HIS HOTEL.
BUT AFTER HE TOOK A HIT...
...HE GOT WILD. *WEIRD* WILD...
...HE...
HE STARTED CHOKING ME.
I THOUGHT HE WOULD KILL ME...
WHAT THE HELL WERE YOU DOING?!
I GET YOUR DRUGS! *I* DO!!
THAT'S NOT ENOUGH FOR YOU, YOU WHORE?!

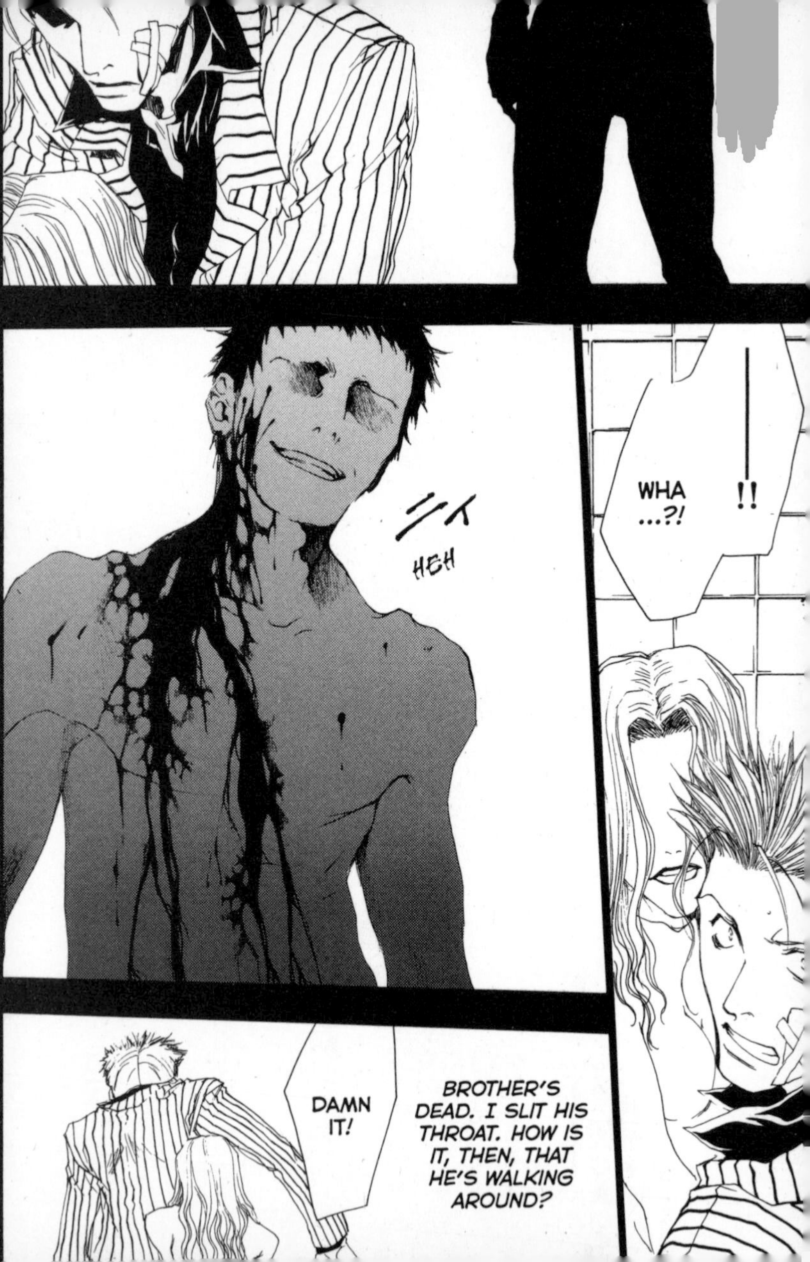
!!
WHA ...?!
ニィ
HEH
BROTHER'S DEAD. I SLIT HIS THROAT. HOW IS IT, THEN, THAT HE'S WALKING AROUND?
DAMN IT!

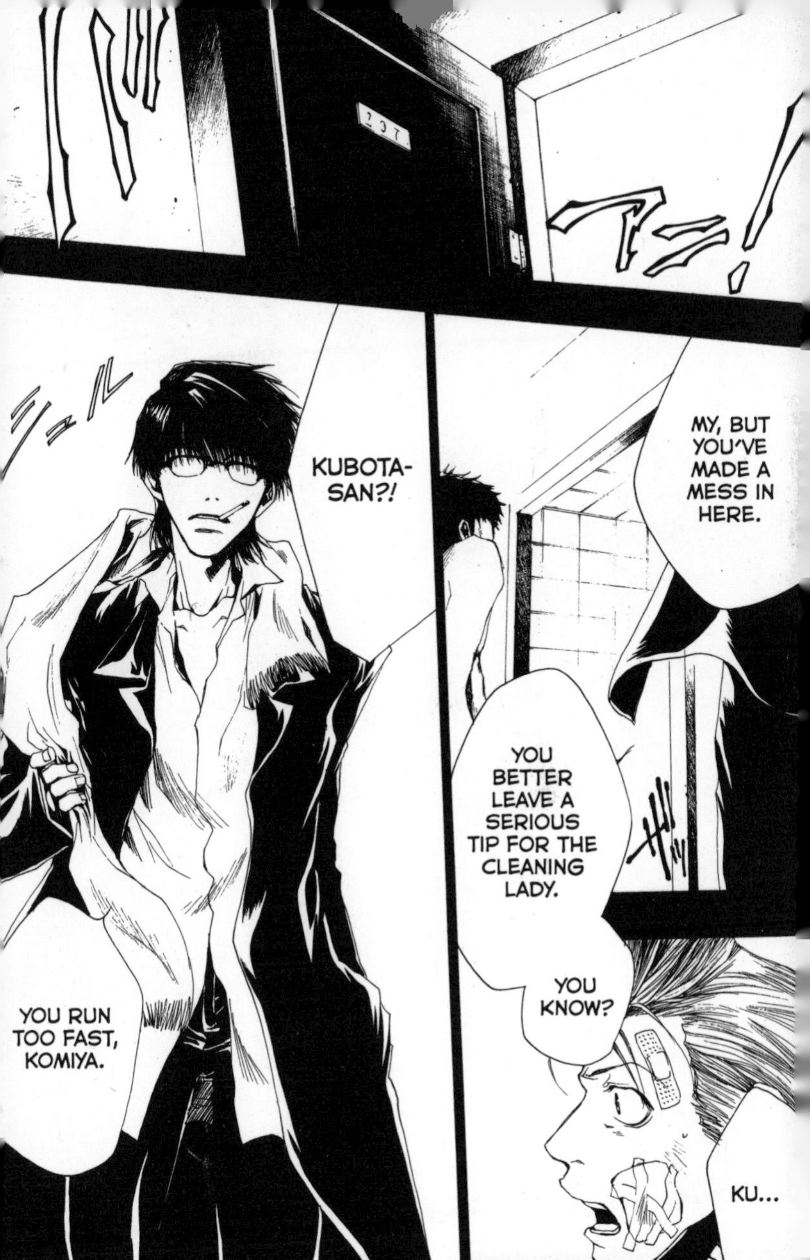

MY, BUT YOU'VE MADE A MESS IN HERE.
YOU BETTER LEAVE A SERIOUS TIP FOR THE CLEANING LADY.
YOU KNOW?
KU...
KUBOTA-SAN?!
シュル
YOU RUN TOO FAST, KOMIYA.

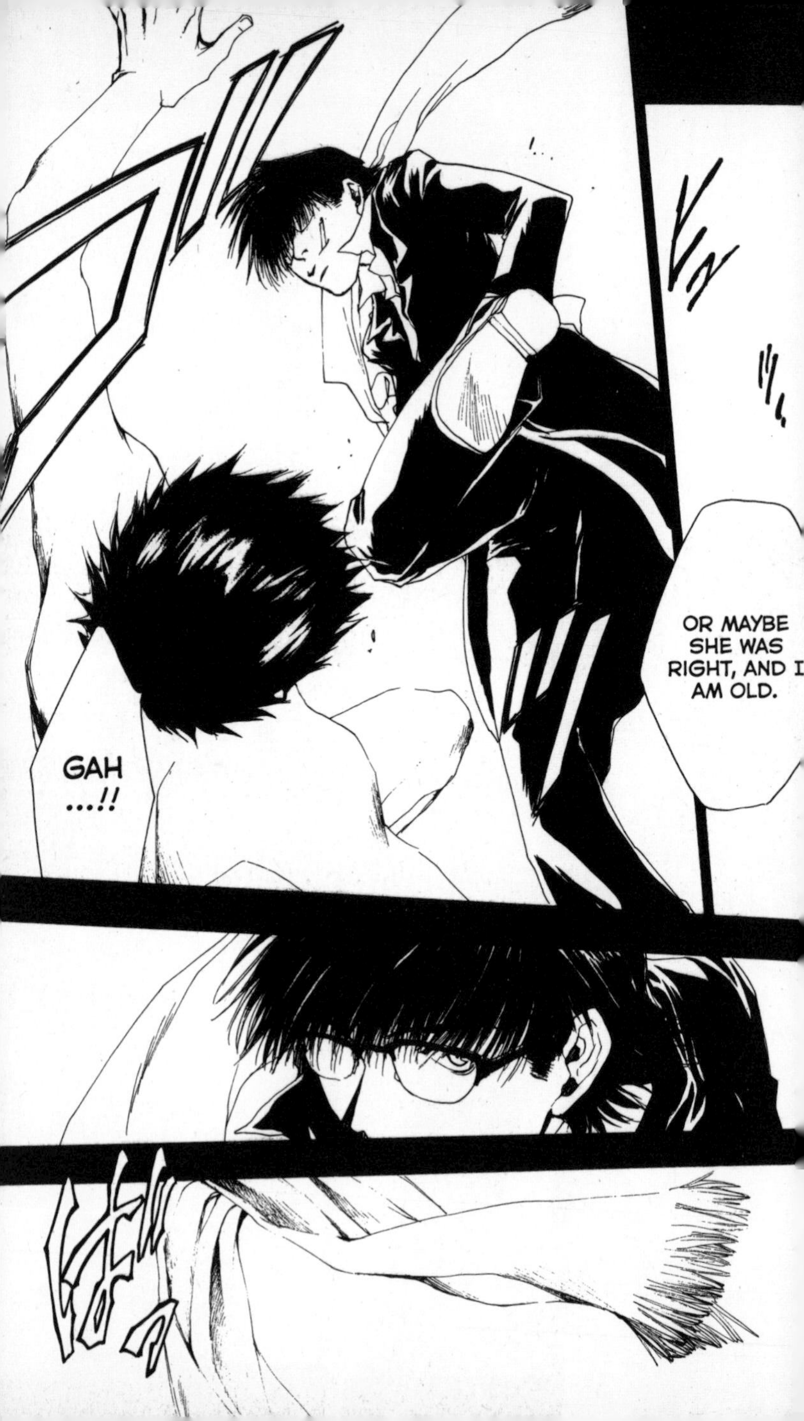
OR MAYBE SHE WAS RIGHT, AND I AM OLD.
GAH ...!!

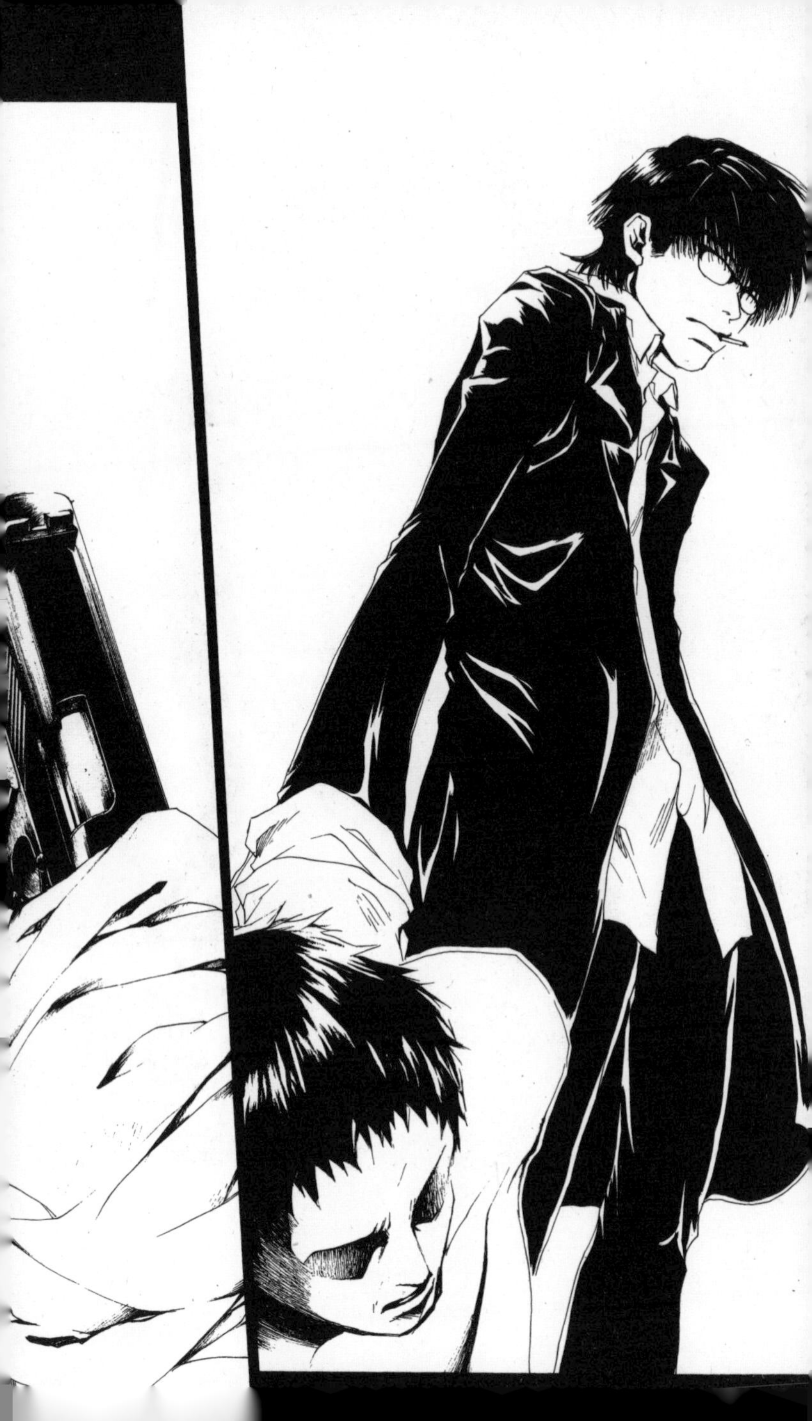

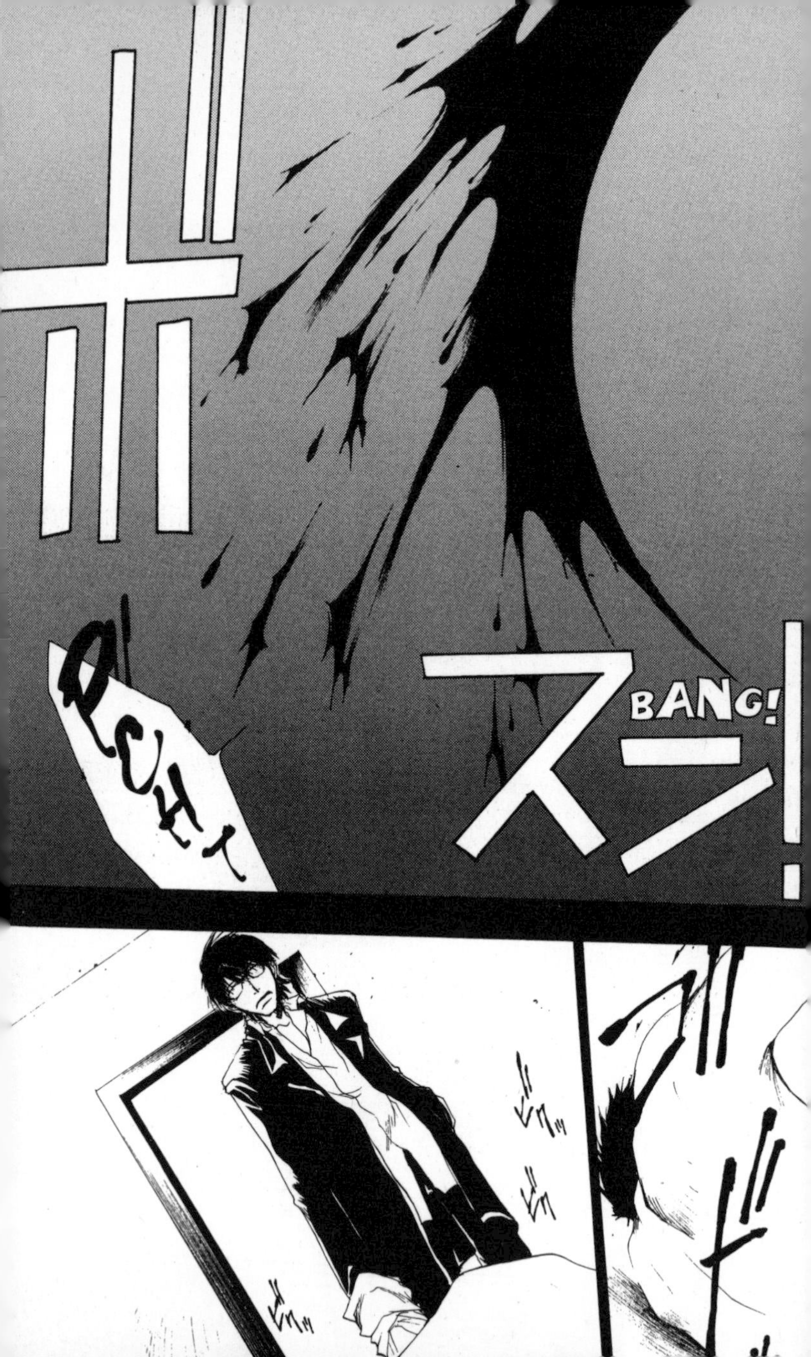
BANG!
PCHT

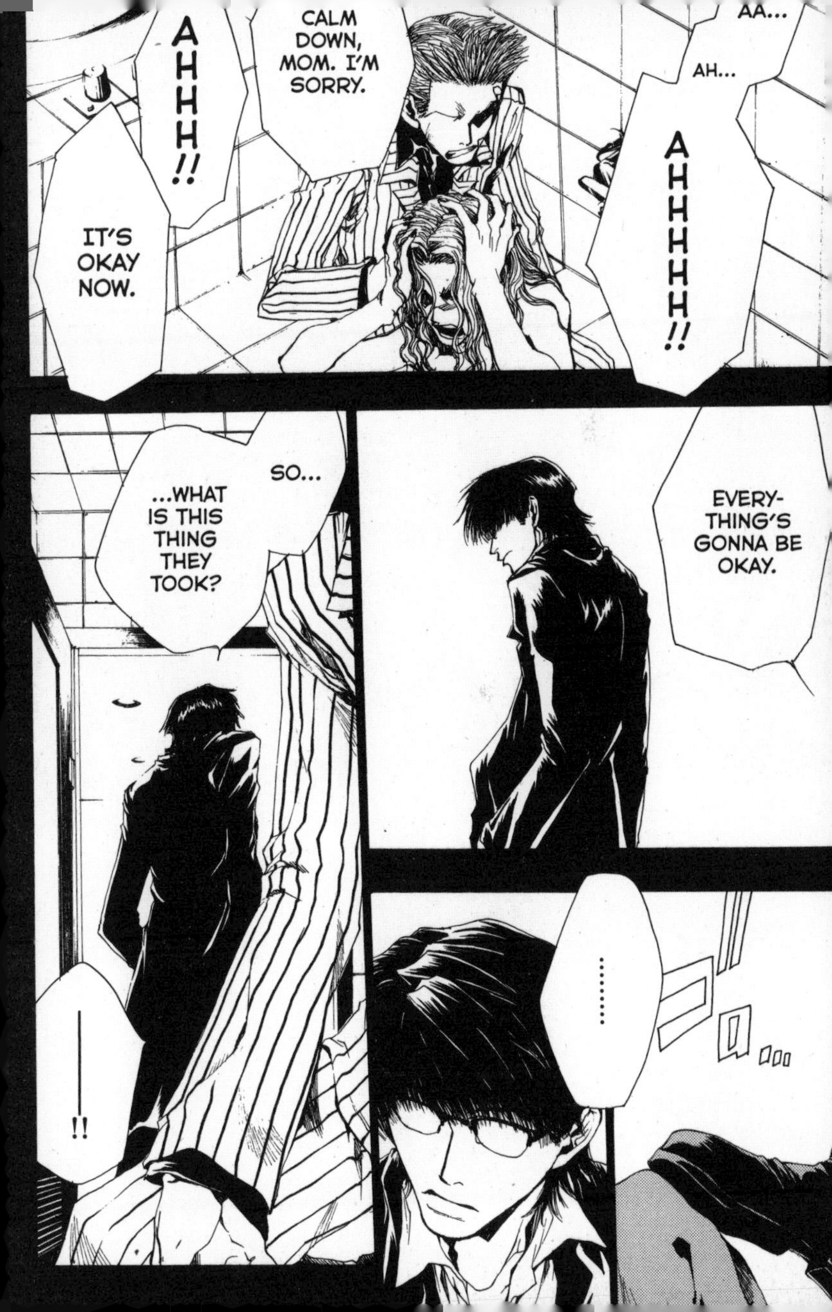
AA...
AH...
AHHHHHH!!
CALM DOWN, MOM. I'M SORRY.
AHHHH!!
IT'S OKAY NOW.
EVERY-THING'S GONNA BE OKAY.
......
SO...
...WHAT IS THIS THING THEY TOOK?
—!!

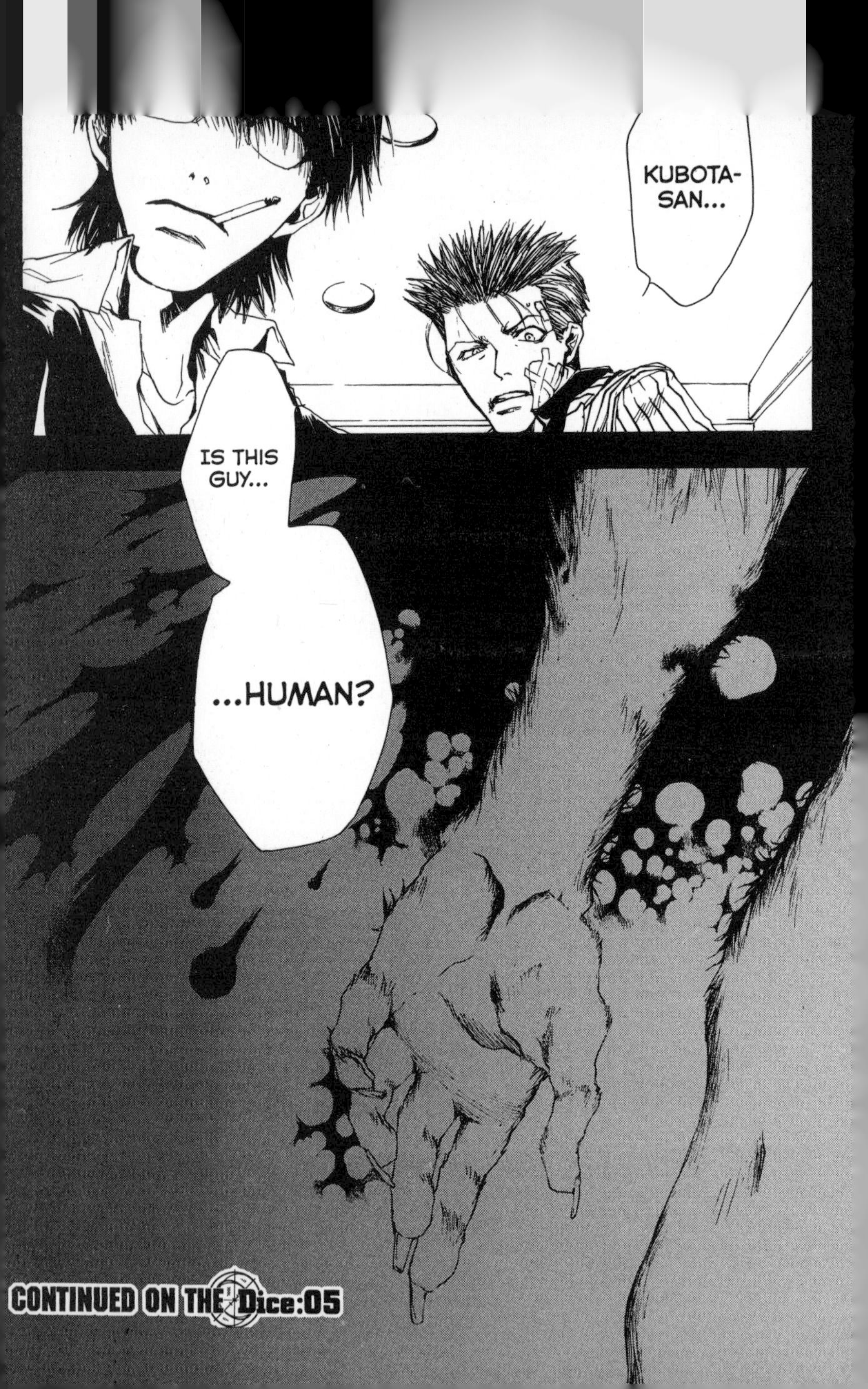
KUBOTA-SAN...
IS THIS GUY...
...HUMAN?
CONTINUED ON THE Dice:05

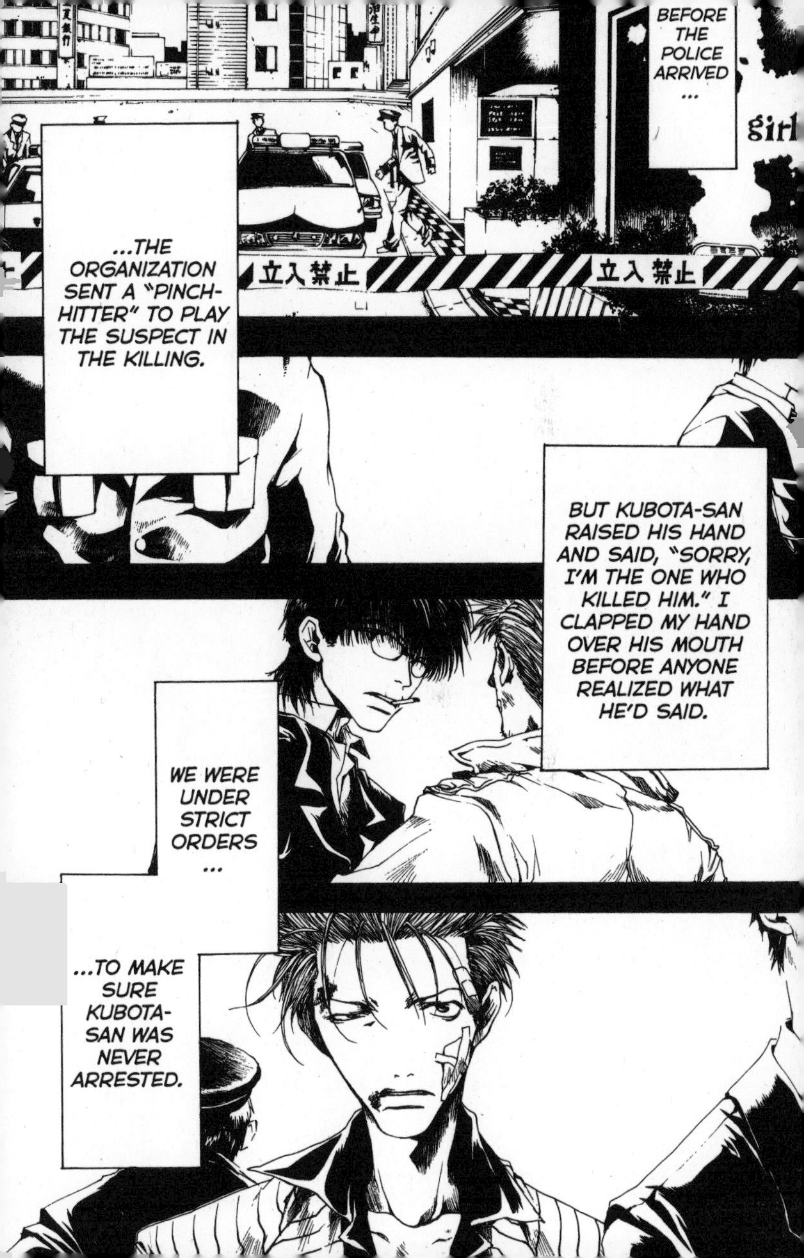

BEFORE THE POLICE ARRIVED ...
girl
...THE ORGANIZATION SENT A "PINCH-HITTER" TO PLAY THE SUSPECT IN THE KILLING.
立入禁止
立入禁止
BUT KUBOTA-SAN RAISED HIS HAND AND SAID, "SORRY, I'M THE ONE WHO KILLED HIM." I CLAPPED MY HAND OVER HIS MOUTH BEFORE ANYONE REALIZED WHAT HE'D SAID.
WE WERE UNDER STRICT ORDERS ...
...TO MAKE SURE KUBOTA-SAN WAS NEVER ARRESTED.

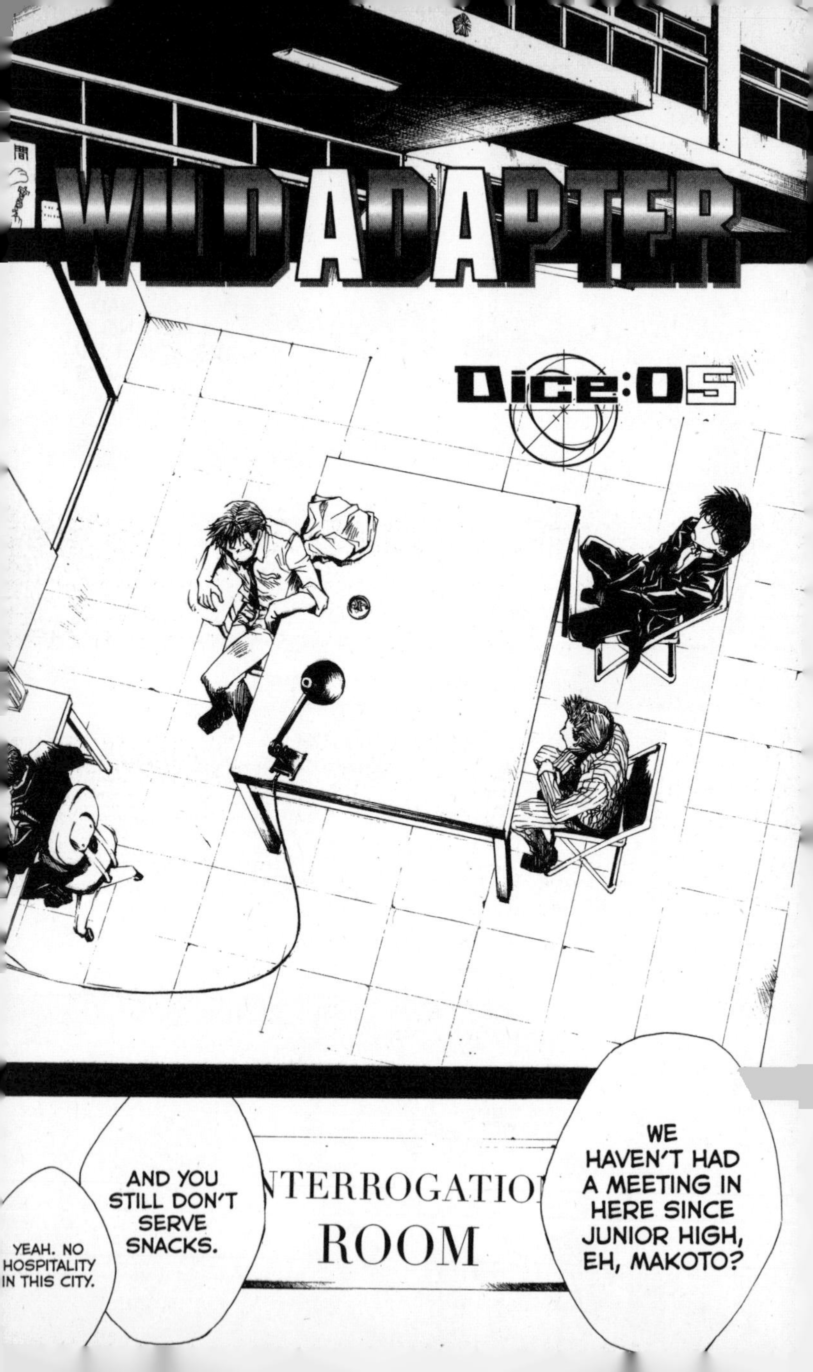
WILD ADAPTER
Dice:05
NTERROGATIO
ROOM
WE HAVEN'T HAD A MEETING IN HERE SINCE JUNIOR HIGH, EH, MAKOTO?
AND YOU STILL DON'T SERVE SNACKS.
YEAH. NO HOSPITALITY IN THIS CITY.

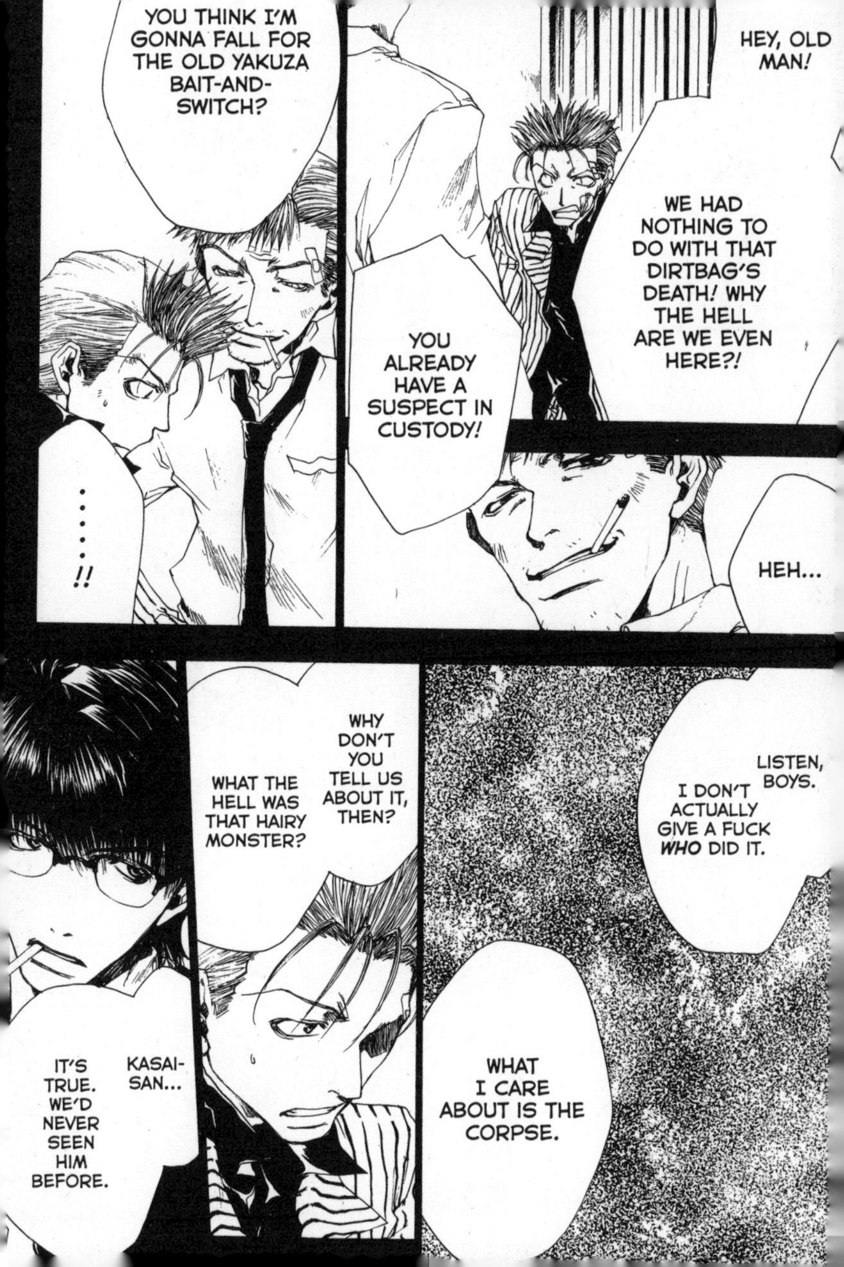

HEY, OLD MAN!
WE HAD NOTHING TO DO WITH THAT DIRTBAG'S DEATH! WHY THE HELL ARE WE EVEN HERE?!
YOU ALREADY HAVE A SUSPECT IN CUSTODY!
HEH...
YOU THINK I'M GONNA FALL FOR THE OLD YAKUZA BAIT-AND-SWITCH?
......!!
LISTEN, BOYS.
I DON'T ACTUALLY GIVE A FUCK *WHO* DID IT.
WHAT I CARE ABOUT IS THE CORPSE.
WHY DON'T YOU TELL US ABOUT IT, THEN?
WHAT THE HELL WAS THAT HAIRY MONSTER?
KASAI-SAN...
IT'S TRUE. WE'D NEVER SEEN HIM BEFORE.

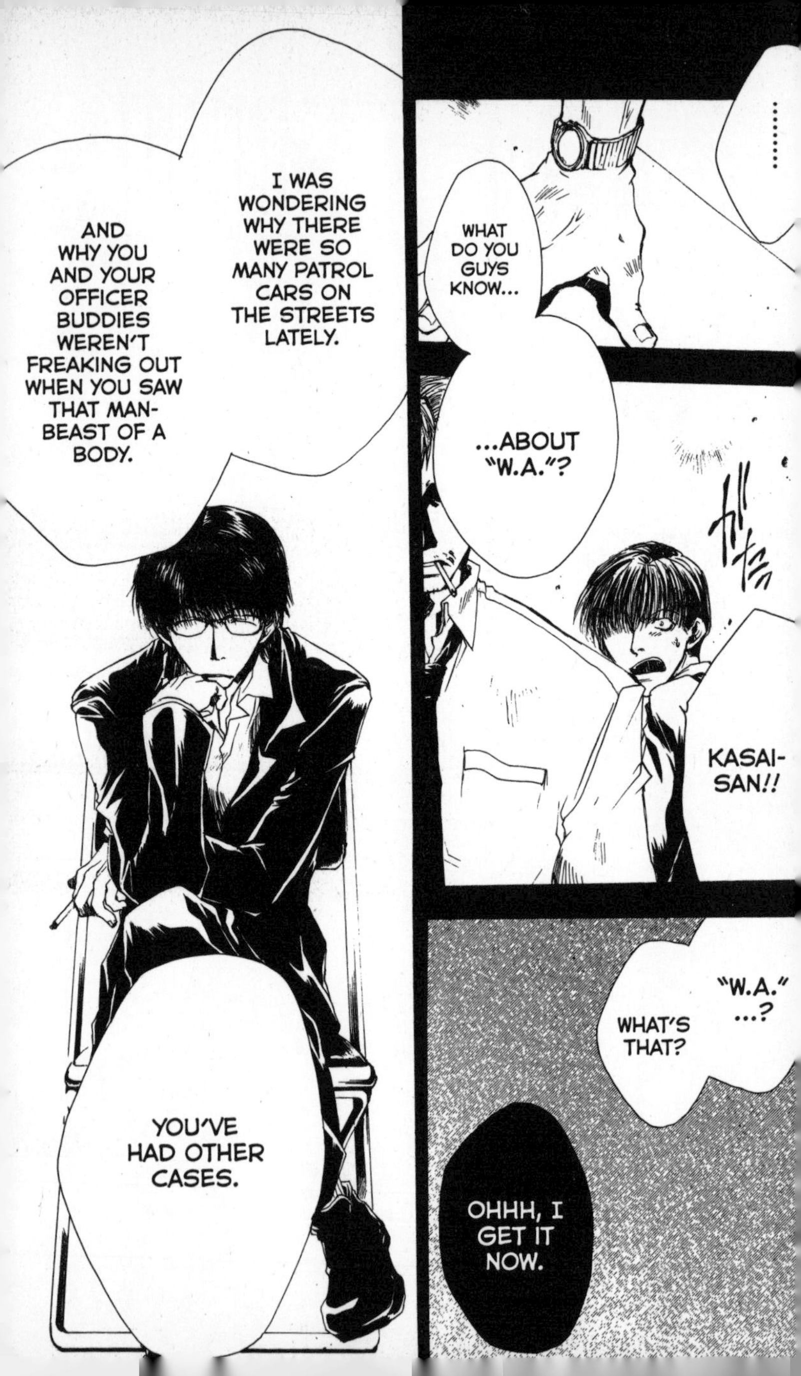
......
WHAT DO YOU GUYS KNOW...
...ABOUT "W.A."?
KASAI-SAN!!
"W.A." ...?
WHAT'S THAT?
OHHH, I GET IT NOW.
I WAS WONDERING WHY THERE WERE SO MANY PATROL CARS ON THE STREETS LATELY.
AND WHY YOU AND YOUR OFFICER BUDDIES WEREN'T FREAKING OUT WHEN YOU SAW THAT MAN-BEAST OF A BODY.
YOU'VE HAD OTHER CASES.

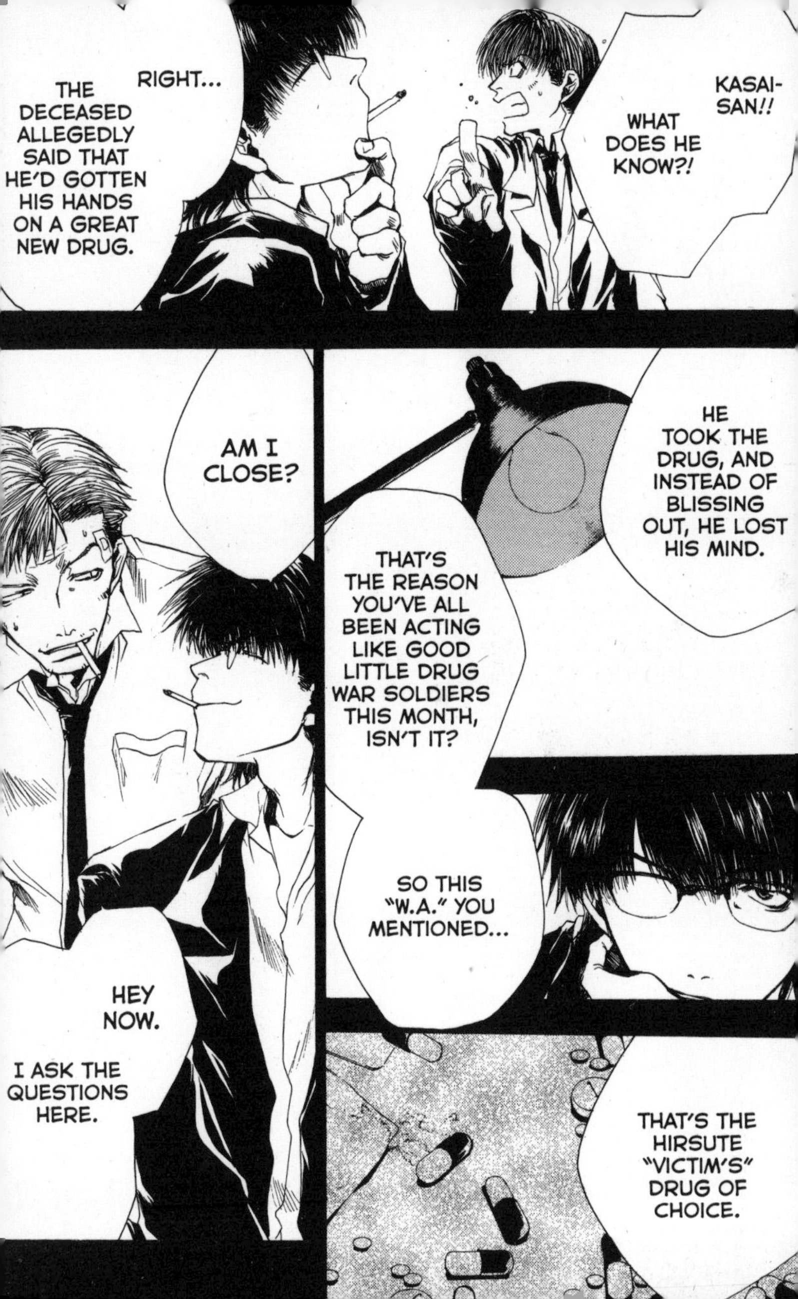
KASAI-SAN!!
WHAT DOES HE KNOW?!
RIGHT...
THE DECEASED ALLEGEDLY SAID THAT HE'D GOTTEN HIS HANDS ON A GREAT NEW DRUG.
HE TOOK THE DRUG, AND INSTEAD OF BLISSING OUT, HE LOST HIS MIND.
THAT'S THE REASON YOU'VE ALL BEEN ACTING LIKE GOOD LITTLE DRUG WAR SOLDIERS THIS MONTH, ISN'T IT?
SO THIS "W.A." YOU MENTIONED...
THAT'S THE HIRSUTE "VICTIM'S" DRUG OF CHOICE.
AM I CLOSE?
HEY NOW.
I ASK THE QUESTIONS HERE.

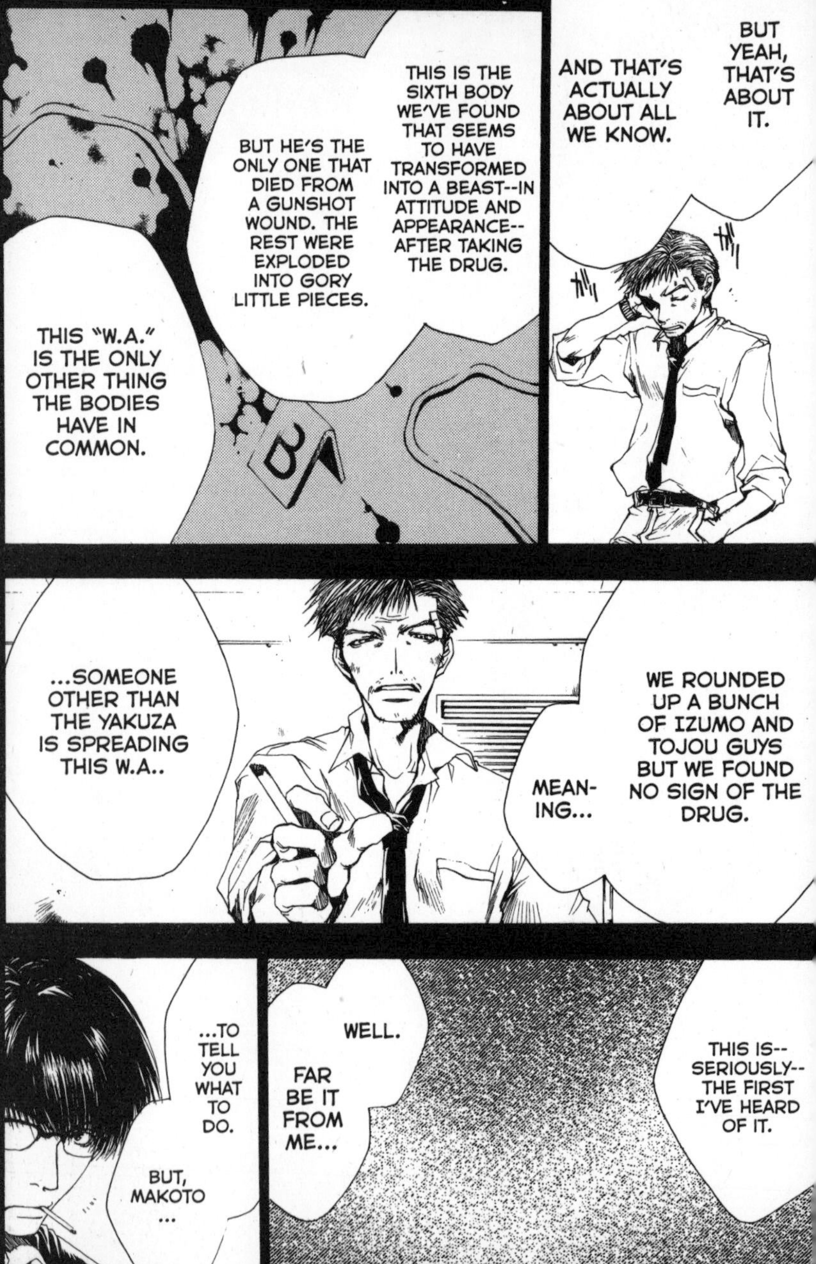
BUT YEAH, THAT'S ABOUT IT.
AND THAT'S ACTUALLY ABOUT ALL WE KNOW.
THIS IS THE SIXTH BODY WE'VE FOUND THAT SEEMS TO HAVE TRANSFORMED INTO A BEAST--IN ATTITUDE AND APPEARANCE--AFTER TAKING THE DRUG.
BUT HE'S THE ONLY ONE THAT DIED FROM A GUNSHOT WOUND. THE REST WERE EXPLODED INTO GORY LITTLE PIECES.
THIS "W.A." IS THE ONLY OTHER THING THE BODIES HAVE IN COMMON.
WE ROUNDED UP A BUNCH OF IZUMO AND TOJOU GUYS BUT WE FOUND NO SIGN OF THE DRUG.
MEAN-ING...
...SOMEONE OTHER THAN THE YAKUZA IS SPREADING THIS W.A..
THIS IS--SERIOUSLY--THE FIRST I'VE HEARD OF IT.
WELL.
FAR BE IT FROM ME...
...TO TELL YOU WHAT TO DO.
BUT, MAKOTO ...

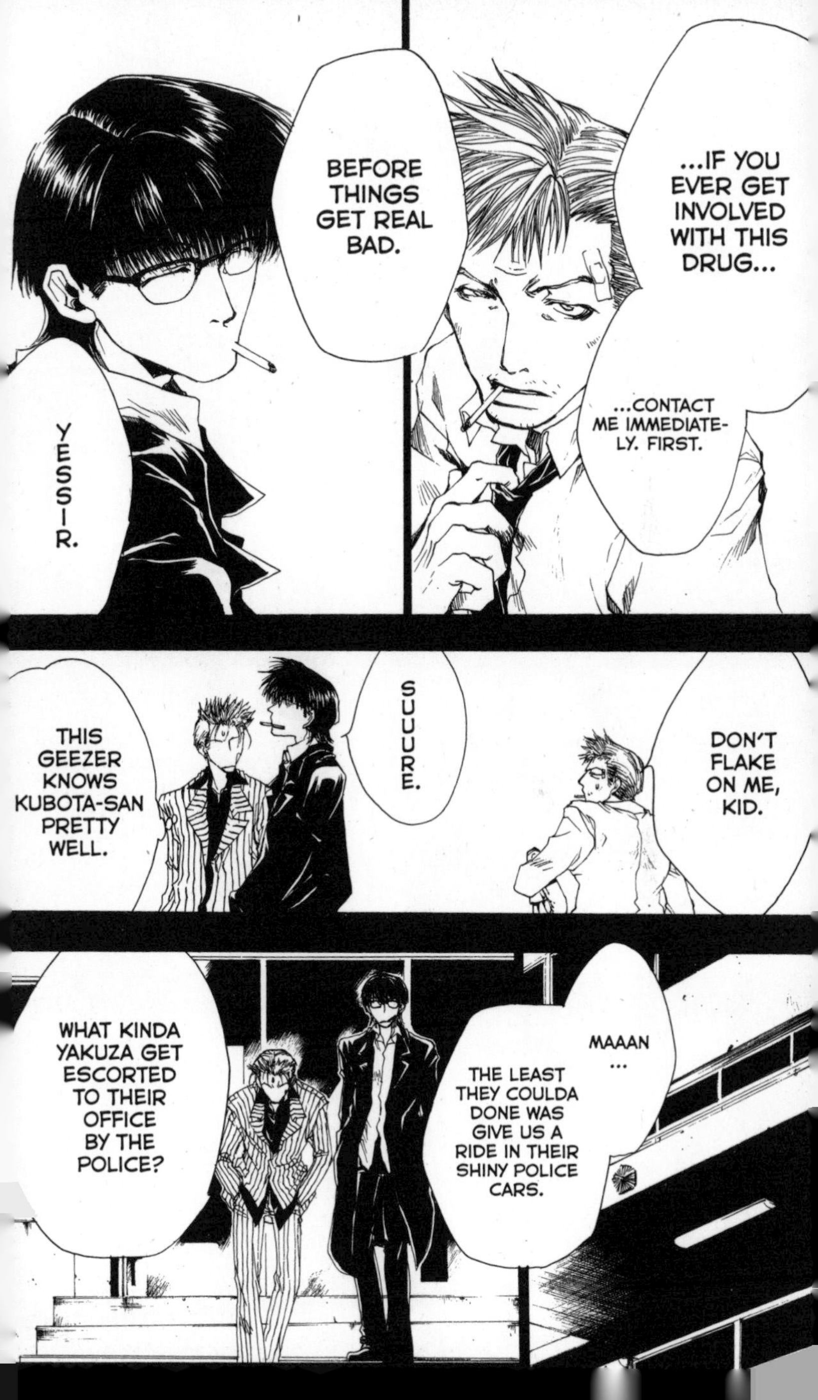
...IF YOU EVER GET INVOLVED WITH THIS DRUG...
...CONTACT ME IMMEDIATE-LY. FIRST.
BEFORE THINGS GET REAL BAD.
YESSIR.
DON'T FLAKE ON ME, KID.
SUUURE.
THIS GEEZER KNOWS KUBOTA-SAN PRETTY WELL.
MAAAN ...
THE LEAST THEY COULDA DONE WAS GIVE US A RIDE IN THEIR SHINY POLICE CARS.
WHAT KINDA YAKUZA GET ESCORTED TO THEIR OFFICE BY THE POLICE?

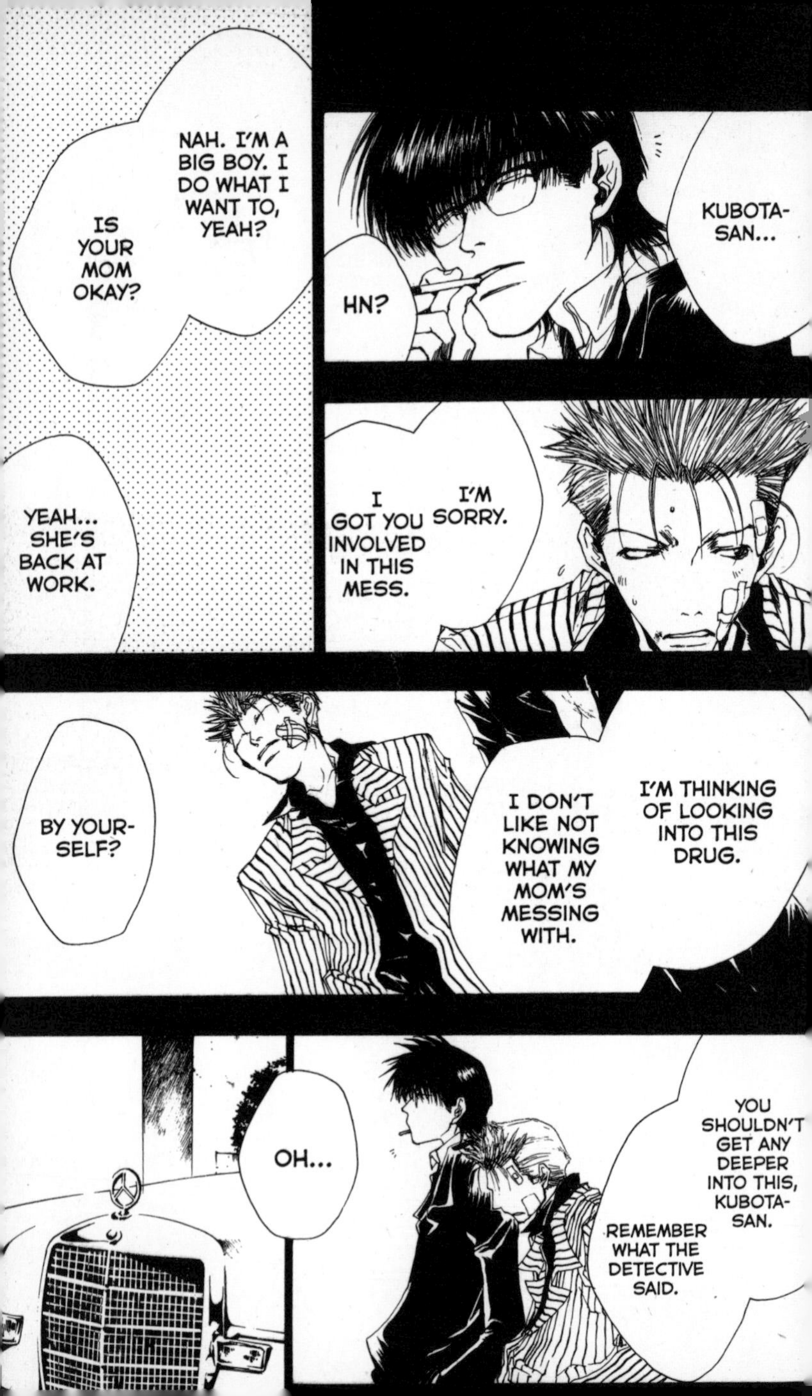
KUBOTA-SAN...
HN?
I'M SORRY.
I GOT YOU INVOLVED IN THIS MESS.
NAH. I'M A BIG BOY. I DO WHAT I WANT TO, YEAH?
IS YOUR MOM OKAY?
YEAH... SHE'S BACK AT WORK.
I'M THINKING OF LOOKING INTO THIS DRUG.
I DON'T LIKE NOT KNOWING WHAT MY MOM'S MESSING WITH.
BY YOURSELF?
YOU SHOULDN'T GET ANY DEEPER INTO THIS, KUBOTA-SAN.
REMEMBER WHAT THE DETECTIVE SAID.
OH...

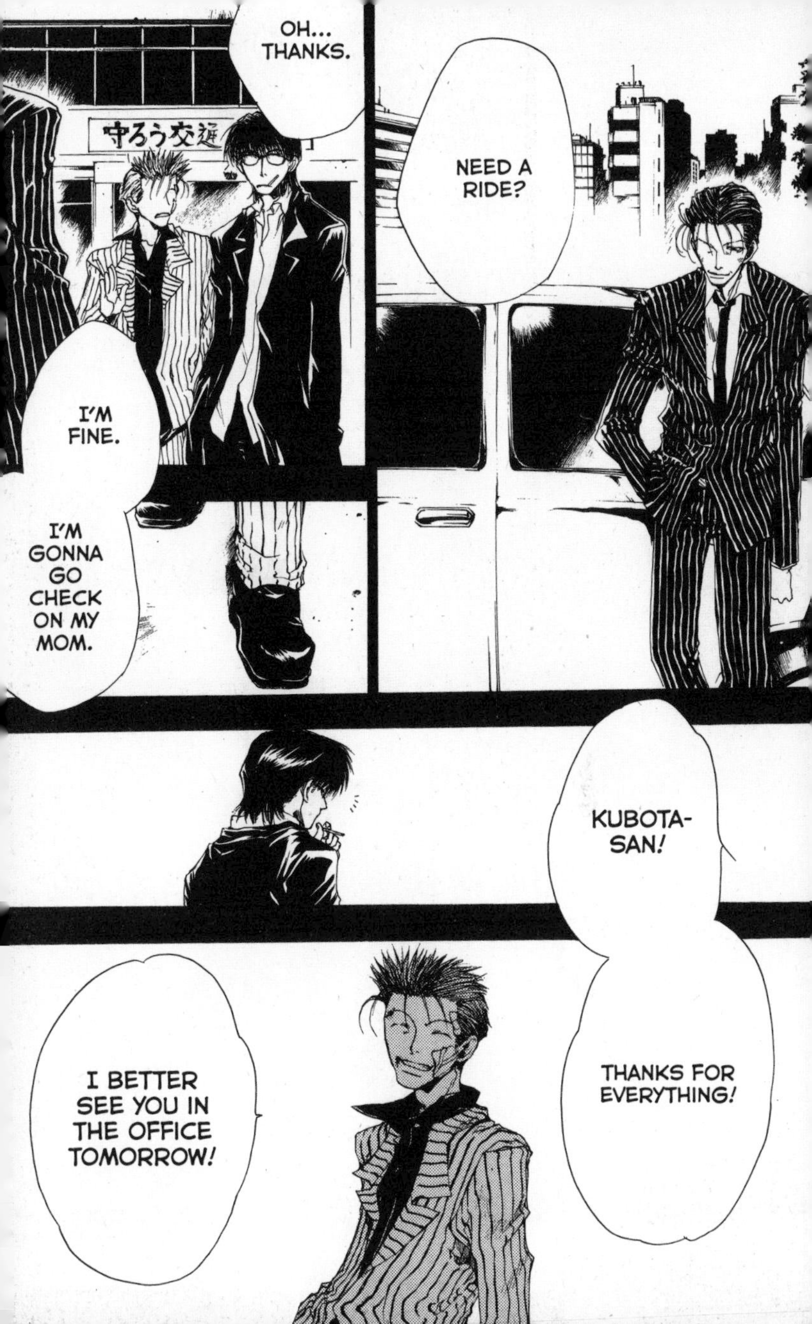
NEED A RIDE?
OH... THANKS.
I'M FINE.
I'M GONNA GO CHECK ON MY MOM.
KUBOTA-SAN!
THANKS FOR EVERYTHING!
I BETTER SEE YOU IN THE OFFICE TOMORROW!

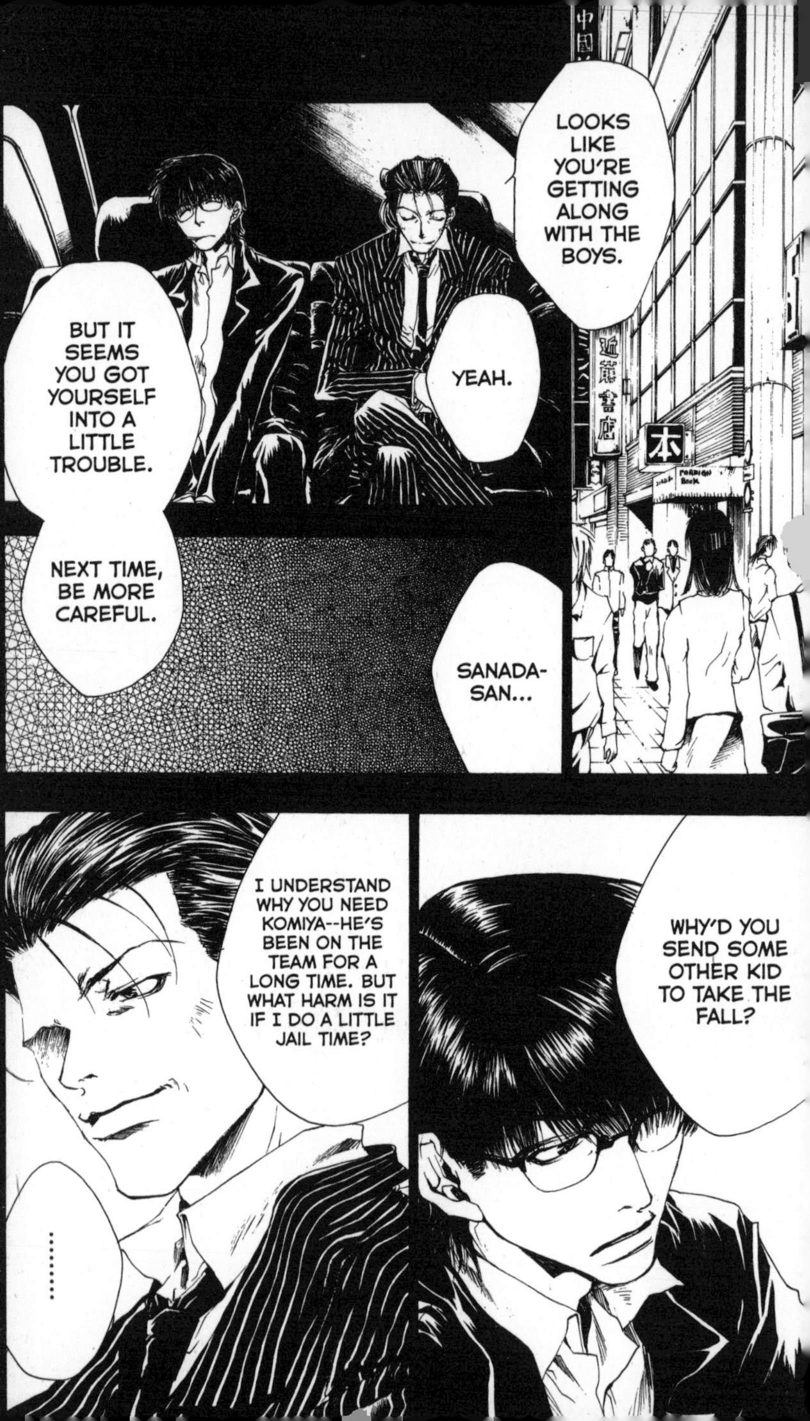
LOOKS LIKE YOU'RE GETTING ALONG WITH THE BOYS.
YEAH.
BUT IT SEEMS YOU GOT YOURSELF INTO A LITTLE TROUBLE.
近藤書店
本
FOREIGN BOOK
SANADA-SAN...
NEXT TIME, BE MORE CAREFUL.
WHY'D YOU SEND SOME OTHER KID TO TAKE THE FALL?
I UNDERSTAND WHY YOU NEED KOMIYA--HE'S BEEN ON THE TEAM FOR A LONG TIME. BUT WHAT HARM IS IT IF I DO A LITTLE JAIL TIME?
....

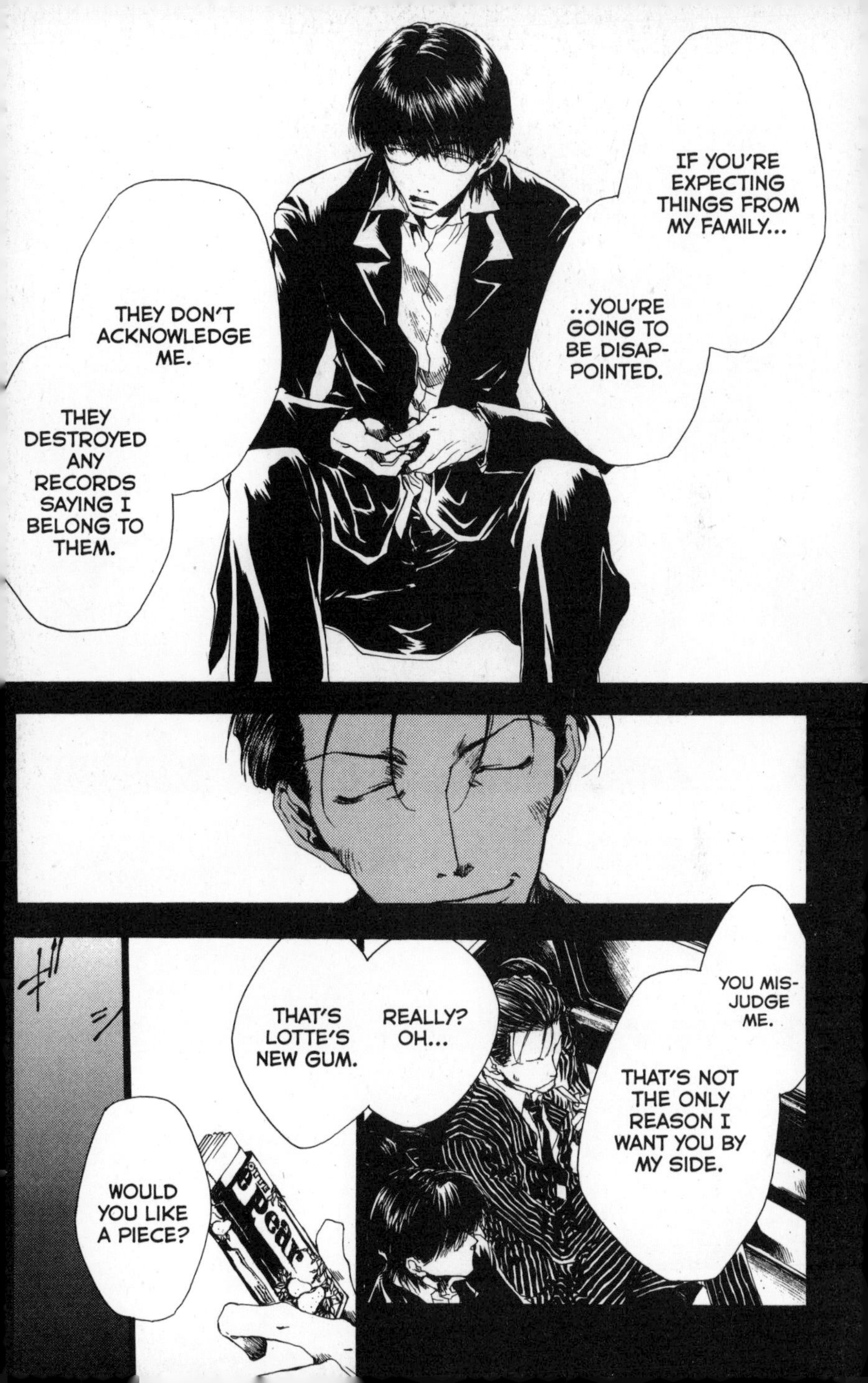
IF YOU'RE EXPECTING THINGS FROM MY FAMILY...
...YOU'RE GOING TO BE DISAPPOINTED.
THEY DON'T ACKNOWLEDGE ME.
THEY DESTROYED ANY RECORDS SAYING I BELONG TO THEM.
YOU MIS-JUDGE ME.
THAT'S NOT THE ONLY REASON I WANT YOU BY MY SIDE.
REALLY? OH...
THAT'S LOTTE'S NEW GUM.
WOULD YOU LIKE A PIECE?

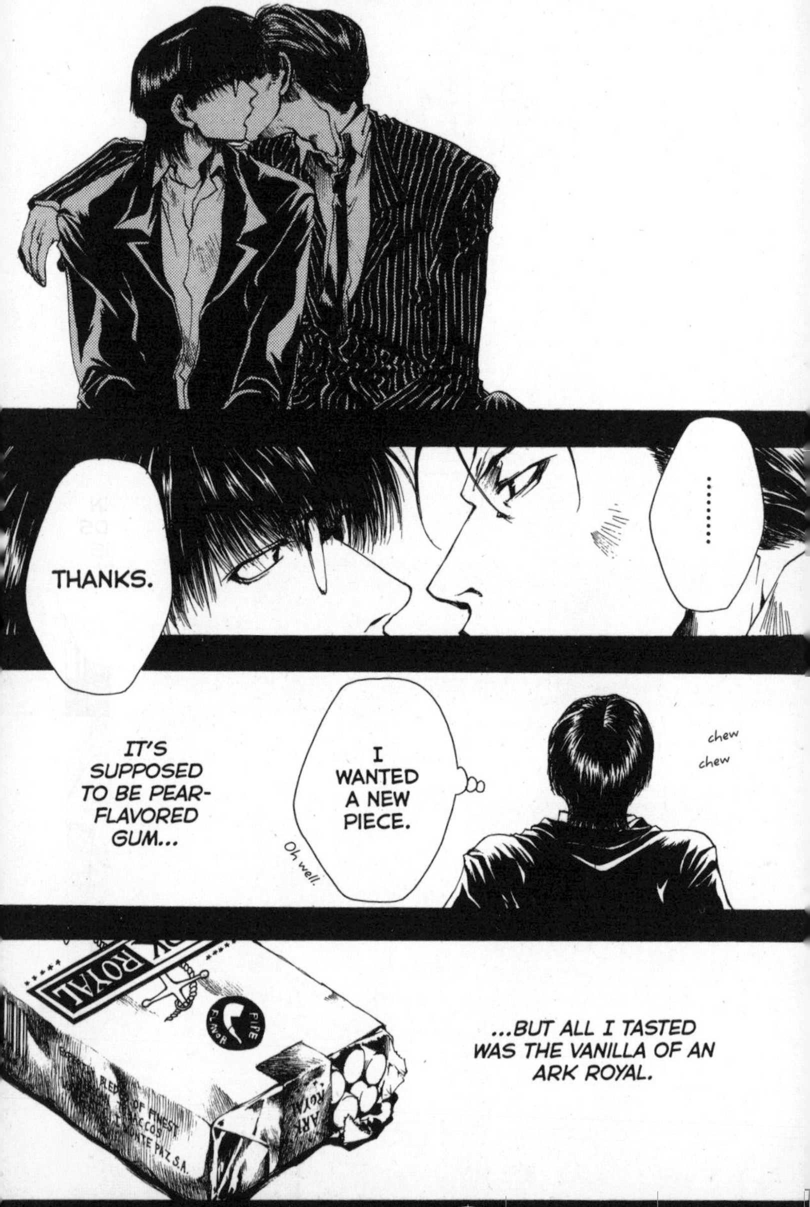
....
THANKS.
chew
chew
I WANTED A NEW PIECE.
Oh well.
IT'S SUPPOSED TO BE PEAR-FLAVORED GUM...
...BUT ALL I TASTED WAS THE VANILLA OF AN ARK ROYAL.
ROYAL
FINE FLAVOR
ARK ROYAL

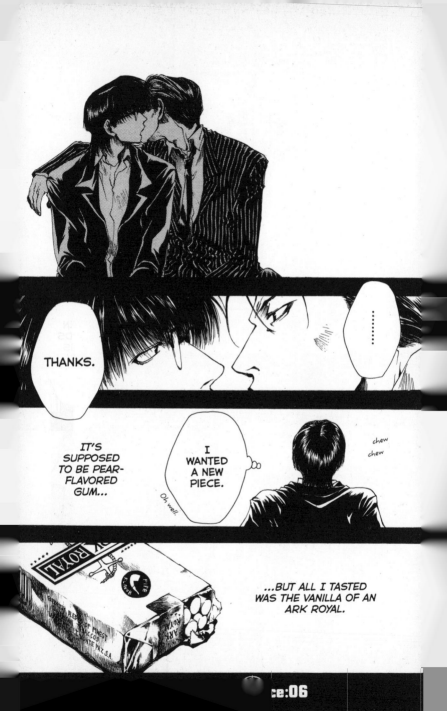

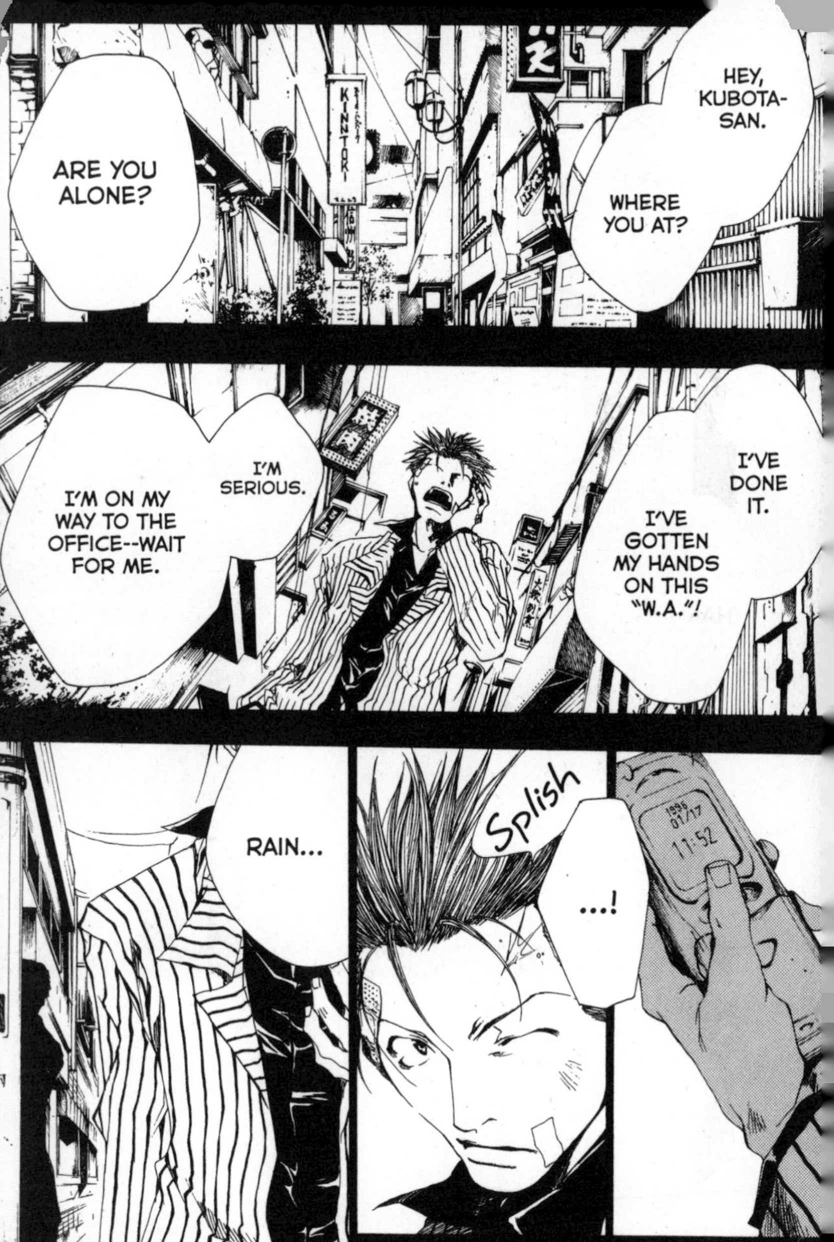
HEY, KUBOTA-SAN.
WHERE YOU AT?
ARE YOU ALONE?
I'VE DONE IT.
I'VE GOTTEN MY HANDS ON THIS "W.A."!
I'M SERIOUS.
I'M ON MY WAY TO THE OFFICE--WAIT FOR ME.
1996 01/17
11:52
...!
Splish
RAIN...

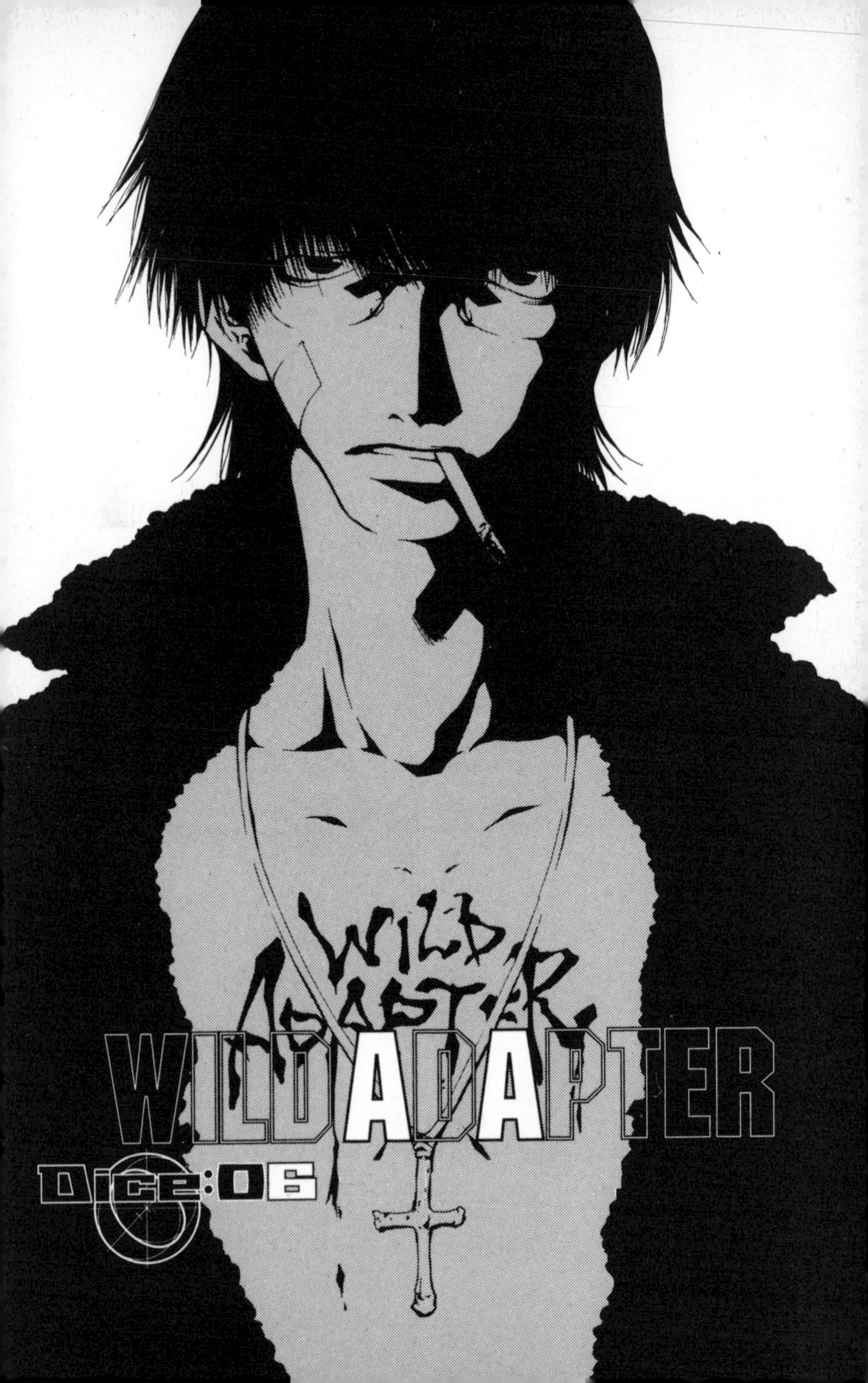
WILD ADAPTER
WILD ADAPTER
DICE:06

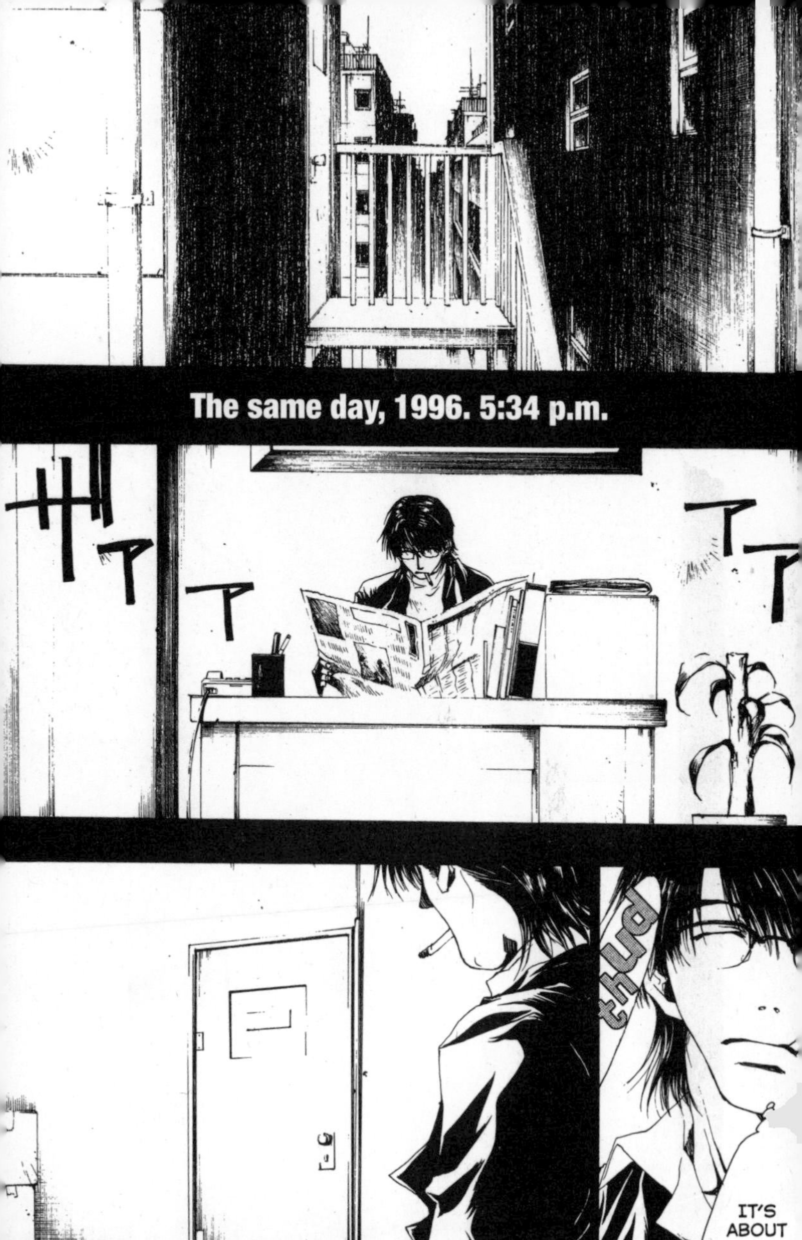
The same day, 1996. 5:34 p.m.
アア
ザアア
thud
IT'S ABOUT TIME...

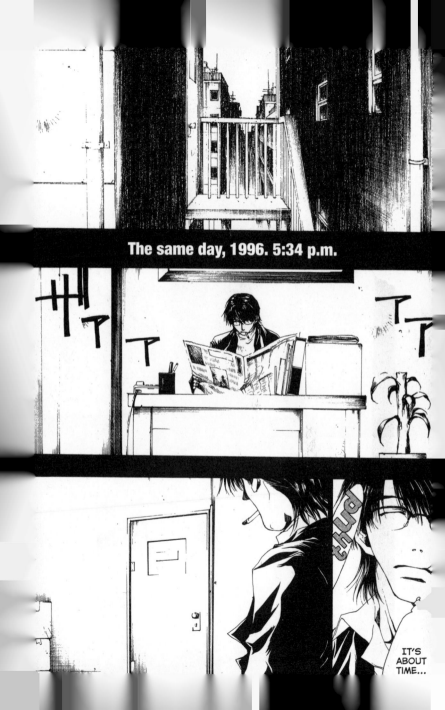

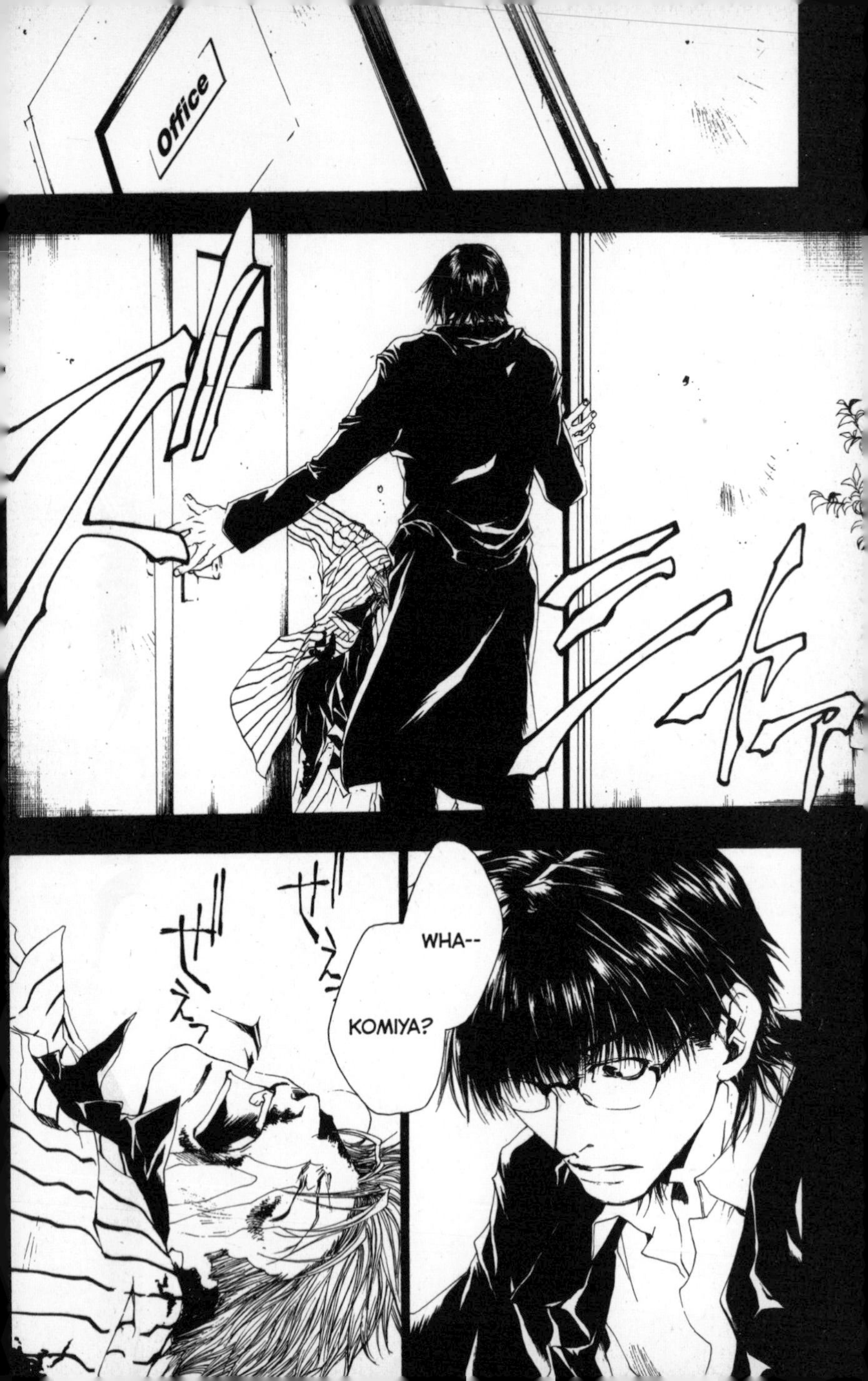
Office
WHA--
KOMIYA?

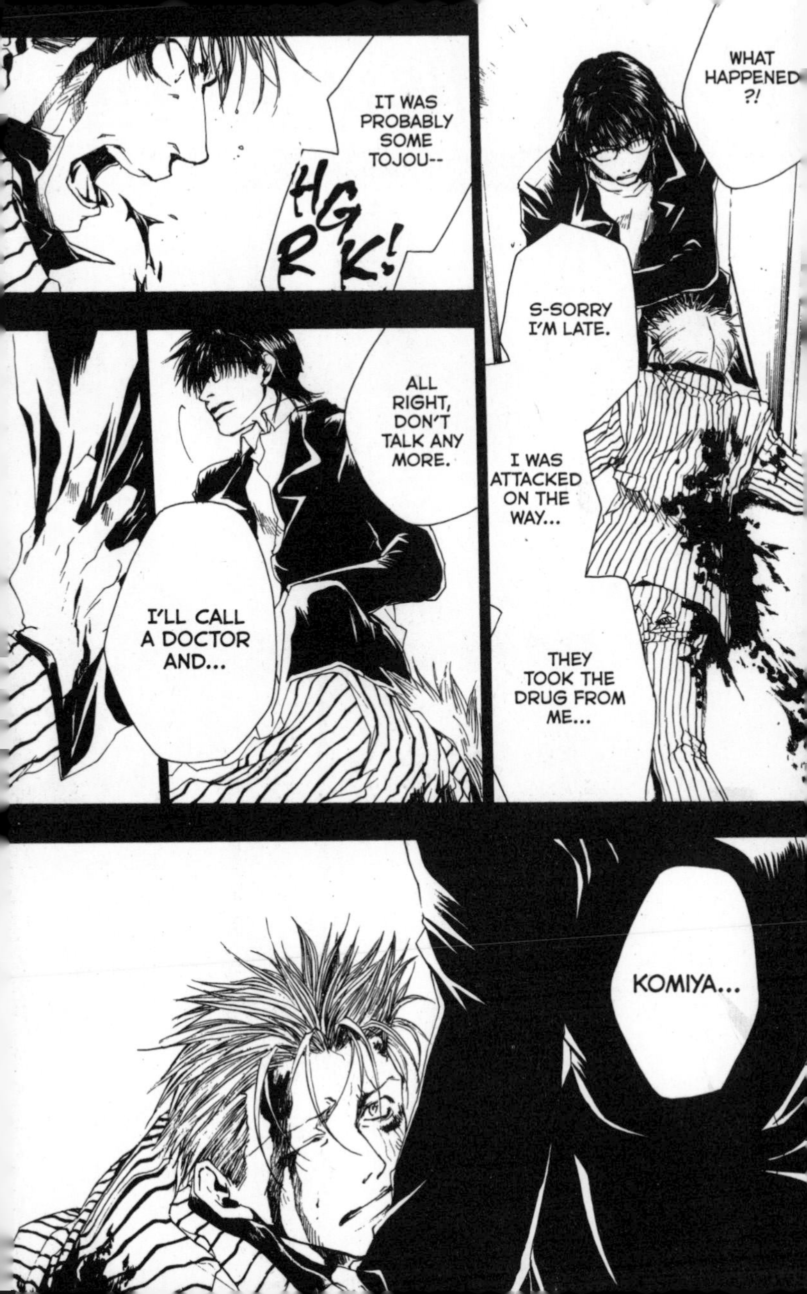
WHAT HAPPENED ?!
S-SORRY I'M LATE.
I WAS ATTACKED ON THE WAY...
THEY TOOK THE DRUG FROM ME...
IT WAS PROBABLY SOME TOJOU--
HGRK!
ALL RIGHT, DON'T TALK ANY MORE.
I'LL CALL A DOCTOR AND...
KOMIYA...

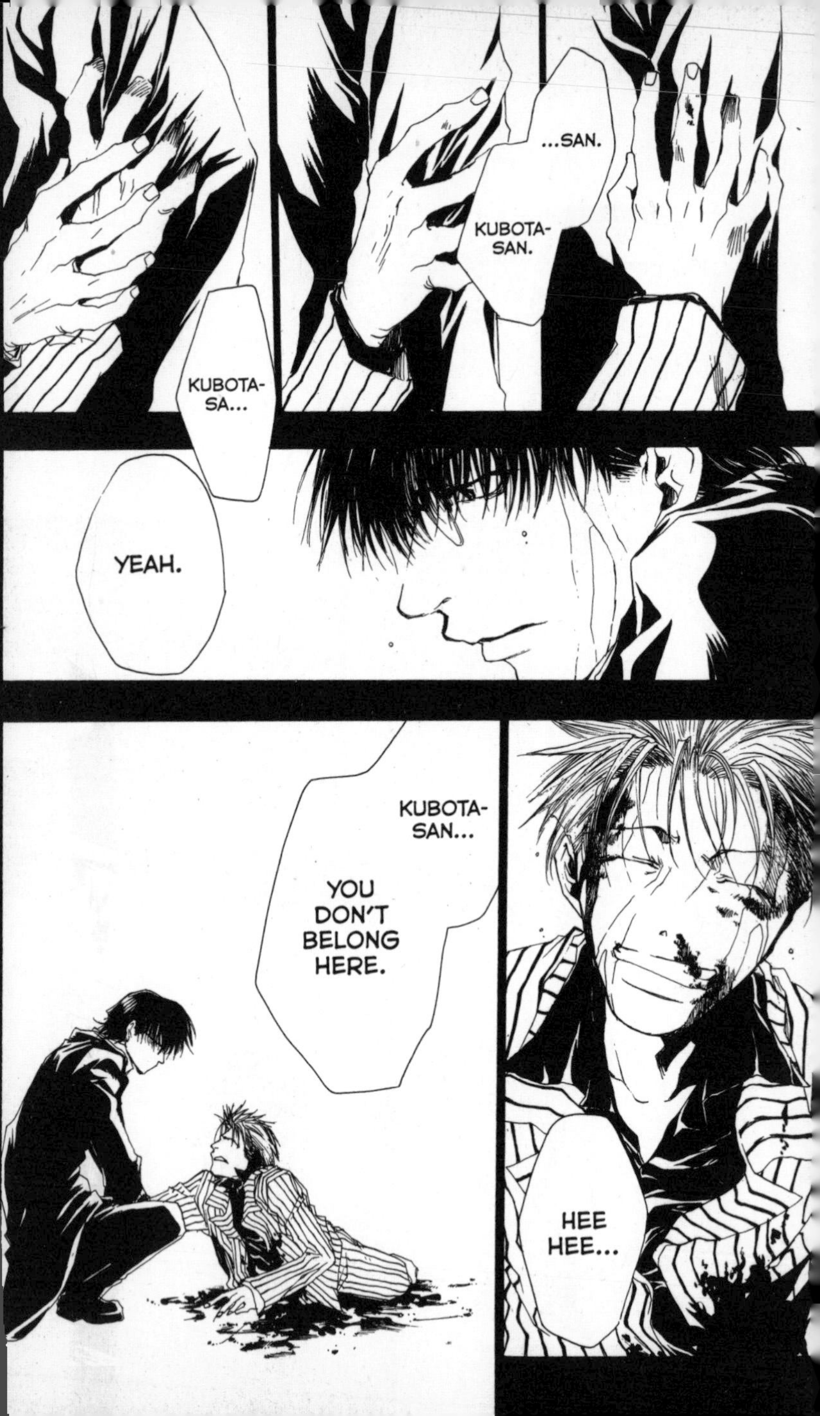
...SAN.
KUBOTA-SAN.
KUBOTA-SA...
YEAH.
HEE HEE...
KUBOTA-SAN...
YOU DON'T BELONG HERE.

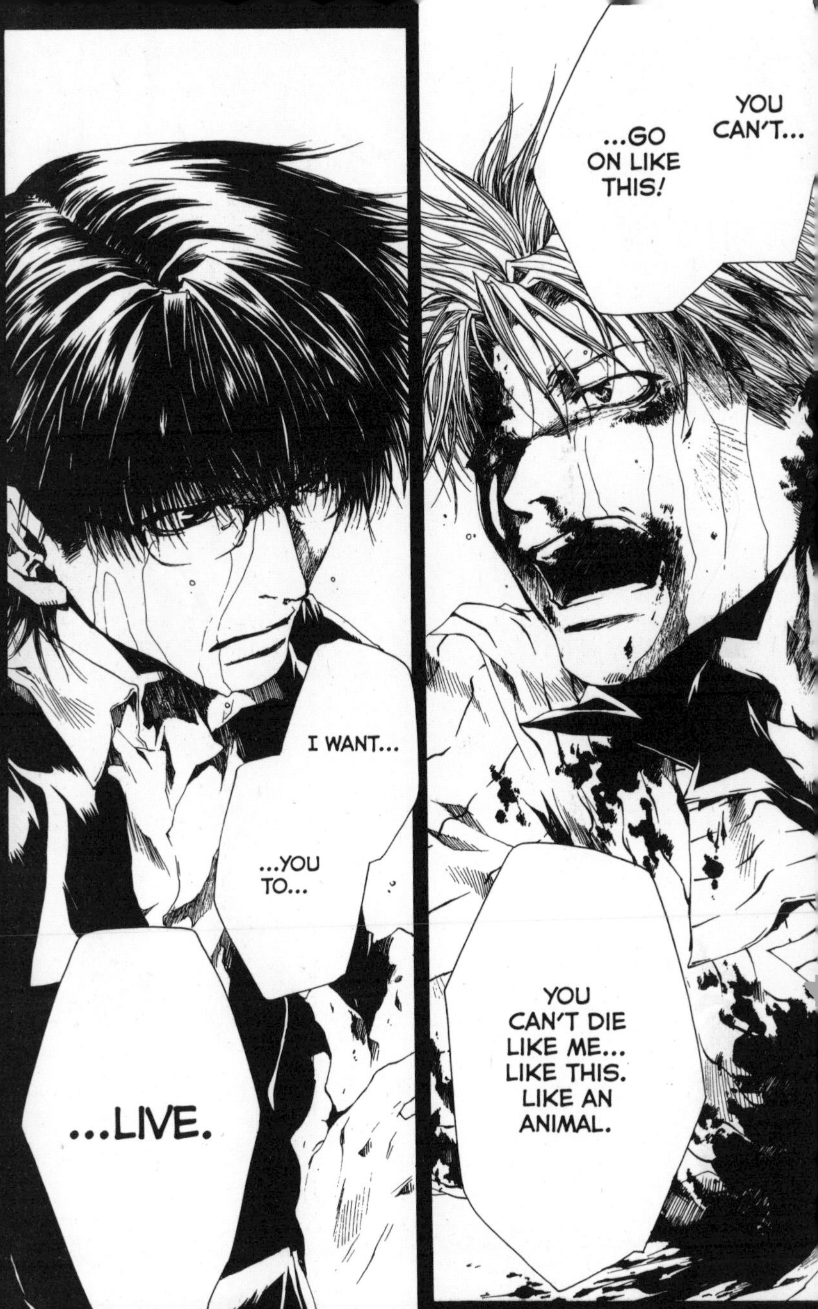
YOU CAN'T...
...GO ON LIKE THIS!
YOU CAN'T DIE LIKE ME... LIKE THIS. LIKE AN ANIMAL.
I WANT...
...YOU TO...
...LIVE.

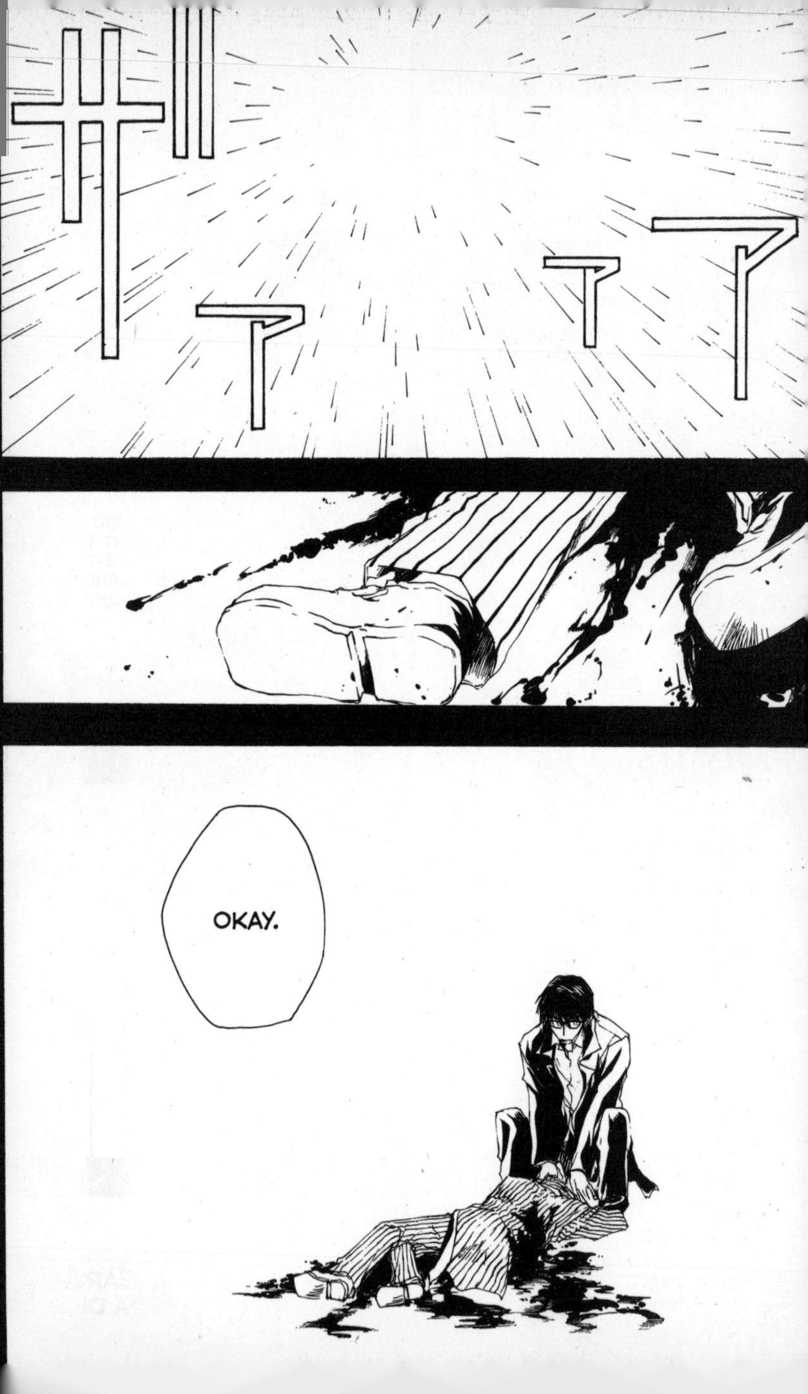
ザァァア
OKAY.

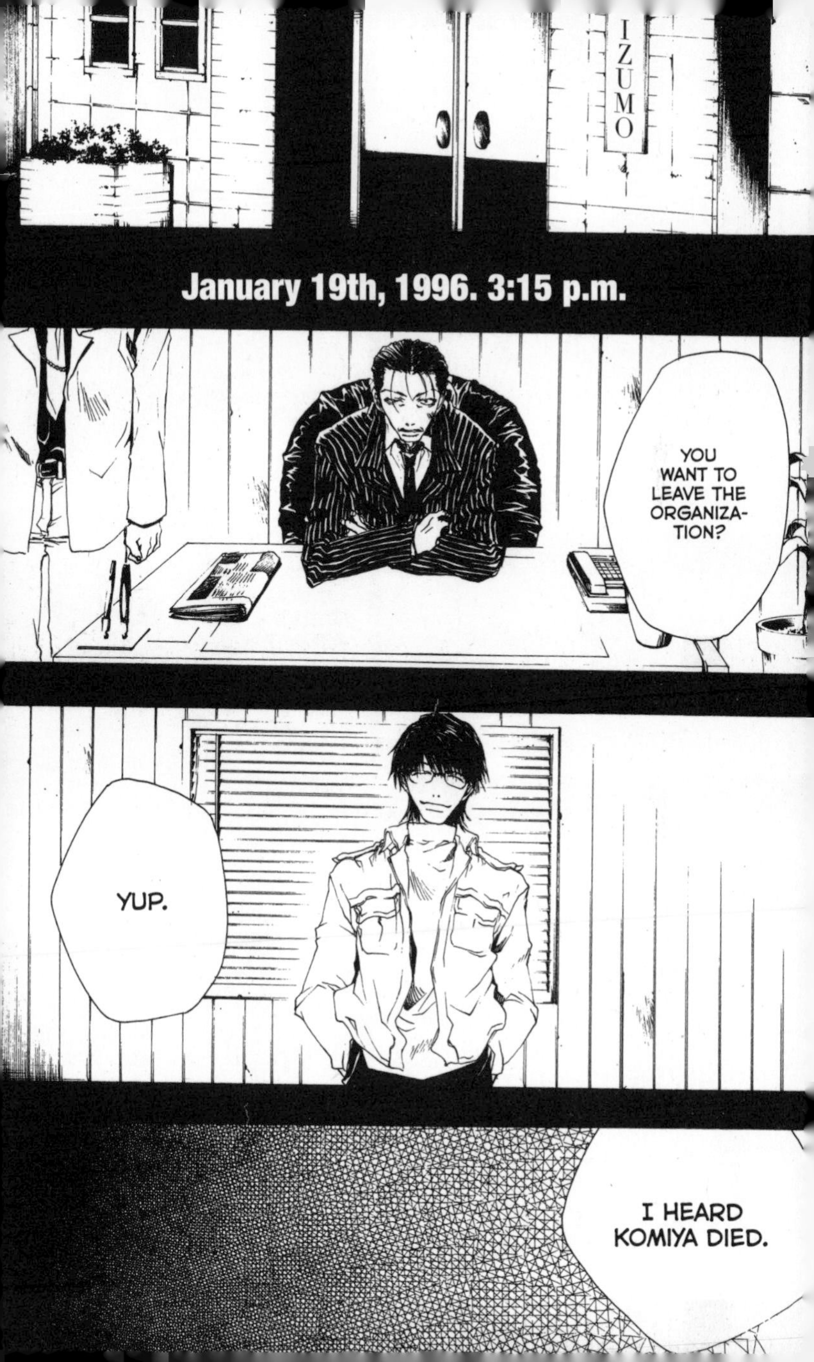
IZUMO
January 19th, 1996. 3:15 p.m.
YOU WANT TO LEAVE THE ORGANIZA-TION?
YUP.
I HEARD KOMIYA DIED.

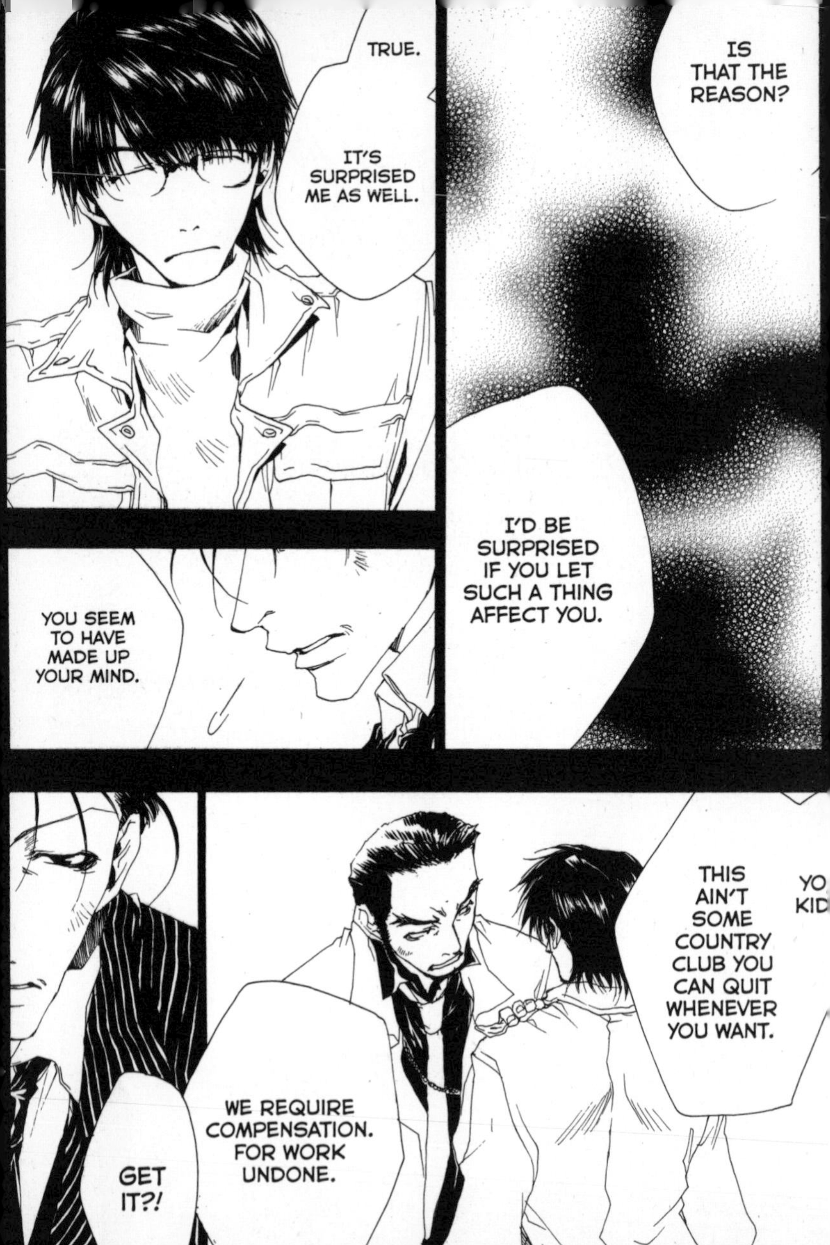
IS THAT THE REASON?
I'D BE SURPRISED IF YOU LET SUCH A THING AFFECT YOU.
TRUE.
IT'S SURPRISED ME AS WELL.
YOU SEEM TO HAVE MADE UP YOUR MIND.
THIS AIN'T SOME COUNTRY CLUB YOU CAN QUIT WHENEVER YOU WANT.
WE REQUIRE COMPENSATION. FOR WORK UNDONE.
GET IT?!

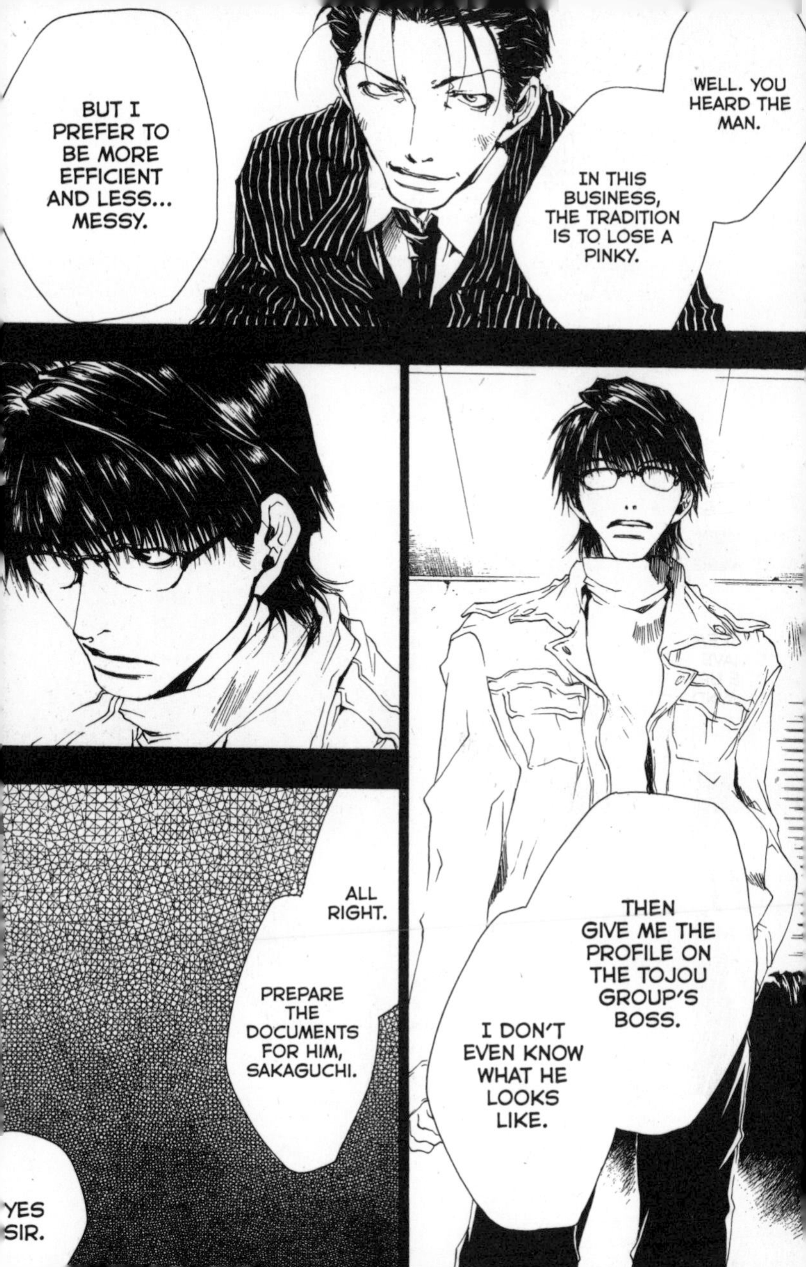
WELL. YOU HEARD THE MAN.
IN THIS BUSINESS, THE TRADITION IS TO LOSE A PINKY.
BUT I PREFER TO BE MORE EFFICIENT AND LESS... MESSY.
THEN GIVE ME THE PROFILE ON THE TOJOU GROUP'S BOSS.
I DON'T EVEN KNOW WHAT HE LOOKS LIKE.
ALL RIGHT.
PREPARE THE DOCUMENTS FOR HIM, SAKAGUCHI.
YES SIR.

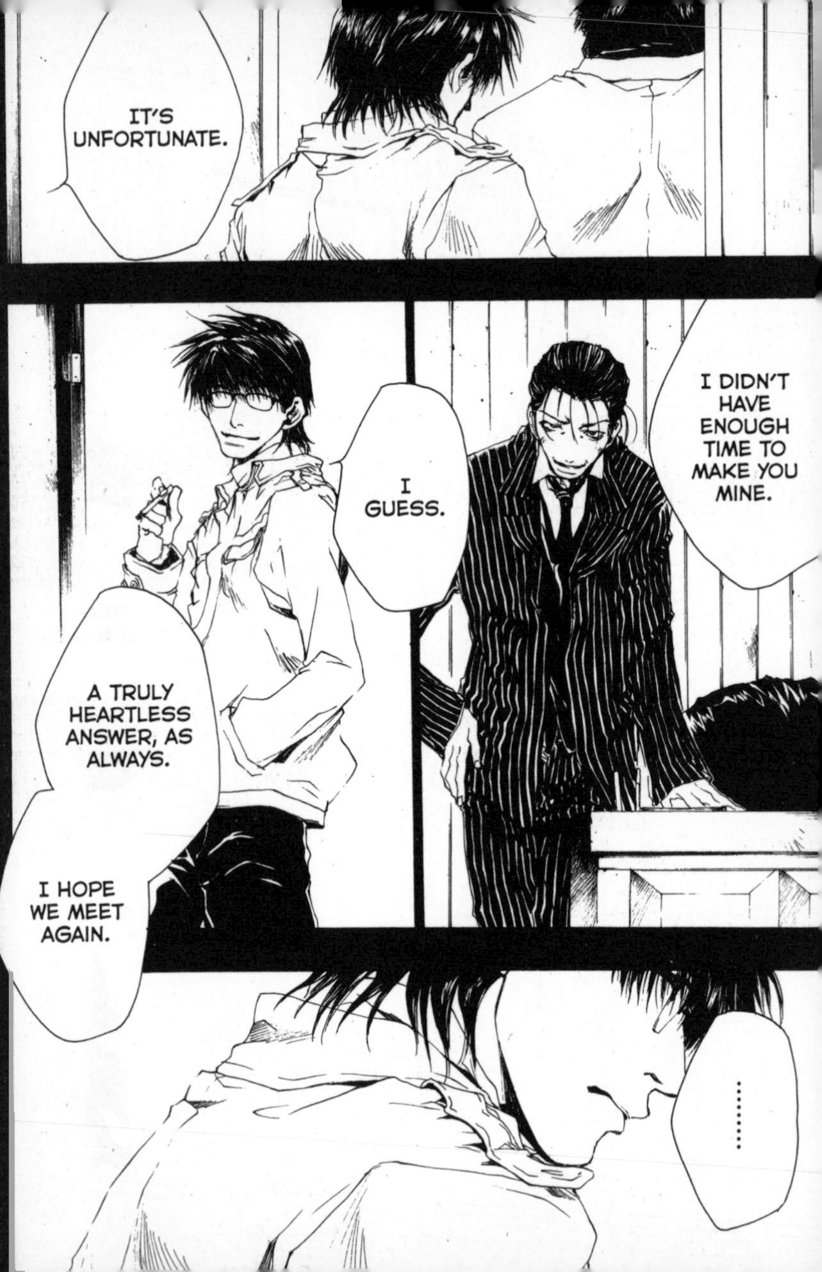
IT'S UNFORTUNATE.
I DIDN'T HAVE ENOUGH TIME TO MAKE YOU MINE.
I GUESS.
A TRULY HEARTLESS ANSWER, AS ALWAYS.
I HOPE WE MEET AGAIN.
……

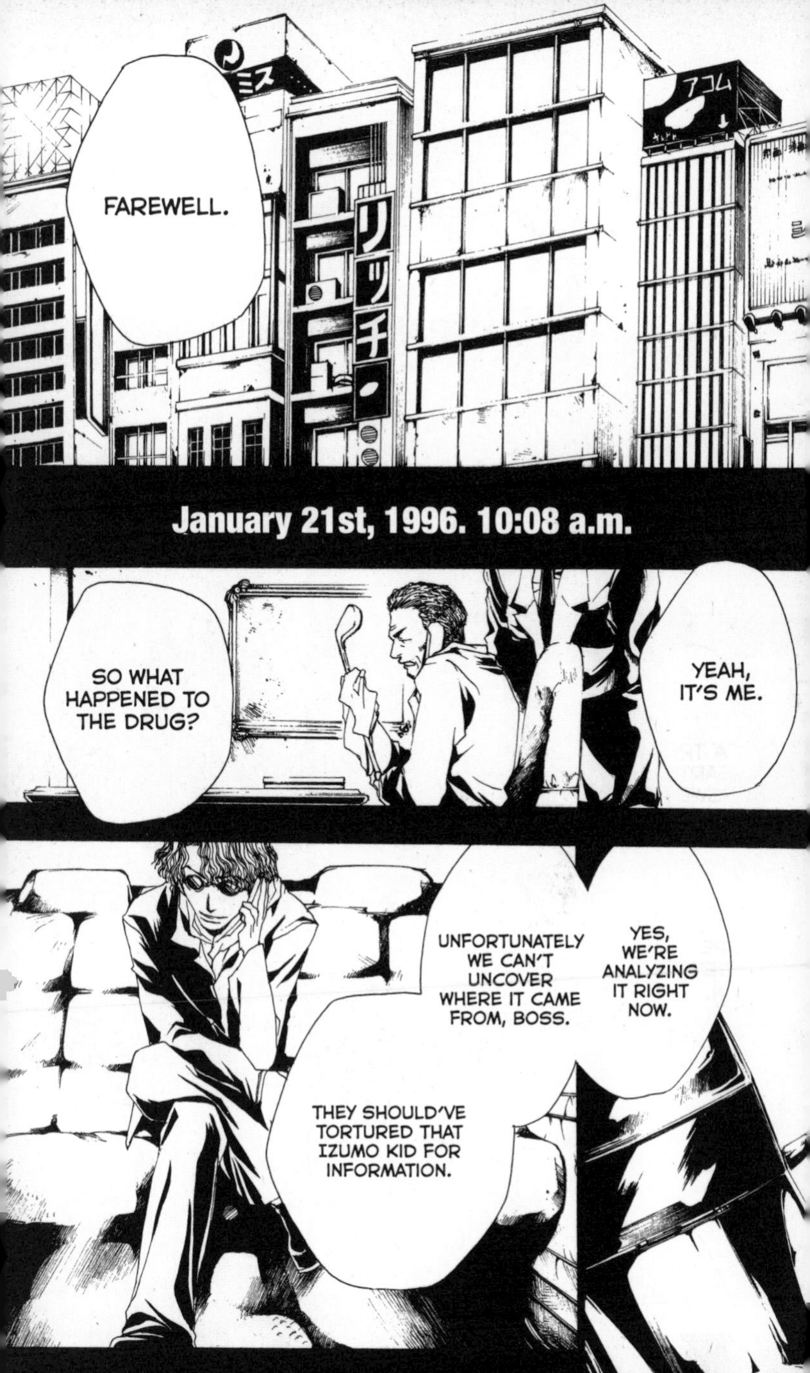

アコム
リッチ
ミス
FAREWELL.
January 21st, 1996. 10:08 a.m.
YEAH, IT'S ME.
SO WHAT HAPPENED TO THE DRUG?
YES, WE'RE ANALYZING IT RIGHT NOW.
UNFORTUNATELY WE CAN'T UNCOVER WHERE IT CAME FROM, BOSS.
THEY SHOULD'VE TORTURED THAT IZUMO KID FOR INFORMATION.

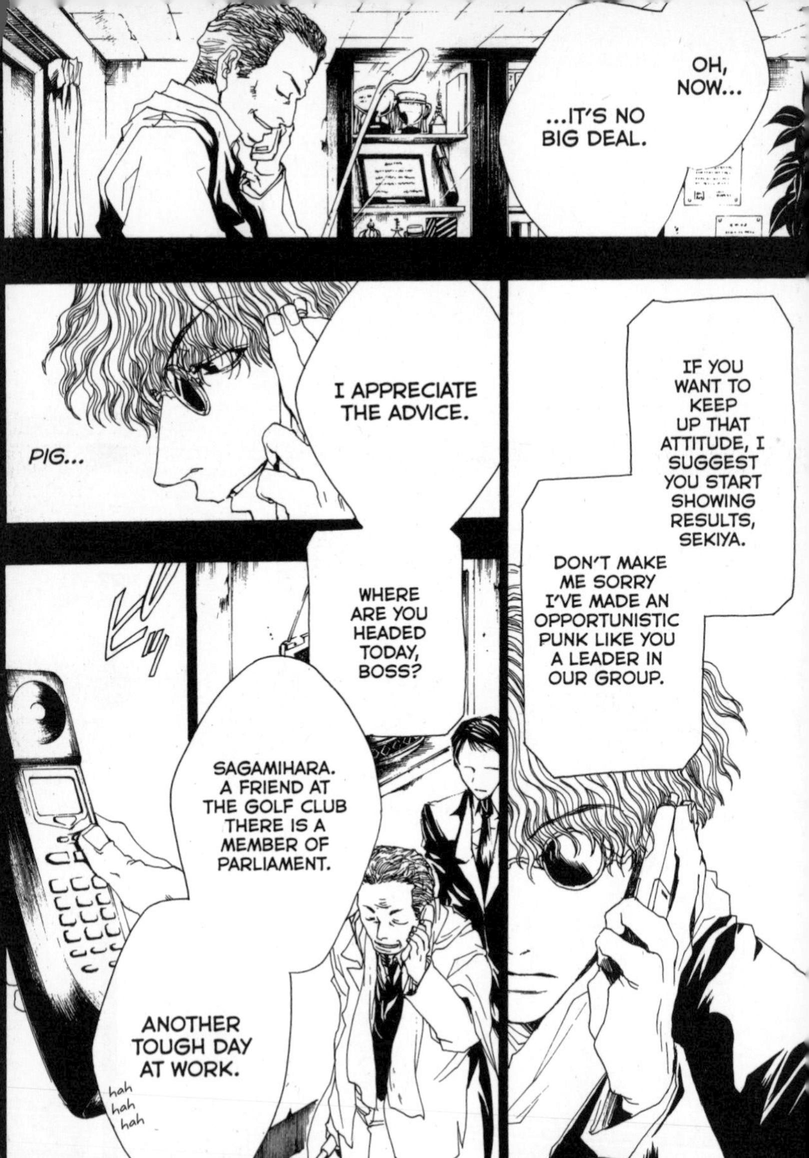
OH, NOW...
...IT'S NO BIG DEAL.
IF YOU WANT TO KEEP UP THAT ATTITUDE, I SUGGEST YOU START SHOWING RESULTS, SEKIYA.
DON'T MAKE ME SORRY I'VE MADE AN OPPORTUNISTIC PUNK LIKE YOU A LEADER IN OUR GROUP.
I APPRECIATE THE ADVICE.
PIG...
WHERE ARE YOU HEADED TODAY, BOSS?
SAGAMIHARA. A FRIEND AT THE GOLF CLUB THERE IS A MEMBER OF PARLIAMENT.
ANOTHER TOUGH DAY AT WORK.
hah hah hah

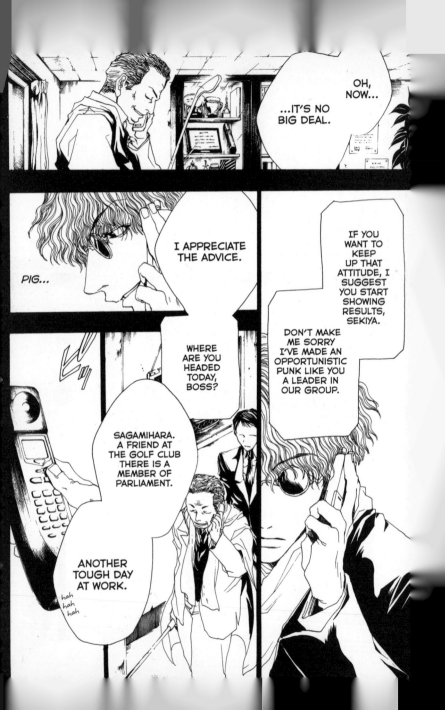

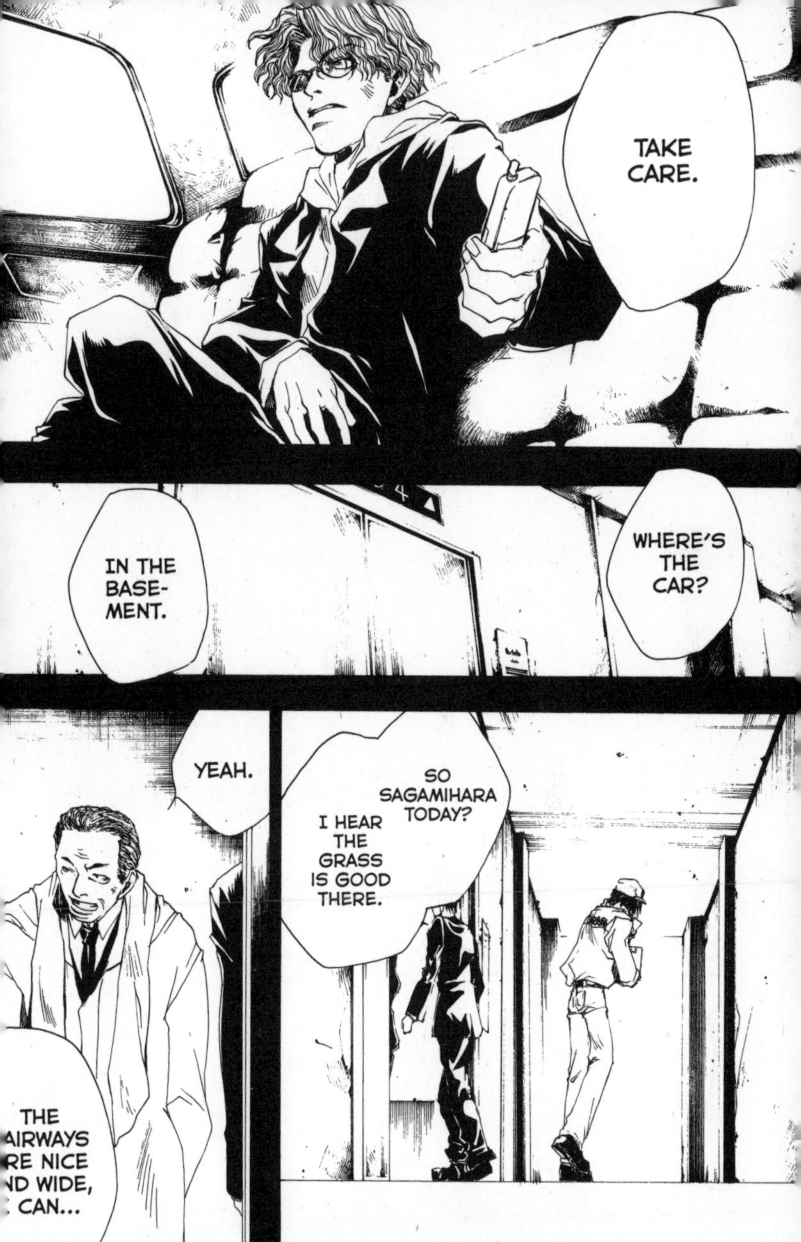
TAKE CARE.
WHERE'S THE CAR?
IN THE BASEMENT.
SO SAGAMIHARA TODAY?
I HEAR THE GRASS IS GOOD THERE.
YEAH.
THE AIRWAYS RE NICE ND WIDE, CAN...

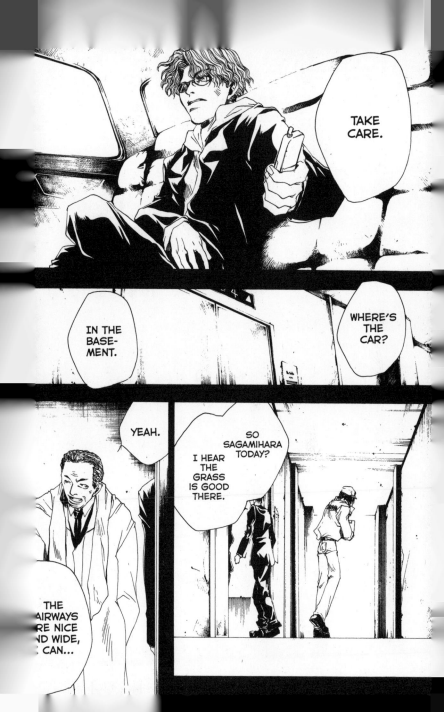

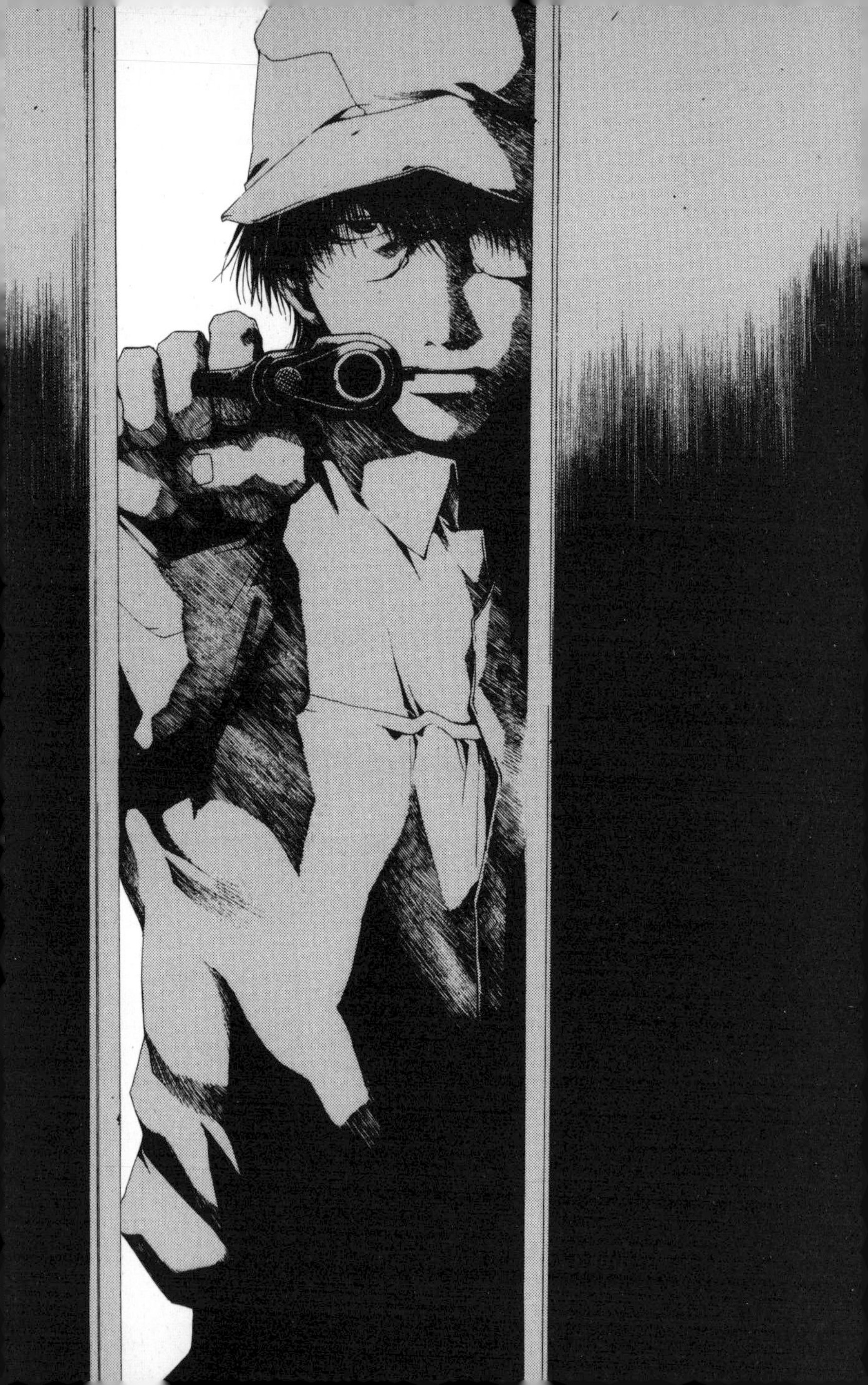

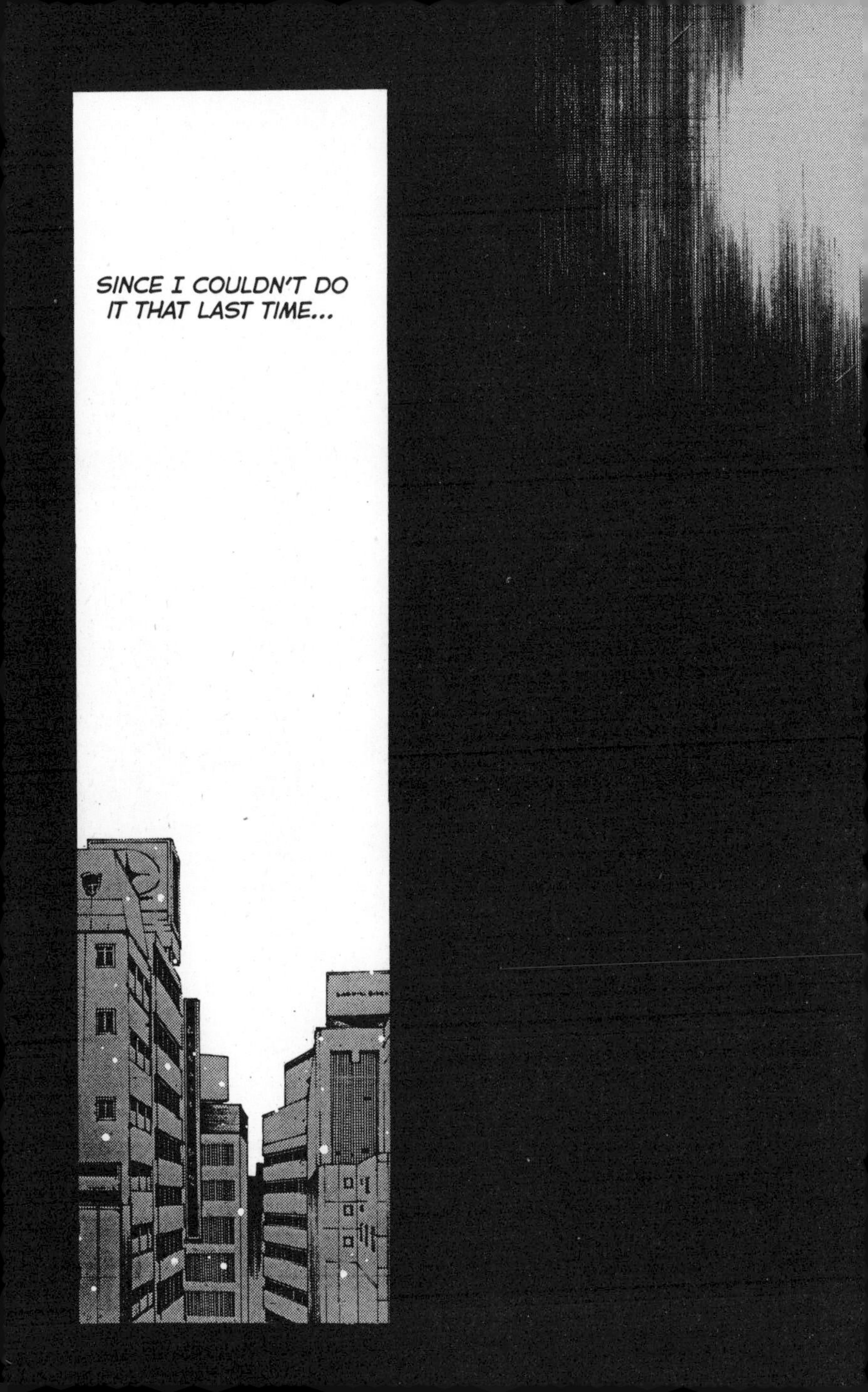
SINCE I COULDN'T DO IT THAT LAST TIME...

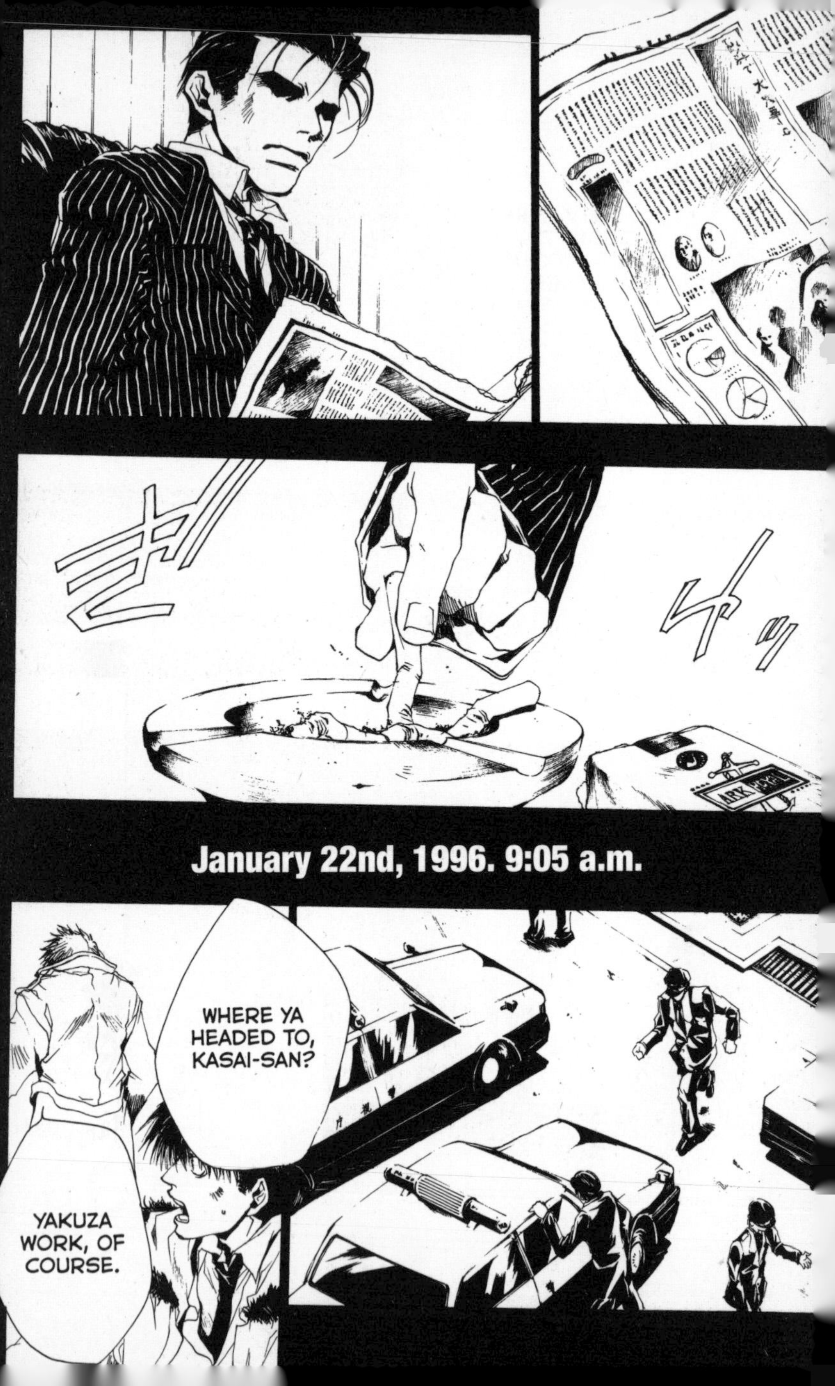
January 22nd, 1996. 9:05 a.m.
WHERE YA HEADED TO, KASAI-SAN?
YAKUZA WORK, OF COURSE.

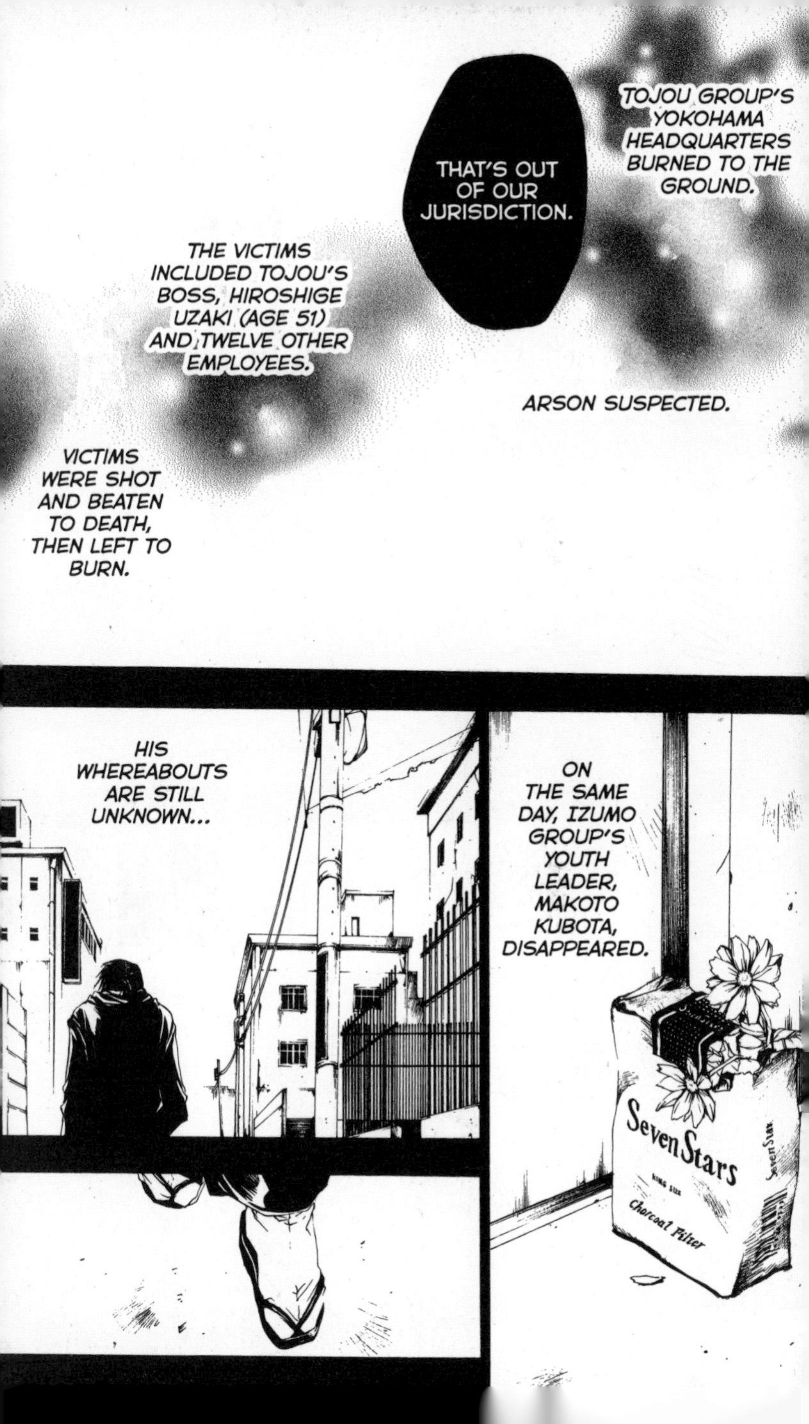
TOJOU GROUP'S YOKOHAMA HEADQUARTERS BURNED TO THE GROUND.
THAT'S OUT OF OUR JURISDICTION.
ARSON SUSPECTED.
THE VICTIMS INCLUDED TOJOU'S BOSS, HIROSHIGE UZAKI (AGE 51) AND TWELVE OTHER EMPLOYEES.
VICTIMS WERE SHOT AND BEATEN TO DEATH, THEN LEFT TO BURN.
ON THE SAME DAY, IZUMO GROUP'S YOUTH LEADER, MAKOTO KUBOTA, DISAPPEARED.
Seven Stars
Charcoal Filter
HIS WHEREABOUTS ARE STILL UNKNOWN...

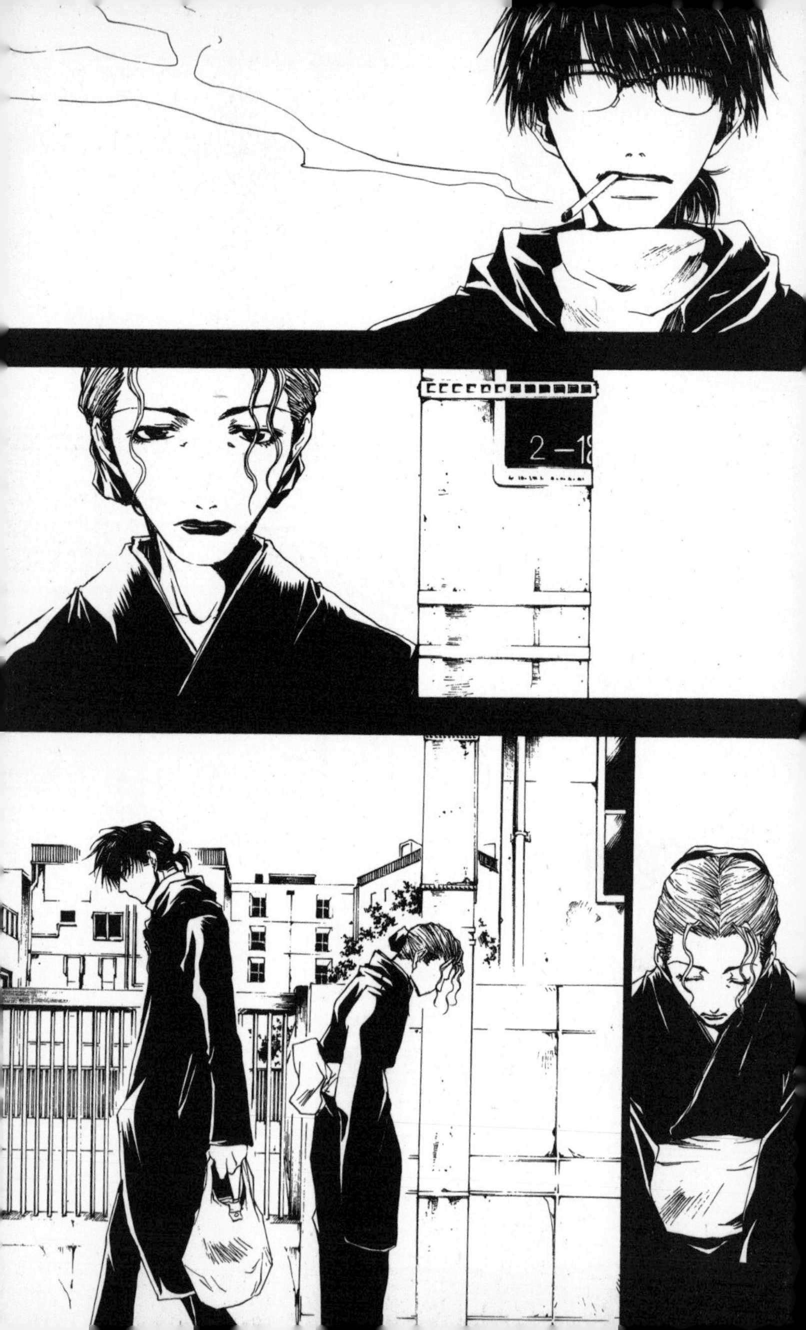
2 –1

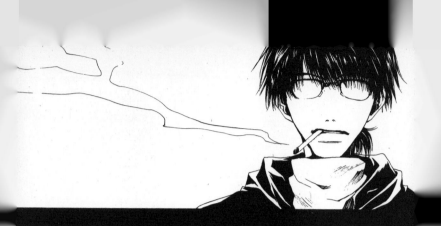

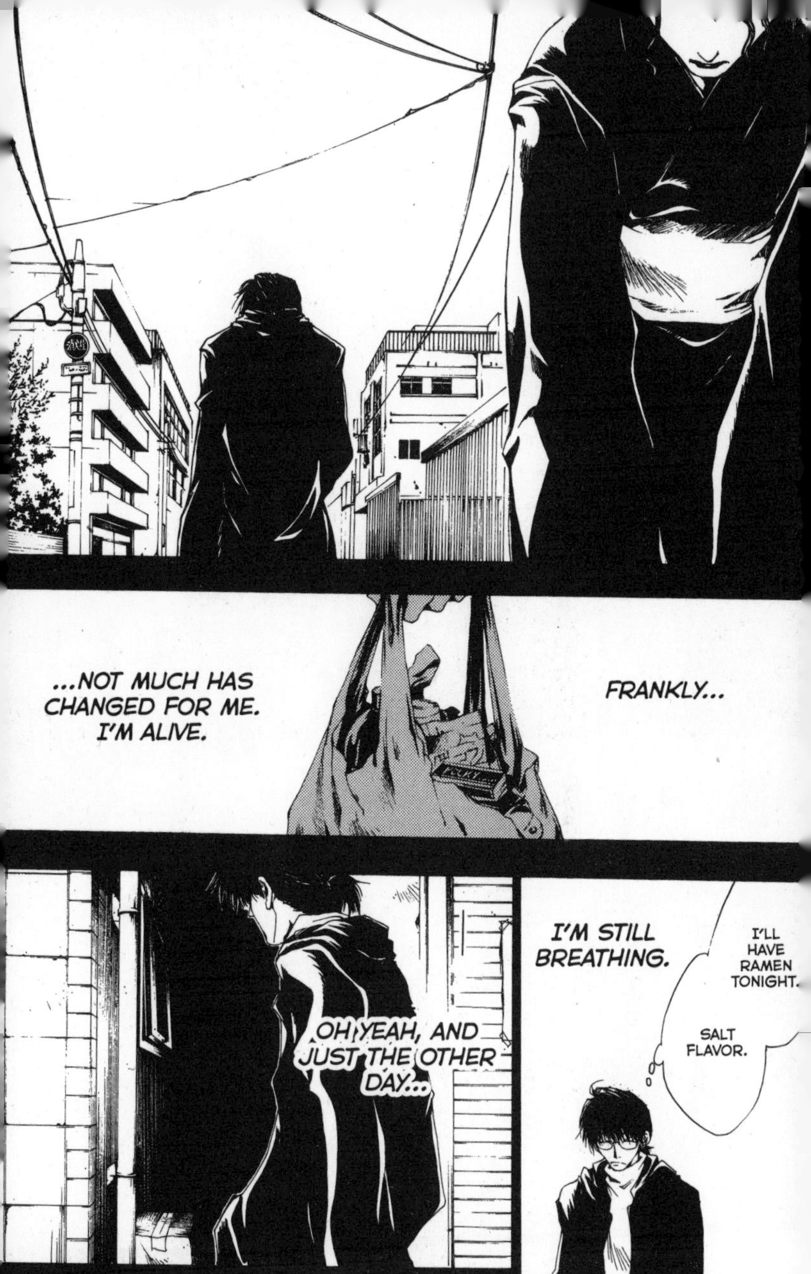
FRANKLY...
...NOT MUCH HAS CHANGED FOR ME. I'M ALIVE.
I'M STILL BREATHING.
I'LL HAVE RAMEN TONIGHT.
SALT FLAVOR.
OH YEAH, AND JUST THE OTHER DAY...

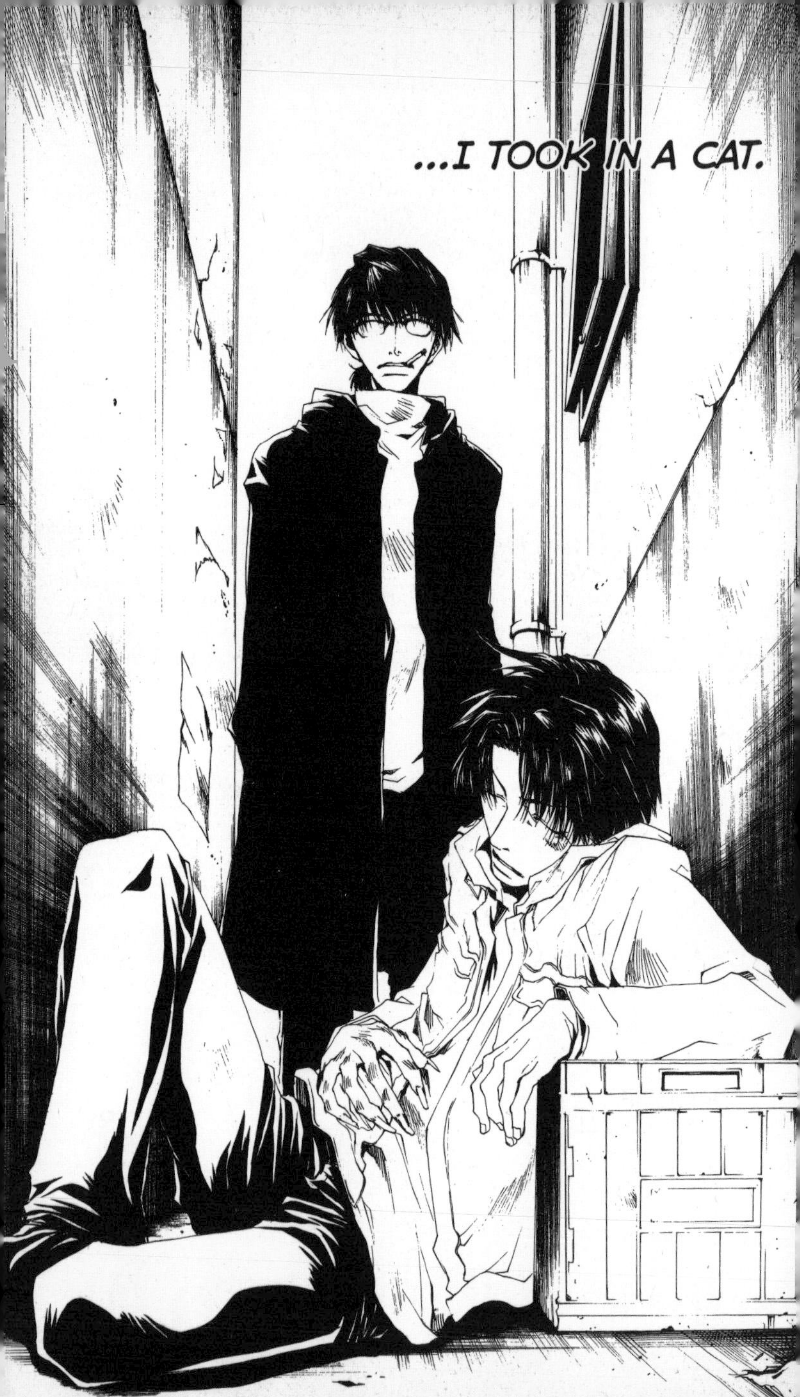
...I TOOK IN A CAT.

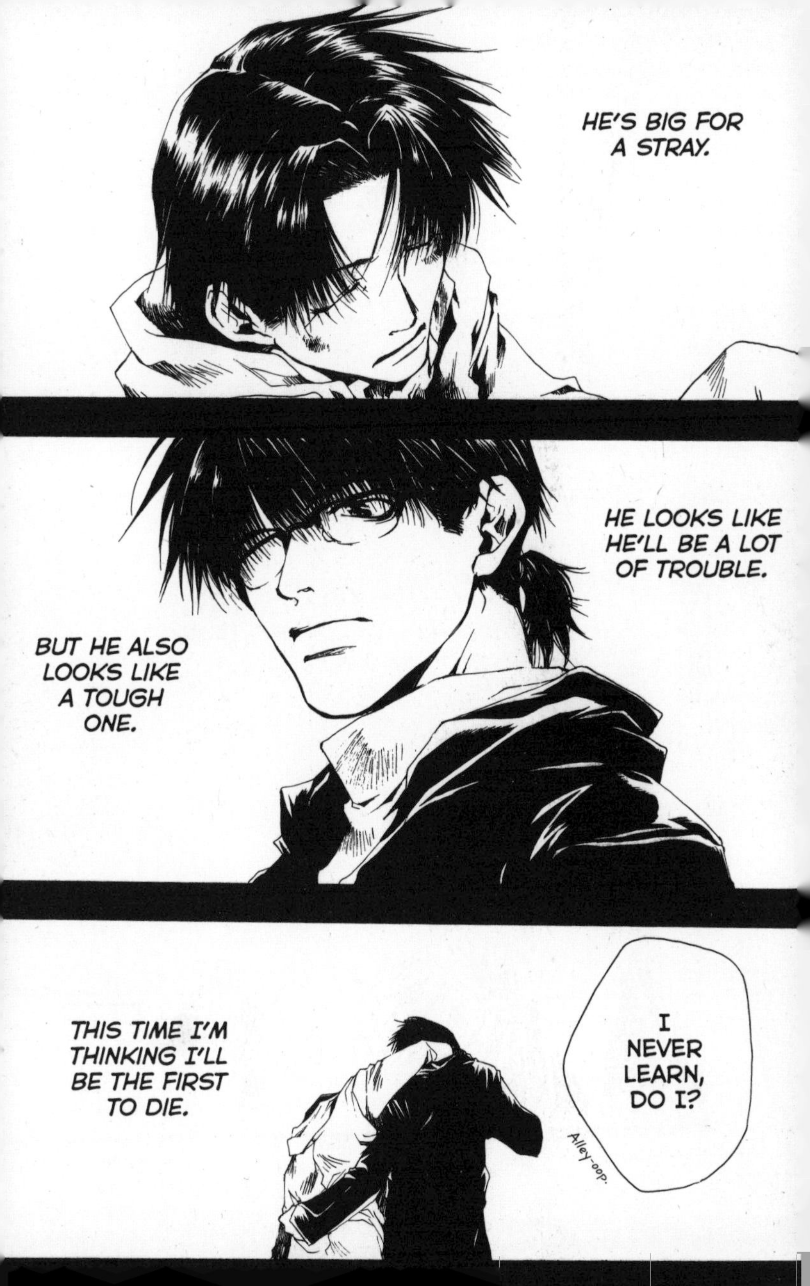
HE'S BIG FOR A STRAY.
HE LOOKS LIKE HE'LL BE A LOT OF TROUBLE.
BUT HE ALSO LOOKS LIKE A TOUGH ONE.
I NEVER LEARN, DO I?
Alley-oop.
THIS TIME I'M THINKING I'LL BE THE FIRST TO DIE.

HE FELT HEAVY, THAT LITTLE CAT.

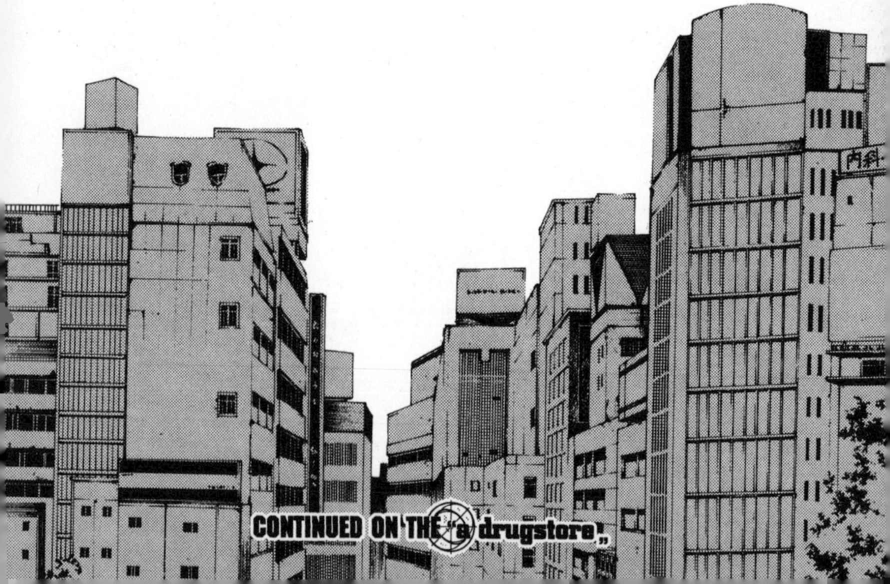
CONTINUED ON THE "a drugstore"

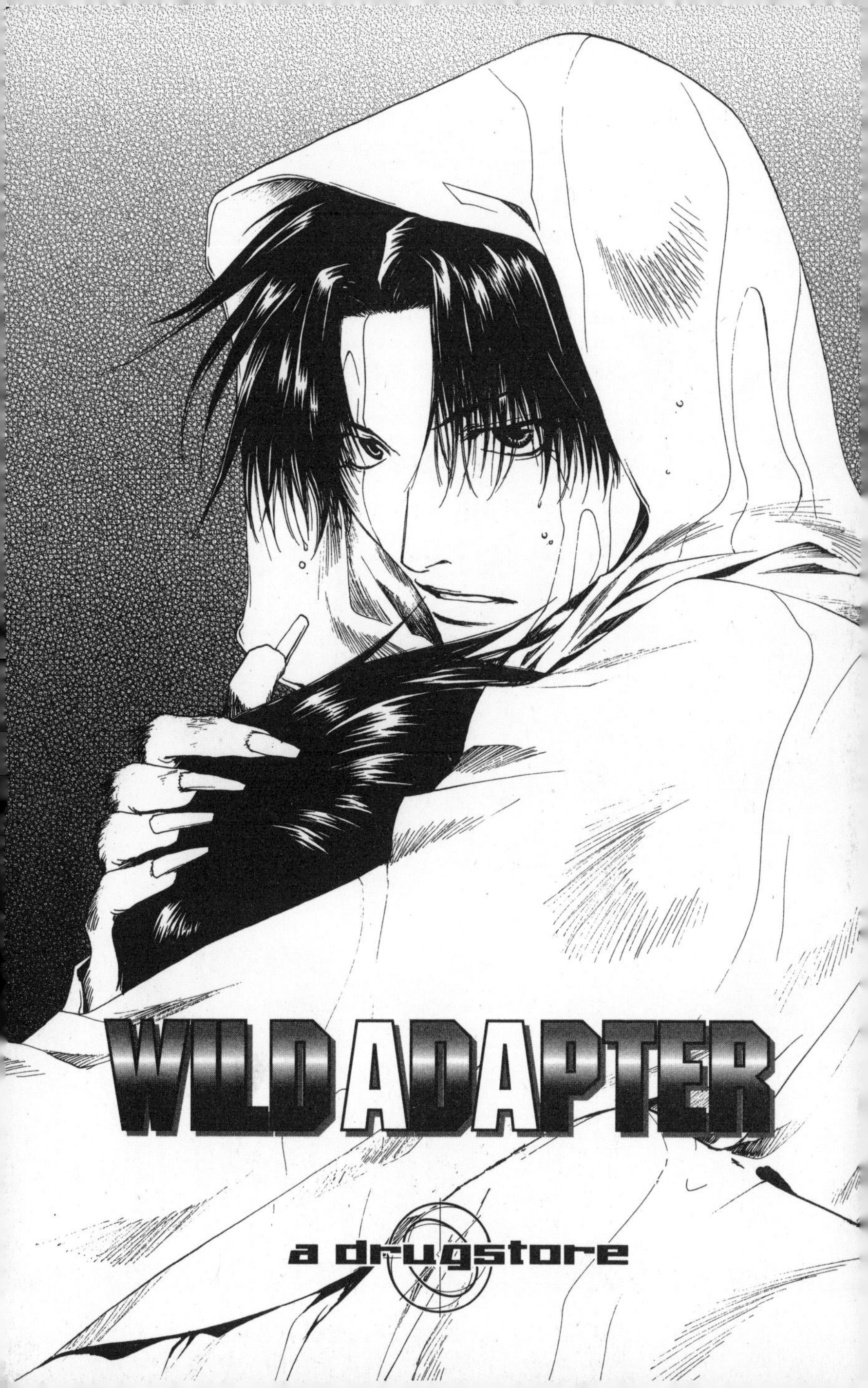
WILD ADAPTER
a drugstore

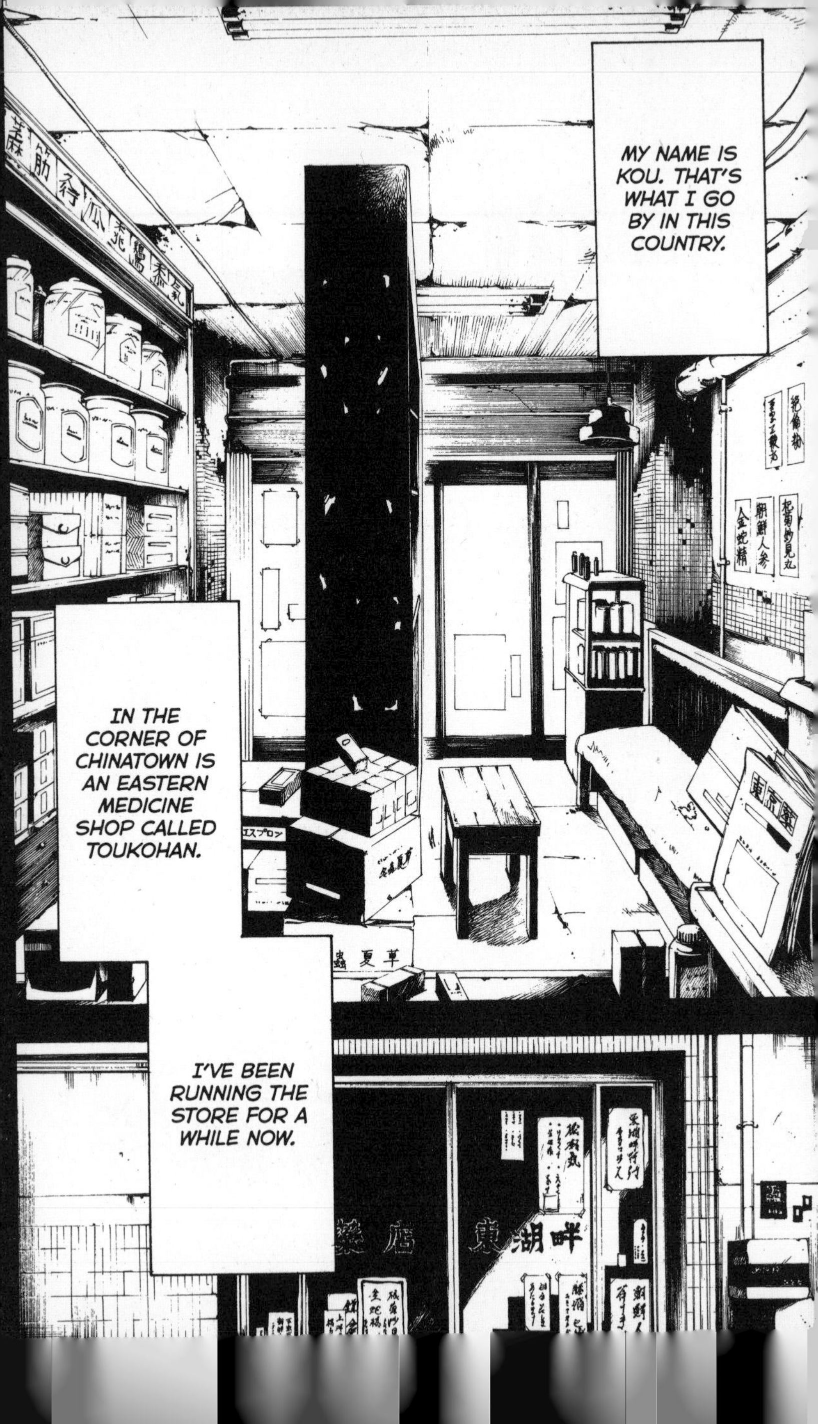
MY NAME IS KOU. THAT'S WHAT I GO BY IN THIS COUNTRY.
IN THE CORNER OF CHINATOWN IS AN EASTERN MEDICINE SHOP CALLED TOUKOHAN.
I'VE BEEN RUNNING THE STORE FOR A WHILE NOW.

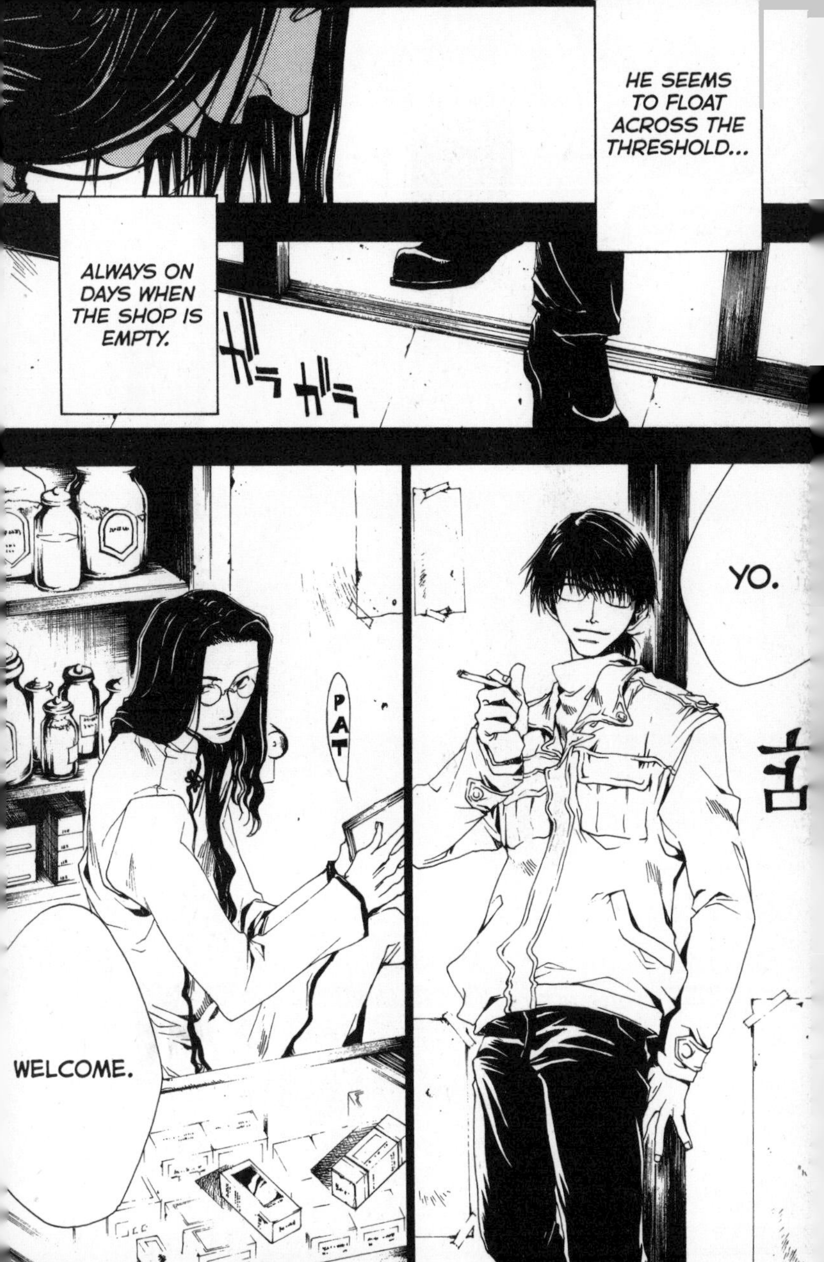
HE SEEMS TO FLOAT ACROSS THE THRESHOLD...
ALWAYS ON DAYS WHEN THE SHOP IS EMPTY.
ガラガラ
YO.
PAT
WELCOME.

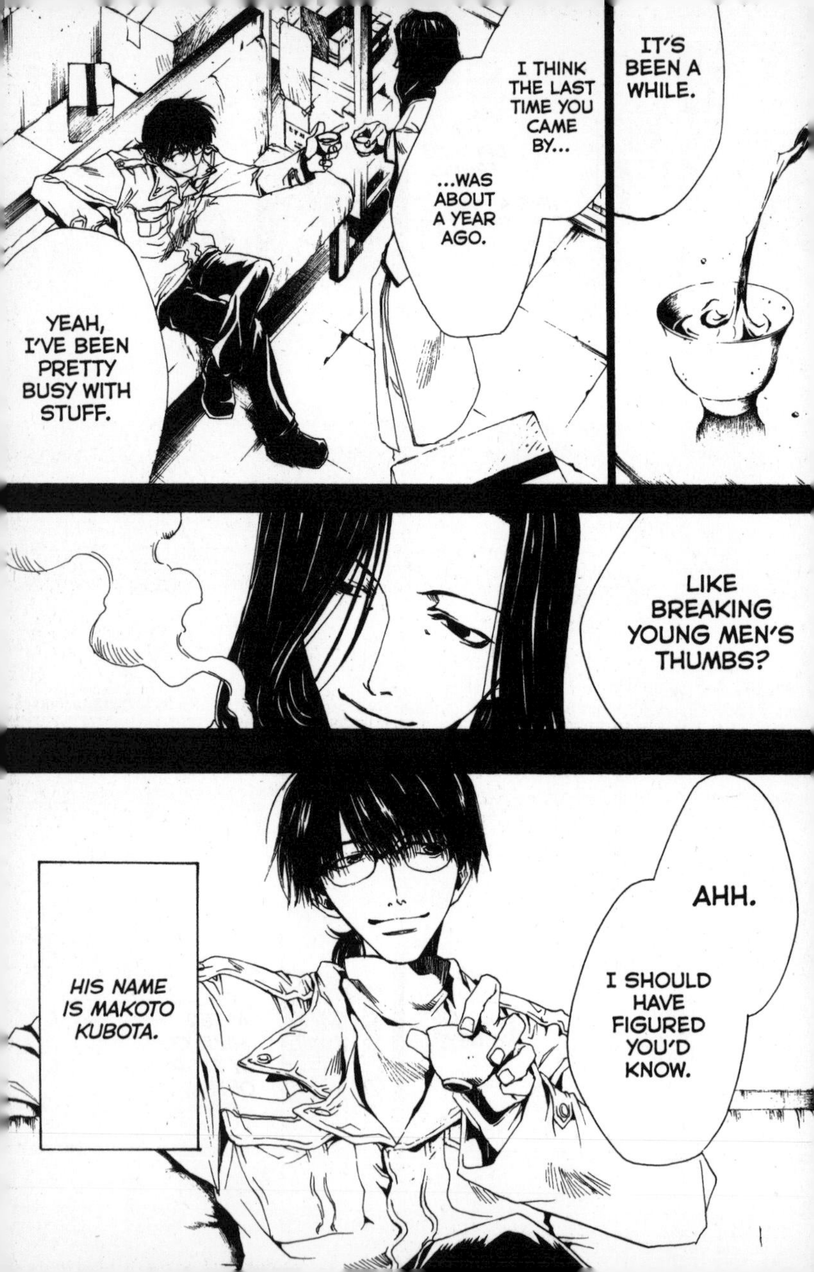
IT'S BEEN A WHILE.
I THINK THE LAST TIME YOU CAME BY...
...WAS ABOUT A YEAR AGO.
YEAH, I'VE BEEN PRETTY BUSY WITH STUFF.
LIKE BREAKING YOUNG MEN'S THUMBS?
AHH.
I SHOULD HAVE FIGURED YOU'D KNOW.
HIS NAME IS MAKOTO KUBOTA.

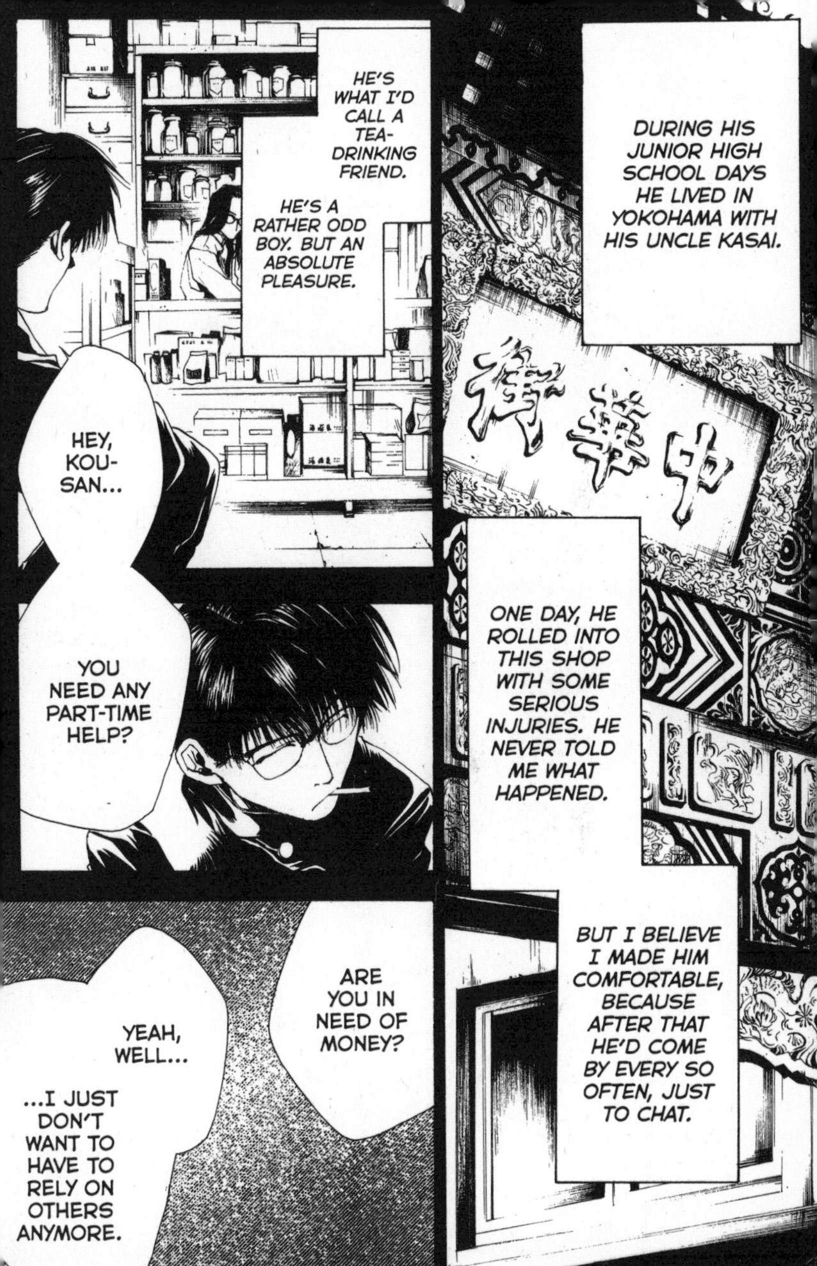
DURING HIS JUNIOR HIGH SCHOOL DAYS HE LIVED IN YOKOHAMA WITH HIS UNCLE KASAI.
中華街
HE'S WHAT I'D CALL A TEA-DRINKING FRIEND.
HE'S A RATHER ODD BOY. BUT AN ABSOLUTE PLEASURE.
HEY, KOU-SAN...
ONE DAY, HE ROLLED INTO THIS SHOP WITH SOME SERIOUS INJURIES. HE NEVER TOLD ME WHAT HAPPENED.
YOU NEED ANY PART-TIME HELP?
BUT I BELIEVE I MADE HIM COMFORTABLE, BECAUSE AFTER THAT HE'D COME BY EVERY SO OFTEN, JUST TO CHAT.
ARE YOU IN NEED OF MONEY?
YEAH, WELL...
...I JUST DON'T WANT TO HAVE TO RELY ON OTHERS ANYMORE.

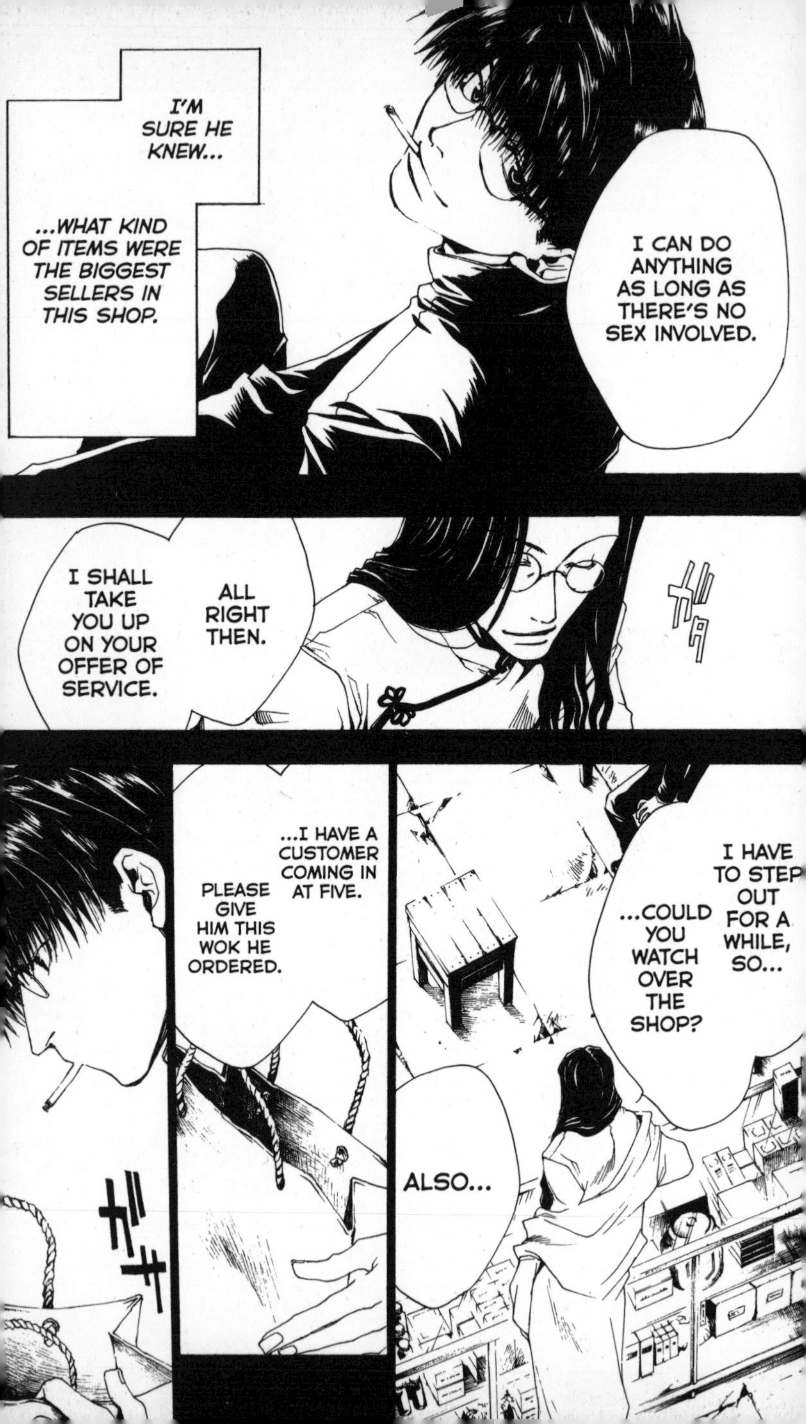
I CAN DO ANYTHING AS LONG AS THERE'S NO SEX INVOLVED.
I'M SURE HE KNEW...
...WHAT KIND OF ITEMS WERE THE BIGGEST SELLERS IN THIS SHOP.
ガタ
ALL RIGHT THEN.
I SHALL TAKE YOU UP ON YOUR OFFER OF SERVICE.
I HAVE TO STEP OUT FOR A WHILE, SO...
...COULD YOU WATCH OVER THE SHOP?
ALSO...
...I HAVE A CUSTOMER COMING IN AT FIVE.
PLEASE GIVE HIM THIS WOK HE ORDERED.

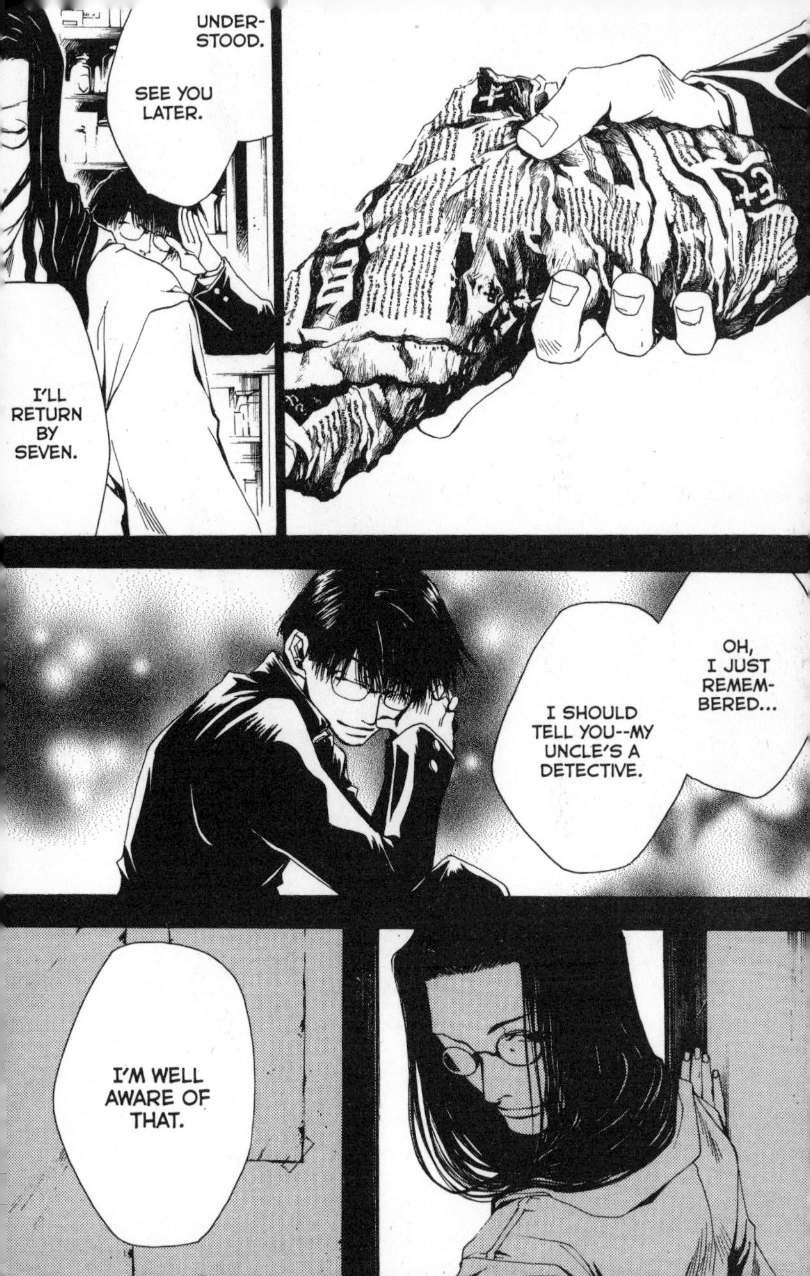
UNDER-STOOD.
SEE YOU LATER.
I'LL RETURN BY SEVEN.
OH, I JUST REMEMBERED...
I SHOULD TELL YOU--MY UNCLE'S A DETECTIVE.
I'M WELL AWARE OF THAT.

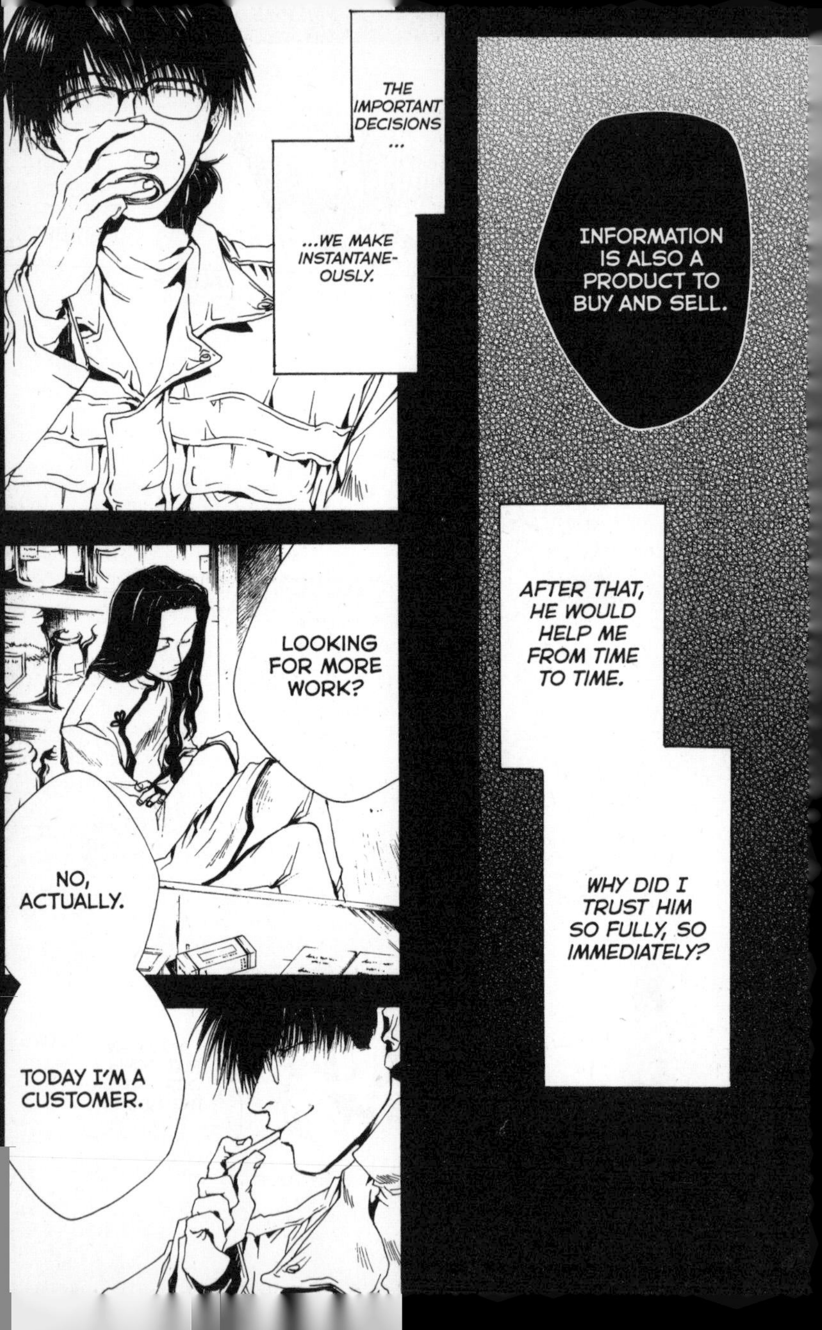
INFORMATION IS ALSO A PRODUCT TO BUY AND SELL.
AFTER THAT, HE WOULD HELP ME FROM TIME TO TIME.
WHY DID I TRUST HIM SO FULLY, SO IMMEDIATELY?
THE IMPORTANT DECISIONS ...
...WE MAKE INSTANTANE-OUSLY.
LOOKING FOR MORE WORK?
NO, ACTUALLY.
TODAY I'M A CUSTOMER.

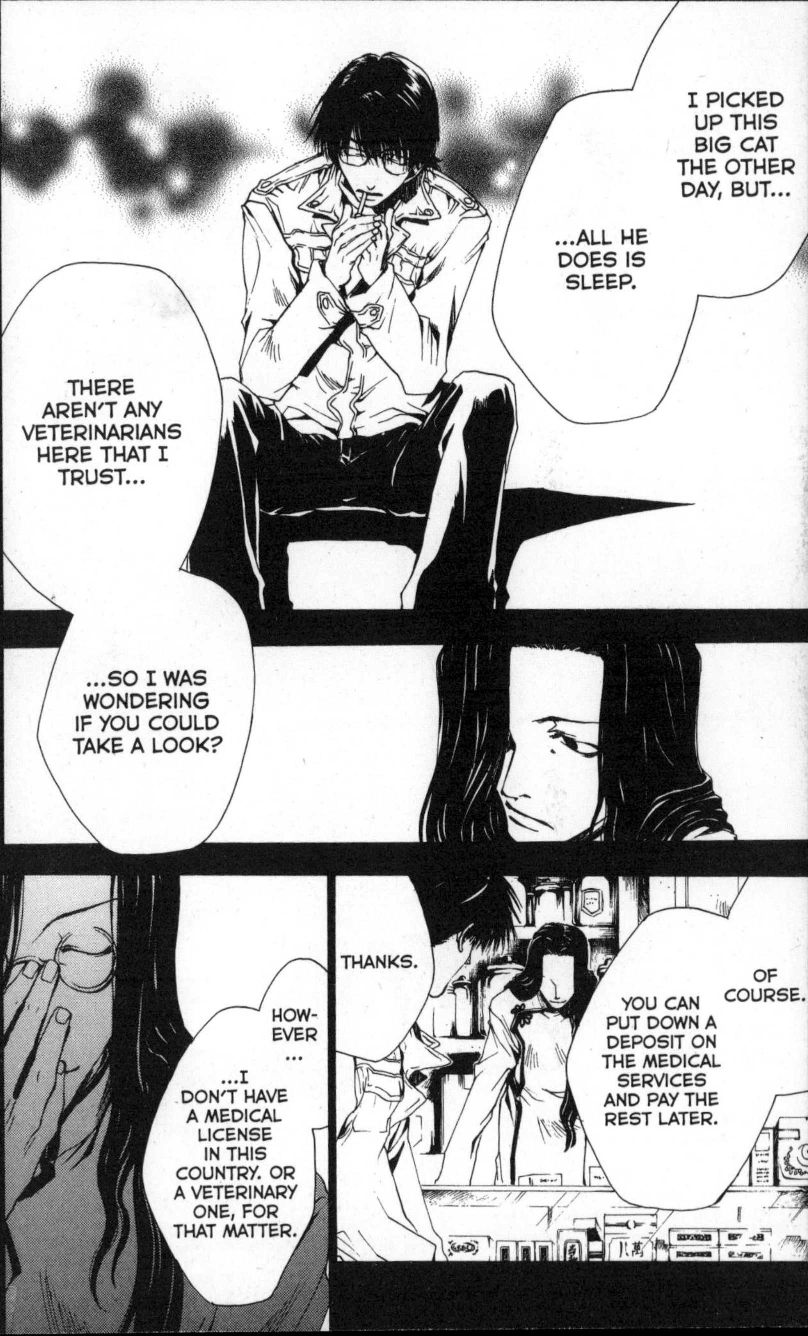
I PICKED UP THIS BIG CAT THE OTHER DAY, BUT...
...ALL HE DOES IS SLEEP.
THERE AREN'T ANY VETERINARIANS HERE THAT I TRUST...
...SO I WAS WONDERING IF YOU COULD TAKE A LOOK?
OF COURSE.
YOU CAN PUT DOWN A DEPOSIT ON THE MEDICAL SERVICES AND PAY THE REST LATER.
THANKS.
HOW-EVER ...
...I DON'T HAVE A MEDICAL LICENSE IN THIS COUNTRY. OR A VETERINARY ONE, FOR THAT MATTER.

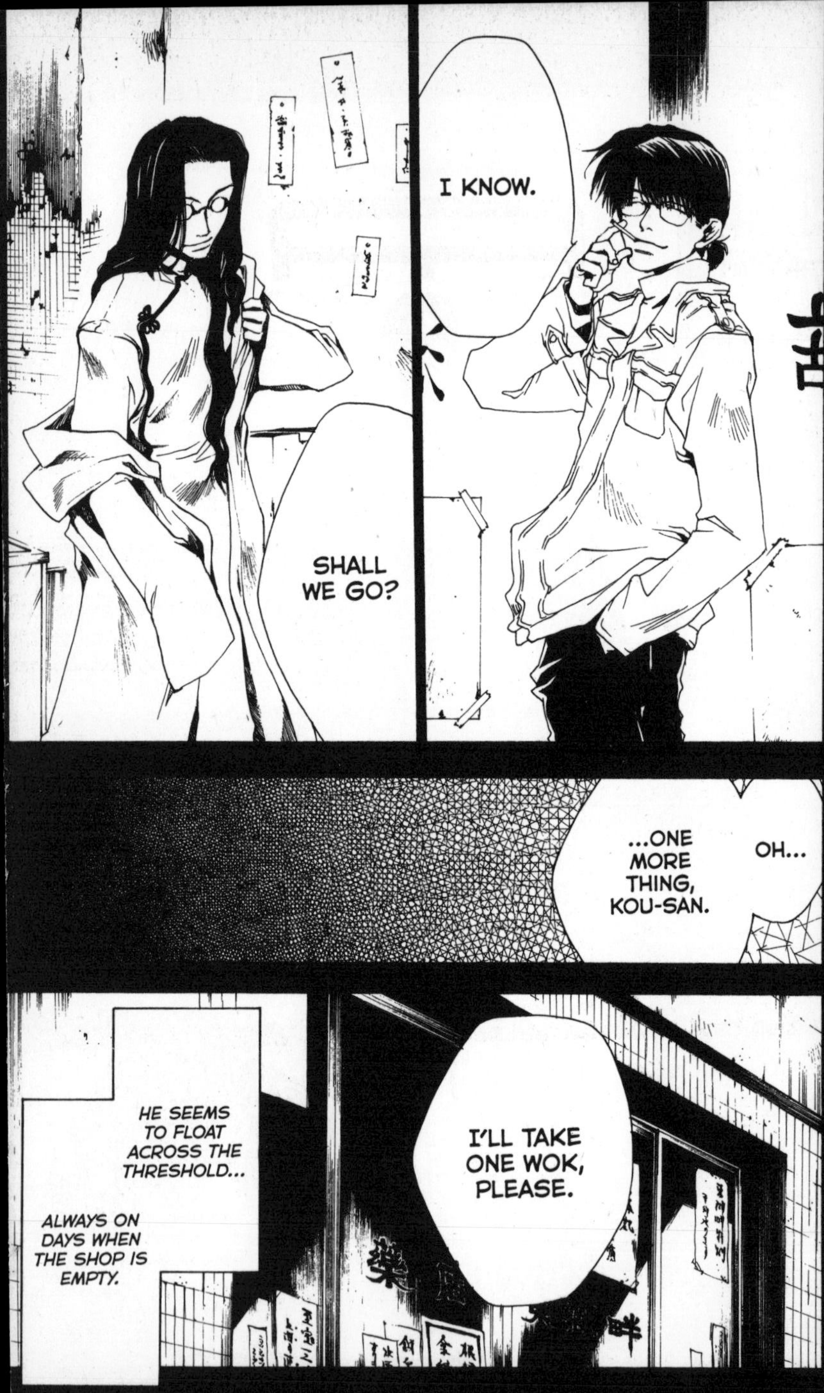
I KNOW.
SHALL WE GO?
OH...
...ONE MORE THING, KOU-SAN.
I'LL TAKE ONE WOK, PLEASE.
HE SEEMS TO FLOAT ACROSS THE THRESHOLD...
ALWAYS ON DAYS WHEN THE SHOP IS EMPTY.

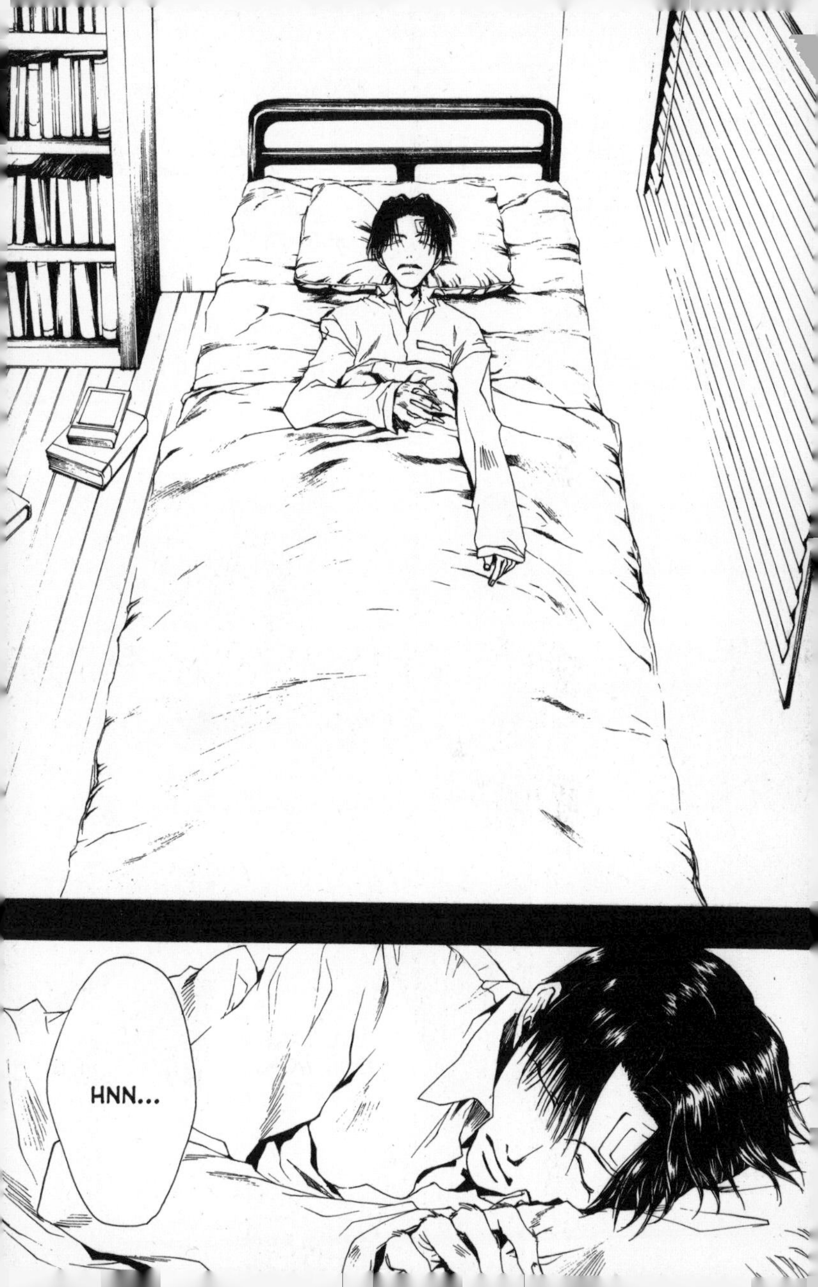
HNN...

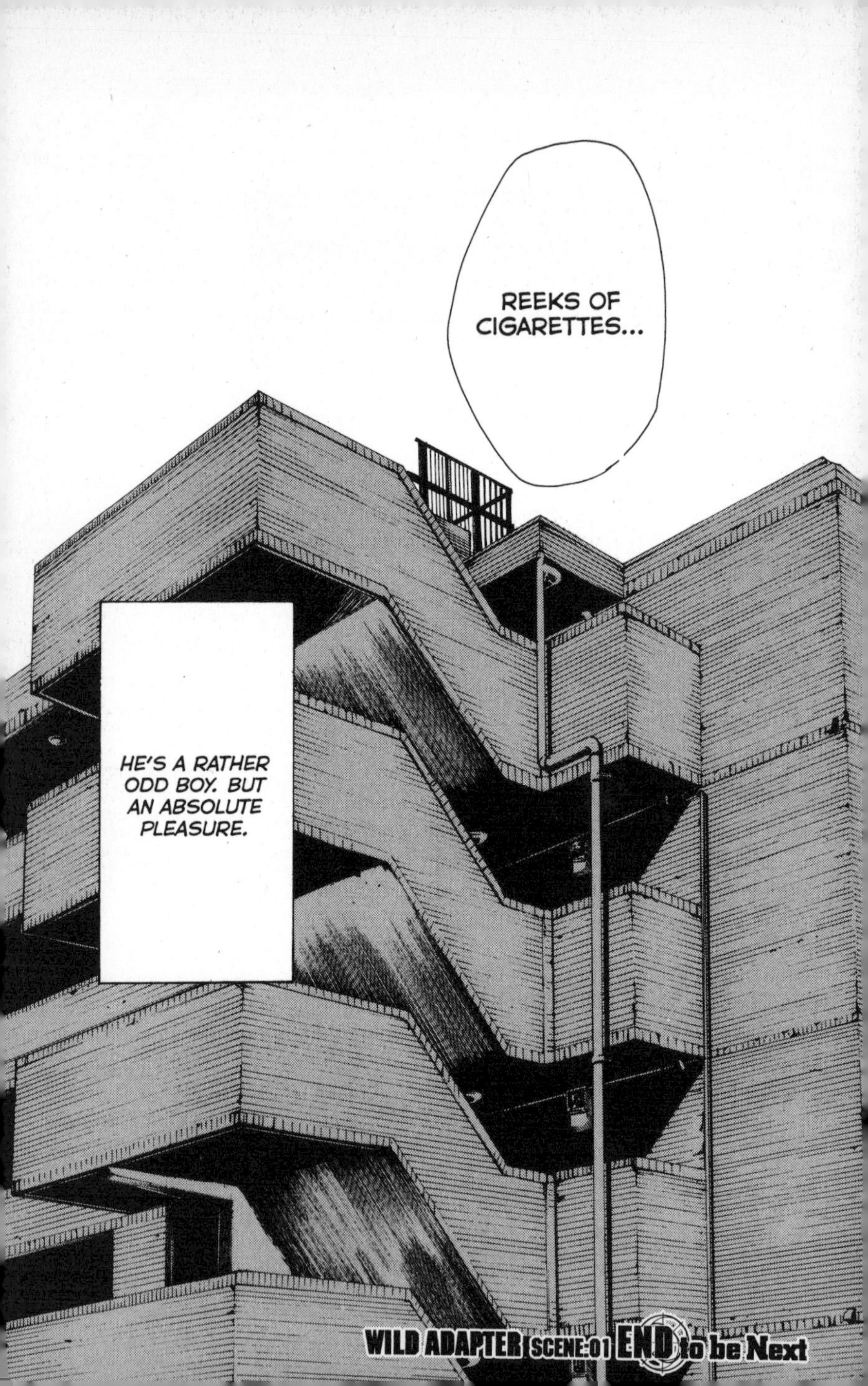
REEKS OF CIGARETTES...
HE'S A RATHER ODD BOY. BUT AN ABSOLUTE PLEASURE.
WILD ADAPTER SCENE:01 END to be Next

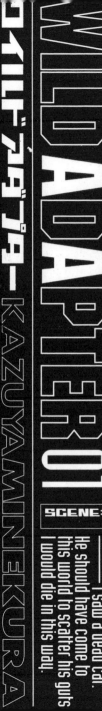

ALL STORIES AND PICTURES by
KAZUYA MINEKURA

Assistant
•
JIRO SUZUKI
KATSUYA SEINO
YUZU MIZUTANI

Total Design
•
HIDEYUKI EBIHARA

Editor
•
KAZUKO OSHIO

Presented by Chara

WILD ADAPTER 01
SCENE:
——I saw a dead cat.
He should have come to
this world to scatter his guts
I would die in this way.

ワイルドアダプター KAZUYA MINEKURA

When this book was finally in print, I read over the first two chapters and was struck with how different the art seemed from what I remembered creating. Still, it was a relief to have the first book out, even if it is only the prologue of the whole story (I like to call it the "Komiya Arc"). It was a bit bold of me to tell my editor that the first three chapters of the story would only be the prologue—I was bolder still to turn the entire first volume into the prologue. But this way I was able to introduce most of the major players in Wild Adapter. Of course one of the most important characters is still a sleeping beauty. But don't worry—Tokito will be an integral part of the action in the next volume. I hope that you've been able to spend enough time with Kubota in this first volume to form an opinion of him, be it positive or negative.

Kazuya Minekura, June, 2001

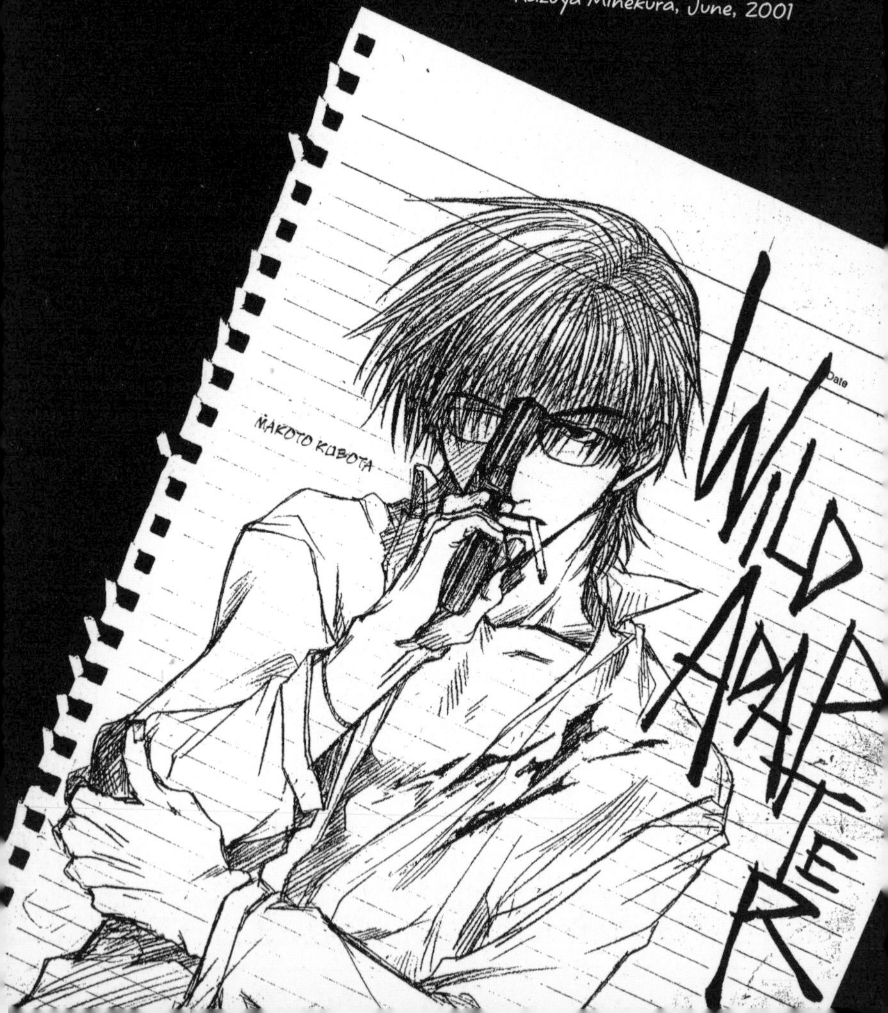

WILD ADAPTER
MAKOTO KUBOTA
Date

In the next volume of

WILD ADAPTE

A year has passed since Makoto Kubota left Sanada and the Izumo Organization in a rain of blood and took in his little "stray cat." Kubota and Tokito have been living together (under ambiguous circumstances), but Tokito is still as wild as ever, and can't seem to remember anything about his past.

When Kubota bumps into a runaway young woman in a convenience store, she has the rare chance to see the way the private lives of these two young men intertwine. But, Saori has to deal with sorting out her personal life and trying to make it out of Yokohama in one piece. Kubota doesn't seem to care for anyone in the world, but he'll throw himself into the middle of a yakuza turf war in order to protect Tokito and learn the secret of Wild Adapter, and if Saori is helped in the process, all the better.

But Sanada is still hot on the trail of his star youth gang leader (and the one that got away), and life is cheap in the back alleys of Yokohama.

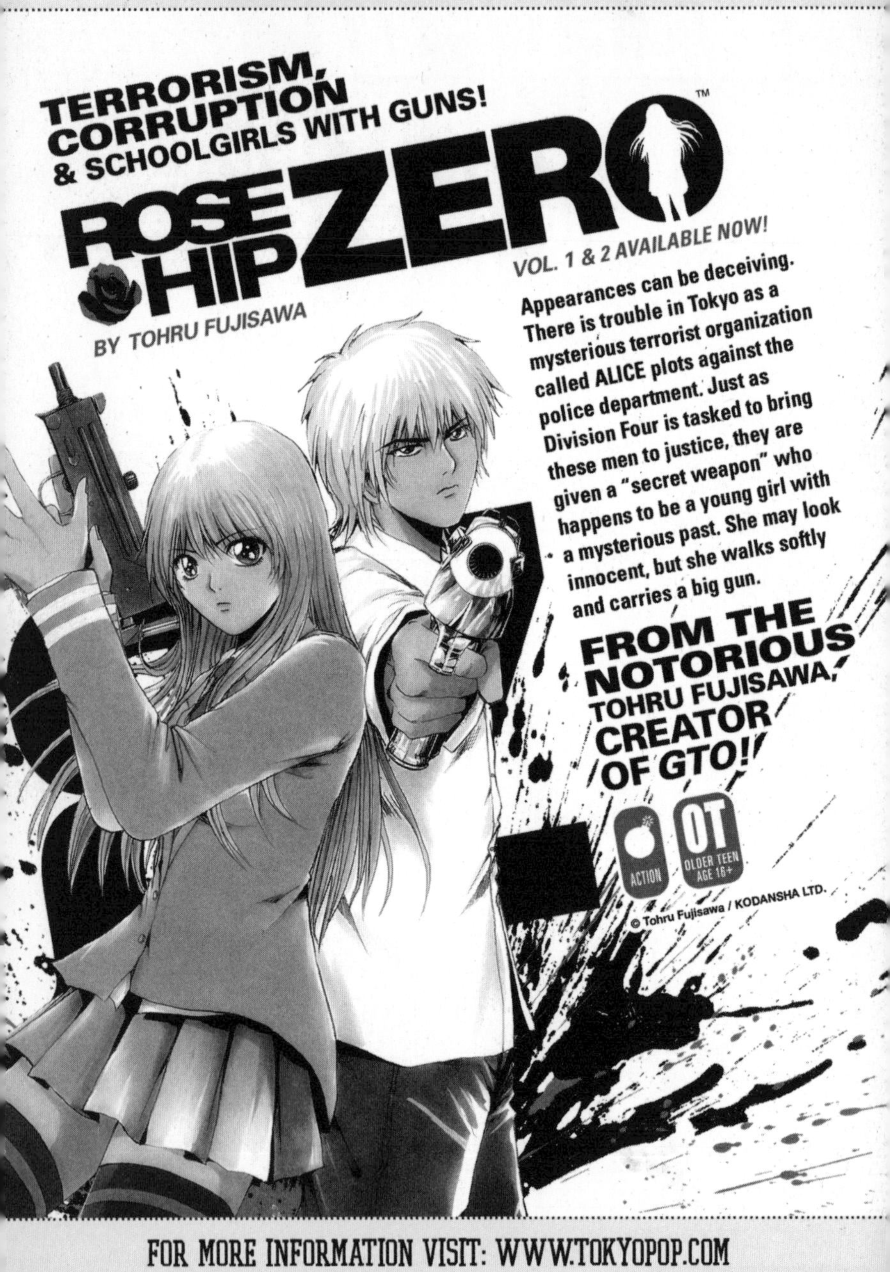
TERRORISM, CORRUPTION & SCHOOLGIRLS WITH GUNS!
ROSE HIP ZERO™
BY TOHRU FUJISAWA
VOL. 1 & 2 AVAILABLE NOW!
Appearances can be deceiving. There is trouble in Tokyo as a mysterious terrorist organization called ALICE plots against the police department. Just as Division Four is tasked to bring these men to justice, they are given a "secret weapon" who happens to be a young girl with a mysterious past. She may look innocent, but she walks softly and carries a big gun.
FROM THE NOTORIOUS TOHRU FUJISAWA, CREATOR OF GTO!
ACTION
OT OLDER TEEN AGE 16+
© Tohru Fujisawa / KODANSHA LTD.

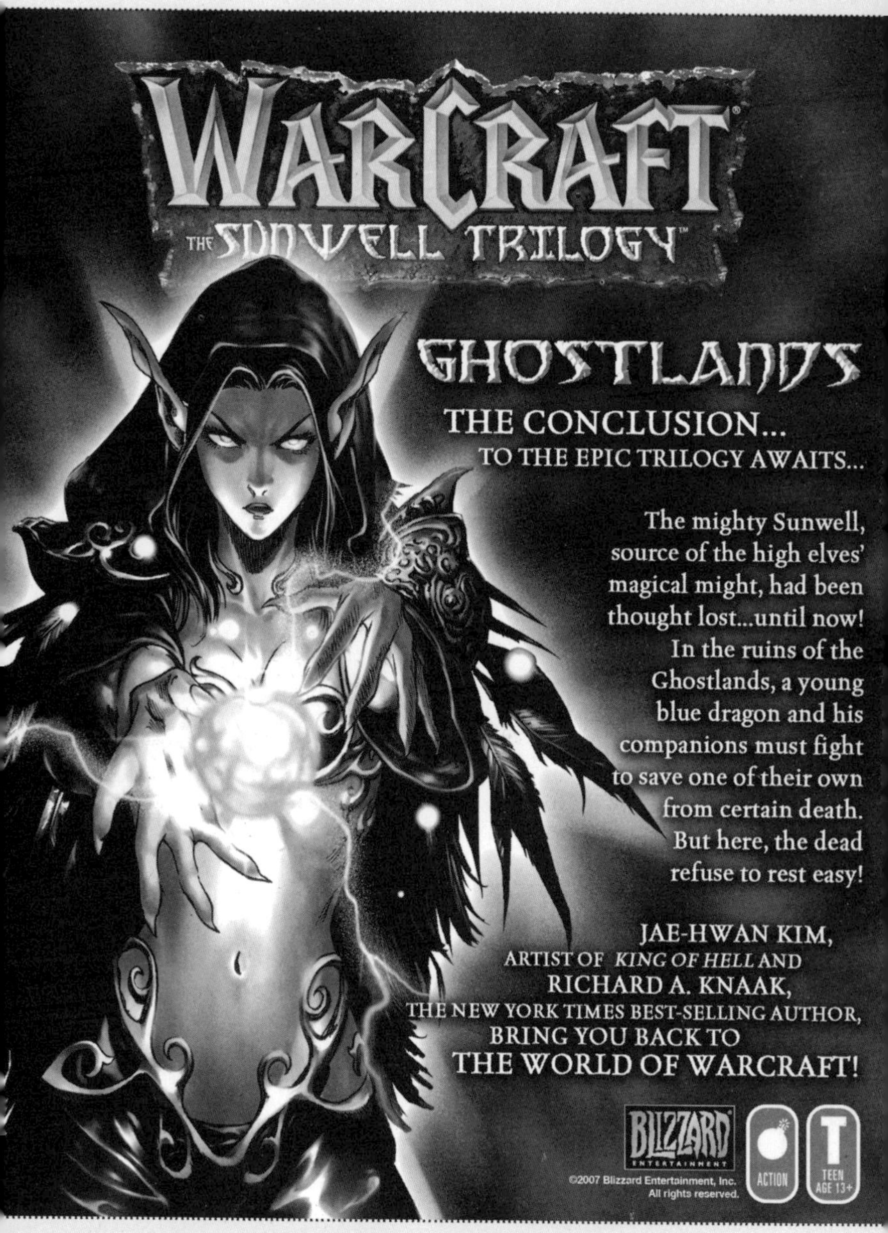
WARCRAFT®
THE SUNWELL TRILOGY™
GHOSTLANDS
THE CONCLUSION...
TO THE EPIC TRILOGY AWAITS...
The mighty Sunwell, source of the high elves' magical might, had been thought lost...until now! In the ruins of the Ghostlands, a young blue dragon and his companions must fight to save one of their own from certain death. But here, the dead refuse to rest easy!
JAE-HWAN KIM, ARTIST OF KING OF HELL AND RICHARD A. KNAAK, THE NEW YORK TIMES BEST-SELLING AUTHOR, BRING YOU BACK TO THE WORLD OF WARCRAFT!
BLIZZARD ENTERTAINMENT
©2007 Blizzard Entertainment, Inc. All rights reserved.
ACTION
T
TEEN AGE 13+

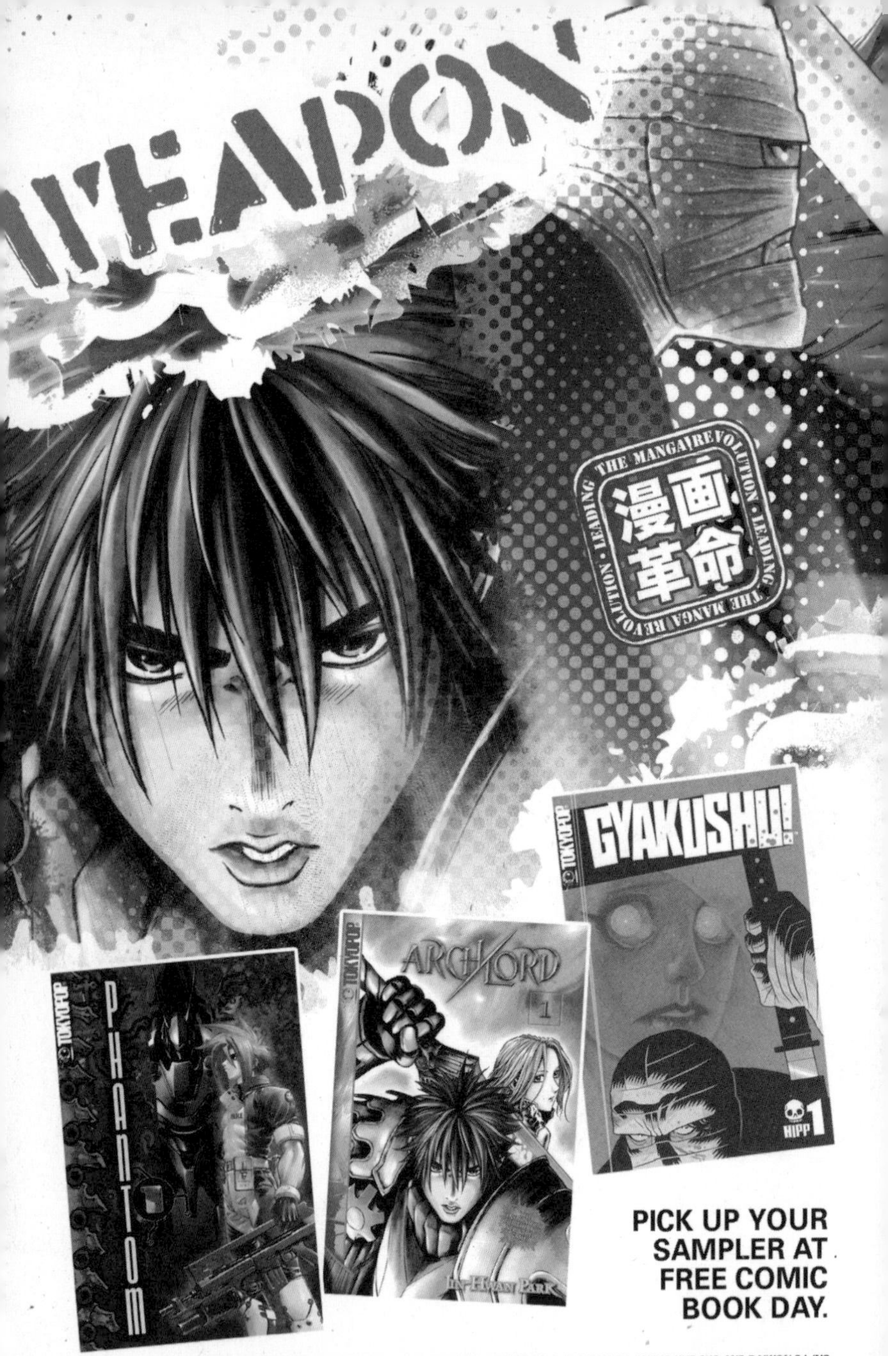

LEADING THE MANGA REVOLUTION
漫画革命
GYAKUSHU!
HIPP 1
ARCHLORD
1
JIN-HWAN PARK
PHANTOM
TOKYOPOP

STOP!

This is the back of the book.
You wouldn't want to spoil a great ending!

This book is printed "manga-style," in the authentic Japanese right-to-left format. Since none of the artwork has been flipped or altered, readers get to experience the story just as the creator intended. You've been asking for it, so TOKYOPOP® delivered: authentic, hot-off-the-press, and far more fun!

DIRECTIONS

If this is your first time reading manga-style, here's a quick guide to help you understand how it works.

It's easy... just start in the top right panel and follow the numbers. Have fun, and look for more 100% authentic manga from TOKYOPOP®!

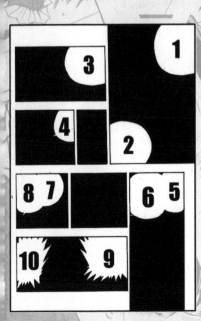